Frederick Oakeley, aged sixteen
Painted by his mother

A Passionate Humility

Frederick Oakeley
and the
Oxford Movement

To
Peter Baker, Duncan Dalais, Simon Hobbs, Roger Kent,
Kevin Mitchell and Tony Pybus
for their friendship

A Passionate Humility

Frederick Oakeley
and the
Oxford Movement

Peter Galloway

First published in 1999

Gracewing
2 Southern Avenue
Leominster
Herefordshire HR6 0QF

ISBN 0 85244 506 7

Typesetting by
Action Publishing Technology Ltd, Gloucester, GL1 1SP

Printed in England by
MPG Books Ltd, Bodmin, PL31 1EG

Contents

Also by Peter Galloway

The Order of St Patrick
Good and Faithful Servants (with Christopher Rawll)
The Cathedrals of Ireland
Royal Service Volume 1 (with others)
The Order of the British Empire
The Most Illustrious Order
The Cathedrals of Scotland

Acknowledgements

Selecting the names of individuals and institutions to whom thanks is due is a fraught process, because of the risk of omission. In the case of this book, there is a further difficulty, in that it began its life as a doctoral thesis, submitted and approved in 1987. The list is comparatively small, because the composition of a thesis is, by its nature, a solitary task. In the intervening years, some of those who assisted with the preparatory research have moved to other fields of work, or retired, or died, but none of these factors seemed to justify the exclusion of their names, and I record my thanks to them.

Gerard Tracey, Librarian and Archivist of the Birmingham Oratory; Dr John Jones, Archivist of Balliol College; Alan Tadiello of Balliol College Library; the Reverend John H. Bishop; the staff of the Bodleian Library; the staff of the British Library; the staff of Keble College Library; the staff of Lambeth Palace Library; Howard Clayton of Lichfield and the staff of Lichfield Joint Record Office; the Reverend Canon Anthony Caesar; Miss Lilian Cornelius of St. John's Church, Duncan Terrace, Islington; Dr Sheridan Gilley of the University of Durham; Dr Peter Nockles; the Right Reverend Dr Geoffrey Rowell, Bishop of Basingstoke, the Reverend Dr Harry Smythe and Peter Meadows of Pusey House Library; the staff of the Royal Commission on Historical Manuscripts; and the staff of Shropshire County Record Office.

Although Frederick Oakeley never married, there are surviving descendants of his brothers and sisters, and among those who helped were the late Sir Atholl Oakeley (1900–87); Dr Henry Oakeley; Miss Mary Oakeley, and especially Rowland Oakeley, a great nephew of Frederick, who celebrated his ninetieth birthday in 1999.

After the thesis had gathered dust for ten years, the Reverend Malcolm Johnson suggested that the subject might well appeal to Gracewing, and one thing led to another. Tom Longford, of Gracewing Publishing, was sufficiently fascinated by Fredrick Oakeley to agree to publish this record of his life and times, and Jo Ashworth rapidly and meticulously transformed the text from a typescript to a book, in time to mark the one hundred and sixtieth anniversary of the licensing of Frederick Oakeley as Minister of Margaret Chapel.

Dr Christopher Rawll, archivist of All Saints' Margaret Street, and always a mine of information about the history of that church and its architecture, willingly encouraged and shared my enthusiasm for researching the life of Frederick Oakeley at a time when we were working on our book *Good and faithful servants* which appeared in 1988.

The Right Reverend Richard Chartres, Bishop of London, kindly agreed to provide a Foreword, despite a heavily-committed diary, and the fact that a tight publishing schedule caused a set of page proofs to land on his desk on the eve of Holy Week.

The Reverend Professor Stuart Hall, as Professor of Ecclesiastical History (1973–90) at King's College in the University of London, patiently guided the formation of my thesis in the years 1983–7 and, in a sense, ensured the appearance of this book.

Preface

When Newman published his *Apologia pro vita sua* in 1864, he spoke of 'a new school of thought arising in the Oxford movement during the period 1839–41, which swept aside the original party of the movement, and took its place. The most prominent person in it was a man of elegant genius, of classical mind, of rare talent in literary composition – Mr Oakeley'. Despite this statement, the Oratorian Louis Bouyer, in his biography of Newman, dismissed Oakeley as, 'a relitively colourless personality.'

The comment is unfair but understandable. Oakeley was comparatively easily eclipsed, partly by his own innate shyness, gentleness and humility, partly by the formidable intellectual genius of John Henry Newman, partly by the bombastic figure of W.G. Ward, who was Oakeley's close friend in their Anglican days, and partly because of the absence of a biography of Oakeley since his death in 1880.

The principal figure in the second generation of the Oxford Movement, Frederick Oakeley had a public reputation that centred on his perfectionist love of exquisitely-performed liturgy and music and, more than forty years after he had left his pioneering experiment at Margaret Chapel in London's West End, R. W. Church, Dean of St Paul's Cathedral 1871–90 and one the early historians of the Oxford Movement, remembered the profound impression that it had made on him. 'Mr Oakeley was, perhaps, the first to realise the capacities of the Anglican ritual for impressive devotional use, and his services, in spite of the disadvantages of time, and also of his chapel, are still remembered by some as having realised for them in a way never since surpased, the secrets and consolations of the worship of the Church'.

Oakeley did indeed have a 'rare talent in literary composition', proved by the more than one hundred and ten articles and books that he wrote. The great majority are articles, and his books are mostly reprinted collections of sermons and lectures. His articles, especially the earlier ones, were not always thoroughly researched, and only served to expose his occasionally defective logic. But there was no doubting the passionate sincerity of belief, the clarity of his argument, and the well-crafted elegant phrasing that always marked his writing. He was not a great theologian and was probably at his best when writing about the practicalities of faith and belief, rather than their theories, but his incisive advice was marked by common sense born of his long experience of parochial ministry.

Frederick Oakeley died in 1880, and although enough is known of his life to make this book possible, there is an element of uncertainty in recording and analysing the life of an individual who is long dead, because there is no possibility of immediate contact either with subject or with those who knew the subject. The passing of time has removed any access to unrecorded memories, and consequently the complete story, although concluded, will never be known. In these circumstances, a biographer can never be sure that the life and reputation of the character who emerges from the pages of his book is complete and accurate, and a representation that both the subject and his friends would have recognised in his lifetime.

I have visited St Mary's Cemetery at Kensal Green, London on a number of occasions, the first being in 1987 when, with the help of the cemetery records and an obliging attendant, I succeeded in finding Frederick Oakeley's dilapidated and forgotten grave. Looking at the memorial that marks the place in which he was laid to rest, I hoped that he would have been content with what I have said about him, even if he did not entirely approve of my conclusions, and respected my efforts to bring his life and his role in the Oxford Movement back into the sunlight.

Foreword by the Bishop of London

The attentive reader of Christmas Carol sheets can often spot the name of Frederick Oakeley at the end of *Adeste Fideles*. He is known best, perhaps, for his enduring translation of a favourite seasonal hymn but this alone is not a sufficient memorial to him. Oakeley translated it for the use of his congregation at the Margaret Chapel, one of his many contributions towards enhancing their liturgical, musical and devotional life. Oakeley is an influential figure of the Oxford Movement's second generation. He was one of the very first to translate the Movement's theological conviction into the practices of corporate worship. He did this in a small proprietary chapel in the parish of All Souls', Langham Place in such a manner, commented Gladstone, that 'its barrenness and poverty passed unnoticed'. R. W. Church reported that many recalled how Oakeley's services 'realised for them in a way never since surpassed, the secrets and consolations of the worship of the Church'.

I am very grateful to Peter Galloway for producing such an accessible and scholarly piece of work, opening up a life often eclipsed by the other giants of the Oxford Movement. He reveals Oakeley's passion for sure, a somewhat reckless energy at times, and one which fuelled a public dispute with my predecessor Bishop Blomfield. Oakeley would certainly have agreed with Newman that 'life is not long enough for a religion of inferences' but demands the very depths of a person's faith and will. Oakeley's humility is also made visible here, though, especially in the moving letters he wrote to old friends – including those to Archbishop Tate.

Pusey knew that 'in Divine things, awe, wonder, the absorbing of infinity, of purity, or of holiness, infuse conviction more directly than reasoning'. The life of Canon Oakeley was similarly infused and itself a translation of the divine invitation: 'O come let us adore Him'.

†Richard London:

Chapter One

Shrewsbury, Lichfield and Highclere

THE EARLY YEARS

It is very pleasant to me to recall the memory of a period which I have always regarded as one of the happiest in my early life.
Frederick Oakeley to George Henry Sumner, 5 May 1875

With the exception of the factual information about the career of Sir Charles Oakeley, the father of Frederick Oakeley, everything that follows in this chapter comes from the old age memories of Frederick himself. Every piece of information regarding his childhood and youth is derived from his own autobiographical and apologetical writings, all of which were written in the 1870s, in the last few years of his life. As there is no biography of his father or of his brothers or sisters, there is no means by which Oakeley's statements about his earliest years can be verified, and we are dependent on his own descriptive accounts of his life at Shrewsbury, Lichfield and Highclere. As they largely describe his personal experiences and reactions to his surroundings and the people that he met, they can only be accepted as they stand, but with the caveat that they were written more than half a century after the events that they describe, with hindsight, and with the powerful editorial traits of the memory in full control. With any individual, the memories of childhood and youth are edited and coloured by time and the experience of succeeding years.

Frederick Oakeley was born on 5 September 1802 at the Abbey House, Shrewsbury, the youngest of the ten children of Sir Charles Oakeley, Bt., and his wife Helena. The Oakeley family were prosperous gentry who had moved around the west midlands of England for several generations, tracing their ancestry back to Roger Ockely of Okley in Shropshire, who lived in the second half of the fourteenth century. The name evolved through 'Okeley' until it assumed its present spelling in the sixteenth century. Richard Oakeley, of Oakeley, was member of parliament for Bishop's Castle from 1623 and a distinguished supporter of the royalist cause in the Civil War. His son, William Oakeley, also member of parliament for Bishop's Castle, was rewarded at the Restoration in 1660 by being appointed high sheriff of Shropshire. His third and youngest son, also named William, was the father of the Reverend William Oakeley (1717–1803), Rector of Forton in Staffordshire and subsequently Vicar of Holy Cross, Shrewsbury, and grandfather of Frederick.[1]

Were it not that the Reverend William Oakeley died when Frederick was only one year old, it would be tempting to speculate that the seeds of Frederick's attraction to the Oxford Movement in his adult life might have been sown in infancy by his grandfather. In eighteenth century England, the eucharist was celebrated only four times per year as a general rule[2] and as late as the 1830s it was not unknown for a devout layman to go to church twice every Sunday, yet to receive the sacrament only twice in the first five years after his confirmation.[3] However, at Forton, there was a monthly celebration of the eucharist as early as 1751, and William Oakeley was one of the few Staffordshire country clergy to maintain Wednesday and Friday prayers in accordance with the rubrics of *The Book of Common Prayer*.[4] He remained at Forton until 1782 when he moved to Shrewsbury to become vicar of the abbey church of Holy Cross.[5] Of his two sons, the elder, William, was born in 1750 and married Margaret, daughter and heiress of Evan Gryffydd of Plas Tan-y-Bwlch in what was then the county of Merionethshire. He died in 1811, leaving an only son, also named William (1790–1835).[6]

The Reverend William Oakeley's younger son, Charles, was born on 27 February 1751. After leaving school at the age of fifteen, he joined the service of the East India Company, and was appointed to a writership in the presidency of Madras.[7] He arrived in India on 6 June 1767 and, after five years as an assistant, he was appointed to the office of secretary to the civil department. In 1777 he was transferred to the military and political department where he remained until November 1780. At that time he found his health to be 'much impaired by too sedentary a life',[8] and he resigned. External affairs intervened to bring about a change in this position. The army of the East India Company found itself faced with an insurrection and retreated to Madras unable to control anything of the surrounding countryside. The arrival of Lord Macartney in June 1781 to deal with the situation, drew a promise from the native ruler of Arcot that the revenues of his state would be assigned to support the expenses of the war. Macartney appointed Charles Oakeley as president of a committee charged with the collection of the revenue. Oakeley rose to the task and the committee was publicly thanked for its efforts, and in 1786 he was placed in charge of the board established to supervise the collection of all the revenues under the jurisdiction of the presidency of Madras.

He returned to England in the autumn of 1789 after twenty-two years in India, 'on account of his family affairs',[9] and was created a baronet on 5 June 1790 for his services. Although he had no desire to seek further employment abroad, his distinguished service in India brought an invitation from the directors of the company to return to India later that year as Governor of Madras. Oakeley proved to be a competent governor and returned to England finally in 1794 to receive a unanimous vote of thanks from the court of directors.[10] In 1777 he had married Helena, only daughter of Rover Beatson, of Kilrie, Fifeshire, 'a woman of great energy and artistic talent',[11] and both he and his wife and their children retired to live in the west country. They took up residence at the Abbey House, Shrewsbury, to be close to Sir Charles' father, now seventy-seven years old and vicar of the neighbouring church of Holy Cross.[12] It was here that Frederick, the youngest of their ten children, was born.

Shrewsbury Abbey was a Benedictine house, founded in the eleventh century by monks from the Abbey of St Martin at Seez. It was dissolved with the other greater monasteries in 1540.[13] Holy Cross Church was the nave of the abbey church, and Abbey House, a large Queen Anne building had been constructed on the site of the abbey itself.[14] There were substantial remains of the abbey ruins still standing in the late eighteenth and early nineteenth centuries, but the remains were swept away in 1836 when Thomas Telford constructed the new Holyhead road close to the south side of the church. As a child, Frederick could remember a number of relics of the abbey, including a stone pulpit which used to stand in the garden of the house; it was later moved to a neighbouring field much to the annoyance of the older inhabitants of Shrewsbury 'who had been in the habit of regarding it with a kind of veneration as a monument of great antiquity and religious interest'.[15] The house and grounds were surrounded by a massive stone wall, another relic of the abbey, also subsequently demolished.

The Reverend William Oakeley died in October 1803 at the age of eighty-six, but Sir Charles and his wife and family were happily settled in Shrewsbury after nine years residence at the Abbey House, and there is no evidence that they contemplated moving at that time. With the coming to power of Napoleon Bonaparte in France, and the prospect of a French invasion, Sir Charles was appointed colonel of the Shrewsbury Volunteers, a local militia formed to act as a last defence against an invading army,[16] and the young Frederick recalled that his nurses made much of the prevailing panic. Whenever he was badly behaved he was rebuked and exhorted to be good with the threat, 'Boney is coming'. 'This fear made such an impression on my imagination that whenever I saw an unusually tall man coming towards me, I fancied it was "Boney".'[17] Sir Charles' connection with the volunteers awakened a kind of military ardour in his youngest son, who took to walking up and down a corridor in the house, wearing a red jacket, beating a drum and humming military tunes.[18]

Frederick Oakeley's most vivid memory of his childhood was of an incident in the summer of 1806 when he was three years old, that was to affect him for the rest of his life. He was sitting in one of the nurseries at the Abbey House, writing a letter to his mother, who was then in London, 'telling her of the arrival in Shrewsbury of "eight caravans of wild beasts belonging to Mr Polito's menagerie".'[19] He went into the adjoining nursery to sharpen his pencil and, on his return, slipped on a step which had just been washed and soaped, and fell, breaking the thigh bone of his right leg. A surgeon was called, and set the broken leg almost immediately, but he had to spend six weeks in bed.[20]

The incident is of interest, partly because it left Frederick Oakeley with a pronounced limp for the rest of his life, and partly because it ensured that his formal schooling was delayed until he arrived at Highclere in 1817. He spent a great deal of time with his mother until he was fifteen years old, making it much more difficult for him to make friends with his peers. His recovery was a long and slow process and he had to be moved about from room to room in the hollow of a chess table. Outdoor exercises were out of the question, although he was taken outside occasionally in a little carriage.[21] He had a remarkable degree of natural resilience since his spirits were never affected by his infirmity.[22]

Sea bathing was increasingly fashionable at the time of his accident and was recommended to Lady Oakeley as a way of strengthening the weakness in her son's leg.[23] She took him away with her every summer between 1807 and 1810, mostly to the seaside. The location of their first journey is unrecorded, though Frederick remembered that he was terrified by 'an immense blue woman in a blue bathing gown . . . waddling towards us with arms outstretched to receive me . . . she sought to entice me into the water by telling me that I should see the pretty fish'.[24] The ruse worked only once and he refused to enter the water a second time unless his mother agreed to accompany him.

Summer holidays with his mother were a source of great happiness to the young Frederick. In 1808 they went to Aberystwyth, by which time, he had overcome his fear of sea bathing, and, although still very lame, no longer needed the chess table and the carriage, being able to walk about with a stick.[25] In the summer of 1809 he went with his mother and his unmarried sisters to Malvern where he enjoyed wandering over the Malvern Hills, though 'I suppose it must have been on a donkey',[26] and then on to Warwick for a visit to his married sister. A further journey to the seaside was made in 1810 with a visit to Penrhyn, though it found little favour with the young Oakeley who remembered it consisting of little more than 'pebble and mussel shells'.[27] From Penrhyn they went on to visit the seat of his uncle William Oakeley, Plas Tan-y-Bwlch, in the Vale of Ffestiniog, where Lady Oakeley did some sketching, one of her favourite pastimes, and at which she was quite proficient. William Oakeley had inherited a slate mine from his father-in-law, and a public house called 'The Oakeley Arms' can still be seen there. From Tan-y-Bwlch they went to Barmouth where the fine sand made up for the shortcomings of Penrhyn.[28]

In 1810, Sir Charles Oakeley decided that the time had come to move from the Abbey House. For several winters past the family had suffered considerable inconvenience from flooding caused by the River Severn which fed a small lake at the back of the house. The lake rose with the river, flooding the ground floor rooms of the house. The approaches to the house were inundated and access was possible only by boat. Tradesmen had to unload their goods from boats moored outside the ground floor windows.[29] Sir Charles searched for a suitable residence in the neighbourhood of Shrewsbury but nothing could be found, so he accepted the offer of the episcopal palace in Lichfield at a very low rent, on condition that he spent a certain amount of money on the necessary repairs to the building.[30] The palace had been rebuilt in 1687 in the classical style that was fashionable at the time but, during the eighteenth and early nineteenth centuries, successive bishops of Lichfield preferred to live the life of country gentlemen at Eccleshall Castle near Stafford,[31] perhaps in the belief that they would be able to maintain a more detached view of the diocesan scene by removing themselves from the centre of ecclesiastical activity. George Augustus Selwyn was the first bishop to return to Lichfield and live at the palace, moving there in 1867. When Sir Charles Oakeley agreed to undertake the conditions of tenancy, the palace had been vacant since the death of Anna Seward, the poet and novelist, on 25 March 1809. She had succeeded her father, Canon Thomas Seward, on his death in 1790, as tenant of the palace.[32]

Frederick Oakeley was eight years old at the time of the move to Lichfield, and had not lived at Shrewsbury long enough to miss the Abbey House, and he remembered looking forward with excited anticipation to the prospect of a change. But the move which might otherwise have been happy coincided with a further period of ill-health, not only for Frederick but also for his mother. The nature of Lady Oakeley's illness is unknown but her son remembered that it was 'lingering'.[33] It continued until the summer of 1811 when she went to London to take medical advice, taking Frederick with her. They stayed at 20 Savile Row, the house of his brother-in-law, for about five or six weeks, the whole of which period Lady Oakeley spent in her bedroom, Frederick being her constant companion.[34] She recovered in due course and returned to Lichfield only for Frederick to develop an internal abscess which was so serious that Lady Oakeley took him back to London in June 1812 to consult a surgeon.[35] It was diagnosed as a lumbar abscess which would swell until it broke, and the prognosis was not good. 'They said also that I should be reduced to a state of alarming weakness and that a hectic fever would supervene which in all probability would be the cause of my death'.[36] The abscess, which broke in August 1813, proved not to be fatal, and in October he went with his mother on a convalescent trip to his sister Georgina and her husband at their home, Sandford Park, in Oxfordshire.[37]

Frederick Oakeley's education began properly in 1814 when he was sent as a day scholar to the grammar school in Lichfield. There was no question of him boarding since his health was still too frail, and even the walks to and from school proved to be a major effort.[38] Until this brief experiment with public schooling, he had been taught entirely by his parents. His father had taught him the rudiments of Latin and arithmetic, while his mother had taught him writing, geography, French and drawing.[39] Frederick believed in later years that his short stay at Lichfield had been of no real benefit to him 'although I understand that the master took all the credit for my subsequent successes at Oxford'.[40]

From the small amount of information that Oakeley gives about his days at the school, it appears that he was lonely and unhappy. It was his first real experience of a school environment and one that he endured rather than enjoyed. Because he was only a day boy, there was no possibility of him being forced to take part in the everyday life of the school, and of making friendships with boys of his own age, both of which might have issued from thorough immersion as a boarder. He had no inclination to join the games of the other boys after dinner, and used to wander about alone while they were at play. 'There were not more than one or two of them with whom I could associate and altogether was by no means sorry when it was found necessary to bring my connection with the school to an end'.[41]

His unhappy experience with schooling at Lichfield is difficult to explain at this distance in time, and Oakeley himself volunteers little information on the subject, although his family and his health are probable factors. He was the youngest of ten children and, if not spoiled, was certainly doted on by his mother and spent much of his time in her company. In all probability his elder brothers and sisters behaved in much the same way, though he says very little about them in his autobiography. He was also unlucky enough to suffer a great deal of ill-health through most of his childhood which only served to increase the close links with his mother and to remove him, in those early formative years, from any outside friendships. Though he was accomplished at performing Shakespeare on his own before an enthusiastic audience consisting of the family servants,[42] this extrovert behaviour in front of those who could be considered friends and supporters was transformed into a deep shyness when confronted with his contemporaries and equals. The pattern of initial withdrawal, loneliness and unhappiness in a new environment was repeated at Highclere in 1817 and at Christ Church, Oxford, in 1820, and this certain shyness in the face of new people or new situations never entirely left him.

He fell ill again in the autumn of 1815 with the recurrence of an abscess, this time on his knee. It was eventually cured, but he was left with a stiffness in his leg which remained with him for the rest of his life.[43] It is unclear from Oakeley's autobiography whether the abscess occurred on the leg which had been broken some ten years earlier, and compounded his difficulty in walking, or whether it was on the other leg, and therefore made walking even more difficult than it was already.

In the autumn of 1817, he was sent away to boarding school. He was fifteen years old, and if a university education was ever to be a reality, he would need a higher and more thorough standard of teaching than his parents were able to give him. Sir Charles and Lady Oakeley were concerned to find the right school for their 'delicate' youngest son, and sought the advice of their third son, Herbert[44] then Domestic Chaplain to the Bishop of London.[45] The recommendation was that he should be sent to board with Charles Sumner[46] at his house at Highclere in Hampshire.[47]

Sumner was born in 1790, the younger son of Robert Sumner, vicar of Kenilworth. After graduating from Trinity College, Cambridge, in 1814, he was ordained deacon at Trinity that year by the bishop of Norwich and secured an appointment as tutor and companion to the two young sons of the Marquess and Marchioness Conyngham. This association may have been highly beneficial for Sumner, and had something to do with his early preferment; the marquess was lord chamberlain and his wife was the mistress of the Prince Regent, later King George IV. In 1826, at the age of only thirty-six, Sumner was appointed Bishop of Llandaff and Dean of St Paul's Cathedral.

Almost immediately after his appointment, Sumner accompanied the Conynghams on a visit to Switzerland. After passing through France and along the Rhone Valley, they arrived at Geneva where they stayed for some months. There, Sumner was introduced to a young Swiss girl, Jennie de Maunoir. After a lengthy engagement, they were married at the English Protestant Church in Geneva in January 1816. Returning to England, Charles was appointed curate of the parish of Highclere, near Newbury in Hampshire, with the large handsome glebe house set in the park as his residence. Sumner intended to continue his career in tutoring as a business, and he needed a large and spacious house for a total household of twelve, with three in the family, three servants and six pupils. There was no lack of pupils and Sumner was able to charge £250p.a. for each, instead of the £200 that he had originally proposed.[48]

Frederick Oakeley left for Highclere on 19 September 1817. He began his schooling with the inevitable period of difficulty but it was overcome and he later recalled that his three years at Highclere constituted a period that was 'one of the happiest in my early life'.[48] Before setting off, he had no worries about his life there since he had no real picture in his mind of what it might be like, and he looked forward to the experience with some anticipation. The small size of the school made the initial settling in period easier than it might otherwise have been, but there were still problems. Oakeley remembered Sumner himself as 'kind and amiable' and well suited to dealing with 'a youth like myself, who had been used from infancy to the care and indulgences of home'.[49] But there were problems with his fellow pupils and the first few days at Highclere were anything but happy. Jennie Sumner who later proved to be a close companion was ill in bed at the time of his arrival. He was shown around the house and grounds by a fellow pupil. 'During the course of our walk I first became conscious of that terrible sense of desolation ... I began to realise the fact that I was in a strange place in the midst of strange companions and at a distance of upwards of one hundred miles from everything and everyone I loved. I left my new acquaintance rather abruptly and went to my room to have a good cry'.[50]

Life did not become easier over the succeeding weeks and he found himself, like many a new boy at a school, the object of some persecution. He had hopefully and trustingly expected a degree of support from his peers and was sadly disappointed.[51] Since the other boys had all been to public or private schools of one sort or another, they had experienced something of the rough and tumble of school life. Frederick was at a disadvantage, not having associated with boys of his own age. Although the behaviour of the other boys at the school was unintelligible to him at the time, he realised with hindsight that he must have presented to them an appearance somewhere between 'a prig and a mollycoddle'.[52] At no time did he complain to Sumner of the bullying, on the assumption that it would increase as a result. On one occasion, when Sumner had gone away for a few days, Oakeley was talking to Jennie Sumner while the other boys were making a considerable noise upstairs. They ignored Mrs Sumner's repeated requests for silence and she reported them to her husband on his return. Sumner assembled the boys and, much to Oakeley's acute embarrassment, turned to him and said that he was glad to find that there was one gentleman in the house. Oakeley thought this a 'somewhat injudicious, although most kindly intended remark',[53] and feared retribution of the worst kind. It did not materialise, and from that point onwards the other boys began to treat him with more consideration. The one factor that eased his difficult early period at the school was the presence of Jennie Sumner. They became friends when he discovered that she shared his love of music, and she appears to have filled the vacuum left by the absence of Lady Oakeley. Frederick ever afterwards remembered the 'relief and consolation which I . . . derived from her kind and genial influence'.[54]

The daily round of work at Highclere was intensive, beginning with a study of the Greek New Testament and a Greek play at 8am, followed by family prayers and then breakfast at 9am. After breakfast, a recreation period of thirty minutes was allowed before the boys went to their rooms to work individually. They met again in Sumner's study at midday before being allowed to spend the early part of the afternoon amusing themselves. Dinner was at 4pm, followed by more work, and at 7pm they would be expected to take their verses or other compositions to Sumner for correction. When this was done, tea was served in the drawing room and then Sumner would read aloud one of Shakespeare's plays or some other standard work or publication of the day. On Sundays they were required to write an exercise on some religious subject or an analysis of one of the sermons they had heard in church. These were read aloud to the assembled school after tea, and Sumner would comment on them. The day ended at 10pm.[55] The school curriculum was inevitably guided by the university curriculum which attached great importance to the knowledge of theology and the classical languages and literature. Within a few months of his arrival at Highclere Oakeley had acquired 'a tolerable facility in the composition of Latin verse, and translated into hexameters and pentameters the whole of Cowper's beautiful lines on receiving his mother's portrait'.[56]

> *Oh that those lips had language! Life has pass'd*
> *With but roughly since I heard thee last.*
> *Those lips are thine – thy own sweet smiles I see,*
> *The same that oft in childhood solac'd me.*

Charles Sumner required a high standard of knowledge from his pupils and was capable of delivering severe criticism for mistakes or faults. Oakeley recalled an occasion when he delivered his exercise one Sunday afternoon, only to be told by Sumner in front of the whole school that he had fallen into the Socinian heresy. Oakeley was quite unaware of such obscure byways of doctrinal history and was quite hurt by the comment.[57] His opportunity for revenge came at a subsequent Greek Testament lesson when he argued, on the basis of Matthew 16:19,[58] that Christ had delivered the keys of the kingdom in a unique way to St Peter alone. Sumner, whose mind had wandered at that moment, feared that Oakeley was developing a dangerous tendency towards Roman doctrine and maintained, on the strength of Matthew 18:18,[59] that the promise was given to all the apostles. Sumner afterwards realised that Oakeley's argument was well-founded and was quick to apologise.

How far this exchange indicates a development in Oakeley's religious thought is impossible to say. But he remembered it for his autobiography many years later, and argued his point 'with somewhat unbecoming vehemence'.[60] Sumner was always careful to avoid teaching doctrine and Oakeley described him as 'singularly reserved and even reticent on the subject'.[61] Any knowledge of doctrine that Oakeley and his fellow pupils gained from Sumner was derived entirely from his sermons and from incidental remarks which opened up to them 'a more earnest appreciation of the realities of the unseen world, than most of us had been familiar with in our previous experience'.[62]

The Christmas holiday of 1817, spent at home in Lichfield, was happy, though less so than he had expected, since the realities of life at Highclere and a life away from home, had inevitably brought about a changed perspective on his home life. Writing many years later, Oakeley made no attempt to analyse this change saying only that he had learned by experience that 'the realities of life do not always correspond with our day dreams and castles in the air'.[63] The return to Highclere early in 1818 was even more difficult for similar reasons, but by the fact that he was returning to a well-established pattern, the

period of unhappiness at the start of his second term was comparatively short. He suffered badly from home-sickness and was much
more unwilling to leave his family at Lichfield since he now knew
what to expect. But he soon recovered and made friends with the
pupils who had bullied him at first. The two elder ones left for good
in the summer of 1818, and when he returned for his second year in
the autumn, he was now in the privileged position of being able to
welcome newcomers, and no longer the victim of what he described as
an 'established and somewhat unmerciful tradition'.[64] From then on
his schooling at Highclere was comparatively painless and, the early
days over, he could write that his life 'was one round of continuous
enjoyment . . . the studies useful and improving without being too
laborious'.[65]

Highclere performed wonders for Oakeley's health. After ten years
as a lame and sickly child, his physical health dramatically improved
to the extent that he could walk several miles a day without difficulty. His lameness was permanent, but in all other respects he
enjoyed good health until the last few years of his life.[66] The house
was beautifully situated and, in Oakeley's estimation, it was 'almost
without rival in England'.[67] The parsonage itself was on the edge of
the estate of Highclere Castle, the country home of the Earl of
Carnarvon, who allowed the boys to use the park without any restriction. The estate consisted of extensive woodland, a lake fringed with
rhododendrons, a garden 'filled with the rarest flowers and plants',
and Siddon and Beacon Hills.[68] In his spare time, Oakeley enjoyed
himself early in the morning by fishing in a stream on Woodhay
Common, riding to Newbury on Sumner's pony, taking long walks
through the woods and climbing Siddon Hill. 'I was also fond of
paying long visits to a good gossiping old woman on Woodhay
Common'.[69]

Oakeley left Highclere in July 1820, nearly eighteen years old, to
go to Christ Church, Oxford, but he never lost his great affection for
Highclere and for Charles and Jennie Sumner. He visited them on
several occasions until they left Highclere in 1822, and thereafter at
their various homes until 1843, when he met them in London for the
last time. As his religious opinions changed through the 1840s he
sensed that Sumner would disapprove of his actions and views and
carefully avoided meeting him for fear of causing any embarrassment. His reception into the Roman Catholic Church in 1845 ensured
a break in relations, but only for a short period. When Jennie Sumner
died in 1849, Oakeley offered his condolences and, though they
did not meet again, Frederick Oakeley and Charles Sumner continued
to exchange friendly letters with each other until Sumner died in

1874.[70] Oakeley visited Highclere only twice after the departure of
the Sumners. After his suspension by the Court of Arches in the
summer of 1845, he went to stay at the house of a relative close to
Highclere, and he took the opportunity to visit the scene of a more
tranquil part of his life. He went to Highclere again, and for the last
time, in 1869.[71]

After Sumner's death in 1874, his son, George Henry Sumner,
began work on an biography of his father, and wrote to Oakeley
asking him to record his memories of the little school at Highclere.
Oakeley replied without hesitation. 'It is very pleasant to me to recall
the memory of a period which I have always regarded as one of the
happiest in my early life ... I used to fancy that Highclere, with its
magnificent park, its gently sloping hills, its densely shaded pine
woods, its glassy lakes, and its hedges of rhododendrons, must be the
most beautiful spot in creation. But as this was at an age when imagination is vivid, and experience limited, I am willing that my opinion
on the subject should be received with the necessary deductions.
However, after revisiting it only a few years ago, I still maintain that
it is almost without a rival in England ... We had the use of the
boats on Milford Lake, could climb bare Beacon, or woody Siddon
without molestation, while those who, like myself, happened to
possess a taste for floriculture, had access, on stated occasions, to the
gardens, with their choice collection of plants'.[72]

In his autobiography, Oakeley attributed his lack of interest in religion during childhood to the fact that he had been raised at a time in
the history of England when the religious education of children and
young people was 'imperfectly understood and still more imperfectly
carried out ... There were none of those expedients and appliances
by which in these days the youthful mind is attracted to things unseen
and ... religion was the one subject which remained a lifeless form,
while all else was invested with the power of reality'.[73] He recalled
that the most serious objection to the enjoyment of religion as a child
was the strict observance of Sunday. No music of any kind, sacred or
otherwise, could be heard outside a church on Sunday, and all forms
of cheerful recreation were strictly forbidden. In the summer months,
the delights of the palace gardens at Lichfield could be set against the
sobriety of the day, but during the winter 'there was nothing whatever to compensate for the absence of all the customary provisions
for the relaxation of the youthful mind'.[74]

Oakeley had a scanty and superficial knowledge of the religion
professed by his parents,[75] though this was due more to his close association with his mother than anything else. Lady Oakeley had been
brought up in Scotland 'among presbyterians' (it is not clear whether

she herself was a presbyterian) and had been taken to India at the age of fourteen 'where the deficiencies of such an education were not likely to be supplied in the thoroughly worldly atmosphere of oriental society'.[76] Her religious character did not develop until a much later period of her life in response to 'domestic afflictions and reverses of fortune'.[77] Sir Charles Oakeley was quite different. Frederick described his father as 'humble, devout and essentially unworldly',[78] and totally unaffected by the twenty years he had spent in Indian society. 'His piety was fervent, sincere and uniform; equally removed from lukewarmness on the one hand, and enthusiasm on the other'.[79] Sir Charles spent an hour in prayer and meditation before breakfast every morning, and when the family lived at Shrewsbury, he attended Wednesday and Friday prayers at the parish church. After the move to Lichfield in 1810 he attended morning prayer at the Cathedral every day, and the dean and chapter set aside two stalls in the choir for the use of himself and one of his sons. He took an active role in the charitable institutions of Shrewsbury and Lichfield, and was abstemious in his habits. Sir Charles won a considerable amount of respect, bordering on veneration and, according to his son, his presence in a company was sufficient to stop all immoral conversation. When he was sixty years old he decided to learn Hebrew with the intention of enabling himself to read the Old Testament in the original.[80]

Frederick could remember saying his daily prayers from a very early age, although they were of 'a thoroughly infantine character',[81] and probably taught to him by his mother. He continued to use them by sheer force of habit, long after they should have been superseded, and it was only during his years at Highclere that he stopped praying that he might be made 'a good boy unto my life's end'.[82] He was taken to church twice a day at Shrewsbury but the family pew was of the large high-walled 'box' variety which was not guaranteed to stimulate or nurture devotion in the very young.[83] His autobiography records that by the time of the move to Lichfield, he had begun to value a somewhat more ceremonial and ornate form of worship than that of a 'protestant parish church' and that the music of Lichfield Cathedral was 'rather of a superior order' and 'had a special charm for me'.[84] This statement should not to be accepted at face value. Whether an eight year old boy was so discerning and demanding in the field of liturgy is a matter of some doubt. Oakeley wrote these sentences long after he had become a Roman Catholic, and his use of the word 'protestant' to describe his grandfather's church in Shrewsbury indicates that he was writing with hindsight in the light of his subsequent career. But the music of the cathedral added materially to his pleasure in attending church, to the extent that 'the purity of my motive may have been vitiated by my natural fondness for music'.[85]

During his childhood years at Lichfield, Frederick Oakeley first came to know that phenomenon with which he was to be intimately acquainted for most of the second half of his life – the Roman Catholic Church – albeit in a slight and shallow way. As a child he knew almost nothing about Roman Catholics other than what he had learned through hearsay, or else had embroidered on the basis of very scanty information. Ignorance of Roman Catholics in nineteenth century England was widespread until the passage of the Roman Catholic Relief Act in 1829. Roman Catholics were thought of as a tiny and arcane body of people practising equally arcane and 'un-English' rites. When John Henry Newman was Curate of St Clement's, Oxford, in the 1820s, he once chided a parishioner who consistently stayed away from the parish church, having no idea that the man was a Roman Catholic priest.[86] Oakeley thought it no exaggeration to say that he and many of his contemporaries knew far more about the manners and customs of the ancient Egyptians or Scythian tribes than of the Roman Catholics.[87] 'I thought that Roman Catholics did not ... number more than about 80 or 100 souls, who were distributed in certain great families over the midland and northern counties. I thought that each of these families lived in a large haunted house, embosomed in yew trees, and surrounded by high brick walls ... I thought they were made up of vast dreary apartments, walled with tapestry; with state bedrooms in which were enormous beds, with ebony bedsteads surmounted by plumes, and which only required horses to be put to them in order to become funeral cars. I fancied ... that there reigned around and within these abodes a preternatural silence, broken only by the flapping of bats and the screeching of owls ... But who and what were the inmates of these dwellings ... They were never to be seen in public places, and if they ever went abroad it must be in company with the aforesaid owls and bats and other such shy and lucifugous creatures'.[88]

Of Roman Catholic churches and priests, Oakeley had a clearer picture since he knew the small suburban chapel about half a mile outside Lichfield on the London road which functioned as the Catholic church for the district and in which 'unmentionable rites' were perpetrated.[89] As a boy he regarded this chapel with contempt, inevitably comparing it with the stately grandeur of Lichfield Cathedral where his early ideas of religion lay.[90] The only aspect of humanity was the modest little presbytery by the side of the chapel 'with its wicket by the side of the road and its narrow gravel walk, edged with neatly trimmed box'.[91] Here lived Dr Kirk,[92] the Roman Catholic priest.

From other reports Kirk was the very model of a priest – simple, innocent, devout and learned. He was an accomplished scholar and
well-versed in French, Latin, Greek and Hebrew, but to the young
Frederick Oakeley he looked like a cross between a 'Jew pedlar and a
quack doctor'.[93] None of his friends would say anything about Dr Kirk
other than that he was a 'Catholic priest', 'and what a "Catholic
priest" might be I thought it safer not to investigate'.[94] These childhood images were eventually laid to rest in 1846, after Oakeley had
become what he had once thought it safer not to investigate. He celebrated mass for the first time in that suburban chapel and made the
acquaintance of Dr Kirk, eighty-six years old and still parish priest of
Lichfield.[95]

Oakeley's ignorance of the Roman Catholic Church was much
strengthened by the fact that it was never mentioned in conversation
at home. It was felt that to raise it in discussion in front of children
would awaken their curiosity on a dangerous subject, and, in any
case, it was as likely for an individual to become a Moslem as a
Catholic. In the nineteenth century, Protestantism was still deeply
ingrained on the English national consciousness, and had been since
the revolution of 1688 which was then still called the 'Glorious
Revolution'. This produced a distrust of Roman Catholics as people
who, by their refusal to join the national church and conform to the
establishment, were long suspected of disloyalty to the state, and
barely tolerated. With memories of the 'Popish Plot', Roman Catholicism was still seen as something essentially un-English, sinister,
and politically threatening; and this was the view that Oakeley held
for several more years. In 1855, ten years after he became a Roman
Catholic, he was still haunted by a verse from the nursery rhyme,
'The House that Jack built', that he had learned as a child in the
nursery.

> *'The Priest all shaven and shorn*
> *That married the man all tattered and torn,*
> *That wooed the maiden all forlorn'.*[96]

During the passage of the Roman Catholic Relief Act in 1829,
Oakeley had breakfast with Sumner, who was by then Bishop of
Winchester, at his house in St James's Square, London. 'The conversation turned on the personal character of Roman Catholics, against
whom I was thoughtless enough to bring some of the more popular
charges. [Sumner] listened in silence, and at length turned towards
me, and said, very calmly, "Oakeley, are you personally acquainted
with any Roman Catholic?" I replied that to the best of my knowledge

I had never spoke to one in my life. "Then", rejoined the Bishop, would it not be better to abstain from talking against them".'[97]

Beyond absorbing this national inchoate suspicion of Catholicism and Catholic priests, Oakeley carried no deep or settled views of religion with him to Highclere, and Charles Sumner's reluctance to speak directly on the subject meant that he arrived at Oxford in 1820 with no more personal religion that that which he had acquired in childhood. But he did carry away from Highclere a distinct memory of one sermon preached by Sumner. Writing in his old age, Oakeley gave two texts for the sermon. In a letter to George Sumner, dated May 1875, he recalled it as being 'What shall I do to be saved?' (Acts 16:30), and that it was the first sermon that he heard Sumner preach.[98] 'I had never before heard one which appeared to me so striking in matter, or was so impressively delivered'.[99] In his 1879 autobiographical memoir, he gave it as 'Lord, what wilt thou have me to do?' (Acts 9:6),[100] stating that it was the only sermon from his childhood years that made any deep impression on him. '(It) opened upon me a view of the Christian's duty which had never before presented itself to my mind'.[101] In neither document does Oakeley indicate the effect of the sermon, assuming that he is referring to a single sermon, on his subsequent life, but it was probably in his mind on the occasion of his penultimate visit to Highclere during the summer of the eventful year of 1845, and he retained the memory of it to the end of his life.

The golden days of Oakeley's youth were almost over. In 1820, he left the arcadian landscape of Highclere and the protective tutelage of George and Jennie Sumner, for the rough and tumble of life as an undergraduate at the University of Oxford.

Chapter Two

Oxford and the Tractarians

THE FORMATIVE YEARS

You have kept your opinions; I have a good deal changed mine.
Frederick Oakeley to Archibald Tait, 1838

Oakeley went up to Christ Church, Oxford in October 1820 to begin life as an undergraduate. His first months there proved to be something of a rude awakening when he realised that the effects of his home life had not been so successfully cured at Highclere as he had at first supposed. He remembered being 'visited by a persecution less violent than that to which I had been previously exposed, but scarcely less trying to a youth who had by no means conquered somewhat excessive attachment to dear number one'.[1] Shy and ill-at-ease freshmen were not in the best position to survive the rigours of the social life of Christ Church in the 1820s and Oakeley soon found himself 'dropped' by those to whom he was introduced or with whom he tried to strike up a friendship. His tutor introduced him to two fellow undergraduates 'and commended me to their good offices, an injunction which they respected by cutting me the first time they met me . . . I soon became so miserable that I did not like to leave my room more than I could help'.[2]

Christ Church in Oakeley's day was probably no worse than any other Oxford college, although it tended to recruit its undergraduates from the ranks of the aristocracy, but its rowdy and bawdy social atmosphere offended the slightly puritanical streak in his nature, and his shyness only made matters worse and he never adjusted to life at the college to the point of enjoyment, as at Highclere. Oakeley attributed this to the fact of Christ Church being the place of his public education,[3] and though there may be an element of truth in this statement, there is more to the story than that. He states that he 'was never at any school at all which could deserve the name. Hence I had to encounter at the age of eighteen those trials which most boys get through and leave behind at the age of eight, the trial of feeling oneself suddenly in an entirely new world, and that a world of the most inconsiderate and unsympathising portion of the rational creation'.[4] This resembles his initial reaction both to the grammar school at Lichfield in 1814, and to Highclere in 1817. Though the latter may not have merited the title of school in quite the same way as Lichfield and Christ Church, Oakeley's reactions on each occasion are too similar to ignore.

His dislike of Christ Church remained, and in his autobiography he recalled its 'boisterous and heartless character', and of his unwilling role as the 'butt of badgering tutors and the sport of overbearing undergraduates'.[5] Making friends, in this case with his fellow undergraduates, was no easier for Oakeley than making friends had ever been, and it was not helped by his attitude. 'I do really think that Christ Church was . . . in my time, the most degraded in respect of all that relates to the true end of our existence . . . I cannot recollect any set of men, however regular in ordinary college duties . . . of whom I do not feel sure that, they were, as a set, addicted to vice and loose conversation'.[6]

Oakeley was so thoroughly lonely that he grasped at the first hand of friendship that was shown, and soon found himself part of a set of undergraduates thoroughly unlike him in every respect, 'but to whom I was attracted by their kindness of manner and the compassionate interest which they appeared to take in my lonely situation'.[7] Whoever they were, and Oakeley says no more than that some of them were of noble birth, they were not interested in academic study, since he soon realised that his association with them was ruining his academic chances. 'I got into the habit of card playing and late suppers; not adverting to the fact that my name went up to the senior censor with those which were in no good odour . . . I also grew irregular at morning chapels . . . [and] began to see all this would not do'.[8] But he discovered that it was much easier to get into a set than to get out, and the effort cost him much sacrifice of feeling since his new acquaintances had developed a genuine liking for him. He succeeded in dissociating himself from them, only to discover that it was too late to join another set, and for the remainder of his undergraduate days, he hovered on the fringes of Christ Church society without ever again penetrating it.[9]

The point of transformation had been reached, and Oakeley began to study hard, rising at 5am or 6am every day to read for two hours before morning chapel and breakfast. Anxious not to leave Oxford without winning one of the university prizes, he entered for everything. Among his friends was Philip Shuttleworth, who later became the anti-Tractarian Bishop of Chichester.[10] Shuttleworth told him to concentrate on Latin verse, for which Oakeley, in his view, had a great talent. He entered for, and gained, the college prize which, though not as prestigious as a university prize, nevertheless gave him great pleasure. The subject was Taprobane.[11] 'The composition', admitted Oakeley, 'was full of defects but my tutor told me that its success was due to a very animated description of an elephant hunt'.[12]

The experience of winning a prize gave him renewed confidence but did little to repair the former neglect of his studies, and he graduated in 1824 with a second class honours degree in *Literae Humaniores*. Both Frederick and his father had expected a first and both men were disappointed with the result. Oakeley's knowledge of divinity (in which all undergraduates were required to be examined) was poor and he came close to being failed. 'I should have been so had I not answered the last question by a happy guess. The examination turned chiefly upon the history of the Old Testament, and the examiner wound up by asking me whether a certain person was king of Judah or of Israel. I had no more idea than the man in the moon, but I said "Israel" which happened to be right and so I got off'.[13]

Oakeley's autobiographical recollection of the religious life of Christ Church was not much different from his general view of college life, although he was remembering Christ Church in the 1820s from the perspective of a Roman Catholic priest in the 1870s. He dismissed the body of tutors as showing little interest in religion, and the profession of any serious views on the subject was regarded as exceptional, extravagant, and not to be encouraged. Those people, and here Oakeley seems to refer to himself, who showed no interest in the 'bad' habits of the general undergraduate body felt obliged to adopt such habits 'in order to avoid the character of consequences of singularity'.[14] Sermons in college chapel were of little help, being of a highly academic nature and concerned only with the interpretation of difficult texts or abstruse points of divinity. 'The services were so managed that it would have been hardly possible for any one to make a good use of them, even had he wished it, and I do not think that such a wish was largely shared. Little or no care was taken to secure even the decent behaviour of those who attended chapel as a general rule; and it was only when that behaviour broke out, as was sometimes the case in the evening, into the most disgraceful irreverence, that authorities interposed to control it'.[15] His memory was confirmed by W. E. Gladstone who remembered that the services at Christ Church were 'scarcely performed with common decency'.[16] The picture of general irreligiousness was not entirely without relief; Oakeley recalled that Vowler Short,[17] one of the tutors, took a deep interest in the spiritual welfare of his students, and he was always spoken of in the warmest terms.[18]

Instead of leaving Oxford after his graduation, Oakeley made a decision that was to affect the rest of his life in a way that he could not have conceived in 1824. Having done less than his best as an undergraduate, he decided to stay at Christ Church and study for a college fellowship as a way of repaying the money that his parents had spent on his education. The financial situation was helped by the fact that he had a mysterious benefactor whose identity he never discovered. From time to time he was told to apply to the college treasurer, and he never came away empty-handed.[19] The decision proved to be the most important of his life and had far-reaching consequences for his future career. He remained in Oxford for fifteen years, and a very formative period it was to be. His academic career proceeded at a steady and successful rate. He won the Chancellor's Latin and English prizes in 1825 and 1827 respectively[20] and the Ellerton Theological prize also in 1827. The winning of the Latin prize was a happy occurrence because Oakeley was required to recite it in the Sheldonian Theatre on the same day that his father was given an honorary doctorate of civil law for his services in India. In 1827 he was elected to a fellowship at Balliol College. In 1830 he was appointed a tutor and catechetical lecturer. In 1831 he was Select Preacher, and in 1834 Senior Dean. In 1835 he was one of the Public Examiners of the university, and in 1837 he was appointed bursar of the college. He might have ended his days as a moderately successful don in the secure and protective environment of the university, or he might have gone to a country living in the gift of Balliol. 'He was just the man to pass a happy and useful life writing elegant and interesting lectures and sermons, and enjoying music and art and good talk without luxury or selfishness, as a distinguished Anglican clergyman'.[21] But other factors intervened to ensure that when he left Oxford in 1839, he was infused with a missionary zeal imparted to him by several years of contact with some of the brightest theological minds in Oxford at the time, and fired with a religious enthusiasm caught from the earliest disciples of what was to become known as the Oxford Movement.

After Oakeley's death in 1880, Thomas Mozley recalled him as 'an elegant and rather dilettante scholar . . . avowedly sentimental rather than decisive in his views, he seemed in a fair way to settle into a very common type of English churchman'.[22] Mozley was in no doubt that the trustees of the Ellerton Theological Prize bore some responsibility for the change in Oakeley.[23] The title of his essay was *What was the object of the Reformers in maintaining the following proposi-tion? "Holy Scriptures is the only sure foundation of any article of faith"*. The essay was never published, Oakeley giving the reason that 'although the class of subject to which it belongs is the most interest-ing possible – the peculiar one is not so much so as to interest friends in general'.[24] Did Oakeley cautiously criticise the the sixteenth century reformers, or merely acquaint himself with their thoughts and actions, and expound them? The latter is more likely since any attack on the Reformation, however mild or veiled, would have been un-likely to secure him the prize in the Oxford of 1827. Oakeley himself traced his hostile attitude to the reformation no further back than a reading of Froude's *Remains*, in 1838.[25]

His first attempt at a fellowship was made at Easter 1826 when he stood for one of two vacancies at Oriel College. He was unsuccessful and the two new fellows were R. H. Froude and Robert Wilberforce.[26] Later in the same year he tried again, this time at Balliol College, but again failed, the successful candidates being Francis William Newman and George Moberley.[27] In 1826, Oakeley became friends with Samuel Wilberforce,[28] brother of Robert, and their friendship lasted until Samuel decided to abandon his prospects of gaining a fellowship and retired to a country curacy in 1828. They both contested the election at Balliol, Oakeley remarking that his chances would greatly improve were Wilberforce to withdraw, but adding charitably, 'the nice thing would be for both of us to succeed; but that I fear is very unlikely and I am inclined to think that success would lose its charm to either of us, in proportion as it conveyed the idea of victory over the other'.[29] Later he wrote, 'I sincerely hope you may succeed if I do not and that we ulti-mately may be established as fellows of the same or of different Colleges'.[30]

Oakeley's search for a college fellowship was set against the declin-ing health of his father. After suffering a paralytic stroke and contracting dropsy of the chest, Sir Charles Oakeley died on 6 September 1826, not living to see the election of his son as Chaplain Fellow of Balliol in March 1827. Oakeley was delighted with the appointment because he had at last made amends for his performance as an undergraduate, and embarked on a career which would provide him with a good emolument and a secure position. In his autobiography he praised Balliol for its qualities which he found superior to Christ Church and Oriel, 'more sedate than the former, and less exclusively intellectual than the latter. Of its moral tone it is impos-sible to speak too highly'.[31] 'There is a great deal of gentlemanlike feeling and good taste . . . generally: and a larger proportion of agree-able young men among the fellows than is the case in most societies'.[32]

To Balliol he went, and for that college he retained a great affection until his death fifty-three years later.

As Chaplain Fellow, Oakeley was required to take holy orders and this was accomplished with little fuss or formality. He was ordained deacon by the Bishop of London in the Chapel Royal, Whitehall; and one week later he was ordained priest in Saint Paul's Cathedral, London, by his old tutor from Highclere, Charles Sumner, now Bishop of Llandaff. Oakeley has left no record of his feelings at the time of his ordinations and the inclination is to say that he was not deeply affected by them. There is no reference in his autobiography, but after he joined the Roman Catholic Church in 1845 they would have ceased to have any meaning for him. His primary ambition was to be a college fellow and the requirement that he should take holy orders was of secondary consideration. 'I consider the chapel duties a great advantage as they give habits of regularity and professional employment which in most cases here in Oxford is wanted. They do not besides compel residence or interfere with my other views though the inducement to reside is to me very desirable. On the whole I am well pleased – not extravagantly ... for that would be unwise and improper'.[33] With his deep childhood impressions of the stately worship of Lichfield Cathedral, it is probable that he conducted worship in the college chapel with seriousness and reverence. But his duties were undemanding since two months later he wrote 'I think of taking pupils to amuse and employ me'.[34] He was now a fellow of an Oxford college and a priest of the Church of England, and at a time when a wind of change was beginning to be felt in both the university and the church.

In the autumn of 1827 Oakeley began attending a series of lectures on the history of *The Book of Common Prayer* delivered by Charles Lloyd, the Regius Professor of Divinity and newly-appointed Bishop of Oxford.[35] Lloyd was a great liturgist and in many ways far ahead of his time. His lectures on the history and structure of *The Book of Common Prayer* led to an examination of the Roman missal and breviary as the principal sources from which the contents of the book had been drawn. Oakeley was certainly present at the lectures and described them as 'very interesting. I think the bishop will publish ere long upon the subject for he has copious materials: and regrets the want of a work in any degree authoritative and satisfactory'.[36] Lloyd's lectures were never printed, but his copious notes in the wide margins of his own prayer book were later used by William Palmer and incorporated in his *Origines liturgicae*, published in 1836.[37]

Lloyd made a deep impression on Oakeley. 'I do remember to have received from him an entirely new notion of Catholics and Catholic doctrine'.[38] Lloyd had spent time in his youth talking with Roman Catholic priests who had fled to England from the worst excesses of the French Revolution. Like others of his generation he developed a new understanding of the Roman Catholic Church, which he conveyed to his students at Oxford. He also introduced the custom of giving private instruction to candidates for holy orders, and the class of pupils that he assembled at Oxford between 1826 and 1828 included all the leaders of the Oxford Movement with the exception of John Keble who had left Oxford in 1823. Within a year of his appointment as Regius Professor, Lloyd began meeting with small informal classes of select students in his own rooms at Christ Church. Among those favoured with an invitation were Newman, Pusey, Froude, Robert Wilberforce, Thomas Mozley, Edward Denison – and Frederick Oakeley. Years later Oakeley remembered the eccentric style with which Lloyd conducted his classes. He carried a coloured pocket handkerchief and constantly indulged in snuff-taking as he sat down, bounced up, and roamed about the room without ever losing the thread of his thought, 'making the circuit of his large class once and again, and acosting its several members, or those at least whom he might choose to select, with a question which in its turn formed the handle of a reply of its own, full of information conveyed in the most attactive form'.[39]

A few years later the content of his lectures might have raised deep suspicion, but not in the peace and quiet of 1827. Lloyd was a man of independent thought and in advance of many of his contemporaries. His experience of the French priests had given him a deep sympathy for the Roman Catholic community in England. One of his students recalled that he made no secret of the fact in his lectures. 'I suppose, Mr Woods, you have been taught from your cradle upwards that it is the special duty of all to abuse Roman Catholics. That, d'ye see? I hold to be a mistake'.[40]

Lloyd's sympathy for English Roman Catholics caused his disgrace and death at the age of only forty-five. A friend and counsellor of Sir Robert Peel, Lloyd voted with Peel on the question of Catholic Emancipation in 1829 and fell into disgrace with the king and with his own clergy; after an impassioned speech in the House of Lords he developed a fever and died three weeks later. Lloyd's influence on Oakeley is clear, but his general influence on the Oxford Movement is less easy to determine. Oakeley was of the opinion that Lloyd's lectures considerably influenced the course of the movement. 'Upon that movement . . . I have no doubt whatever that his teaching had a most important influence'.[41] Yet he continued by saying that he himself derived no definite ideas from Lloyd's lectures on such subjects as the authority of the church, episcopacy and the apostolic succession – subjects with which the earliest *Tracts for the times* were exclusively occupied.[42]

After his election as Chaplain Fellow, Oakeley became friendly with the erratic and eccentric figure of Francis William Newman who had been elected a fellow in the previous year. 'He had doubtless observed in me what made him think that I stood in need of that best and highest kind of paternal charity which consists in the desire and attempt to gain over our friends to the side of truth. He invited me to take walks with him and wrote me several long letters designed to draw my attention to important matters to which he evidently felt that I was more or less a stranger'.[43] Though grateful for his friendship, Oakeley was critical of some (unspecified) opinions of Francis Newman. 'He is a very amiable man with some (as I believe) errors of opinion and without much chance of correction. But he is thoroughly conscientious and good-hearted'.[44] Oakeley showed Newman's letters to his friend Richard Hurrell Froude, 'whom I looked upon as the pink of orthodoxy'.[45] Froude, much to Oakeley's surprise, said that the letters contained a great deal of excellent advice which Oakeley should follow, but the friendship did not last long. Francis Newman became more and more erratic in his opinions and eventually left the University in 1830 to lead a strange wandering life, wrapped up in a highly individual spiritual pilgrimage.[46] The link between the two men is not of importance in itself, but the story reveals a friendship not only with F. W. Newman, but also with Froude, so providing two possible lines of friendship to Newman's brother, John Henry Newman.

According to Newman's papers, Oakeley first came to the attention of John Henry Newman in 1826, when the latter was a candidate for election to a fellowship at Oriel College. Newman, who had been elected a Fellow of Oriel in 1822, wrote to his sister Jemima,[47] enclosing a list of candidates including the name of Oakeley. In March 1827 he wrote to his mother telling her that, 'Young Oakeley was elected a Fellow of Balliol the other day'.[48] By the early months of 1829, Oakeley and Newman were both members of a small and exclusive dining club consisting of about fifteen members of the university, each one entertaining the others to dinner in his room about every two weeks. The club was well established by 3 March 1829 when Newman recorded in his diary that he 'dined with club at Oakeley's rooms'.[49] According to Newman it survived until after his return from a tour of southern Europe in 1833. There are other brief references in his papers to dinners of the club at which Oakeley was present, in June 1830, May 1831 and November 1832, and doubtless they saw each other on many other occasions in between.

Throughout his life, Oakeley accorded Newman a considerable

degree of respect which Newman often failed to reciprocate, and there are traces of a patronising intellectual arrogance in Newman's earliest references to Oakeley. If the latter was ever aware of this, it did not affect his esteem for Newman to whom he looked often for guidance and advice. A letter from Newman to his curate Isaac Williams (Newman had been appointed vicar of the university church of St Mary the Virgin in 1828) gives an example of his attitude to Oakeley. 'Please will you go to O. at Balliol . . . and, after buttering him sufficiently, ask him to take my select preaching turn . . . or to change with me'.[50] A lengthier and rather gossipy letter to Froude in June 1834 reveals a good deal more, not only of Newman's attitude to Oakeley, but also of Oakeley's character. 'Simple Oakeley when the wax paper was put into his hand . . . sat down and began to answer the . . . paper of Logic which he had not yet got up – and was in consequence most egregiously floored. I saved him from going in a second day, but not even Jupiter himself can undo the past. Well – a day or two before he went up, I examined him (not for the first time) in his Divinity, in which he was . . . most miserably deficient . . . I advised him to withdraw before worse came of it. When he had withdrawn we heard that his Logic itself would have plucked, had he proceeded . . . but this is not all. At the end of last term . . . he was told he must appear in the Collection Tower . . . and be examined in the Articles to make up to the consciences of the Tutors their not having lectured him in them according to the Statutes. No wonder he was completely done . . . His turn to appear had come, and he was not in his rooms; so when he did at length appear Denison and Greswell set on him for inattention – he had the folly to respond – a battle ensued – in which he clearly showed he had lost his temper, for he would maintain that he was right and they were wrong'.[51] This is not typical of Oakeley. He was not naturally aggressive or contumacious, and this letter perhaps only indicates an early display of the ill-timed impetuosity that was to cause him so much trouble in later years.

Despite the friendship with Newman, Oakeley played no role in the early years of the Oxford Movement. His surviving writings make no mention of the Assize Sermon of 14 July 1833, which Newman later decreed to be the beginning of the movement, and he dismissed the early *Tracts for the times* as a phase of the movement 'which never presented any features of attraction either to my own mind or to that of others whom the movement eventually absorbed into itself'.[52] Although he was well acquainted with Newman and Froude, he was not a member of the 'Oriel Party' of 1826–33, and therefore not closely involved with the theological debating that went on in the Oriel

Senior Common Room. In his antecedents, Oakeley was the archetypal Protestant Tory, like every other Fellow of Balliol. 'I was supposed to be not only a Protestant and a Tory like the rest, but to be utterly incapable of ever becoming anything else'.[53] The first sign of a rebellion against this typecasting occurred in 1829 at the time of Catholic Emancipation. A by-election was held to select a candidate to represent the university in parliament, the opposing candidates being Sir Robert Peel and Sir Robert Inglis. It was a long-standing custom that the college fellows voted corporately, and any breach was regarded as virtually unpardonable. Oakeley had promised Bishop Lloyd that he would support Peel and when this was discovered 'I found myself the victim of sour looks and unpleasant innuendoes in the Balliol common-room'.[54]

This was followed by a phase when Oakeley rather half-heartedly and not very happily embraced evangelicalism. It probably began at the end of 1830, not long after Francis Newman had left Oxford, and lasted until about 1835. After his appointment as a college tutor, Oakeley had become acquainted with a number of undergraduates, one of whom was of a strongly evangelical disposition. This undergraduate 'made it his business to talk to me on religious subjects and, while seeming to act as a disciple, either designedly or unintentionally became my teacher . . . I could not but feel that . . . there was an appearance of earnestness and reality in the evangelicals which was wanting in most of the high churchmen who up to that time had happened to come in my way'.[55] Oakeley was a close friend of two undergraduates during his period as a college tutor, one of whom was Archibald Campbell Tait (1811–82), the future Archbishop of Canterbury. Whether this unnamed undergraduate evangelical can be identified with Tait is uncertain. Tait was of presbyterian upbringing and went to Balliol in 1830. He became a close personal friend of Oakeley, to the extent that they spent several long vacations together in Scotland and Europe. Many years later, he wrote of Oakeley in those years: 'his mind was opened wide to religious impressions, and the influence of Bishop Sumner and his friends had given him a strong bias to the evangelical school. This continued more or less all through my undergraduate days'.[56]

Oakeley found himself becoming 'critical and reserved, constantly craving after a standard of life for which I seemed to find no practical counterpart except in persons of a certain type which did not happen to be the type of those immediately around me. I got out of humour with Oxford, its studies, its conversation and its people and longed for parochial work in some other region. I thought of taking a small college living in a dreary part of Huntingdonshire'.[57]

He did not go to Huntingdonshire and by about 1835, this period of unrelieved gloom seems to have ended. More important matters were beginning to occupy his attention. In March 1835 a bill was introduced in parliament to dispense with subscription to the Thirty-Nine Articles as a condition for admission to the university. This brought forth a firm declaration of principle from Oakeley in the form of a public letter to the Duke of Wellington, chancellor of the university. It was his first published work since the Latin and English Prize Essays of 1825 and 1827. *A letter to his grace the Duke of Wellington* shows a firm stand against the proposed bill. It pleased Newman and brought Oakeley more into line with the nascent Oxford Movement, as Oakeley was firmly of the opinion that subscription of the Thirty-Nine Articles should remain. 'Nothing can ... be more desirable, than that young men should be induced to turn their attention to the leading subjects involved in the articles of the Church of England before coming to the university'.[58] There was no need for those subscribing to know everything contained in the articles. It was sufficient for them to know that they contained the 'well-considered and generally acknowledged doctrines of the Church'.[59] The articles provided the sole and sufficient basis for the faith of those thousands who had neither the time nor the capacity for deep enquiry. This was not to say that the authority of any particular church was to be ranked with scripture, but only that such carefully formulated and inspired views of scriptural truth were of far greater authority than any private interpretation of the word of God. 'This I take to be the middle way of the Church of England, equally removed from popery ... and ultra-protestantism'.[60] Oakeley could see that if the bill were to pass, the university would be opened to dissenters of all denominations including those, 'whose tenets I believe to be utterly irreconcilable with spiritual and evangelical religion'.[61]

Newman was delighted. The bill, sponsored by the Earl of Radnor, had produced a flood of pamphlets pouring from the presses into the Oxford common rooms, all defending the link between the church and the university. The leading role was taken by the Tractarians although all other parties joined the fray, and the great majority stood firmly against abolition. Newman acted as the co-ordinator of the Tractarian opposition, and on 23 March, asked Henry Wilberforce[62] to write a pamphlet on the dangers of religious indifference at Oxford. The pamphlet[63] was produced in May and unfortunately turned out to be a forty-page attack on R. D. Hampden,[64] the 'broad church' Principal of St Mary's Hall. Newman was uneasy about it, and when he invited Oakeley to contribute to a collection of pamphlets on Hampden, subscription to the articles, and related topics, Oakeley refused, saying that he would join only if Wilberforce's pamphlet was omitted. He did not contribute, and went ahead with his own *Letter*, but Newman was pleased nonetheless, feeling that Oakeley could now be counted a supporter. 'You should read Oakeley's pamphlet. He has committed himself'.[65]

A letter to his grace the Duke of Wellington brought Oakeley some prominence in Oxford, and he was sufficiently well thought of by Edward Pusey (1800–82), Regius Professor of Hebrew, to be invited to join the governing committee of the Theological Society in November 1835. The invitation was an honour for Oakeley since, apart from Pusey, the committee was to consist of Keble, Newman, the Regius and Lady Margaret Professors of Divinity, and the Archdeacon of Oxford. The object of the society was to promote 'knowledge of the several branches of theology, and to further full, clear and definite knowledge by references to original sources', and it was to be promoted 'according to the peculiar character of our Church, by combining the study of Christian antiquity with that of Holy Scripture'.[66] Oakeley gave at least one lecture to a meeting of the society, on the rise and progress of Jansenism, and Pusey later employed him to translate the anti-Pelagian treatises of St Augustine. 'I have looked over Oakeley's translation of the de Pecc[atorum Meritis et Remissione] . . . I think he has often turned difficult passages happily'.[67]

The events of 1835 brought Oakeley into a much closer relationship with Newman and Pusey, partly because of the Theological Society and partly because of their common dislike of the proposals to abandon subscription to the articles as a condition of admission to the university, but the year may have been something more of watershed than he was aware. It was about the same time that his evangelical phase drew to a close, with no real sadness on Oakeley's part. 'It deprived me of almost every social comfort without any adequate religious compensation. The influence of the Tractarian movement was now beginning to be felt in Oxford and exactly met my difficulties'.[68] Oakeley's growing attachment to the movement in the period 1835–9 is not easy to chronicle. But not everything that was going on in his mind during those years was subsequently recorded on paper and, like others who pursued the same path, hindsight enabled him to see everything in those early years as little more than a preparation for his conversion to the Roman Catholic Church in 1845.

Another significant factor in Oakeley's development was the arrival of the ebullient, irrepressible and tempestuous figure of William George Ward who, for better or worse, became Oakeley's closest friend and colleague for the next ten years. Ward was elected a Fellow of Balliol College in 1834, and appointed mathematical lecturer. He could be a volatile individual who was either loved or hated by all who knew him. Most of his contemporaries agreed that he was an excellent mathematician and metaphysician, though they were a good deal more critical of his knowledge of history and theology, and certainly of his temperament. One described him as 'a stormy petrel with wings of an albatross, which he flapped with stentorian power in the faces of all who presumed to differ from him'.[69] Another remembered his 'bright and attractive conversation, his bold and startling candour, his frank, not to say reckless, fearlessness of consequences, his unrivalled skill in logical fence, his unfailing good humour and love of fun'.[70]

Despite the obvious differences between the two men, Ward and Oakeley became firm friends and almost inseparable companions through their remaining years as Anglicans, and continued as friends until Oakeley's death in 1880. A contemporary described them thus: 'Their friendship was the more remarkable from their difference of manner and gifts – the one so impetuous, so logical ... the other so distrait, quiet and silent. They were always associated in the Tractarian politics, and the element of eccentricity in both, yet of so opposite a kind in each, seems to have given a sort of dramatic effect to their intercourse. The contrast extended to externals: Ward's large figure, heavy tread, loud voice and hearty laugh, being the antithesis to Oakeley's spare frame, halting step, shy and reticent demeanour'.[71] Unlikely companions as they might have been, the bond between the two men grew much stronger when they had both thrown themselves heart and mind into the Tractarian movement after 1839.

In February 1836 Richard Hurrell Froude, friend of Newman and Oakeley, died from consumption at the age of thirty-three. Newman was heartbroken by the death of his friend, but his distress was partly diverted by his plans for the building of a church at Littlemore, a small village a few miles outside Oxford. Despite its distance, Littlemore was part of the geographical parish of St Mary the Virgin, and Newman gave the most scrupulous attention and pastoral care to the people of the village, walking there every day. Almost from the date of his appointment as Vicar of St Mary's, he had planned to build a church to serve the people of the village. Eventually the church of St Mary the Virgin and St Nicholas was consecrated on 22 September 1836.[72] Whether or not Oakeley was present at that occasion, he was, by 1839, certainly familiar with and fond enough of the internal arrangements of the church to want to reproduce the layout when he began to reorder his own church in London.

On Trinity Sunday 1836 a further honour came to Oakeley when he was invited to preach at a general ordination by the Bishop of Oxford in Christ Church Cathedral, and among those ordained deacon on that occasion was Archibald Campbell Tait. The text of his sermon was Luke 9:59–62, 'Follow me'. It is a standard ordination sermon about the responsibilities of those to be ordained, but there is an interesting allusion to the power of sacramental grace. After referring to the 'two especial sacraments of the Gospel', he continued, 'For even of these, as we know, the benefit may be frustrated by the ill disposition of the recipient; and collision with the world will weaken, and in time destroy, their effects; so that one of them must quickly be succeeded by the other; and the other oftentimes repeated'.[73] This was a very Catholic interpretation of sacramental grace and it seems that Oakeley was urging not only greater frequency of communion, but also for communion to be first given at a much earlier age. It is impossible to say what the significance of this statement in one isolated sermon might be, but it certainly marked a movement away from his theological position in the early 1830s, a time when his sermons 'contained less and less of the sacramental theory and finally ignored though without contravening it'.[74]

This is only an indication of his changing beliefs and his growing interest in the work of the Tractarians. Clear, unmistakable milestones are still difficult to come by at this stage. There is a curious statement in his autobiography to the effect that he began to feel that the principles of the movement were in some way compatible with the religion of his childhood. 'It fell in with the views and habits of religion in which I have been brought up and taught me that I might be as earnest as I pleased without abandoning them'.[75] This is an extraordinary statement. If the phrase 'brought up' refers, as it seems, to his childhood and adolescent years, then this contradicts his earlier declared position that he arrived at Christ Church in 1820 with no more deep or settled ideas of religion than those with which he had arrived at Highclere in 1817. 'I did not carry with me any very deep or settled ideas of religion'.[76] His habits from those days are easier to identify. Virtually daily attendance at Holy Cross, Shrewsbury and at Lichfield Cathedral, and at least weekly attendance at the parish church in Highclere. Did Oakeley feel some kind of conflict between his childhood religion, such as it was, and his earnest evangelicalism, which was resolved by Tractarianism? A possible explanation might be that Oakeley, when referring to his childhood religion, is speaking only of his love of the music and ceremony of Lichfield Cathedral. The stately formality of its worship would have contradicted his earnest and enthusiastic evangelicalism with its emphasis on personal conversion, salvation by faith and its relative dismissal of external worship. Somehow Tractarianism bridged the gap between these two apparent opposites teaching him that they were not mutually exclusive, that personal conviction was not the antithesis of a love of liturgical formality. Tractarianism gave Oakeley great peace of mind. 'It was sometime indeed before the teaching of the school . . . presented itself to me in this light, but happily for myself I did not quit Oxford till it had produced something like a permanent effect'.[77] The move towards a 'permanent effect' cannot easily be chronicled in the years 1835–9. In the eyes of some observers, Oakeley had committed himself to the Tractarian cause as early as January 1837, though not all the time. 'Jones and Oakeley are regular Newmanites, and hate moderate men . . . Oakeley says if he writes at all, it will be for the Oxford Tracts. He is more virulent in old Jones' company than out of it'.[78]

In 1837 Oakeley was appointed preacher for the University of Oxford at the Chapel Royal, Whitehall, an appointment then seen as a first step to higher office. The chapel had been designed as the banqueting house of Whitehall Palace, and opened in 1622. It was the only building to survive the destruction of the palace by fire in 1698. Converted into a Chapel Royal it remained such until 1890, apart from a period as the chapel of the Horse Guards from 1809–1829. Oakeley's duty was to preach in the chapel on alternate Sundays, alternating with the preacher from the University of Cambridge, at that time Henry Philpot.[79] The appointment was made by Bishop Charles James Blomfield of London in his ex-officio capacity as Dean of the Chapels Royal. The bishop consulted Edward Pusey about a suitable appointee, and Pusey discussed the matter with Newman indicating that a popular preacher was needed. Newman was in little doubt as to who should be appointed. 'Oakeley is the safest card'.[80] When the appointment was finally decided and made public Newman was delighted. 'What a good appointment Oakeley's is to the Whitehall Preachership! You will have very elegant and interesting, and very bold and apostolical sermons from him'.[81] The letter was addressed to J. W. Bowden, one of his closest friends, and from the wording of the letter, presumably an attender at the Chapel.[82] Oakeley was similarly delighted. 'The appointment was both honourable and lucrative and was peculiarly acceptable to myself as affording me an excuse for resigning the office of college tutor which I thoroughly disliked. My friends at home too looked forward to the prospect of high preferment which they expected to come of my having to preach before royal personages and cabinet ministers and were also glad of anything which would be likely to draw me away from the religious connections in which they found I was more or less involved'.[83] Oakeley's tenure of the Whitehall preachership lasted until the spring of 1839 by which time he was firmly committed to those very connections that his friends at home had hoped he might shed. His two years at the chapel did not require residence in London, so he continued to reside at Balliol College, being drawn closer and closer into the orbit of the developing Tractarian movement while preaching apparently non-controversial sermons before distinguished congregations at Whitehall. Apparently the acoustics of the building were so poor, that the greater part of the congregation did not hear his sermons. Among those who attended regularly was Sir Robert Peel, and when Oakeley left in 1839, he presented him with a copy of his published collected sermons. Peel replied that he would be glad to acquaint himself with them as, though they had been preached in his presence, he had not heard a word of any of them.[84]

By the beginning of 1839, Oakeley and Tait, once close friends, were beginning to tread separate paths. Whatever influence Tait might have exercised was waning, and the influence of Ward, Newman and Pusey was growing. In the winter of 1838, correspondence between Tait and his former tutor showed a divergence. In the course of a letter dealing with an entirely different subject, Tait remarked, 'You must be aware that for some time back (owing, I always supposed – I hope erroneously – to your own wish) I have not seen so much of you in private as I once did, and as I have always desired'. To which Oakeley replied, 'It seems to me we have agreed far better since we have met less. Disputing with friends I cannot bear, and yet, as we do not quite agree on essential matters, and each feels strongly his own way, dispute we must. You have kept your opinions; I have a good deal changed mine'.[85] Oakeley and Tait were beginning to part company, but it proved to be only a temporary separation. Eighteen years later, when Oakeley had become a Roman Catholic priest, and Tait had become an Anglican bishop, and both in London, the two men resumed their friendship, and remained in touch until Oakeley's death.

The change of Oakeley's religious opinion is apparent in two of his works, published at the beginning and at the end of his term of duty at Whitehall. *Remarks Upon Aristotelian and Platonic Ethics* was published in 1837, the preface being dated 3 March of that year, and was dedicated to Keble. The work is an examination of the ethics of the classical age as compared with Christian ethics, 'to recommend the study of heathen ethics in the spirit of the church'.[86] Oakeley concluded that the two sets of ethics were not contradictory, divine revelation correcting and completing what man's reason could do towards teaching him his duty. The purpose of ethics was the formation of a character in man answerable to the end of his existence,[87] and systems of ethics ought 'to be measured by its tendency to effect this great object'.[88] Heathen philosophy was not wrong but imperfect. It was fundamentally flawed by the absence of any supreme and infallible authority, a lack which was made up in Christianity by revelation, 'beyond all an infallible rule; and before all a divine monitor'.[89] This is the first glimpse of his desire for an absolute authority. It was the absence of any regularity and consistency in teaching on the part of the Church of England that led to his increasing disillusionment with the church of his upbringing. He branched out from his study of ethics, for no immediately apparent reason, to talk about the study of divinity as an academic subject. Having won the Ellerton Theological Prize, Oakeley felt that the less divinity had to do with examinations and academic honours the better.[90] 'Divinity is, of all subjects, that which least bears to be mixed up with any but the highest considerations. I cannot help being suspicious of such things as Theological Prizes and scholarships'.[91] The one end of the study of Divinity should be, not the gaining of a prize, but the 'amendment of the heart'.[92]

The last section of the *Remarks* is an interesting, if slightly muddled, reference to the work of the sixteenth century English reformers. He began by praising the reformers as boldly seeking the truth and, 'instruments, in God's hands, for the production of the reformed Catholic system; the precise exemplification of Aristotle's "mean excellence".'[93] Oakeley found the philosophy of Aristotle to be most in harmony with the moral system of the gospel because both represented man's moral nature as capable of advancing indefinitely towards its perfection.[94] As it stood, the Church of England acted as a guard against all extremes. 'It better secures true obedience than popery; true independence than ultra-protestantism; the right use of human reason, than the rationalistic system; the reality and depth of feeling, than the enthusiastic'.[95] He then continues, strangely, by saying that he could discern evidence of these four extremes within the Church of England. 'And thus the true Church, although a Via Media . . . is . . . a mass of compromise and inconsistency . . . statements, the most seemingly incomparable, it throws out with a recklessness of consequences, an indifference to the chance of misrepresentation . . . It is a character which eminently pervades the formularies of our Church when viewed in their combination'.[96]

It is difficult to guess the precise significance of this statement found in a book about classical ethics. The years 1835–9 were a transitional period between evangelicalism and tractarianism and this book appeared at the half-way point. When Newman wrote Tract 90 in 1841 he did so with the intention of trying to prevent those younger members of the movement who were looking towards Rome from joining that Church. The intention of the tract was to Catholicise the Thirty-Nine Articles, the historic formularies of the Church of England. Oakeley was a leading member of that Romeward group, and here, in 1837, he is already critical of the articles, if that is what he means by 'formularies of our Church'. He describes them as 'a mass of compromise and inconsistency' though from 1841 onwards he would use the word 'uncatholic'.

By the summer of 1839, Oakeley had committed himself to the Tractarian cause, and was quite convinced that a consistent, regular and authoritative system of teaching was the only answer to this annoying state of compromise and inconsistency, and he found this in the teachings of the Catholic (though not yet Roman Catholic) Church. At the end of his term at the Chapel Royal, he published a volume of the sermons that he had preached there during his two years as Oxford Preacher.[97] The volume is of interest less for the sermons than for the fifty-seven page preface which shows the extent to which Oakeley had developed in the preceding two years. Reading through the sermons, Oakeley felt impelled to say that they presented 'a very imperfect copy of his thoughts'.[98] He excused himself from preaching about his thoughts at the Chapel Royal firstly because he shrank from using that medium for the discussion of any subject which might be deemed controversial or political, secondly because he judged the distinction between religion and irreligion to be more important, and thirdly because his convictions had only strengthened during the course of his ministry.[99] Now, he had arrived at 'the deep and deliberate conviction, that the Church doctrine, the Church discipline, the Church ordinances and the Church temper, are all parts of a coherent whole, none of which can rightly or safely be separated from the rest'.[100]

The emphasis on doctrine, discipline and ordinances is a recurring theme in Oakeley's writings, and his desire to see definite and consistent teaching led him to Catholicism and the Roman Catholic Church. 'The Church system (is) not the outward form or "accidental garb" of religion, it (is) a portion of its very body and substance'.[101] 'Is it not with the Church system, as with Christianity itself, that the burthen of proof is with its opponents. It exists; and it is for those who deny its apostolicity, to show how, and when, it originated. And no account can, as the author conceives, be given of its origin, which does not connect it with the apostles, and through them with the divine head of the church'.[102] He drew a distinction between what was Catholic and what was Roman, regarding the latter as a corrupt accretion. 'The former is . . . pure, the latter base'.[103] He redefined the word 'protestant' which, in its ordinary and contemporary meaning denoted opposition to the Roman Catholic Church, to mean an opposition to popery and things Roman, but not to catholicism which he saw as 'an essentially divine principle'.[104] He does not say clearly what he understands by the word 'catholicism' and, at this stage, it may have meant little more than the superstructure of the Roman Catholic Church, but he was certainly beginning to see it in a new light. The Church system, to use his words, 'is undoubtedly calculated to supply . . . constant and nutritious food . . . Its daily services; its frequent communions; its weekly fasts; its holy anniversaries; all this certainly bears the semblance of an attempt to realise heaven upon earth'.[105]

Whatever Oakeley is referring to here, he is not speaking of the Church of England in 1839. The hint of a desire for the certainty of authority, first mentioned in the *Remarks*, is taken a stage further here with Oakeley praising catholicism for regarding man as the humble recipient of heavenly truth. Whereas protestantism 'esteems him, as even the most enlightened heathens disliked to esteem him, in the light of a critic, and a framer of his own creed'.[106] Oakeley had divided Christianity into two religious systems, one from God, and the other from man,[107] and he saw traces of the latter in protestantism, particularly 'the right of private judgement; a principle which, if carried out to its legitimate extent, is utterly irreconcilable with anathemas against religious error'.[108] He condemned Calvinism for its tendency 'to insulate and individualise privileges and promises, which the Church regards as common to a divinely-constituted visible body'.[109] It had an unfortunate proneness to dwell upon individual feeling and experience[110] and an impatience with the 'common' prayers of the church.[111] 'It all conduces not to selfishness but to thought of self'.[112] Oakeley attributed all this to the neglect of fasting[113] and directed the attention of his readers towards the first few pages of *The Book of Common Prayer* and its prescriptive rules on the subject.[114] This man-made system, of which traces were to be found in protestantism, was unevangelical as well as being uncatholic, 'in that it has a tendency to encourage tempers of the mind which are plainly not the tempers of the Gospel'.[115] Nothing was more characteristic of the gospel as a practical rule, 'than its tendency to draw off man's contemplation from self to something external of self'.[116] He was aware that he might well offend many of his readers by the position he had declared in the preface but made no apology for doing so. He had attempted 'to speak to the hearts of those who are not altogether and upon principle opposed to the high church theology. The chance of finding an echo in one single breast is . . . well worth even the certainty of seeming to speak in the language of presumption and egotism'.[117] This is the first evidence we find of a bold streak in Oakeley, which might be described as either heroic or foolish, according to opinion, and which was to become much more evident after 1841.

Some of Oakeley's contemporaries were critical of the preface and the most notable was Bishop Charles James Blomfield of London.[118] Whatever high preferment Oakeley might have been expected to gain as the result of his tenure of the Whitehall preachership was effectively ended by this publication which brought the first of many expressions of episcopal displeasure from the Bishop of London. Blomfield had agreed to let the book be dedicated to him, without knowing the content of the preface. This was not because Oakeley had deliberately concealed it, but because, in all his innocence, Oakeley had not imagined that it could in any way upset the bishop. Blomfield thought otherwise and wrote angrily to Oakeley saying that he had been placed in a position whereby he might be thought of as approving the contents of the preface as well as those of the sermons themselves, and insisted that the dedication be removed immediately. Oakeley replied that printing was too far advanced to allow such a change, and hoped that the bishop would permit deferment of the execution of his order until such times as a second edition was called for. Blomfield did not reply and, as a second edition was never called for, the matter was dropped. Long afterwards Oakeley believed that his subsequent difficult relationship with the bishop was due partly to that incident. 'I am not sure that the serious misunderstanding between the bishop and myself, from which I afterwards suffered so much, may not have been due in a measure to the circumstances in question'.[119]

In spite of his praise of Catholicism, there was, as yet, still no question of Oakeley showing anything but complete loyalty to the Church of England. 'Consider the greatness of our religious privileges; that in this country alone of all the world, there is established a branch of the Christian Church, at once catholic and reformed. There are countries across the sea where the Roman Catholic Religion prevails; where Christian truth is well-nigh obscured by the corrupt translations of men ... we are Catholics without being Roman Catholics, and Protestants without protesting against the truth which, with all the corruptions, Rome holds'.[120] This statement needs to be compared with the statement in the *Remarks* where he speaks of the formularies of the Church of England as 'a mass of compromise and inconsistency', as further evidence of his uncertain attitude towards the position of the Church of England.

His admiration for fasts, frequent communions and 'holy anniversaries' supposes some experience of the practices of the Roman Catholic Church. He had moved a long way from the days of his child-

hood when he had believed Roman Catholics to be a few darkly mysterious families scattered over the midland and northern counties of
England. The lectures of Bishop Lloyd in the autumn of 1827 had given
him a new understanding of catholics and catholic doctrine, and he had
made at least two trips to Europe, possibly collecting lasting impressions of continental catholicism. In 1828 he travelled with his brother
Edward[121] through the Netherlands to Cologne, up the Rhine to
Switzerland and home through France.[122] 'I remember to have been
impressed, almost as it were against my wishes, with the exceedingly
religious appearance of the Flemish towns. Of course I thought it all
superstition, and so on; but even then, I drew comparisons between the
aspect of things abroad and at home, to the great advantage of the
former. Churches open and frequented at five or six in the morning . . .
and a decided air of reverence in the people'.[123] He repeated the journey
in 1834 with Archibald Tait. There was a predisposition in Oakeley to
be fascinated by the externals of catholic worship. He had spent seven
years attending Lichfield Cathedral weekly if not daily, and the stately
grandeur of its architecture and music must have left its mark on the
mind of a child between the ages of eight and fifteen. There was something of a compulsive worshipper about him, and several years before
his involvement with the Tractarians one of his friends described him,
with exaggerated cynicism, as 'so impressed by worship and devotion,
that if he should come upon a temple filled with a multitude prostrate
before an idol, he would throw himself down amongst them'.[124]

Oakeley admitted in the preface to the Whitehall sermons to having
imbibed his new opinions by study, by reflexion, and by conversation
with his friends, and also by the teaching and examples of certain
members of his own University, 'who have . . . been actively engaged
in calling the attention of the church in this nation to the theology of
the primitive times, and of her own earliest age'.[125] Apart from
Newman and Pusey who fall into this category, Oakeley changed his
position partly because of a reading of Froude's *Remains*. Froude and
Oakeley knew each other well in the years before Froude's death in
February 1836. They would have known each other, at least by sight
and by name, at Easter 1826 when they both competed (with others)
for two vacant fellowships at Oriel College. Froude was successful
and Oakeley was not, but the two of them maintained their acquaintance. In March 1827 Oakeley told Wilberforce that he had seen
Froude on several occasions. 'He is as good-natured . . . as usual'.[126]
On thinking of a visit to Bishop Sumner in Monmouthshire in July of
that year, Oakeley considered the possibility of crossing the Channel
to Somerset 'whence I hope to see Froude and some friends'.[127] In the
same month, Samuel Wilberforce wrote to Froude telling him that 'our

little splendid friend'[128] had won the Ellerton Theological Prize. Oakeley and Froude were both present, and met each other, at Bishop Lloyd's lectures later that year,[129] and both were members, with Newman, of the dining club of 1829–33. Though they knew each other well, Oakeley derived little from Froude's religious standpoint in those years. His bias was still towards the evangelical school, and this was reinforced in the period 1830–5. Furthermore, the consumption that was to kill Froude in February 1836 had begun to manifest itself in January 1832, and much of the remaining four years of his life was spent abroad in warmer climates in an effort to improve his health. Oakeley's friendship with Froude probably did not extend much beyond the years 1826–32 and, of his own admission, it was never very close. 'I enjoyed at one time the privilege of constant intercourse and familiar acquaintance with him . . . yet I have no claim whatever to be considered his intimate friend. We were not, indeed, at that time, in anything like complete religious accord; and I remember his once saying to me . . . "My dear Oakeley; I believe you will come right some day; but you are a long time about it".'[130]

Oakeley's 'coming right' was not to happen until three years after Froude's death. After some thought, Newman decided to publish selections from Froude's papers, and the first two volumes appeared in March 1838 with two further volumes appearing in 1839. Froude condemned the reformation, describing the English reformers as a set with whom he wished to have less and less to do, and he dismissed John Jewel, the sixteenth century Bishop of Salisbury, as an irreverent dissenter. Froude hated the reformation because it stood for state interference with religion, but his private journal, published in the first volume, expressed his views in such an infantile way, that the book aroused strong condemnation and opposition. The work gave Oakeley a completely new aspect on the reformation, much in the same way that Lloyd's lectures had given him a new aspect on the Roman Catholic Church, and it foreshadowed much of what he was to say in his article on Bishop Jewel published in 1841. 'My notions on the English reformers and reformation, were first gleaned from Mr Froude's *Remains* and the preface of his editors . . . it was from those honoured teachers that I first learned to think disparagingly of the work of the English reformers'.[131] Ward was delighted with the *Remains*, admiring their frankness and extremism, and was drawn into the Tractarian movement because of its anti-reformation stand. He openly committed himself to the movement in the latter part of 1838[132] to be followed by Oakeley in the first few months of 1839. From this point onwards, the two men were to be inseparable companions.

After his resignation of the Whitehall preachership, Oakeley returned to Oxford. During the remaining four or five months of his residence in the university, he regularly attended the early morning service at St Mary's, and Newman's parochial sermons on Sunday afternoons, considering himself 'avowedly committed to the teaching of the Oxford divines'.[133] Ward was a source of great comfort and consolation to him at the time. 'I was largely indebted to the sympathy and support which I received from my friend Mr Ward as well as to the light which he threw upon a course of religious teaching comparatively new to me by his masterly grasp of the truth and singularly lucid methods of explaining and enforcing it'.[134]

During those last few months at Oxford, Oakeley's position at Balliol become more and more uncomfortable as the movement began to fall under a cloud of official disapproval. Oakeley aroused the enmity of Dr Richard Jenkyns,[135] the old-fashioned and eccentric master of the college, 'in whom were represented old manners, old traditions, old prejudices, a Tory and a Churchman, high and dry, without much literature, but having a good deal of character'.[136] Jenkyns hated both popery and puritanism with a perfect hatred, and the sight of Ward and Oakeley, two of the senior fellows of the college, falling prey to the insidious charms of the Tractarians, was sufficient to arouse his wrath. 'He felt ... that in exchanging Lowchurchism for the Highchurchism of the Tractarians, which he regarded as the direct road to popery, I had only escaped Scylla to strike upon Charybdis'.[137]

Oakeley's personal relations with Jenkyns were perfectly cordial, and the Master, who instinctively reacted against Ward's pugnaciousness, always remained on affectionate terms with the scholarly and sensitive Oakeley, even throughout the legendary civil war in 1843. During a debate on the question of rebuilding part of the college including the Master's House, Oakeley proposed that the task of design should be entrusted to his friend A. W. N. Pugin, 'so well-known for his pre-eminent skill in Gothic architecture'. Although an accomplished architect, Pugin was a convert to the Roman Catholic Church and, in the eyes of the Protestant establishment, he had compounded this sin by publishing an attack on the proposal in 1839 to build a memorial in Oxford to the English reformation martyrs Cranmer, Ridley and Latymer. A furious debate took place between the Master, who attempted to veto the choice of Pugin, and the Fellows, led by Oakeley and Ward, who regarded this pretended veto as an infringment of their constitutional rights. Oakeley attempted to play the role of the peacemaker between the Master and the Fellows, but to little avail. A compromise agreed that the Master's House should be repaired but not rebuilt.[138]

It was tribute to the nature of Oakeley and Ward that, after both men had resigned their fellowships in 1845, their subsequent correspondence with the irascible Jenkyns was always couched in terms that were warm and friendly.

In February 1839, one of Oakeley's last links with his childhood was broken by the death of his mother. Lady Oakeley was seventy-six years old and had suffered from heart disease for several years, but her death came suddenly. Although his mother's death caused him sadness, its timing was appropriate. Frederick Oakeley was on the threshold of a substantial change in his career and opinions, a change of which his mother was aware and of which she did not approve. 'I could not help feeling . . . that my intercourse with her had for some time been slightly but perceptibly restrained by her want of sympathy with my religious views'.[139] After the death of Sir Charles, Lady Oakeley had continued to live at the episcopal palace in Lichfield with those members of her family who were still unmarried. But her death meant the final break-up of the family home, and almost the end of Frederick's links with the town of his formative years. The sole exception was a prebendal stall at Lichfield Cathedral. The stall of Dasset Parva had been given to Oakeley by Bishop Ryder[140] in 1832. The attached income was the smallest of all the prebendal stalls but Oakeley was pleased to be given this official link with a building in which he had worshipped since the age of eight. The duties of the prebendary were of the lightest character since he was required to do no more than to preach on the sixth Sunday after the Epiphany, which, in *The Book of Common Prayer* calendar, occurred only very rarely. 'And as there was always a preacher ready to take it for a guinea the actual duty was even less onerous than the nominal'.[141] In fact Oakeley was far more diligent in his duties at the cathedral than required and, as he enjoyed preaching, he frequently offered to take the turns of other preachers 'whom I found very willing to give them up. I used to preach with a real desire of doing good but discovered after no long time that my sermons were no better understood than if they had been in Greek. I soothed my wounded pride by saying to myself that the inhabitants of cathedral cities were the stupidest people in the world, and I am not sure that I was altogether wrong'.[142]

The death of his mother and the departure from the palace of the remaining members of his family, together with the increasing discomfort of his position at Balliol, was instrumental in persuading Oakeley that there was no longer any reason to remain in Oxford. He was offered, and accepted, a small and undistinguished proprietary chapel in the west end of London. He was licensed on 5 July 1839 and went to residence in August. 'I received an offer which I certainly should not have accepted at any former period but which the circumstances of the time at which it was made to me invested with a peculiar interest'.[143]

Chapter Three

The Oxford Movement goes to London

MARGARET CHAPEL

The whole place was so filled by the reverence of Oakeley's
ministrations and manner, that its barrenness and poverty
passed unnoticed.
William Ewart Gladstone

In August 1839 Oakeley moved to London to take charge of Margaret
Chapel, a small and undistinguished proprietary chapel. 'When I went
to tell the Master of Balliol that I had resolved on taking Margaret
Chapel he remarked that of all kinds of clerical duty in the world he
himself would most dislike that of a proprietary chapel in London. I
could not help feeling that I entirely agreed with him though I felt also
that there was one thing in the world even worse which was a college
meeting at Balliol in the divided state of opinion which had recently
grown up between himself and the Fellows, and the Fellows with one
another. So to Margaret Chapel I went'.[1] During his years at Margaret
Chapel, Oakeley formally remained Chaplain Fellow of Balliol College,
but his chaplaincy duties were deputed to W. G. Ward, who officiated
as deputy chaplain and read morning and evening prayers in the chapel.

Margaret Street is in what is now called the West End of London,
though in Oakeley's day it would have been called West London. It lies
150 yards to the north of Oxford Circus, and runs parallel with Oxford
Street, connecting Wells Street to Cavendish Square. The street was laid
out in 1734 and named after Lady Margaret Cavendish (d. 1785), only
daughter of the second Earl of Oxford and Mortimer, and wife of the
second Duke of Portland. In 1839 it was not a particularly attractive,
elegant or fashionable street and neither was the area in which it was set.
In Oakeley's words, it 'was devoid of romantic interest and ecclesiastical prestige as any other member of that peculiarly dull family of

highways which occupies the neighbourhood of Cavendish Square . . . Two parallel lines of moderate dwelling houses, most uninterestingly uniform and almost depressingly dismal. Towards its eastern and more unfashionable end . . . it subsided into buildings of a more motley character – lodging houses, houses of public entertainment, shops and carriage manufactories';[2] and it was towards the eastern end of the street, 300 yards from Regent Street that there once stood the edifice known as Margaret Chapel.

Although the early history of Margaret Chapel is obscure, it was occupied by a succession of marginal sects. It was built about 1760 for a group of Deists under a Dr Disney and remained a centre of Deism for some years, before being occupied by a group of Bereans or Barclayites, founded by John Barclay at Edinburgh in 1773. Barclay taught a modified form of Calvinism, stressing its mystical and supernatural aspects. He had some success for a while, but his movement, mostly confined to Scotland, melted away after his death in 1798 and his followers mostly merged with Congregationalism. He is known to have founded Berean communities in London and Bristol, and Margaret Chapel may well have been one of them, but it did not survive for long. In 1776 the chapel was occupied by The Reverend David Williams with the intention 'of including in one congregation all earnest and pious men, without reference to creed, faith and doctrine'.[3] Sectarian groups and congregations rested for their security and future on the persuasiveness and vigour of their minister or preacher and his powers of oratory, and Williams' form of religion attracted much attention at first. But it was a vague religion, without creeds and without liturgy, and his beliefs, which appear to have been very much the products of his own mind, were of such an eccentric and individual nature that they hardly formed the strong and deep foundations for a church to flourish and survive for any length of time. His following declined and the chapel was eventually closed. It was subsequently acquired on leasehold, the freehold being owned by the Crown, about 1789, and reopened as a proprietary chapel of the Church of England. It continued with a succession of resident clergy, as an independent chapel within the parish of St Marylebone. Little is known of these resident ministers beyond their names and the dates of their tenure at the chapel. The building was sometimes called Margaret Street Chapel, but was usually known as Margaret Chapel.

At some date before 1829, the lease of the site and building was bought from the Crown by Henry Drummond[4] who appointed William Dodsworth to the chapel in March 1829 to propagate the views of the nascent Catholic Apostolic Church, otherwise known as the Irvingites. In subsequent years they erected their own churches, but in the early years of their existence, they sought to spread their views and beliefs within the Church of England. Dodsworth himself went through several religious phases. He began his religious life as an Evangelical, moved on to Irvingism, and left Margaret Chapel in 1837, a convinced Tractarian. He left to become vicar of the new parish of Christ Church, Albany Street, about a mile to the north of Margaret Chapel, there to effect the principles of the Oxford Movement. He moved a stage further in 1851, becoming a Roman Catholic after the Gorham Judgement. The nature of his ministry at Margaret Chapel is relevant in that he presaged something of the work that Oakeley was to accomplish there. In 1835 he introduced the observance of saints' days. There is evidence of a frequent celebration of Holy Communion, possibly weekly, including one on the feast of the Epiphany,[5] and a daily 8am service.[6] Establishing a link between Oakeley and Irvingism is an impossible task. But the Catholic Apostolic Church which succeeded Irving was marked by heavy ritualism, and Drummond was instrumental in building the massive church in Gordon Square, London, which became the central church of that denomination. Dodsworth's liturgical innovations, although modest, might have predisposed the chapel for Oakeley.

Dodsworth was succeeded for a short period of no more than two years by Charles Thornton, 'a good scholar and an able man'.[7] Thornton's ministry was brief and undistinguished and he resigned, apparently through ill-health, in the spring of 1839. Not much more is known of him or his ministry beyond some rather disparaging comments by Oakeley who described Thornton as 'a very estimable young clergyman, of weak health, who soon broke down under its weight',[8] and the chapel as 'almost deserted'[9] under his ministry. This may or may not be true. Information regarding the life of Margaret Chapel before the arrival of Oakeley in 1839 is sparse, but it is not unknown for new incumbents to downgrade or even denigrate the work of their predecessors.

The circumstances surrounding the appointment of Oakeley are not clear, but there is good reason to suppose that Edward Pusey may have played a role in Oakeley's appointment to the chapel as he did in his appointment to the Whitehall Preachership. Charles Thornton was a cousin of Pusey,[10] and Philip Pusey, Edward's brother, was a regular worshipper at the chapel. According to Oakeley, Bishop Blomfield experienced some difficulty in attempting to fill Thornton's place,[11] and this accords with the appointment of Oakeley. Blomfield was a difficult man and, though the incident of the preface to the collected Whitehall sermons had caused great annoyance, he licensed Oakeley to the chapel on 5 July 1839, only a few months after publication. Either Blomfield was very forgiving, or he was indeed finding it difficult to replace Thornton, or both. Possibly Oakeley offered his own candidacy though this is unlikely in view of the preface. More probably Pusey himself recommended the appointment of Oakeley. Whatever the circumstances Blomfield accepted the recommendation, according to Oakeley, 'not I believe without some misgivings'.[12]

Oakeley consulted his friends on the prospect of working at the chapel, notably Isaac Williams,[13] Newman's curate. Williams gave his approval, thinking that it would provide a Tractarian foothold in London. 'I thought the chapel was a sphere best suited for him, and where he might do us much good – his choice being between that and a college living, of which he had then the option. And he took the chapel on my advice. Little did I foresee the issue and the change that was to come; but I represented to him that his abilities suited him well for stating our views and principles in London'.[14]

Margaret Chapel was a proprietary chapel, the lease being owned by Henry Drummond who apparently played little if any role in its religious life. He owned the lease throughout the whole of Oakeley's ministry but there is no evidence that he interfered with the work being done there. Proprietary chapels were not consecrated or made over for the use of worship in perpetuity because they were the private property of the owner. The officiating clergyman derived his right to officiate from the licence of the bishop of the diocese, revocable at pleasure. This was usually not granted without the approval or consent of the vicar or rector of the parish in which the chapel was located. Proprietary chapels had no defined geographical parish and lay outside the jurisdiction of the incumbent of the parish church. They could occasionally be sources of embarrassment if the licenced priest was a popular preacher, and cause incumbents to rant and fume at the existence of these conventicles within their parishes. Margaret Chapel was the centre of a district of some two thousand souls within the parish of All Souls, Langham Place but it was already well established before the construction of All Souls in 1822–4, and had a school attached.

The chapel itself was not of a high architectural order, and the one surviving drawing of the exterior gives it the appearance of an eighteenth century meeting house for Dissenters. 'Exteriorly it was like an old-fashioned Methodist Chapel of the early days before Nonconformists had begun to affect Gothic architecture'.[15] Another observer described it as a 'simple, ugly building'.[16] Oakeley's reaction was even more forthright. 'When I first beheld the interior of the building in which my duties were laid out for an indefinite period my heart sank within me'.[17] 'A more unpromising arena for a Catholic experiment could scarcely be imagined'.[18] The chapel was 'a complete paragon of ugliness . . . it was low, dark and stuffy, it bore no other resemblance to the Christian fold than that of being choked with sheep pens under the name of pews ... it was begirt by a hideous gallery, filled on Sundays with uneasy schoolchildren'.[19] Access was by means of two entrance doors on Margaret Street, which opened into two narrow passage ways along the east and west walls of the chapel, giving access to the pews and to the sanctuary area. The pews stretched almost across the width of the chapel, there being no central aisle, leaving the two corridor aisles, scarcely wide enough for two people to walk abreast, to lead to the sanctuary area. The furnishing of this area was typical of its date; it was occupied by an enormous three-decker pulpit reaching almost to the ceiling. 'The chapel ... although poetically supposed to have been dedicated to St Margaret, really owed its well-known designation to no saint whatever, but to a lady of title; and, certainly, in 1839, when I first became acquainted with it, its antecedents and characteristics savoured of any calendar rather than that of the Church'.[20]

In spite of his initial dismay, Oakeley was pleased to have an independent sphere of operation, which would give him the opportunity to put into effect the Tractarian principles that he had learned at Oxford. The field might be disadvantageous, but it gave him scope for a line of religious experiment quite different from what could be and what was being attempted in Oxford itself, though in strict keeping with Oxford principles. During the years 1839–41, his primary occupation was the transformation of this shabby little chapel into a centre and model of liturgical and musical excellence. 'Here it was he became the originator of the first or earliest "ritualistic" services'.[21] 'Here were conducted services which were so attractive with the High Church party that the chapel may be said to have been the centre from which the reforms extended'.[22] Oakeley's innovations were modest when measured against the 'ritualistic' standards of the later nineteenth century, but various reminiscences of his work at Margaret Chapel reveal that he engendered a atmosphere of devotion, reverence and holiness in this humble little building.

The changes that Oakeley introduced were quick in coming and not entirely without opposition from the congregation. He decided to re-order the interior of the chapel and, since he was supported by a sufficient number of the congregation, work began almost as soon as he had taken up residence. The first target was the large three-decker pulpit, this 'three-headed monster'[23] as Oakeley afterwards recalled it. Beginning with a clerk's desk, it was completed by a reading desk and a pulpit, each rising above the other in ascending scale, the pulpit forming the apex of the series. Oakeley remembered the structure as a means by which 'the preacher was elevated on a kind of throne, as if in parody of that which surmounts a Catholic altar, and here he stood, claiming as it were the adoration of the people'.[24] This statement was made in 1865 and shows a much more Catholic eucharistic theology than that which he must have possessed in 1839. Neither Oakeley nor any other priest of the Church of England would have contemplated reservation of the Blessed Sacrament, let alone in an altar tabernacle. Permanent reservation was not to be seen in the Church of England until John Mason Neale introduced it at the convent of the Society of St Margaret in 1857.[25] But Oakeley had acquired sufficient knowledge of Tractarian principles to appreciate and uphold the centrality of the eucharist. His first action was to remove the three-decker, 'to get rid of this monstrosity',[26] as he called it, and to reveal the small communion table completely hidden behind it. The pulpit was removed to the epistle side of the chapel and the reading desk to the gospel side. Oakeley found that he had more support from the congregation than he might have guessed possible. He was cordially supported by several members of the congregation 'who bore the change with more equanimity than might have been expected'.[27] His chief supporter was Edward Bellasis,[28] a young barrister who showed his approval by donating £30 to be used as Oakeley thought fit. Thereafter Bellasis remained a constant friend, especially during the last difficult months at the chapel in 1845. Bellasis's arrival at the chapel was fortuitously almost contemporary with that of Oakeley. Bellasis had started to attend the chapel in the spring of 1839 because of its daily 8am morning service, and Oakeley arrived there within a few weeks. 'It was at once plain', wrote Bellasis, 'that he did not mean to content himself with the squalid condition of the chapel . . . All this I entirely approved of and assisted him in'.[29]

The dismantling of the 'monstrosity' of a pulpit was not greeted with unanimous approval, and the most vociferous objections came from Adamson, the elderly chapel clerk, who had known the chapel almost from its beginnings. He lived in a set of rooms adjoining the chapel, and communicating with it by means of a doorway into the gallery. Adamson was a great trial to Oakeley throughout his six years ministry. From Oakeley's accounts, he emerges as a rather difficult and crusty old man whom Oakeley endured with great patience. He wore a brown wig[30] and had a tendency to gossip,[31] and he described the demolition of the three-decker as 'insufferable'.[32] Dethroned from his ancient and eminent position, he looked about for some way of regaining his privilege, or at least a portion of it, and Oakeley caught him a few days later erecting a pew for himself in a remote corner of the chapel. When this plan was frustrated by prompt action, 'he had no alternative but to subside into the general body of the congregation, and there assert his ancient right by reciting the responses with vociferous obtrusiveness'.[33] 'He never succeeded in bringing his "Amen" into a proper tone of subordination'.[34] Adamson never recovered from the shock of his dethronement and was so determined on revenge that he was in the habit of telling visitors to the Chapel that 'it tries to go as near Rome as ever it could'.[35]

To the aged and immovable Adamson, brought up in the latitudinarian and erastian Church of England of the eighteenth century, Oakeley's modest changes smacked of Rome and popery. But nothing of the sort occurred to Oakeley. 'I can honestly say that the motive which actuated me in trying to improve upon the ceremonial practice ... was to give worship as much reverential beauty as was consistent with the strict observance of such rubrics as were plain and incontrovertible, and the free interpretation of others which seemed to me to admit, without undue straining, of a more catholic sense than that which they commonly received ... I must maintain that the ritual of Margaret Chapel, whatever may be said for or against it, was simplicity itself ... no Catholic, however uneducated, could possibly have mistaken the communion service at Margaret Chapel for high mass ... we never dreamt of using any vestment but the surplice. As to a chasuble or cope, or even an embroidered stole ... I would have no more thought of assuming any one of these than of mounting the pope's tiara'.[36] This gives the lie to Welch's statement that Oakeley 'delighted in vestments',[37] at least to the extent that they were worn at Margaret Chapel during the years 1839–45. By his statement, Oakeley did not even adopt the practice of wearing a stole over his surplice, although Bloxam had begun the practice at Littlemore after reading Palmer's *Origines Liturgicae*.[38]

It was never Oakeley's intention to introduce Roman Catholic ceremonial at the chapel or to build up a nest of crypto-Roman Catholics among the congregation, or to persuade them to leave the Church of England for the Roman Catholic Church, though he did try to accomplish the last in the period immediately following his departure in the summer of 1845. 'It is a great mistake to suppose that the principle object of this chapel was to obtrude upon people new and strange ceremonies, or to elevate the merely formal side of religion to the exclusion of the practical and the devotional ... nor was the object ... to dissatisfy Anglicans with the system in which they found themselves, but rather to give that system all the advantages of which it seemed capable'.[39] This was standard Tractarianism as exemplified by Newman in Tract 90.

Oakeley was supported in his endeavours by his assistant William Upton Richards[40] and by most of his congregation. Though there might be doubt as to the size of the congregation on his arrival in 1839, there is no doubt that he had made a success of Margaret Chapel by the time of his departure in 1845. 'The chapel had a strong appeal because the devotional atmosphere of its worship, quite apart from liturgical and musical innovations, made it unique in the Protestant London of the 1840s. Oakeley gathered around himself a congregation strong in their loyalty to him, and their devotion to the principles for which he stood. Margaret Chapel was the first practical demonstration of Tractarianism, and Oakeley began a completely new aspect of the Oxford Movement in 1839. The still essentially theological movement in Oxford was now complemented by a liturgical movement in London, and Oakeley's appointment has been seen as the spread of the Oxford Movement to London.[41] It was principally because of the activities of Oakeley at Margaret Chapel that the irascible Bishop Blomfield fulminated against the liturgical practices of the Tractarians.

Oakeley took up residence at 74 Margaret Street, a large house on the other side of the street from the Chapel, in August 1839, and by the end of September, the three-decker pulpit had been dismantled. The small communion table was revealed to the gaze of the congregation for the first time, and was adorned and beautified as much as possible. Oakeley wasted no time and was firm in his opinion of what needed to be done and in his intention of doing it, standing or falling 'by the religious principles he had learned from persons greatly his superiors in learning and ability'.[42]

Though Oakeley may have learned much from Newman and his friends in certain areas, he learned little of liturgy or the internal decoration of a church from that source. In his reordering of the sanctuary at the chapel, he copied as far as possible the appearance of the church of St Mary and St Nicholas at Littlemore. That church owed its appearance to the work of John Rouse Bloxam,[43] Newman's curate at Littlemore. Bloxam was an amateur architect and an antiquarian enthusiast, and he was knowledgeable in ceremonial matters, and Middleton ascribes the revival of ceremonial in the Church of England to the work of Bloxam at Littlemore.[44] Littlemore Church had a small stone cross behind and above the altar, and in 1837 Bloxam added two wooden candlesticks, copied from those on the altar at Magdalen College Chapel, as well as two standard candlesticks. He also added a bible bound in crimson, in two volumes, to stand on the altar, and a wooden alms dish. Oakeley admired this arrangement and copied it at Margaret Chapel, though the matter of the cross caused some problem. 'The doubt now seems to be whether the cross is to be immediately over the altar, or some way above it . . . Does it strike you it would look strange as a single object on the wall? I am decided in favour of having it in relief, and of the same colour with the wall. At Littlemore you remember it is, as it were, on the altar'.[45]

On 1 October Oakeley wrote to Bloxam enclosing an unbound bible in sheets asking for it to be bound 'just like that which stands on the altar at Littlemore. Mr Wyatt is I believe to send me a package containing candlesticks etc. to be here for St Luke's Day, and if the bible could be got ready to come in it, it would be very nice. But it is almost too much to expect'.[46] One of the surviving pictures of the interior of the chapel as it was in Oakeley's day is dated 1845. It shows the east end of the chapel as it was before being substantially altered by William Upton Richards, Oakeley's assistant and successor. It shows the altar standing against the east wall between two high round-topped windows, and against wooden panelling. It is draped with a heavy Laudian-style frontal, on the front of which is a sunburst with the monogram 'IHC' at the centre. Two tall baroque candlesticks stand at the back of the altar, some way in from each end. On the outer side of each candlestick, at each extremity of the altar, are two cushions on which rest two books. Presumably this is the two-volume bible bound in crimson. In the centre of the table is a large salver type alms dish (the 'decent bason' of *The Book of Common Prayer*) standing on its rim against the wall. Behind it and above can be seen the shadowy outline of a cross. A large chalice with lid, and an equally large flagon stand in front of the alms dish. Before the altar, and at each end are three large and ornate kneelers. Apart from this picture, there is a surviving description bearing out most of these details of the sanctuary arrangements as they were after 1839. 'On entering, one was at once struck by the extreme simplicity of the arrangements. There was a communion table, covered by the usual crimson velvet, but without the large crimson cushions or pillows which were common in churches, and in the centre was a dwarfed wooden cross of plain wood, such as one would look for in the cell of an anchoret. On either side of the cross was a low candlestick containing a thick wax candle ... The short candles usually placed upon the altar were exchanged at Easter, Christmas and Whitsuntide for candles about ten feet high, and above the wooden cross appeared an arc of evergreens and exotics. Along the front of the galleries little wax candles were placed alternately with bouquets of flowers on brackets and some gilded ornaments were added to the altar cloth. During Advent and Lent and Passiontide candlesticks and all were taken away'.[47]

Such were Oakeley's alterations to the sanctuary of Margaret Chapel, and he wasted no time in preaching to the congregation about the importance of the appearance of the church building as a way of manifesting Christ. 'The Church witnesses to Christ everywhere, not in her creeds alone, ordinances and ritual; but in the very form and decoration of the material temple'.[48]

Oakeley's supporters in the congregation included a number of influential people, among them Edward Bellasis (1800–73) and James Hope (1812–73), both barristers, the latter having been an undergraduate with Oakeley at Christ Church; Alexander George Fullerton (1808–1907), a diplomat, and his wife, Lady Georgiana Fullerton (1812–85); Alexander Beresford Hope (1820–87), a wealthy high churchman and later Member of Parliament for Cambridge University; Robert Williams (1811–90), another Member of Parliament; George Richmond R.A. (1809–96); Samuel Wood (1809–43), uncle of the second Viscount Halifax (1839–1934); the future Prime Minister, William Ewart Gladstone (1809–98), and his brother-in-law Lord Lyttleton (1817–76). Gladstone was a regular worshipper at the chapel on Sunday evenings and occasionally during the week.[49] But he had known the chapel during the days of Dodsworth and his attendance was not due entirely to Oakeley's ministry. There is less information about the opposition to Oakeley's reforms. Adamson the clerk was one, and there were others, notably a Mr Carus Wilson. 'The chief things he objected to were the cross which he said was "obviously made a religious use of", and what he called the pope's banner in the window, viz., the lamb and the flag'.[50] The 1845 picture of the sanctuary shows a representation of the lamb bearing the banner of victory in the lower left-hand section of the window to the left of the altar, and this seems to be the focus of Mr Carus Wilson's objection. Oakeley was an advocate of glass painting, and it would seem, from his article in *The British Critic* of the following year,[51] that he painted several Christian symbols on the otherwise clear glass of the east windows of the chapel.

Another strong and early objection took the form of a protest against the use of bags instead of plates for the collection of alms at services. 'We were told on high authority that this was a Romish practice'.[52] Oakeley believed that it would encourage the practice of secret alms giving better than an open plate. The objectors were mistaken in their belief that it was a Roman Catholic custom since that church used both bags and plates. A more serious objection might have been made on the ground that *The Book of Common Prayer* specifically ordered, not a bag but a basin as the receptacle for the alms. Oakeley decided that the matter was not worth a fight, and compromised between bag and basin. The alms were collected in bags which were then deposited by the collectors into a large alms dish held by Oakeley at the communion rail. Even this did not satisfy some objectors and, within a few days, Oakeley was summoned to London House (then in St James's Square) by Bishop Blomfield, to answer the charge of 'worshipping an alms dish by gazing upon it with an amount of intentness which ... could not be understood to signify less than an act of mental adoration'.[53] Oakeley replied to this charge by saying that the alternatives were to look up or down, or to look left or right, but that the most natural and reverent course was to look at the dish itself.[54] In the end, all the contestants being weary of the fight, the bags, the basin and Oakeley's method were left undisturbed. Towards the end of his life, after many years experience as a Roman Catholic priest, Oakeley changed his views on the subject of dishes and bags as he discovered 'that there are people who prefer the bags simply because they conceal not the motive of the giver but the smallness of the gift'.[55]

Oakeley was often in trouble with Bishop Blomfield and he was summoned to appear before the bishop at London House on more than one occasion. 'I almost trembled whenever I heard the postman's rap which I used to think was twice as loud as usual when he came charged with a missive from an ecclesiastical superior'.[56] The bishop summoned Oakeley to appear before him on matters which now seem trivial but which were then seen as ominous signs of a new movement which threatened to change the nature of the Church of England. Three other controversies will suffice as illustrations of the wearisome and exhausting interchange that continued between Oakeley and the bishop for six years.

The first illustration concerns the two candles on the altar. Blomfield did not object to their presence, but insisted that they should not be lit unless needed for the purposes of light. Oakeley obeyed, but 'felt a peculiar satisfaction when a November fog gave me a plausible reason for lighting the two candles during the morning service, and I suspect also on some occasions I was apt to exaggerate rather than underrate the haziness of the atmosphere'.[57]

The second illustration concerns the use of flowers on the altar. Oakeley was summoned to London House and charged, initially, with placing flowers on the table. Fortunately Edward Bellasis had gone on a tour of ten city churches and found, that in nine cases it was customary to place flowers in various parts of the church at Easter and at other great festivals. Armed with these facts, Oakeley conveyed them to Blomfield as respectfully as he could. The bishop replied that he objected not to the use of flowers, but the implied symbolism in the use of colour; Oakeley was using red flowers on martyrs' days, white flowers on virgins' days, and so on. This Blomfield refused to countenance and Oakeley undertook to have no more than one arrangement of flowers on the altar, and to ensure a mix of colours.[58]

The third illustration concerned the use of vesture. By his own admission Oakeley did not think of using anything but a surplice, but even this caused the bishop to fret, and he insisted that if a surplice was worn for preaching at the morning service, then a black gown should be used in the evening, 'and thus neutralise Rome by Geneva'.[59]

One innovation, introduced at some date after Easter 1841, was the adoption of the eastward facing position during celebrations of holy communion. Instead of standing at the north end of the altar, Oakeley began the practice of standing on the western side, facing east. This was again something that he would have learned and copied from the practice of Bloxam at Littlemore, where the eastward position had been in use since the consecration of the church.[60] If Oakeley was not quite the pioneer of the eastward position, he was one of the earliest to adopt it. Thomas Carter, later Rector of Clewer, remembered it as a great novelty that attracted considerable attention at the time. 'I can still recall the surprise it gave me. It was at the old Margaret Street chapel, on the site of which All Saints' Church now stands. Oakley (sic) was then Vicar (sic) and a good deal of talk was caused by this new departure in celebrating. I went often on purpose to see him celebrate, as a great many others did. It struck one with a new idea of the service'.[61]

Although the chapel gained a reputation for being a centre of ritualism, Oakeley's work bore little resemblance to the ritualism that emerged in the Church of England in the second half of the nineteenth century, and Bishop Blomfield was not entirely unsympathetic to Oakeley's ideas. He did not think the liturgy of the church perfect and incapable of improvement, but no changes were worth the expense of the peace of the Church.[62] Oakeley's changes were a threat to the peace of the Church and therefore had to be opposed. But his compromises with Oakeley show that he had some feeling for what Oakeley was trying to do. His *Charge* of 1842 with its emphasis on matters of ritualism shows strong evidence of his encounters with Oakeley. He ordered surplices,[63] and allowed unlit candles,[64] though the order on surplices was withdrawn later after protests from the clergy of Islington.[65] But there is a clear reference to Oakeley's views on the colour of flowers. Blomfield thought that it was worse than frivolous to decorate the communion table with flowers especially when the decoration varied daily 'so as to bear some fanciful analogy to the history of the saint commemorated'.[66]

In 1842, Blomfield again summoned Oakeley to explain himself. 'I have again heard strange reports about Margaret Chapel, and must request you to answer the following queries. 1. Have you ever used in Margaret Chapel, and are you in the habit of using, in the Oratory of Margaret Street Establishment, the Roman Breviary? 2. Is any Roman Catholic book of devotions ever put into the hands of the Choristers who form a part of that Establishment, when social or domestic worship is celebrated? And does that Book so used (if used) contain a Litany to Our Lady? 3. Are crucifixes used in this Institution, as stimulants to private devotion? I must further request you to let me see the sermon which you preached on Sunday 13 November on a portion of the Epistle for the 6th Sunday after Epiphany'.[67]

For all the sparring that went on between the two men, Oakeley was consistently loyal to his bishop, and episcopal directions were promptly, if regretfully, obeyed. But his life at the chapel was difficult, and if we accept Oakeley's statement that hardly a week passed by without a summons from London House (almost certainly hyperbole) it is a wonder that he survived six years at the chapel. More than twenty years later he wrote, 'duty was rendered very difficult, and life very uncomfortable, by having to defend ourselves against directions which presumed such a want of common sense, and to confide in authorities who evidently had no confidence in us. Still we bore the trial longer than we might have been expected, under the consciousness of good intentions, and for the sake of many sincere and earnest persons who seemed to be attached to our ministry'.[68] This was written when memories of Bishop Blomfield still rankled. But in his memoirs, written almost at the end of his life, Oakeley displayed an admirable degree of charity towards the bishop and admitted that much of the blame lay with himself. 'I am convinced that my relations with Bishop Blomfield were as painful to his lordship as they were to me. I am sure that in all his dealings with me he was actuated by a conscious sense of duty, while I am not so sure that on my side I was as careful as I ought to have been to make due allowance for the difficulty of his position'.[69]

Oakeley's primary interest, at least during the two years from the summer of 1839 until the summer of 1841, was the reordering of the interior of Margaret Chapel and various experiments with liturgical change. It was only after the summer of 1841 that he began to interest himself in historical theology and became marked as a leader of the Romeward group of Tractarians. The question arises as to what kind of theological or historical research or thought underlay his actions at the chapel. His primary interest was in the field of liturgy, but where did it originate, and how did it develop?

The origin is clear. A mixture of the atmosphere of spiritual devotion to be found in the chapel of Newman's monastery at Littlemore combined with the decoration of Littlemore Church had left its mark on him. The 'monastery' chapel made a deep impression on Oakeley and, ten years after becoming a Roman Catholic, he still remembered it with emotion and affection, spending his time there 'assisting at the hours in the dark little chapel, with its high red curtain, its crucifix, and its air of impenetrable seclusion'.[70] But where did Oakeley go from there, and what had he really learned of Tractarianism? In November 1839, Oakeley published a sermon entitled *Christ manifested to the faithful through the Church*. It was preached to his congregation on the twenty-fifth Sunday after Trinity, shortly after the internal reordering had been completed. In general it showed that he had a high theology of the church and a fascination with things Roman. At the beginning of the preface to the sermon he stated that he desired 'nothing less than that it should be taken to be controversial',[71] and controversial it was. He castigated the so-called 'Glorious Revolution' of 1688 as nothing more than 'a rebellion', and the deposition of King James II and VII as 'a very great sin'. He believed that English theology had 'deteriorated' during the eighteenth and early nineteenth centuries by 'the adoption of low secular views of the church as if it were a mere worldly and secular political institution'. The Church of England had abandoned 'the earnest and glowing doctrine of the ancient Church' for the 'chilling speculations of modern times'.[72]

Oakeley does not expound the words 'chilling speculations' though he is probably referring to the rationalism and liberalism of the eighteenth century. When he speaks of 'low secular views of the Church', we have an echo of the fundamental Tractarian belief in the Church as an institution ordained of God and therefore outside any secular authority. He continued by expressing his support for another Tractarian position, that of regarding the Church of England as the apostolic church in England. But he did not believe that it would ever act as such, or become the focus of unity, 'so long as we shrink from putting forth her powers, and acting up to her provisions'.[73] The Church of England had maintained the creeds of the primitive church and she continued to express the doctrine of atonement by the 'richest jewel in the church's bridal coronet, the service of the holy eucharist'.[74] The eucharist, with the other sacraments of the church, constituted 'the most signal token of our Lord's presence in his church'.[75] The perpetuation of an unbroken succession of ministers in the form of the bishops linked the church with 'the power imparted by our Lord to his apostles'.[76] The maintenance of the church's holy days in *The Book of Common Prayer* was, to Oakeley's mind, another link between the Church of England and the primitive church, and encouraged his desire to celebrate them with greater frequency than hitherto. He divided them into two classes, 'the one directly commemorative of our Lord himself; the other of his blessed saints; in which number may be included also the holy angels of the most exalted kind of sanctity'.[77] From here he moved to the position of the Blessed Virgin Mary, noting that 'the Church elsewhere' bestowed divine honours on her, which were the exclusive prerogative of Christ himself. But it should never be forgotten that 'even that more than reverence wherewith some are fain to regard that Holy Virgin . . . had its origins . . . in the love of the Saviour'.[78]

This reference to the Blessed Virgin Mary is the first occasion in his writings that Oakeley mentions her, and he does so by way of apology for those who would accord her more than her due share of reverence. The attack on those who led the 'Glorious Revolution' of 1688 and deposed the 'lawful' king, and his dismissal of eighteenth century theology is a stage towards his attack on the English Reformers which was to appear in the summer of 1841, and a stage further away from the sermon of 1838 when he spoke of those countries in which the Roman Catholic 'religion' prevailed where Christian truth was 'well-nigh obscured by the corruptions of men', and where he praised the Church of England as both Catholic and Reformed. In that same sermon he spoke of the 'Roman Catholic Religion', but by November 1839, he is calling it 'the Church elsewhere', though he still tends to distance himself from Rome. He still believed that the Church of England had everything within it that was necessary for it to be regarded as a part of the Catholic Church. There was no need to leave it, but rather there was a duty to enable it to realise its full potential.

By the spring of 1840, Oakeley's work at the chapel had settled into a regular routine, and he began to try his hand at writing articles. Between April 1840 and October 1843, he published thirteen articles in *The British Critic*.[79] The journal was founded in 1793 as a monthly general review but was reduced in 1825 to a quarterly because it could not compete with other magazines. In its third and fourth series, from 1825, it became primarily a theological journal in content and perspective. Each edition consisted of about fifteen long articles totalling two hundred and sixty pages. Started in 1793 as a review of all worthwhile publications in the field of knowledge, it moved, with a change of editors in 1814, to longer reviews of fewer works. Newman began to write for it in 1836, and he assumed the editorship in 1838, having secured the dismissal of his predecessor by a carefully calculated piece of manoeuvring.[80] From that date it became the literary journal of the Tractarians until it ceased publication in the autumn of 1843.

Oakeley's first article entitled *The Church Service* was published in April 1840. It begins with a familiar Tractarian theme, the catholicity of *The Book of Common Prayer*, and showed that its rubrics could be interpreted in a Catholic sense. He repeated his argument that being a catholic did not imply or require obedience to Rome or full acceptance of all the doctrines of that Church.

The first part of the article is effusive in its praise of *The Book of*

Common Prayer, speaking of it as 'an object for the weary eye to rest on, a witness for individual error, and a genuine guide in difficulty, as well as a pledge that as a Church we were not forsaken'.[81] Oakeley recounted his debt to Bishop Lloyd's lectures on liturgy, noting that his work did not die with him. Here he may be referring to himself and his work at the chapel, or possibly to William Palmer's *Origines Liturgicae*, published in 1836. When Lloyd first began to encourage his students to buy copies of the breviary and missal, only three or four copies could be found in Oxford. By 1840, Mr Parker, the Oxford bookseller found it worthwhile to import considerable numbers of Roman and Parisian Breviaries each year 'whence we infer . . . that the ancient services are coming to be studied, not merely as matter of literature . . . but for purposes of private devotion. We do not share . . . the apprehension of those who regard facts like this as indicative of a popish leaning in the rising generation of English Churchmen'.[82]

He praised the Roman Breviary for 'its deep and varied application of Scripture',[83] remarking on the dissimilarity between the Roman and the Parisian Breviaries, the latter being more in accord with the general doctrine of the Church of England. As an example, he quoted the Parisian Breviary as being much freer from the direct invocation of saints, and other such 'uncatholic peculiarities',[84] and he repeated his assertion that there was 'no danger to our own purer branch of the Church Catholic from this increased attention to the Offices of the Church abroad'.[85] Oakeley argued that a better knowledge of the liturgies of the Roman Catholic Church would lead to a more charitable estimate of the devotional system of that Church which he himself clearly admired. But he still preserved his distance from Rome of which he thought 'more in sorrow than in anger'.[86] In his praise of *The Book of Common Prayer*, Oakeley drew much support from Tract 86 by Isaac Williams in the series *Tracts for the times*. Far from thinking of using the Roman Breviary himself, Oakeley saw the publication of the tract as 'a corrective of the possible evils of the present increased interest in the continental liturgies'.[87] In an elegant and poetic style, he criticised those who preferred Catholic liturgy to the 'homelier, but not therefore less wholesome fare which a merciful providence has set before us'.[88] Oakeley accepted the fact that Froude had come under strong criticism in this respect, but he defended him against those who attacked the *Remains* for their Roman leanings. In the spring of 1840 Oakeley was quite sure that Froude had had no intention of moving in the direction of Rome. Those who presumed so had taken certain passages completely out of context and away from surrounding material which might have explained them 'whence it has been supposed that the writer was desirous of breaking away from the wholesome restraints of the system under which providence had placed him'.[89] This may be true, but Oakeley showed that he was unfamiliar with Froude's mercurial temperament, describing him as 'peculiarly docile and sober'.[90] In 1865 Oakeley attempted a precise calculus of where Froude's views would have taken him had he survived. On that occasion he found it impossible to come to any firm conclusion.[91]

After extolling *The Book of Common Prayer*, Oakeley passed to a critical examination of its contents. He began with the service of holy communion, remarking on the penitential nature of the earlier portion of the liturgy which set it apart from all other liturgies, adding that in the liturgy of the American Episcopal Church, 'certain notes of joy have found their way among the opening sentences of Morning and Evening Prayer'.[92] He noted the practice in certain churches, irregular though it was, of beginning the service with a psalm or a hymn. Oakeley believed this to show 'that Christians see their position in their own Church, an awkward one from which they would fain escape if they would'.[93] Nevertheless he felt this to be entirely appropriate to what he described as the 'anomalous' condition of the Church of England.[94] He speaks of the 'great suitableness, to our ordinary needs, of the old Catholic system',[95] but the suitability of the penitential tone of *The Book of Common Prayer* to the Church of England. No one but Oakeley himself can give a satisfactory explanation of what he means, in April 1840, by the phrase 'old Catholic system'. It would seem to be a slightly romantic image of the medieval church in England, before the Reformation, free from the distorting work of the Protestant reformers and later Roman 'corruptions'. This is typical of many of Oakeley's ponderous statements and contrived arguments.

He continues by noting the lack of use of the second post-communion prayer, with its more joyful sentiments, probably not realising that the first post-communion prayer was not a post-communion prayer at all but formerly a part of the medieval canon abolished by Cranmer who wished to avoid any sacrificial connotation. Oakeley thought that the absence of the use of the second prayer was 'a kind of silent testimony to the fact that we are in a degraded condition'.[96] To this he added the absence of Palm Sunday and the feast of the Transfiguration; the recital of the Gloria in Excelsis while kneeling; the use of the word 'table' instead of 'altar'; the disuse of the practice of anointing at baptism and confirmation; and the loss of the octaves, with the exception of the highest festivals. But however imperfect the services of the Church of England might be, 'better surely far . . . is our lot who rejoice too little . . . than theirs in the degenerate Church of Rome who rejoice, if not too much, yet more surely than becomes their condition'.[97]

Oakeley thought that he could discern an underlying plan, namely that these various points witnessed to the fact 'that we really are not worthy of all the great things the Church designs for us, and so must take "a lower room", and wait until we are called up higher'.[98] He was sharply critical of *The Book of Common Prayer* when it gave the sovereign precedence over the clergy in the litany, 'a peculiarity but too significant of our condition'.[99] This is another echo of the Tractarian belief in the Church as a divine society, ordained of God, and therefore outside the jurisdiction of any temporal authority.

The whole article is shot through with Oakeley's contradictory attitudes towards the Roman Catholic Church and its doctrines. He speaks of 'the degenerate Church of Rome' and then shows that he believes in the doctrine of transubstantiation when he speaks of 'the change which the holy elements undergo as consecrated by the priest'.[100] Yet there is something of Newman's via media in his thoughts when he speaks of the 'laxity in one form or another as the common feature of the popish or ultra-Protestant systems', and of Protestantism as having 'something about it which somehow falls in with the pleasant doctrines of popery'.[101] He yearned for primitive Catholicism which was 'imaginative and ascetic', whereas Popery was 'imaginative without being ascetic', and Protestantism was 'neither imaginative nor ascetic'.[102] The substructure of his views was that *The Book of Common Prayer*, the normative rite of the Church of England for nearly three hundred years, contained 'all the essentials of Catholic truth . . . with the loss, here and there, of the more jubilant and filial language, together with some of the more ennobling privileges of a former period',[103] and he hoped that the actual practice of the Church would be brought more into line with what he judged to be a much broader theory. 'The English Church, has, we maintain, the principle of true Catholicity within it. We desire that this principle be carried out into all the details of the system; for, come what may, we will never, God helping us, go over to Rome so long as we have the creeds and the sacraments, and the outline of a perfect Catholicism in our ritual'.[104]

This is the first clear statement given by Oakeley about his requirements for staying within the Church of England. He wrote this in the spring of 1840. In the autumn of 1845 he was received into the Roman Catholic Church. We can be sure that the Church of England still possessed, at that date, the creeds, the sacraments and 'the outline of a perfect Catholicism' since neither the text nor the rubrics of *The Book of Common Prayer* changed in those years. The obvious conclusion is that Oakeley changed his own requirements. But how many seeds of change were already present? Oakeley has admitted his admiration for the devotional aspects of the Roman Catholic Church, and explicitly declared his belief in the doctrine of transubstantiation. Yet he also speaks, like a typical Protestant minister, of the 'degenerate Church of Rome' and all her 'corruptions'. One wonders, reading his protestation of loyalty to the Church of England, whether his protest is a little too loud? Perhaps the siren-like call of Rome was having a greater effect on Frederick Oakeley than he either realised or was prepared to admit.

The Church Service is a declaration of Oakeley's belief in the paramount importance of liturgy, a position which set him apart from the Tractarian leaders. None of his contemporaries, with the possible exception of Bloxam who was interested more as an antiquarian than as a pastor, concerned themselves much with liturgical change. Both Newman and Pusey, with their scholarly theological minds, were unconcerned and unsympathetic to what they saw as trivial liturgical changes which might offend or provoke. This included the wearing of coloured stoles or any unusual postures or gestures. 'Pusey thought that the reassertion of Catholic truth must not be hindered by unnecessary provocation in ceremony, and that the simplicity of English practice was appropriate to the penitential state of divided Christendom'.[105] It should be noted that Pusey, as a Canon of Christ Church, had no church in which to engage in liturgical experiment, nor indeed did Newman since the university church of St Mary the Virgin was under the eye of the university authorities. In any case, Newman had shown his lack of interest in matters ceremonial by allowing Bloxam a free hand to order the interior of Littlemore Church. So it was left to Oakeley in his obscure proprietary chapel in London to begin the liturgical phase of the Oxford Movement.

The Church Service continued with what can only be an exposition of the liturgical practices at Margaret Chapel introduced by Oakeley since September 1839. Oakeley urged a daily service, whether office or eucharist is not specified, but almost certainly the former, and the keeping of holy days. The church itself should be kept open every day and 'from (its) internal structure and arrangements . . . assist the devotions of the worshippers'.[106] 'Why put upon the most high neglects which we should be ashamed of in the presence of an earthly sovereign . . . How much does it look like a preference of self to God . . . when churches are poorly appointed, while all the treasures of nature and contrivances of art are lavished upon private dwelling houses';[107] but he urged the use of symbolism, 'the intense and cleaving power of dramatic representation', only to the extent of maintaining consistency with the duty of obedience to the rubrics.[108] He added a further recommendation that liturgical changes should not be attempted if it would cause risk to Christian peace and unity'.[109]

Having delivered these preliminary cautions, he passed to detailed suggestions. His first point was the use of the cross in church, hedged about with a curiously quaint degree of Victorian reserve. An image of the cross should be placed in every church in a place sufficiently conspicuous to assist the devotions of the worshipper. But it was to be a 'mere' cross and not a crucifix which Oakeley thought of as 'bordering upon the irreverent'. The crucifix should only be used for very private contemplation 'under certain trying circumstances, say, for instance, a surgical operation'.[110] Additionally he recommended the use of other Christian symbols, such as the lamb with the banner of victory, the descending dove as a representation of the Holy Spirit, the anchor, the triangle, the pelican and the fish. He advised his readers that the most appropriate method of displaying these symbols was to paint them on to the windows, which is what he appears to have done at the chapel. At least four of these symbols are displayed on the east windows of Margaret Chapel in the 1845 drawing.

Oakeley was well ahead of his time in suggesting that greater use should be made of the variety permitted by *The Book of Common Prayer*. The use of the introductory sentences should be guided by their appropriateness to the Church's seasons. The Te Deum should be replaced by the Benedicite during Advent and Lent. During Lent itself the Church should be 'clad in mourning; purple coverings are most popular'.[111] Some distinction should be made between Holy Week and the rest of Lent, and between Good Friday and the rest of Holy Week. On festivals, the altar coverings and pulpit hangings should be 'of unusual richness', and flowers should be woven into wreaths and placed on the altar, the colours being chosen with care: white for the Virgin Mary as the sign of sinless purity; purple or crimson on the saints days to signify martyrdom; and on All Saints' Day and the feast of the Holy Innocents white should be intermingled with red as a memorial of virgin innocence. Oakeley had a good sense of liturgical arrangement and colour, and he could be credited with the reintroduction of liturgical colour into the English parish church. He was, perhaps, less accurate in his prediction that the cultivation and arrangement of church flowers would be a suitable occupation for the Christian poor, and one wonders how many hard-pressed parish priests would agree with his final thought on the subject. 'The decoration of the chancel however, should be the especial privilege of the minister himself'.[112]

Two candles should be placed on the altar, though in April 1840 Oakeley was not prepared to press his belief that they should be lit, in case it caused offence. He was unwilling to wear vestments for the same reason, though he was quite sure that they were permitted by the Ornaments Rubric.[113] Members of the congregation should be encouraged to reverence the altar, and likewise the minister whenever he approached or passed it; and Oakeley thought it in accordance with the rubrics to celebrate the eucharist at the centre of the altar, and facing it.[114]

Oakeley concluded his survey by reminding those of his readers who might think his suggestions trivial 'that care about minutiae is the peculiar mark of an intense and reverent affection', and, more importantly, that the raison d'être behind it should be understood and appreciated. For all his fussiness in the matter of liturgy, there was a side to Oakeley that saved it from being the sham display it could otherwise have been. It all meant a great deal to him, but for the right reasons. 'There is something quite revolting in the idea of dealing with the subject of external religion as a matter of mere taste. It is far too intimately allied with all that is high and awful, to admit of being approached lightly, or even unguardedly discussed.[115]

The remainder of his article deals with the classification of festivals, eves and vigils, and the rules regarding the transference of those feasts that fell on a Sunday. There is little of interest or note here. Oakeley recommended the use of *An Ecclesiastical Almanack* which would 'furnish much valuable aid to those who are desirous of supplying what is incomplete, and interpreting what is obscure, in the rubric of our own church, from the rules and practice of the church universal. All who wish to regard our church as Catholic, rather than Protestant, or National, will rejoice in every attempt to remind us of the points in which we agree, rather than disagree, with our brethren of the Church abroad'.[116]

The Church Service tells us much of what Oakeley considered important in the field of liturgy, and what he had done at Margaret Chapel during the previous few months. Probably little deep academic knowledge lay behind the article, if only because of the shallow bibliography of books reviewed. Apart from Tract 86, he lists two books of hymns from the Parisian Breviary, a book of private devotions by John Cosin, the seventeenth century bishop of Durham, and *An Ecclesiastical Almanack*, none of them a great work on liturgical history. But this lack of depth does not undermine the significance of the article: namely the progress and development of his interest in liturgy. Some of his thoughts on the subject are original, though based more on common sense than extensive reading. His views on the use of liturgical colour for example are unlikely to derive from Roman Catholic usage, since that Church was itself in the process of standardising its own use of liturgical colour as local usage disappeared or was suppressed.[117] Oakeley still endeavoured to maintain a distance between the Churches of England and Rome. He tried to uncover 'ancient Catholic ritual' by stripping away later 'corrupt Roman accretions', a task not unlike that attempted in a later age by Percy Dearmer, perhaps without knowing fully what he was looking for. Historians of the Oxford Movement, as well as Oakeley's contemporaries, remember him chiefly for the extraordinarily profound atmosphere of devotion to be found during the services at Margaret Chapel, more so than for any scholarship or research or academic ability. He has been described as 'the first to realise the capacities of the Anglican ritual for impressive devotional use, and his services, in spite of the disadvantages of the time, and also of his chapel, are still remembered by some as having realised for them, in a way never since surpassed, the secrets and the consolations of the worship of the Church'.[118] Gladstone remembered the chapel as 'so filled by the reverence of Oakeley's ministrations, that its barrenness and poverty passed unnoticed'.[119] Ollard described Margaret Chapel as 'the first church in London where a real attempt was made to raise the standard of the Church's services'.[120] 'Oakeley accomplished more than most Tractarians in making the sacramental principle a living reality for the people he served. Among the leaders of the movement only Keble and Newman were his peers in the practical apostolate'.[121] These judgements on Oakeley's work are much closer to the truth than an assessment which sees in him merely 'the first touch of the aesthetic interest which so many were to identify with the Oxford Movement'.[122] His work was much deeper than a shallow 'aesthetic interest'. In his *Oxford Church Movement*, George Wakeling, a regular worshipper at the chapel in Oakeley's day, called it 'a spot to which people could point as a proof that the Church Movement was a vital and real one, not resting in mere books, but to be seen and known of all men by its works'.[123] Wakeling's book is basically a collection of sketches and anecdotes, but he shows that Margaret Chapel created a vivid impression on his mind which was still with him more than half a century later. He adds further details of the daily life of the chapel. Matins and Evensong were said daily at 8am and 5pm respectively, the congregation being summoned by the ringing of a half-cracked bell in the small turret above the front gable of the chapel. The sound of the bell was hardly louder or more penetrating than the blow of the blacksmith's hammer in the forge at the back of the chapel, 'a perpetual accompaniment to the week-day services, to which we got quite accustomed'.[124]

The chapel was 'fairly full' on weekdays, and there was no mistaking 'the hearty and unanimous response, the reverent and earnest behaviour'.[125] This feeling of unanimity was continued outside the chapel after service, and the 'hearty greetings and handshakes were a sight to see; it was like a rallying point for all friends of the movement'.[126] His statement that the congregation included 'many of the highest and most learned in Church and State',[127] is an exaggeration, but there was a sprinkling of the well to do and well connected, as well as the poor. Gladstone was a frequent worshipper at the chapel, and a supporter of Oakeley, yet in a rather self-contradictory letter, he described himself as 'little more than an occasional visitant and external observer', but added 'the experiences of the old Margaret Chapel are never to be forgotten', and that the congregation was 'of all I have seen in any country or communion, the most absorbed in devotion'.[128] Wakeling lists Gladstone's brother-in-law, Lord Lyttleton, among the congregation, though Gladstone could recall no members of the aristocracy apart from Lady Georgiana Fullerton[129] and no politicians apart from Mr Ponsonby, later Earl of Bessborough.[130] This is contradicted by Oakeley who remembered 'many members of the aristocracy, and more than one personage in high official position'.[131] Possibly Oakeley and Wakeling may have been a good deal broader in their definition of the word aristocracy. But there is no reason to doubt Oakeley's statement that the congregation 'seemed to find in its quiet, orderly and reverent services . . . a relief from the turmoil of the world'.[132]

The old chapel must have seen a good share of excitement and anticipation as the place of the origin of the liturgical aspect of the movement. It is not difficult to imagine Oakeley poring over his almanacs, checking for feasts of saints, and for the nature of the saint to determine the colour of the flowers that he would arrange in the sanctuary; then standing at the door hoping for the descent of a friendly fog to enable him to justify the lighting of the altar candles; then waiting in trepidation the next morning for a summons to London House to explain such acts to the irascible Bishop Blomfield.

The early days were not without their lighter moments, especially with the old clerk still smarting from his 'dethronement' and liable to seek revenge at a suitable opportunity. An amusing incident took place early in July 1840. The clerk lived in a house contiguous with the chapel, and his rooms connected, by doorway, with the gallery of the chapel. He kept a family of cats in his rooms, but took little care to ensure that they stayed there and, occasionally, the family diffused itself throughout the chapel, mewing at embarrassing moments, such as during the readings. Oakeley entertained the suspicion that the clerk kept these cats 'as ministers of his wrath and avengers of his insulted dignity – a sort of legion or train of obsequious furies to be let loose at pleasure'.[133] On one occasion, one of the cats perched itself on the balustrade of the gallery. The clerk, who realised that matters had gone far enough and that there was a real danger that the animal might leap down on to the head of some unsuspecting member of the congregation, 'proceeded from his place by stealthy steps to arrest the culprit . . . The cat, hearing a measured tread behind, chose with ready instinct, the only practicable alternative; and accordingly, by a strong leap, descended headlong into the sanctuary, only just clearing the head of an eminent divine . . . The animal, on gaining the ground and finding herself in so unusual a situation, was seized with a fit of despair, and, by another strong leap clearing the altar rails, she rushed in terror through the building and made her exit through the door'.[134]

The eminent divine in question was none other than John Henry Newman who wrote to his sister telling her of the incident. 'While I was sitting in my surplice at the altar in Margaret Chapel on Sunday, during the first lesson, a large cat fell from the ceiling, close down at my feet narrowly missing my head. If I am not mistaken, it fell on its back. Where it came from no-one I have met can tell . . . I had heard a mewing since the beginning of the service. Mrs Bowden, who observed a large cat at St Mary Maggiore in Rome, suggests . . . it as additional proof that, in the clerk's words, the chapel in Margaret Street goes as near as ever it can to Roman Catholics'.[135]

Oakeley's love of the Roman Catholic Church and its practices received new impetus in August 1840, four months after the publication of *The Church Service*, when he spent a two week holiday in Normandy. On his return he reported to Pusey that he was; 'much pleased altogether' by what he saw of the Roman Catholic Church. He 'saw and heard a good deal of the Church which was interesting', visiting a hospital at Caen, run by the Soeurs de la Misericorde. 'They live within the precincts of the Hospital and have daily matins and vespers (which is now very uncommon in France). I understand that many were of rich and noble families, and that they were there for life. They have a Superioress and a Chaplain: the former recites the daily Office, the latter celebrates the Mass on Sunday'.[136]

Oakeley had nothing in England with which to compare his experience in Normandy, since the first Church of England sisterhood did not come into being until 1845, the year of his departure for Rome. For the first two years of his ministry at Margaret Chapel, Oakeley lived alone at 74 Margaret Street until, in the autumn of 1841, he was joined by two friends, George Bridges (1818–99) and George Tickell (1815–93), both of whom later became Jesuits, and the three men attempted to live a kind of monastic existence. Oakeley later admitted that it was a complete failure because they started at the wrong end. 'We started with excellent intentions but in entire ignorance of the principles upon which such institutions depend for their permanence and therefore for their success . . . Instead of subordinat-

ing external austerities to the subjugation of the will and affections,
(we) supposed the essence of the religious life to consist in surrounding ourselves with privations and discomforts. We put up for a time
with scanty meals, chilly rooms, carpetless floors, and other such
mortifications, but soon found they were too much for us'.[137] The
three 'monks' also adopted the unwise plan of admitting the errand
boy as a lay brother, without examining him for any sense of voca-
tion, and allowed him to stay in the house and to dine with them. As
the boy grew up, he began courting a girl living in a house opposite.
The girl's father objected saying that the errand boy was not a suitable match for his daughter, whereupon 'the errand boy somewhat
indignantly replied that he was quite a gentleman, and mentioned as a
proof of it that at the house where he was staying, he regularly dined
every day with the gentlemen upstairs'.[138]

For all that it may have been built on sand, this monastic community survived until the autumn of 1844, when one of its members
departed for Rome. When W. G. Ward visited the house at Christmas
1841, during one of his frequent visits, he found to his delight that
the residents were keeping the full round of monastic offices in a
small room of the house which Oakeley had fitted up as a chapel.
'On Christmas Eve we had our own service in the public chapel, at
nine o clock in the evening attended by about 150 people, with beautiful music and very nice short lecture; we then went over to his
house and recited vespers and compline. Then to tea, and after tea
the nocturnes for Christmas Day, so as to begin lauds as nearly as
possible at midnight. Next morning at seven he had his boys over,
and we opened with the 'Adeste Fideles' and his family prayers,
which are as nearly as may be translated from prime. Our own
service took up the rest of the day, but in the evening we had again
vespers and compline. We have had the whole of some offices for
many days, and I can't tell you how delighted I have been. I had no
idea before the exceeding beauty of the Catholic service as a
whole'.[139]

Chapter Four

Of music and choirs

FREDERICK OAKELEY AND THE CHORAL REVIVAL

The singing beautiful; one old version psalm to an old Gregorian
tune quite marvellously beautiful.
Samuel Wilberforce to Miss L. Noel, 6 May 1844

In his biography of Sir Herbert Oakeley, Edward Murray Oakeley described his uncle Frederick as 'the best musician in his generation of the family'.[1] Parallel with his interest in liturgy, was an abiding love of music.

If Frederick Oakeley has any single claim to fame, it is probably in his enduring translation of *Adeste fideles*, one of the abiding classics of Christian hymnody. The hymn is universally sung, but the name of Frederick Oakeley, in this context, is almost completely forgotten. *Adeste fideles, laeti triumphantes; venite, venite in Bethlehem*, is a seventeenth or eighteenth century hymn of French or German origin, but there are no surviving manuscript copies earlier than about 1743. It was popular in France and may have been composed there about 1700. There are, or were, several different translations of the Latin text, but the one which has outlived the others is that written by Oakeley in 1840 for his congregation at Margaret Chapel. He did not publish it but, with minor alterations, his version was included in Murray's *Hymnal* of 1852,[2] and Murray has ensured Oakeley a permanent place in the history of English hymnology.[3] As the hymn stands today, the words of stanzas 1, 2, 6 and 7 can be traced to the work of Oakeley,[4] although other changes have been made to his text during the period of time. When Julian was compiling his *Dictionary of hymnology, setting forth the origin and history of Christian hymns* in 1873, he wrote to Oakeley who obligingly replied with the text that he had devised for Margaret Chapel in about 1840. 'I send you the *authentic* form of the hymn "Ye faithful, etc" It has been changed in some books without my asking'. The last comment is almost certainly a euphemism for 'without my permission'.

> *Ye faithful approach ye,*
> *Joyfully triumphing*
> *O come ye, O come ye, to Bethlehem.*
> *Come and adore ye, born the King of Angels,*
> *O come let us worship,*
> *O come let us worship,*
> *O come let us worship Christ the Lord.*
>
> *God of God,*
> *Light of Light,*
> *Lo, he disdains not the Virgin's womb.*
> *Very God, begotten not created.*
> *O come let us worship, etc.*
>
> *Sing quires angelic,*
> *So sing exulting,*
> *Sing all ye citizens of heaven above.*
> *Glory to God in the highest.*
> *O come let us worship, etc.*
>
> *Yea Lord we greet thee,*
> *Born this happy morning,*
> *Jesu to thee be glory given*
> *Word of the Father*
> *In our flesh appearing.*
> *O come let us worship, etc.*[5]

Oakeley could not remember when he had written it, except that it was 'about 1840', and that he had made the translation 'for the use of the congregation of Margaret Chapel where the "ritualistic" movement originated in London'.[6]

Oakeley's autobiography contains a number of references to his interest in music, beginning with the time in childhood when he broke his leg, and learned to play the piano at the age of four. 'I could play "God save the King" and "Mother Goose" with one hand ... I was passionately fond of music and was not long in acquiring by constant practice, the power of transferring to the pianoforte, airs and even long pieces of music which had made an impression upon me and to which as time went on I was able to add the appropriate bass, without having any theoretical knowledge of music. This was the beginning of a faculty which has proved a delightful resource to me throughout my life'.[7] When he was eight, the organist of Lichfield Cathedral 'was wont to allow him .. to play the chant in the Psalms on weekdays'.[8]

The one factor that eased his early difficult months at Highclere was the presence of Jennie Sumner who shared his love of music. She would entertain him by playing the piano herself or occasionally allowing him to play.[9] Through his years at Oxford, 'he still delighted in playing the piano at a time when a man's performance on that instrument in public was interpreted, in university circles, as a mark of degeneracy'.[10] As Chaplain Fellow of Balliol, he made an attempt to improve the quality of worship in the college chapel, but with little result. Only New College, Magdalen and Christ Church maintained endowed choral foundations; in the other chapels, services were read by the chaplain and could be extremely dreary. There was little that Oakeley could achieve at Balliol.

Oakeley shared his love of music with W. G. Ward, a Fellow of Balliol from 1834, who had a fine singing voice and a great love of Italian buffo songs.[11] Long before he was attracted to the Oxford Movement, Ward often went to the Catholic Chapel at Spanish Place in London, where the music and solemn ceremonial raised his feelings to God.[12]

Oakeley cannot claim the entire credit for reforming and extending the use of church music in the early nineteenth century Church of England. Choirs already existed in cathedrals and in a handful of Oxford and Cambridge colleges. By 1838 at least two parishes in England and one in Ireland had surpliced choirs.[13] But these were isolated and atypical examples set up in response to local situations. Oakeley's efforts at Margaret Chapel took place within the rising Oxford Movement, and it was that movement which produced not only a liturgical but a choral revival as well. Both were partly gestures of protest against long-standing neglect in the conduct of divine worship. The choral revival was intended to stimulate congregational chanting of the psalms and responses – sections of the service which had hitherto been read'.[14] As with liturgy, Newman himself gave no personal lead, though he was a keen musician and often found recreation in playing the violin; it was Oakeley who led the way. 'The reforms which Oakeley instituted there [at Margaret Chapel] may with justification be regarded as providing the foundation upon which the choral revival was built'.[15]

Unable to accomplish anything significant in the chapel at Balliol, Oakeley arrived at Margaret Chapel with total freedom to implement his vision. Shortly after his arrival, he obtained the services of two individuals to help him in this venture. The first was a Master Willing, until then a chorister at Westminster Abbey.[16] 'He and I used to chant the daily psalms, the choir taking up the alternate verses, and this arrangement was kept up in the morning and evening of every day during the six years of my administration'.[17] One member of the chapel congregation later recalled that 'just outside the altar rails were two small desks, one for the officiating clergyman, and the other for two little surpliced boys who chanted with him the alternate verses of the psalms and canticles, the others being taken up by the congregation assisted by a small choir in the gallery'.[18] Oakeley also obtained the services of Richard Redhead,[19] a chorister of Magdalen College, Oxford, and a pupil of the organist Walter Vicary.[20] Redhead became an organist of distinction in Tractarian circles throughout most of the nineteenth century.

The first indication of what was happening at Margaret Chapel appeared in 1840 when he published his *Church Music: A Selection of Chants, Sanctuses and Responses*, prefaced by an 'Advertisement' by Oakeley. His choir consisted of four or five boys with good singing and hearing ability, who had been trained for only a few weeks. This, Oakeley believed, was sufficient to form a choir for chanting daily psalms. As long as they had aptitude and a natural taste for music, no previous knowledge was required, and the boys would soon find the exercise more of a pleasure than a task.[21]

What prompted Oakeley to introduce this cathedral style of worship to Margaret Chapel? Partly his own musical interests; and partly because he was a part of the Oxford Movement's attempt to introduce a note of dignity to worship;[22] to recover the use of that which had been lost in parochial worship. 'It is surely to be lamented that a practice so ancient and edifying as that of choral chanting, should . . . be confined almost exclusively to cathedrals'.[23] He believed that its survival in those places was due solely to the mainte-nance of daily worship. Without a daily service, chanting was almost out of the question. Where divine service was celebrated only once each week, nothing ought to be attempted beyond the Venite and the canticles – those parts of the services which were invariable.[24] 'Habitual use is necessary towards the excellence of chanting'.[25] Chants should not be elaborate but 'of a simpler and severer kind'[26] being merely intonation. Elaborate chanting was 'of the nature of a corruption'.[27] Oakeley advised his readers that the introduction of chanting into parish churches would cost less in time, trouble and money than they might have guessed.[28] The only essential item was a person able to chant and instruct a cathedral choir, that is a choir of boys. Somewhat optimistically, Oakeley was convinced that this was not an impracticable condition, and that it would become progressively easier as chanting became more widespread'.[29]

The musical innovations in use at the chapel during the period 1840–3 were on a scale then unknown in parochial use, but quite simple by modern standards. They were as commensurately adventurous as Oakeley's liturgical innovations, but attracted less controversy. The versicles, responses and litany were sung to the setting by Tallis. The psalms for the day were sung to Anglican chants. Metrical psalms and hymns were sung to twenty-six tunes, three of which were compositions of Redhead, and the rest in common use elsewhere. Three settings of the sanctus were used during Communion, one by Jonelli, one by Gibbons, and the third specially composed by Redhead. Other metrical psalms and hymns were occasionally introduced and sung from printed leaflets.[30]

Oakeley's first article on the subject, entitled *Chanting*, appeared in *The British Critic* for October 1840. He began with the theme of the barrenness of church buildings and worship. 'Cold as our age is, still it has enthusiasm enough left to fire at the notion, that, while private persons have their dwellings and pompous retinues, the house of God may be scantily equipped, and his services economically administered. The comely vest, and the costly chalice, – the train of chanters and the company of priests – these are points of decent and orderly arrangement, which would surely approve themselves to our instinctive love of the beautiful and the becoming'.[31]

He surveyed the origin and development of chanting in England,[32] bemoaning the time when 'day by day and seven times a day, the voices of her people were attuned to the words of the psalmist',[33] and describing its survival in cathedrals as 'a favourable accident'.[34] He continued with a survey of antiphonal psalmody in the Roman Catholic Church,[35] concluding with the remodelling of the antiphonary by Pope Gregory the Great – the origin of Gregorian chanting as it came to be known. Oakeley made the valid point that intonation contained a lesser degree of individual expression than reading or singing. Therefore it was much superior since it restricted the chanter from attempting, consciously, to create an effect on his hearers, which was not the intended end of prayer and praise. 'The very essence of religion consists of withdrawing our thoughts from the creative . . to the great object of all our devotions'.[36] Chanting, by its nature, worked against 'the tendency to self-contemplation and congregation worship'.[37] Music, in a liturgical context, served 'to guard the holy treasure of divine words from irreverent gaze'.[38] Such music should be simple and not have a skilfully-wrought and delicately-rounded character of its own to tempt'. Gregorian tones were perfect since they were 'mere unmeaning sounds, as dissociated from the words which animate them like a flame from heaven, and awaken their voice like airs of the morning'.[39] The psalms were never intended to be outlets for enthusiasm and, therefore it was not surprising that Gregorian chanting was not more popular, 'particularly with musicians and the class of person who liked fashionable preaching and comfortable pews'.[40]

Oakeley followed *Chanting* with another article in July 1842 on the use generally of psalms and hymns in worship. Hymns, at least in the Church of England, were an early nineteenth century creation, and certain sections of opinion viewed them as crude representations of Christian faith and doctrine. They received a much more sympathetic reception in eighteenth century Methodism through the efforts of John and Charles Wesley. The use of hymns in the Church of England at the time was almost unknown, and metrical psalms were the only form of popular singing in widespread use. They were psalms with order changed and words adapted, enabling them to be sung as hymns. But even these scriptural hymns had their critics, and Oakeley was inclined to agree. He saw them as 'spoiled psalms',[41] because they were not only translated but also paraphrased versions of the original words of the psalm. 'When we sing the psalms in verse we are using what is in fact a step farther from the original; what has been more or less twisted ... into a shape not merely new, but uncongenial'.[42] He believed that the psalms should be used for the purpose of meditation whereby, 'they become the means of creating a series of mental images, and so form a continued incitement to faith ... They contribute more from being merely suggestive, and not plain declarative of the gospel mysteries'.[43]

Hymns were quite different. Oakeley saw them as 'direct vehicles of specially Christian enthusiasm. Who is not conscious that the Te Deum .. unlocks and gives free play to the feelings which during the Psalms have been more or less restrained'.[44] It should be stated that Oakeley's understanding of hymns was very limited. He was familiar with the two volumes of versified psalms much in use in the Church of England: Sternhold and Hopkins (1562), and Tate and Brady (1696), known respectively as the 'Old Version' and the 'New Version'. When Samuel Wilberforce visited the chapel in May 1844, the 'Old Version' was in use.[45] But many years later Gladstone thought he could remember the New Version being used exclusively.[46] Oakeley was also familiar with what he called the 'Ecclesiastical Hymns' (i.e. those found in *The Book of Common Prayer*, but not based in Scripture), such as the Te Deum, the Gloria, the Benedicite, the Sanctus, and others. He also knew the hymns in the Roman Breviary. But of the eighteenth century developments in hymnology, from Isaac Watts, through the Wesleys to Augustus Toplady, Newton, Cowper and others he makes no mention. Their hymns were very much the product either of Methodism or of the Evangelicals within the Church of England and early in the nineteenth century they were still subject to prejudice and hostility. It has been suggested that Oakeley made translations of Latin hymns to offset the influence of evangelical hymnody,[47] but there is insufficient evidence to arrive at a firm conclusion. If he did, then the only two to have survived are 'Adeste fideles' and 'In passione Domine', the latter written by St Bonaventure as the Matins hymn for an office of the Holy Cross.

In 1843, Oakeley and Redhead produced a fully-pointed psalter, entitled *Laudes Diurnae*, set out with unharmonized Gregorian chants. In his book *The choral revival in the Anglican Church*, Rainbow states that nothing but Anglican chant was used at Margaret Chapel from 1840 until the publication *Laudes Diurnae*.[48] But this cannot be the case since Gregorian tones were certainly in use in the Chapel by July 1842, when Oakeley declared that his enthusiasm for them was not shared by Redhead who used them 'less often than I liked'.[49] This may have been due to the fact that Redhead himself knew nothing of plainsong.[50] Although Redhead was the nominal author of *Laudes Diurnae*, the book is mostly the result of Oakeley's efforts.

Laudes Diurnae was based on *Cantica Vespera* by Vincent Novello, organist to the Roman Catholic chapel of the Sardinian embassy in London. Novello's work was intended for the use of Roman Catholic churches, similarly engaged in the revival of Gregorian chant.[51] *Laudes Diurnae* was full of faults. 'Oakeley made no attempt to correlate the verbal stresses of the English prose to . . . the implied musical stresses. He simply set one syllable to each note of the mediation and ending of the chant, and the rest to the reciting note . . . the result was neither faithful to the accepted character of the chant nor satisfactory to an uninformed singer'.[52] 'It was the venture of a bold, determined, but inevitably uninformed amateur'.[53] The primary intention of *Laudes Diurnae* was to encourage the congregation to join in and, with that object, it may have been successful. Oakeley himself knew that it had drawbacks, and described it as 'a little book . . . of humble pretensions'.[54] He admitted that objections might be made on the grounds that it compelled the use of the same chant for the same psalm, but it was a start. 'The reformation of the English chant must be a work of time . . . we must acquire the substantial qualities before the remoter results can be expected to sit easily and gracefully upon us'.[55]

How far the book persuaded the chapel congregation to learn Gregorian chanting is uncertain, but it was sung distinctively, as a member of the congregation recalled. 'The chanting was very abrupt, rapid and emphatic. It was a brisk sort of Gregorian, very different in style from anything I ever heard before or since'.[56] Newman was impressed; he spent two Sundays at the chapel in October 1843, and pronounced himself 'very much pleased with the chanting'.[57] Edward Bellasis described the services as 'very nice, and [in January 1844] Oakeley has commenced intoning parts of the service more after cathedral fashion'.[58] Gladstone remembered the singing at the chapel as 'the heartiest and warmest I ever heard'.[59] Oakeley's old friend Samuel Wilberforce, now Archdeacon of Surrey, who had known the chapel in the days of William Dodsworth, went there again in 1844, was severely critical of what he found, and declared that he would never go there again. 'All was so odd as to provoke the attention to separate details; instead of the true devotional purpose. Oakeley's sermon was poor and barren in the extreme'. But for the music, he had nothing but praise. 'The singing beautiful; one old version psalm to an old Gregorian tune quite marvellously beautiful'.[60]

Chapter Five

The point of no return

OAKELEY AND 'BISHOP JEWEL'

I am very sorry it had offended nice people. I cannot bring myself to lament it; indeed it was so very deliberate . . . on my part.
Frederick Oakeley to Thomas Mozley, 31 August 1841

1841 was a watershed in the history of the Oxford Movement, the great event of the year being the publication of Newman's tract *Remarks on Certain Passages in the Thirty-Nine Articles*, the ninetieth and last of the *Tracts for the times*. Newman wrote it with the intention of keeping within the Church of England those Tractarians who were pulling strongly in the direction of Rome; it served only to increase the momentum, and to bring down opprobrium on the movement. The year began quietly for Oakeley, now happily and successfully in his second year at the chapel, with a new article in *The British Critic*. He had now become a regular contributor to the journal, and his third article *Ancient and Modern Ways of Charity* appeared in the issue for January 1841. The content of the article would give heart to many a social reformer. It begins with a fierce denunciation of the iniquitous system of pew rents and the scant concern of the Church of England in his own day for the plight of the poor. Oakeley compared the Church of England in 1841 with its 'glorious' past as an integrated part of the Roman Catholic Church, using doctrine, liturgy and church architecture to show why it was that Roman Catholics concerned themselves with the poor. This is the first time that Oakeley uses the words 'Catholic Church' instead of 'Catholic system' or 'Catholicism' as before. His concept of the 'Catholic Church' at this stage, was still completely hypothetical, existing in his own mind and the minds of the other Tractarians, deriving from the undivided pre-Reformation Church.

Oakeley saw concern and sympathy for the poor exercised by two groups as far apart from each other as the North and South poles. One group was 'the Catholic Church', and the other that which he called 'the extreme levellers'. Having used the words 'Catholic Church', Oakeley was sensitive enough to add a word of explanation, realising that not all his readers were capable of making the intellectual leap necessary to separate 'Catholic' from 'Roman'. 'Fear not that we are sliding or trying to entice you into an advocacy of or an alliance between papal Rome and Irish democracy. We are not speaking of Rome, but of Catholicism, whether in Rome or in ourselves'.[1] Hitherto, Oakeley had identified the fundamental Catholicity of the Church of England, and the 'degeneracy' of the Roman Catholic Church. Now he declares that there is a core of 'Catholicism' which both churches hold in common, and continued his theme of the undeveloped 'Catholicity' of the Church of England. 'When we go back from the deeds of the English Church in the past and even present time, to her unheeded provisions, and still further to her theoretical capabilities, still less pretence remains for questioning her claim to be considered as essentially the Church of the poor'.[2]

He strongly attacked the insularity of the Church of England and its erastian nature, and expressed his admiration for the universality of Catholicism. 'One of the principal errors to which we seem at this time exposed, is that of identifying heresy with mere dissent, which is indeed the natural consequence of identifying the Church with the establishment ... the basis of Christian union is not nationality but Catholicism ... We overlook ... our peculiar corruptions and dangers ... and occupy, in protestations against Rome, a great deal of the time, which could better employed in trying to regain principles, to which, with all her faults, Rome had been, on the whole, a faithful witness'.[3]

So Rome no longer had 'corruptions' but 'faults', and on the whole she maintains 'a faithful witness. It is now the Church of England that has 'errors', 'corruptions' and 'dangers'. Oakeley has changed his attitude towards Rome since all his talk of 'degeneracy' and 'corruption' in *The Church Service* of April 1840. In a matter of only eight months, he has adopted a softer and kinder view of the Roman Catholic Church, and a harder and more critical view of the Church of England. The article is primarily concerned with the plight of the poor and so the references to Rome are slight and incidental. But his vigorous attack on the faults of the Church of England set the scene for another and much more swingeing article six months later, Oakeley declared that he felt far more sympathy with the individual 'be he who he may', that was moved to indignation by the miserable condition of the poor, especially those in the towns, 'and who uses all means (short, of course, of violence,) to get their grievances acknowledged and redressed', than with the whole host of aristocratic Whigs, liberal Conservatives, dining philosophers, luxurious democrats, paper philanthropists and moderate reformers'.[4] Oakeley saw Catholicism as a radical spiritual movement which seemed, ostensibly and paradoxically, to curtail the equality demanded by the Chartists of his own day, and to infringe the existing social order upheld by the Tory party, though in fact, it encompassed more than all the equality of the one and more than all the subordination of the other. 'And why? because (the Catholic) gives you the substance for shadows; and, secondly . . . because he discriminates between this world and the next. The equality which he contemplates, being in respect of things spiritual and eternal, is complete beyond power of increase by the addition, or of diminution by the severance of anything which is merely of this world . . . He shows the rich, that the good things of this world are nothing to be proud of; and the poor that they are nothing to envy'.[5]

Oakeley was not a social revolutionary; as the son of a baronet, the possibility was remote, though not impossible. He had no thought of overturning the existing social order, and such revolutionary thoughts as he did have were strictly confined to the area within the framework of the church. He had no objection to the existence of the country house and the estates, and the wealth of the aristocracy and gentry, but he was severely critical when such privileges were carried into church on Sunday, and he urged the abolition of cushioned private pews. 'Look at the high-walled and well-furnished pews, in which the rich seclude themselves from observation, where all should be public, and indulge in pleasant postures where self should be forgotten . . . the larger part of the building is occupied with galleries for the genteelly-dressed and profitable pews; and well may you ask for the palpable evidence of that Blessed Gospel which has 'lifted the poor out of the dust and the beggar out of the mire'.[6]

He reserved equally strong criticism for the design and layout of the church buildings of his own day which he likened to 'schools of instruction rather than houses of prayer',[7] with a 'commercial, utilitarian look about them, like the rest of things'.[8] With strong echoes of Margaret Chapel, he attacked churches that were 'choked with boxes and their walls seamed with galleries; their dominant pulpits and degraded altars' all of which spoke of 'instruction rather than prayer, self-exaltation rather than sacrifice, effect rather than reality, earth rather than heaven'.[9]

He concluded the article with a reference back to his earlier theory that there was an essential Catholic core to both the Roman and Anglican Churches, and these Catholic 'elements' should be separated from their 'noxious adjuncts' and brought into coalition with each other.[10] This sounds much like an advanced plea for unity on common ground and, but for his criticisms of the Church of England and his uncritical attitude towards the Roman Catholic Church, we might take it as such. But by the end of 1840 Oakeley was beginning to show too much impatience with the ways of the Church of England for it to mean anything but a growing consideration for the Roman Catholic Church.

Any reaction that there might have been to the article was quickly overwhelmed by the storm which greeted the publication of Tract 90 a few weeks later. The tract was a crisis point in the history of the Oxford Movement, and historians have seen events and incidents either leading up to it or away from it. Much has been written about it, and Newman himself, in his *Apologia pro vita sua* gives a detailed account of the development of his mind which led to the publication of the tract on 27 February 1841, six days before his fortieth birthday. The tract was entitled *Remarks on Certain Passages in the Thirty-Nine Articles* and was written in order to show that 'while our Prayer Book is acknowledged on all hands to be of Catholic origin, our Articles also, the offspring of an uncatholic age, are through God's good providence, to say the least, not uncatholic, and may be solicited by those who aim at being Catholic in heart and doctrine'.[11]

Behind this formal statement lay Newman's genuine concern for those of his disciples who were attracted to Rome, and a desire to head them off by showing that it was quite possible to be both a Catholic and a member of the Church of England. It was possible to subscribe the apparently uncatholic Articles of Religion without any breach of conscience. He took fourteen of the Articles and, by a feat of intellectual gymnastics succeeded in proving that they did not really mean to say what they most plainly said. His fundamental argument was that the Articles attacked not the doctrine but the contemporary corruption of the doctrine. They dealt with an existing condition with which the framers of the Articles were familiar, and not with the doctrinal basis of that condition. For example, Article 22 condemned the 'Romish doctrine' of purgatory, images, relics and invocation of saints, yet, argued Newman, 'Romish doctrine' was not that of the primitive church, nor was it that of the sixteenth century Council of Trent which condemned the same kind of superstitious corruption as did the Article. The Articles were designed to counteract certain abuses, not the official position of the Roman Catholic Church as defined by the Council of Trent, and they could not be viewed as a repudiation of Trent because their formulation preceded the publication of the Tridentine Decrees.

The tract inevitably caused a furore among most sections of opinion within the Church of England. The Articles were commonly held to be a statement of 'true' doctrine against the 'corruption' of the Roman Catholic Church. To see them used as a means of securing a rapprochement with Rome was beyond belief, and the authorities of the University of Oxford agreed. The Hebdomadal Board formally censured the tract on 16 March. Newman was surprised but unrepentant, at the angry outburst that greeted the tract, and justified his reasons. 'The tract was necessary to keep our young friends from stumbling at the Articles and going to Rome'.[12]

The tract was clearly intended for the second generation Tractarians headed by Oakeley and Ward. As Oakeley, at the age of thirty-eight, was only two years younger than Newman, the phrase 'young friends' was probably more an allusion to the theological immaturity of Oakeley and Ward, rather than their youth.

At least for a while, Tract 90 had the desired effect. It refreshed and reassured Oakeley who admitted to Pusey that he had had difficulty in accommodating his beliefs to the Thirty-Nine Articles. 'There are persons about me ... who have long felt considerable perplexity about certain passages in the 39 Articles and who certainly could not, except upon the supposition of a Catholic interpretation of those Articles, consciously subscribe them. I will not at all shrink from saying that I participate in this difficulty myself'.[13] Oakeley realised that the tract would cause trouble in certain quarters but declared that he would stand by its contents and its author. 'I have long appreciated that sooner or later there must be a struggle between the two maintainers of two entirely opposite principles ... it requires no great foresight to see what will be the consequences'.[14]

Oakeley writes as though he expected a showdown. One of the two conflicting principles of which he writes is certainly Catholicism. What the other might be is open to debate. 'Everything else' would be unsatisfactorily vague, and 'Protestant' is not a word to be found in his writings at this stage. Probably not the Evangelical party since Oakeley had only recently passed through that phase himself and, as a party, they were as concerned as the Tractarians to improve the quality of worship; thus far they had much in common. Oakeley's opposite principles are Catholicism and probably that part of the Church of England which placed emphasis on its status as an Erastian, national church. Whatever it might be, his description of them as two opposing principles is a new development. He believed that Newman, in writing Tract 90, was endeavouring to avoid a conflict between these two principles, and because it had occurred in spite of his efforts, it must be by providence.[15]

In the light of this statement it was not surprising that any hope that the controversy surrounding Tract 90 might dissipate was not to be realised. If Oakeley regarded the publication of the tract as providential, then Ward would go further. 'The men for whom it was mainly written would have something to say about it, and they would not be disposed to minimise the expressions in it which had provoked Low Church or Latitudinarian criticism', and the important effect of the tract was to make Oakeley and Ward 'keenly conscious of its separate temper and aims, which were not those of Pusey and the older men'.[16] Newman no doubt hoped that Tract 90 would exercise a calming influence on his 'young friends'; it did nothing of the kind. The tract provided Oakeley and Ward with a powerful new weapon in their armoury. Oakeley especially was deeply affected by it, witnessed by the fact that he wrote about it, quoted from it, and supported it, in his remaining four years in the Church of England. It became, for him, something of a regimental standard, a colour to be defended at all costs on the field of battle. Newman wrote the tract with the intention of preventing his 'young friends' from going to Rome. There is no evidence that, in February 1841, Oakeley intended to do anything of the kind. He was fascinated by the Roman Catholic Church; its music and liturgy appealed to all his sensitive aesthetic interests, and he would have liked to import at least some of its aspects into the Church of England. But in 1841, he was still content to remain in the communion of the Church of England. In the succeeding four years, Tract 90 proved to be a significant factor in disturbing that contentment; to Oakeley, it was evidence that he was right.

Both Oakeley and Ward published pamphlets in defence of the tract. Ward published three between mid-April and mid-June, and Oakeley published his on 10 July. Oakeley's *The Subject of Tract XC* was written, ostensibly, to prove that Newman's arguments did not propound an unprecedented view of the Thirty-Nine Articles. 'The present collection of extracts is brought forward for the purpose of showing that such is not the case'.[17] Newman's views had a perfectly respectable and historic ancestry. Oakeley repeated his belief that the controversy surrounding the publication of the tract was providential, since 'persons are driven upon this course in spite of themselves'.[18] On a note of contempt, he sarcastically attacked those who criticised Tract 90, by declaring that his pamphlet might be seen as 'being unfair to our Church to represent her as a witness to doctrines so very much above the average pitch of her theology and so entirely at variance with her occasional teaching; it is also highly inexpedient, and especially at a time when many of her members are known to be tending in the direction of Rome'.[19] Nevertheless Oakeley was sure that destiny was being fulfilled. 'The apprehension of possible results though (in the estimate of many) disastrous, must not defer us from a course manifestly right in itself'.[20]

As ever, Oakeley's tract was marked by elegant style and fluent argument, but his knowledge of history and historical theology left much to be desired. He viewed the sixteenth century English Reformation, at least initially, as an essentially political act, quite unlike the Continental Reformation which he saw as an indignant protest against existing corruptions.[21] The English divines were forced into legislating on points of doctrine 'under all the advantages of persons who had been educated in the system they were now obliged to oppose'.[22] They were hampered in their work by a series of conflicting and embarrassing interests, particularly the pressures of the Continental Reformers on the one side and 'the known sentiments of the English nation' on the other; Oakeley calls them 'the old English Catholics'.[23] 'The object of the original framers and subsequent revisers ... was to form a National Church on the most comprehensive basis',[24] and, so argued Oakeley, 'there is no one side in the Church of England, at this moment, the representatives of which are, under existing circumstances, in any situation to dogmatize or condemn'.[25] Oakeley's fundamental argument in support of Tract 90 was that the Articles had been framed with the intention of including both Roman Catholics and Protestants, and though these two wings were separated by 'fundamental and irreconcilable' differences, yet each side could subscribe to the Articles 'while believing a doctrine which, in the judgement of the other, was a serious error'.[26] *The Subject of Tract XC* should be seen, not as a worthwhile piece of historical research that contributed significantly to the debate on the Thirty-Nine Articles, but as a typically Oakeleyan expression of what he wished to believe, and a personal contribution to support the embattled Newman.

In objective and guarded tones Oakeley admitted that Tractarianism did lead to what its opponents might call 'popery'. But he saw it as no more than the 'full and consistent carrying out of sacramental theology'. If this course of action led in the direction of Rome, then it was only because 'the impressive and consolatory idea of a visible Church is more fully realised in Rome, than among ourselves'. But this was not at all to say or to imply 'that it ought to terminate there, or that it will'.[27] When *The Subject of Tract XC* was reprinted in December 1844 amid very different circumstances and emotions, Oakeley added a note to the effect that he no longer felt so equivocal in this matter.

His attitude to the Roman Catholic Church was set out in a very long letter to Pusey at the end of March 1841. It shows how divided he was in his feelings, and no real evidence of an intention to move towards Rome. 'I still trust that a very painful sense of our Church's actual state in very many ways is not inconsistent with a dutiful attachment to her and an earnest desire to find in her the resting place which the Church Catholic is meant to be. And on the other hand, that a most reverential estimate of those Catholic principles which Rome professes, may be combined with fullest acknowledgement of her actually uncatholic practice in very many instances and which is so much more inexcusable in her than in us'. Continuing the theme of Tract 90, he declared that the sure way of preventing conversions to Rome was by showing members of the Church of England 'that their own Church has really that within her which Rome more palpably exhibits . . . Our present object must be to build up our own Church in Catholic truth, to shew the greatest tenderness towards all her most devoted members, to stir up in ourselves and others the practical duties of religion; and to leave the future alone'.[28]

Oakeley might have been concerned to leave the future alone, but he was in the process of mounting a full scale attack on the past. He told Pusey that his feelings of love and loyalty towards the Church of England were encouraged 'by connecting it with times before the Reformation and exhibiting sympathy with the tone of her ancient saints . . . sympathy with Rome, in certain great points of principle, as well as mere doctrine (or, I may say, sympathy with the ancient Church of England) seems the necessary result; all of which I say by way of shewing that a certain tone of feeling is not necessarily defective in love as well as duty to our own Mother; taking, that is, our Mother as the ancient and famous English Church of which the essence I trust lived through the Reformation'.[29]

It was clear that Oakeley believed the Roman Catholic Church of his own day and the pre-Reformation Church in England to be, in essentials, one and the same. If so then despite his earlier protestations of loyalty he was moving in the direction of believing that the Roman Catholic Church in 1841 presented a more faithful picture of the undivided pre-Reformation Church than did the Church of England. His use of material language to describe the 'ancient and famous' English Church implies that the Church of England of his own day was a poor and under-nourished child by comparison.

Oakeley warned Pusey that there were many people who would not remain within the Church of England if the duty of remaining was founded upon a belief in its intrinsic superiority to the Roman Church. 'Such persons (whether in error or not), seem to deserve especial consideration, for what (human) hope is there of elevating the tone of our Church: (which we all equally desire), if we lose from it the more Catholically disposed of its present members?'[30]

Oakeley believed that it would be no sin or error to join the Roman Catholic Church, telling Pusey so in June 1841. Ward had published three extreme pamphlets in defence of Tract 90 and, as a result, Bishop Blomfield inhibited him from preaching at Margaret Chapel. Oakeley leapt to the defence of his friend. 'The view I understand Ward to go upon, is this, and I quite agree in it; that idolatry being in, and not of, Rome, it could be no sin to join Rome, except as it would involve leaving what is believed a branch of the true Church. It would of course be a sin to leave the Church of England, as long as she is felt to have the "notes of a true Church".'[31]

Pusey recommended that Ward should set everybody's mind at rest by pledging himself not to join Rome under any circumstances. Ward refused, and Oakeley supported him saying that if some authoritative pronouncement in the Church of England were to commit that church to heresy, 'in that case any one must look to Rome for sacramental blessings; of which upon such sad hypothesis, the Church of England would cease to be the appointed channel'.[32]

At the time of the publication of Ward's last pamphlet on 21 June, a curious triangular correspondence took place between Blomfield, Tait and Oakeley, due to a misinterpretation by Oakeley of a remark by Blomfield, which he took to mean that the bishop supported Tractarianism. The episode shows that for all that their paths had diverged, Oakeley and Tait still retained something of their affection and friendship for each other. Tait was one of the four university tutors who had publicly protested against Tract 90, and when Ward's pamphlets appeared, he proposed to go further and censure Ward. Oakeley, in a firm but friendly message, warned Tait that their friendship would be in serious jeopardy if he proceeded. 'I am quite ready then, and should under certain circumstances feel myself bound to say, that I read or heard read, the whole of Ward's last pamphlet before it was published – that I strongly recommended the publication of it, and that as it stands, I entirely concur in the sentiments it expresses'.[33]

During one of his frequent visits to London House, shortly after the publication of Tract 90, Bishop Blomfield expressed to Oakeley his hope that peace and caution would be allowed a chance and that the peace of the church would not be disturbed by any proceedings arising from the publication of the tract.[34] Without any evidence, Oakeley took this to mean that the bishop was opposed to any formal attempt to censure either the tract or Ward's pamphlets. He repeated his conversation with Blomfield to Tait in the presence of a third party, possibly Ward, and either or both of them repeated the conversation in university circles as proof that Blomfield disapproved of the decree of censure of Tract 90 by the Hebdomadal Board. Blomfield wrote to Oakeley demanding that he repeat in writing what had been said during the course of their conversation. Oakeley replied, with the caveat that his memory of their meeting was 'very distant'.[35] The incident quickly fizzled out a short time later when Oakeley's celebrated article on Bishop Jewel appeared in *The British Critic* for July 1841.

John Jewel (1522–71) was Bishop of Salisbury from 1560 until his death. His fame rests chiefly on his celebrated work in defence of the claims of the Church of England published in 1562, *Apologia Ecclesiae Anglicanae*, which established itself as a classic. Oakeley's article took the form of a review of a reprint of Jewel's book, giving him the opportunity to express his opinions on the Reformation. They can be summed up quite briefly; he had scarcely one good word to say about it. Everything before the Reformation was right and everything since was wrong. 'Painful and humiliating, we must ever feel, is the record of that angry struggle, which . . . has been the means of dividing against itself the kingdom which should be united against the world . . . the means of disturbing the peace, and infringing the unity of the Christian body'.[36]

Oakeley admitted that it might not have been possible to avoid the Reformation: that there were grounds on which it might possibly be defended: that it could be argued that it was productive of some benefits; and that it might work with everything else to the good of the church. But that was as far as he went in praise of the Reformation and his readers received a shock when he delivered the punch line. 'We cannot but esteem it, when viewed in its leading principles . . . as involving . . . far too much of intrinsic evil, to be a legitimate subject of triumph . . . we have so accustomed ourselves to regard the separation as inevitable, that we have almost ceased to esteem it as an evil, if we have not gone the still further length of hailing it as a boon, and glorying in it as a privilege'.[37] His argument, that the union of the whole church under one visible government was the most perfect state to which the church should aspire, was fair enough, but he spoilt it by then singing the praises of the Roman Catholic Church in a way rarely seen from a clergyman of the Church of England. 'We were united, and now are not. And the history of this great struggle for religious independence . . . is . . . the record and progress of that deplorable schism'.[38] If Rome and the Church of England were part of one and the same church, then the sins of Rome should be a source of sorrow not of pride, to Anglicans. He did not claim that active and visible union with the see of Rome constituted the essence of a Church, but 'at the same time we are deeply conscious that, in lacking it . . . we forgo a greater privilege. Rome has imperishable claims upon our gratitude, and . . . upon our deference. She is our 'elder sister' in the faith; nay, she is our Mother; to whom, by the grace of God, we owe it that we are what we are . . . may we never be provoked to forget her, or cease to love her, even though she frown upon us, and to desire "if it were possible", to be at one with her'.[39]

No one can fault Oakeley for boldly and fearlessly proclaiming what he believed to be the truth, but one wonders if he realised that statements of this kind caused apoplexy in the common rooms of Oxford and the episcopal palaces of early Victorian England. On reading a passage like this, it is hardly surprising that Newman and Pusey were alarmed by the activities of Oakeley and the nascent 'Romeward' group.

After this sweeping statement, Oakeley proceeded to attack Bishop Jewel and all his works, which he described as 'one continuous strain of invective and apology. His words are like nouns defective in all cases but the accusative'.[40] Widening his field to lament the absence of any practical or devotional writings in the Reformation years, he remarked that 'an ill-natured person might almost suspect that, as their sermons were certainly philippics, so their very prayers were anathemas'.[41]

Oakeley made something of a show of Jewel's inability to stand firm on any principle whatever, and attacked him for wavering between Catholicism and Protestantism. 'He was a staunch Protestant when Protestantism was in vogue . . . in time of trial, away went his Protestantism all in a moment; among kindred spirits and in calmer time, he was again a Protestant'.[42] This was quite unfair to Jewel who was a faithful member of the Church of England and had known nothing else since his earliest days, being only twelve years old at the passage of the Act of Supremacy. He had no love either for the continental Reformers or for the Catholic Church. On the accession of Queen Mary I in 1553 he wrote, as public orator of the university of Oxford, a fairly general letter of congratulation on behalf of the university. But he declined to attend mass and was removed from his fellowship. Under pressure he subscribed to a Catholic test but afterwards escaped to Switzerland and made a public confession of his frailty in subscribing.

Jewel was only one example, albeit a more prominent one, of many clerics who were caught on the horns of such a dilemma in the brief reign of Queen Mary I. But this was not enough to excuse him in the eyes of Oakeley for whom 'standing firm' was the ultimate test of loyalty and faith. 'In these mawkish and simpering days, these days of conciliatory tactics and well-rounded periods, one gets more and more to admire what somebody has called ... "a good hater"; a down-right self-denying hater, (not of persons, but) of principles; deeply satisfied as we are that they who hate nothing, love nothing ... we had rather see a person zealous "unto death" for Protestantism, than for nothing'.[43]

Oakeley had written his article sure in his verdict that Jewel was 'guilty'. and then proceeded to 'select' the evidence needed to prove his case and secure a conviction. His article is in no sense an objective analysis of the very real pressures under which Jewel and many of his contemporaries found themselves in the life of the sixteenth century Church of England. The unsympathetic Oakeley announced his intention of 'exposing' Jewel's theology by reference to his life, private letters and more controversial publications.[44]

Bishop Jewel is one-sided but very cleverly written. He made a clear distinction between the earlier Reformers, and their successors, regarding Ridley and Latimer as martyrs, and Jewel as an apostate.[45] He has a point here, since both Latimer and Jewel were warned of their imminent arrest. Latimer chose to stay, and Jewel fled to Switzerland. This damned Jewel in the eyes of Oakeley. He strongly condemned certain aspects of Jewel's life, writings and actions, and then produced excuses for such failings which, far from excusing Jewel, only served to portray him as a coward and a failure; which was Oakeley's intention. He condemned Jewel's flight to Switzerland, and then made the allowance: 'How can you tell whether, being a Catholic, you might not have signed the Confession of Augsburg ... with fire and faggot staring you in the face?'[46] Alluding to the martyrdom of Ridley and Latimer by burning, he implied that Jewel was less than heroic in choosing escape and he deprecated the high respect in which Jewel was held by the Church of England. 'There is a duty and an object to preserve intact the illustrious fame of the saints and martyrs of the church. Groundless canonisation is high treason against the royal prerogative of that noble army; and random eulogy is a petty offence in the same department of crime'.[47]

Given his liturgical reforms at Margaret Chapel, Oakeley was naturally critical of Jewel's 'antipathy to the whole principle of external and symbolical worship as involved in the use of church vestments and ornaments, with such accompaniments of ceremonial religion'.[48] Since he had spent two years embellishing his chapel on one side of Margaret Street, and trying to establish a monastery on the other, he took grave exception to what he described as Jewel's 'bitter invective' against such externals, and he quoted, with evident distaste,

Jewel's letter to Peter Martyr (1500–62), the Anglo-Italian Reformer, about monasteries being levelled to the ground and the altars being consigned to the flames.[49]

Oakeley then passed to Tract 90, quoting it as showing that the Church of England presented a more faithful image of Catholicism than the continental Protestant communions, both in liturgy and in the Articles. But, as might be expected, he went further than Newman. He was thankful for what Newman had done in showing that a Catholic might conscientiously subscribe the Articles but nevertheless 'here and there they wear a less Catholic aspect, and were certainly framed by persons of a thoroughly uncatholic spirit . . . There seems too much reason to apprehend that, without some more stringent test of Catholicity than we are likely to obtain, or ought, perhaps, under existing circumstances, to desire, our own branch of the Church must remain . . . the apparent representative of a different principle'.[50] Here were the signs that, although Tract 90 was gratefully received, Newman's efforts were not enough and Oakeley was already beginning to move past its position. Even with Newman's Catholic interpretation of the Thirty-Nine Articles, Oakeley was beginning to question the ability of Catholics to remain within such an overtly 'uncatholic' Church.

The article went from bad to worse in the eyes of the his less sympathetic readers. Since Protestantism was, according to Oakeley, 'characteristically the religion of corrupt human nature',[51] he doubted whether the Church of England would be able to realise its full potential as a Catholic Church, certainly not for some time to come, though he was sure that it would do so given time. His thoughts of the tenacity of the principles of Catholicism, propagated by the Tractarians, read like a piece of war propaganda. 'The hold which in a very short time they have taken on the affections of people in this country, is something, of which not everyone has an idea. All weapons forged against them seem to fall to the ground.; and they are where they are, despite all which has been done and more which has been muttered, against them'.[52]

Oakeley adopted the argument that the English Reformation had nothing to with the Continental Reformation. The Reformation in England was due entirely to secular influences, and was a protest against the power and authority of Rome and the hierarchy. If it had any characteristic feature of its own, it was due less to the unbiased doctrinal peculiarity of its authors than to accidental circumstances; and that the preservation of certain outward features of divine worship was due to the personal wishes of Queen Elizabeth I.[53] He quoted Newman as the authority representing a party which had come into existence to support the maintenance of Catholic doctrine, yet remaining within the Church of England. 'This may be considered as represented in the preface to the second part of Mr Froude's Remains'.[54] But he went further than Newman had done and set himself up as the judge of the Reformation. 'We do hold it of supreme importance to determine whether, or not, the English Reformers be trustworthy witnesses to Catholic doctrine'.[55] Oakeley took Jewel as a typical Elizabethan bishop, a copy of whose work resided in every parish by the command of Archbishop Bancroft in 1610. He set out to prove that Jewel was at least in sympathy with Continental Protestants, admitting that he had been led to think as much by his reading of Froude's *Remains*. 'On public grounds . . . no less than for our own private satisfaction, and . . . out of tenderness to Mr Froude's memory, as well as deference to his judgement, we have been led to look . . . into the works and biography of that writer'.[56]

Oakeley believed that to cling to the authority of Jewel and his fellow English Reformers, as individuals, would be to deal unfairly with Roman Catholics, 'other branches of the Catholic Church',[57] by making common cause with a set of writers 'with whom . . . we can have no sort of sympathy'.[58] Oakeley took Jewel to task in a number of areas dear to his heart, 'the apostolical succession, the divine virtue of the sacraments, the power of the keys, the visibility and indefectibility of the Church Catholic, and the like. On these subjects . . . we find Bishop Jewel siding, not with the Catholics, but with the Protestants'.[59] On the question of grace through the sacraments, one quotation will suffice: 'Not a word . . . of the direct conveyance of divine grace by the sacraments. Not a hint at the mysterious virtue, the transforming, invigorating efficacy, which the natural elements acquire through the act of consecration, and of which they are the appointed media to the soul'.[60] To hold to the authority of Jewel would be to exhibit 'a very distorted and unreal representation of the Catholicism to which we desire to attract (the unprejudiced); holding before them a phantom which will elude their grasp, a light which will cheat their pursuit . . . disquieting them in their present home, without furnishing them with a shelter? This should be well considered'.[61]

Oakeley had indeed considered it well. *Bishop Jewel* was an inflammatory piece of work, especially appearing so soon after the publication of Tract 90, but Oakeley was in no mood for compromise. The influence of Froude's *Remains* had, on his own admission, led him to think disparagingly of the English Reformation and there is a sense in which Oakeley felt that he was taking up the torch, as well as the pen, laid down by Froude. 'It should be remembered that it is not we who have been the first to suggest the doubt and open the enquiry; and not so much in the way of formal proof, as of strong expression of individual feelings, which, however satisfactory to the person himself, have died with him'.[62]

Oakeley continued Froude's view that the English Reformation was a stain on the history of the English Church, and called for the 'unprotestantizing (to use an offensive, but forcible, word) of the national Church'.[63] Though his sentiments were expressed a shade more elegantly than those of Froude, the shock waves were almost as deep and as extensive, but more inside the Tractarian fold than outside. The *Remains* were published in four volumes and enjoyed a much wider circulation, whereas Oakeley's views were confined to one article. His final paragraph flung down the gauntlet. 'We cannot stand were we are; we must go backwards or forwards; and it will surely be the latter . . . we must recede more and more from the principles . . . if any such there be . . . of the English Reformation. Those principles are Catholic or they are not. If they be Catholic, let them be so proved, and we will shrink from no penance, which may be exacted as the price of unsettling men's minds. If they be not Catholic, then, no matter whom we alienate, or to whom we give cause of triumph, they must be abandoned'.[64]

On the subject of the *Remains*, Newman had jumped to the defence of Froude to whom he was closer than anybody else in his lifetime. He was not so ready to spring to the defence of Oakeley, partly because the bond was less strong, and partly because of the continuing furore over Tract 90. The Tract was published on 27 February, and Newman had certainly seen the script of *Bishop Jewel* by 6 April when he wrote to his brother-in-law, Thomas Mozley.[65] 'Oakeley has written a very able one on Jewel, but when it got into type I was scared, considering the present row (over Number 90). I will send it to you, It struck me whether it might do . . . But after all I really do not know'.[66] Part of the reason for Newman's uncharacteristic indecisiveness was a changeover in the editorship of *The British Critic*. Since the autumn of 1840, he had contemplated the possibility of handing over the job to someone else and, at the time that Oakeley was completing his article, he was in the process of passing the job to Thomas Mozley. As the retiring editor, final decisions on material to be included in the July issue should be made not by Newman but by Mozley. Having read Oakeley's article, Newman passed it to Mozley for a final decision and later declined to accept any responsibility for it. Mozley was a genial and tolerant individual, but also careless and lazy, and without much depth or perception.[67] He was Rector of Cholderton, a parish on Salisbury Plain, about twenty miles from the nearest railway station, 'a fact which would provide him with an automatic excuse for missing deadlines or failing to do library research'.[68] Mozley's uncritical acceptance of *Bishop Jewel* was bad enough, but the storm which greeted its appearance was made worse by two articles of his own. One article attacked Sir Robert Peel (the prime minister) as a shifty and untrustworthy politician, and the other launched into Dr Godfrey Faussett, the Lady Margaret Professor of Divinity at Oxford and a long time opponent of the Tractarians. Newman had also suggested, disastrously as events proved, that Mozley should ask Ward to contribute more articles.[69] From the summer of 1841, Oakeley and Ward came to dominate *The British Critic* and its editor faraway on Salisbury Plain, and the content of the journal lurched sharply towards the expression of the views of these Romeward-looking clergy.

In his memoirs, published more than forty years later, Mozley recalled that perhaps he did not read the article carefully enough, except here and there; that he personally knew little of Jewel or his works, and that what he did know he disliked; and that Oakeley's reputation as 'a singularly gentle, modest and humble-minded man' provided a kind of security that the article would not go too far. Reading through the article again, he would say no more than that he found certain passages to be 'imprudent'.[70] Poor Mozley came in for severe criticism from his wife Harriet, who was Newman's eldest sister.[71] 'I have said all along that Jewel is worse than Faussett, and I told J. H. N. so. Tom is quite aware that judgement, both public and private, is against him . . . I have not read more of Mr O's article . . . but I am strong against it, and the opinion is quite as general everywhere'.[72]

Mozley's inactivity showed a deplorable lack of understanding of the responsibilities of editorship, quite apart from the anxiety it caused to the principal Tractarians. Keble was initially pleased by the sentiments in *Bishop Jewel*, and wrote to Newman saying that he 'particularly liked' Oakeley's article.[73] Newman was worried and he was still preoccupied with defending Tract 90. Pusey was appalled. He was on a visit to Ireland when he read the article and wrote directly to Newman. 'I am grieved that he [Oakeley] and Ward think it necessary to act as "public prosecutors" against the Reformers. It is surely not leaving it an open question, if *The British Critic*, which is supposed to express all our opinions, engages in such a crusade against them', and he rightly saw that the journal was now more or less committed to the position of Oakeley and Ward. 'I do not see how, according to any etiquette, *The British Critic* could in another number, apologise for the Reformers, and, if not, then it is committed to the view of a certain section [of the movement]'. But his deepest worries were caused by Oakeley's final statement about urging people to go forward without giving them any indication of the way by which they should travel. 'I should think this indefiniteness in itself very injurious: it is one thing for ourselves privately to feel or to say that . . . we have not cleared our views as to the power of the keys, or to confess that we or many have much to learn, another to set persons adrift, tell them that they are to go forwards some whither, urge them on and give them . . . neither chart nor compass. And why may not such as I, if we can, think the English Reformers meant to be Catholic? . . . It makes one heavy-hearted and think that one's office is done'.[74]

Newman received many letters from his friends and acquaintances, all of which expressed varying degrees of alarm about the future of *The British Critic*. He was in serious doubt about the wisdom of appointing Mozley as editor and appears to have contemplated the involvement of Frederic Rogers,[75] a promising young lawyer with a clear and incisive mind, hoping that he might succeed where Mozley was failing, in curbing the excesses of Oakeley and Ward. But Rogers himself was in despair as to what to do. 'A line which will satisfy Oakeley, Ward, Keble and Wilson[76] seems permanently hard to find, independently of the particular difficulties about Mozley. I am afraid your notion of my getting general influence in the review is rather hopeless. I feel far too perplexed and mistrustful myself to have any chance of keeping together half-a-dozen different sets of writers all pulling ways which I don't understand'.[77]

William Palmer (1803–85), a fellow of Worcester College, and a supporter of Newman during the affair of Tract 90, was alarmed by Oakeley's attitude. Palmer was a Tractarian as long as the movement was anti-Roman; *Bishop Jewel* was the first indication that it was not, and he echoed Pusey's concern about its unsettling effect. '[Oakeley] shows a spirit of hostility towards the Reformation . . . and anything but a friendly spirit towards the Church of England . . . [He] has no right to speak doubtfully on such important questions; if he cannot say firmly where the Church is, he ought to remain silent until further study had enabled him to speak decidedly on a point of such great importance and on which it is deeply criminal to unsettle the minds of others without necessity'.[78]

The correspondence drifted on until the end of July, when Pusey wrote to Newman again, reporting Palmer's concern. Pusey was not simply a mouthpiece for Palmer; he himself was anxious that *Bishop Jewel* would sow seeds of doubt in the minds of many, and certain that his picture of a degraded Church of England would send many others into the arms of Rome. 'Oakeley's writings are very painful to me ... They would be the very strongest temptation to go over to Rome ... and they will, I fear, much aggravate our difficulty in retaining many who are so tempted ... he does exhibit the Reformers in such a degraded light; puppets, set in motion not by any deeds of their own, but by Henry's lusts: going as little a way as they could, but moving because they must ... it is certainly unutterably degrading to our poor Church, if not such a mark upon her, that people would think it a duty to leave her'.[79] Pusey was rightly dismissive of Oakeley's scholarship, doubting that he had sufficient historical knowledge to support his arguments, and that he was merely theorising on the facts of others. He was as concerned as Frederic Rogers about the future of *The British Critic*. 'I do not see how *The British Critic* can take both sides without destroying the impression produced by unity; so there seems no alternative, but either saying nothing about the Reformation or that *The British Critic* should be the organ and representative of Oakeley's section'.[80] If we take this comment by Pusey as it stands, two conclusions can be drawn. Firstly, that by July 1841, there was a quite distinct group of Tractarians in existence, distinct enough for Pusey to refer to them as a 'section', and, secondly, that Pusey may have regarded Oakeley as the leader of that section. In his *Apologia pro vita sua*, Newman supported this by speaking of Oakeley as the most prominent member of the group.[81]

Newman himself was being pulled in two directions. As the undisputed leader and intellectual genius of the Tractarians, everybody took their complaints and feelings to him. On one side lay Pusey and others of his mind, devoted to the Church of England and convinced that Catholic truths and principles were best obeyed by remaining within her. On the other side lay Oakeley and Ward, representing a new and younger generation of Tractarians for whom the outward majesty of the Roman Catholic Church, was an almost irresistible lure, and who were, in the later words of Newman, 'urging the wheels of an unbalanced logic in the direction of Rome, although without as yet any definite idea of going thither'.[82] Newman tried to keep everyone happy. He endeavoured to dispel Pusey's anxiety by saying that although he agreed with Oakeley's attitude to the Reformers, he did not see the need for saying so in public, and that he would try to put a stop to any further attacks. But there was the continuing problem of a paucity of suitable and available writers for *The British Critic*. 'Every Review must depend on the men who will write for it. It is a great difficulty to get men to write. Oakeley and some others are ready writers, and have more time on their hands than we have, and this has thrown it upon them ... I assure you I shall try all I can to turn it into the literary channel, and if my will has its way, I will put a stop to all attacks on the Reformers . . . I certainly will represent the matter strongly to Oakeley and Ward, but they have but one thought in their mind. Their mind is possessed with one subject'.[83]

Even with Newman's hint that he was by no means certain of his will prevailing over the combined wills of Oakeley and Ward, especially since they now had a pliable editor in the shape of Mozley, Pusey was satisfied. 'It is a great relief that you mean Oakeley and Ward to be quiet; it is surely a diseased state of mind to be so taken up with one subject, and that a sort of persecution of the memory of those whose dross, we trust, God has cleared away. I should think that negative position of taking a line against persons, a very dangerous one, and very unhealthy to humility in a young man'.[84] Newman thought this to be too hard on Oakeley and Ward and did not believe that they were strongly critical of the Reformers merely for the sake of being critical, 'but as a feeling that our Church cannot be right till they are exposed, till their leaven is cast out, and till our Church repents of them. I think it would do better if they left all this to time. Truth will work'.[85]

Apart from Pusey, Palmer and Rogers, objections to *Bishop Jewel* were raised by Bishop Bagot of Oxford,[86] who, like many others, was generally in sympathy with Tractarians until he began to see the activity of the Romeward section. He conveyed his concern to Pusey who was able to reassure him that 'it is Mr Newman's earnest wish that the Review should be free from anything objectionable; he was alive to people's feelings about it, and will do what in him lies to meet them'.[87] The most perceptive assessment of public feeling came from Keble who, despite his earlier statement that he liked the article, had now had time to consider the reactions. George Dudley Ryder[88] had talked to Keble about the possibility of writing an article on Cranmer for *The British Critic*. Keble urged caution and delay. He advised that it should not appear in the October issue so soon after *Bishop Jewel* in July. Further derogatory articles would only serve to increase public disgust more with the review than with the Reformers. A separately published documentary history of the English Reformers would do much less damage than an even slightly critical article in *The British Critic*. It would serve to 'get rid of the rather conceited appearance of endeavouring to dethrone the Reformers from the place they have occupied in public opinion for three centuries by a few attacks in a periodical'.[89]

Newman took much of the criticism directed against *Bishop Jewel* on his own shoulders. In common with many other periodicals of the day, articles in *The British Critic* were unsigned. Any correspondence, favourable or otherwise, usually went to the editor, and although Newman was not, technically, the editor at the time of the publication of the July issue, he had been so for some years until quite recently, and in the minds of many he was still closely linked with the journal. Furthermore he was a public figure in the university of Oxford and more accessible than a parish priest somewhere on the Salisbury Plain. Moreover, in so far as the Tractarians constituted a movement, and in so far as that movement had a leader, he was it. Working on the traditional principle that the man at the top takes ultimate responsibility for the behaviour of his subordinates, Newman took the full force of the criticism directed against the author of the anonymous article. As he had promised Pusey, he spoke to Oakeley and told him that a number of people were offended by *Bishop Jewel*, but it seems that Oakeley was unaware of the upset at their meeting which took place before the end of August 1841. He was, in any case, quite unrepentant. 'I am very sorry it had offended nice people. I cannot bring myself to lament it; indeed it was so very deliberate ... on my part'.[90] What passed between the two men is not on record, but evidently Newman was a master of tact and diplomacy, because Oakeley recalled that he 'could not make out' whether Newman approved or disapproved of the article.[91]

Oakeley must have been aware of something of the hostile reaction to his article, because *The Record*, a weekly anti-Tractarian newspaper had printed a strong attack on the article in a number of its issues early in August. The attack had centred on Oakeley's attempt to exonerate the memory of Thomas Becket from the charge of having rescued a priest charged with murder from the jurisdiction of the civil courts. Jewel had used this incident to charge Becket with the 'wilful maintenance of manifest wickedness in the clergy'.[92] Oakeley was indignant on hearing 'the blessed saints and martyrs of the Most High thus slandered by these teachers of yesterday'.[93] *The Record* was indignant: 'Here we find the title of martyr, aye, and of blessed saint and martyr, given to a man who would refuse it to a Latimer and a Ridley', and the call to unprotestantize the Church of England was the final insult. 'We need not beg our readers to mark these things. They must impress themselves on every mind which has any just zeal for the purity of the truth of God, or of our Church, thus dishonoured by these her false sons'.[94]

The charge of being a 'false son' was sufficient to provoke Oakeley to write a letter to *The Record* in defence of the stand he had taken in support of Becket. 'I must contend that it is a slander upon Becket's memory, to represent this proceeding as an act of indulgence towards a profligate clergyman'. That Becket's resistance to King Henry II 'was not due to any desire on his part, of upholding laxity in the clergy, must be plain to any unprejudiced reader of his history . . . Bishop Jewel's imputation is certainly slanderous, though I am aware that he did but echo the current opinion of his time'.[95]

The succeeding events seem to show that Ward had played a less than honest role in the affair of *Bishop Jewel*. Before writing to *The Record*, Oakeley had asked Ward to get Newman's permission. It appears that Ward asked Newman if he would have any objection to a letter being sent to the paper on the subject of Becket's character. It also appears that Ward gave no indication that Oakeley would be the author, or that it would be in direct response to passages in *Bishop Jewel*. Mozley was worried by the letter, of which *The Record* printed only certain passages, and wondered what should be done. 'Is this discreet either on Oakeley's account, or fair to *The British Critic*? It looks like a soldier stepping out of the ranks and breaking the phalanx. He will have plenty of opportunity of saying what he likes in the latter'.[96] If Newman's reply is accepted as an accurate statement, then Ward was very selective in what he told Newman. 'Oakeley's letter to *The Record* arose from a blunder. Ward asked me beforehand whether I should object to it – but he did not say that the letter was to appear to come from any other connection with the B. C. which made all the difference. I thought it was a letter on Becket's character and had no notion the B. C. was to be [brought] in'.[97] Is it possible that Oakeley himself had any part in this deception? It is possible but unlikely. Oakeley's contemporaries have produced sufficiently similar testimonies of his character for us to believe that, despite a tendency to be impulsive in expressing his views, he was essentially loyal to Newman, honest in his behaviour, and incapable of duplicity. Ward was the opposite of Oakeley. As Oakeley was shy and gentle, so Ward was pugnacious and quick-tempered, always launching himself with relish into a verbal fight, without much regard for the rules. He may have been excited by the prospect of controversy surrounding his friend and urged him to respond in writing to the criticisms of *The Record*. While obeying Oakeley's request that he seek Newman's permission, Ward may have thought it necessary only to obtain the most general approval from Newman, and quite unnecessary to give any details.

Whether to gain approval, to test his reaction, or simply to inform him, Oakeley sent a copy of *The Subject of Tract XC* to his old friend from undergraduate days, Philip Shuttleworth, who had recently been appointed Bishop of Chichester. Shuttleworth had previously been Warden of New College, Oxford, and a was a strong opponent of Tractarians. Oakeley remembered him from their days together at Christ Church as 'a first rate Latin scholar and a prize man'.[98] It was Shuttleworth who had advised Oakeley to abandon his attempts to gain a prize in English and concentrate on Latin verse. On the advice of Dean Chandler of Chichester Cathedral, Shuttleworth had appointed Henry Manning to the vacant archdeaconry of Chichester in later December 1840. But, fresh from the battlefield of Oxford, Shuttleworth was no friend of the Tractarians, and he addressed a long and stern letter to the his old friend expressing his 'deep sorrow' at the content of the article. He objected to the 'undoubting and trenchant tone' of Oakeley's statements about the reformation, many of which showed 'a real want of sound evidence'. Had Oakeley, when describing the reformation as a purely political event in England, forgotten the 'affecting prayer' of Cranmer on the day of his martyrdom, and was the thrusting of his 'unworthy hand' to the flames done solely for political reasons? In stating that a denial of the eucharistic sacrifice was an heretical tendency, could he quote one word in the Articles, the Liturgy or the New Testament in which the Eucharist was, even by implication, called a sacrifice? The canons and the prayer book spoke not of an altar but of a communion table, and the Saviour had spoken not of a sacrifice but of a simple commemorative rite. 'St Paul tells us by this service we show forth our Lord's death till he come, and in alluding to the irreverent celebration of the eucharist in the Corinthian Church, he uses expressions perfectly irreconcilable with the idea of its being of a sacrificial nature. And yet if your assertion is correct, our canons are heretical, the prayer book is heretical, St Paul is heretical and + + + + + ! ! ! You assert that the Church Catholic is the ordained channel of blessing from God to men. Strip this assertion of its oracular character, and look for its warrant to scripture, and you will find not one single word to bear you out . . . You assert the power of effective absolution as placed in the hands of the clergy. The New Testament contains no such doctrine nor was it taught even by those occasionally unsound men the Early Fathers. Read the epistles of Cyprian for instance . . . You quote abundantly from Bishop Montague (and others of his kind): but one sentence of St Paul would be worth all their books put together. Of scripture, in the course of your argument you take no further notice than you do of the Koran . . . I am sure, my dear Oakeley, your intentions are upright. I have seen too much of you to have any doubts on this point. But you remember the sentence pronounced on those who preach another Gospel. This is a serious question and not to be dealt with lightly. Under that judgement I fear that your party are falling. Sure I am that your case must be made out by much stronger arguments than I have met with, before I can believe it to be reconcilable with our only rule of faith, the inspired scriptures'.[99]

Shuttleworth's letter forms the longest and most direct surviving challenge to Oakeley's views at this time, and it was written by a long-standing friend. Shuttleworth was a Low Churchman, and he wrote from the standpoint of the divine inspiration of scripture as the sole authority. But he wrote firmly and kindly to his old friend, and Oakeley replied to his comments by taking not the slightest notice.

Chapter Six

An unbalanced logic

ARTICLES LITURGICAL AND HISTORICAL

I have been fifty times startled by passages in his articles for The British Critic, but I have always made it my rule to let everything pass that I thought could be defended whether I liked the first blush of it or not.
Thomas Mozley to John Henry Newman, 28 January 1842

If Thomas Mozley knew what was happening in Tractarian circles and elsewhere, particularly the anxiety caused by *Bishop Jewel*, it made no difference to his use of Oakeley as a regular contributor to the pages of *The British Critic*. As Newman had told Pusey, the main difficulty facing the editor of any periodical, was filling the pages of each issue, and finding suitable and available writers to undertake the task. For all that his articles could be inflammatory and headstrong, Oakeley was a fluent and elegant writer, and that was not to be lightly dismissed. His strident anti-Reformation position was due partly to what he had learned from the equally strident Froude, but Oakeley was a convert to the Tractarian movement, and a fairly recent convert at that. Converts are known to be more extreme than their new-found cause, and they often proclaim it with a vigour and an enthusiasm that can cause embarrassment to their more settled elders. Nevertheless, Oakeley had time to write for *The British Critic*, and for the easy-going Mozley, that was good enough.

The journal had begun its life as a general review, remaining such until the days of Newman's editorship. From that time, its contributors started to deliver lengthy articles, and so it continued after the appointment of Mozley in the summer of 1841. Mozley had not the time carefully to read and check these lengthy articles. He was also broadly in sympathy with the position of Oakeley and Ward, and many of their articles were too technical in their subject matter for him fully to understand them. 'My first troubles were with Oakeley and Ward. I will not say that I hesitated much as to the truth of what they wrote, for in that matter I was inclined to go very far, at least in the way of toleration . . . Oakeley was out of my reach altogether in liturgies and ritual. I could only put my point on a salient point of his articles here and there. This I did, and he submitted, evidently intending, however, to persevere and come round in the end'.[1]

Oakeley wrote thirteen articles for *The British Critic* between April 1840 and October 1843, of which six are wholly concerned with liturgy, and two touch upon the subject here and there. After the storms surrounding *Bishop Jewel*, Oakeley returned in the issue for October 1841 to the theoretically innocuous and more tranquil pastures of liturgy, with an article entitled *Rites and Ceremonies*.

The genesis of the articles lies in a correspondence between Oakeley and Mozley which had begun before the end of August 1841. Mozley had asked Oakeley to write an article on a subject unrecorded in their surviving correspondence. It seems that Mozley rarely thought about filling the pages of an issue until the previous issue was in print, and his offer to Oakeley took place against the background of *Bishop Jewel*. Newman had spoken to Oakeley on the subject and doubtless he had spoken to Mozley as well since the two men were brothers-in-law. Newman had decided to tell Oakeley to steer well clear of the dangerous and emotive area of the English Reformation, and Mozley suggested a different topic for his next article. Whatever it was, Oakeley felt unsure of his knowledge of the field to attempt an article. 'Perhaps it was not from liking to pledge myself to what I was uncertain about. If so it was a prudent measure: for, alas when I came to try my hand upon the subject I could not satisfy myself though I feel as if something might come of it sooner or later. Meanwhile a nice French book fell into my hands'.[2]

The book in question was *Institutions liturgiques* by the Abbé Prosper Gueranger, and it gave Oakeley the idea for an article on ritual and ceremonial which he had first explored, superficially, in *The Church Service* in April 1840. He sent the completed article to Oxford to be vetted by Newman, but felt there was no need to consult Mozley on the change of subject, because I felt the subject sufficiently like that you had booked me for, not to be likely to clash with others'.[3]

Oakeley's article on liturgy derived mainly from his work at Margaret Chapel, where he had satisfied his desire to produce a Catholic liturgy by making the fullest use of the capabilities of the rubrics of *The Book of Common Prayer*. The first fruits appeared in *The Church Service*, and *Rites and Ceremonies* showed how far his interest had widened and deepened. On 28 July 1841 Oakeley and Ward had visited St Mary's College, Oscott. The college was founded in 1794 in a country house then some miles from Birmingham, though now part of Birmingham itself, as a school and a seminary. By 1838 increased numbers had justified a move to a new and purpose-built complex about a mile and a half east of the old site which became known as Old Oscott.[4] Oakeley and Ward visited the chapel, the decoration and stained glass of which were by Pugin.[5] At the same time, they took the opportunity to visit the new Roman Catholic Cathedral of St Chad in Birmingham, also by Pugin. The cathedral (built in 1839–41) had been consecrated only a few weeks before the visit in the presence of the nine Roman Catholic bishops in England,[6] as the cathedral church for the vicar apostolic of the Midlands District. The visit had been brought about through the good offices of the likeable and slightly eccentric figure of Ambrose Phillips de Lisle (1809–78), a wealthy Roman Catholic landowner in Leicestershire. Phillipps de Lisle was a friend of the same John Rouse Bloxam who had designed the interior of Littlemore Church in 1836, and whose designs Oakeley had copied at Margaret Chapel in 1839. Bloxam, a fellow of Magdalen College, invited Phillipps de Lisle to Oxford and introduced him to Ward. Phillipps and Ward struck up a friendship and a visit to Oscott was arranged, Bloxam and Ward arranging for Oakeley to be included. The two 'Romeward' Tractarians were very impressed by what they found. 'Oakeley and Ward both concur with me in expressions of delight at the truly Catholic ethos of St Mary's College, Oscott'.[7]

The beauty of the college chapel and the cathedral church added to Oakeley's desire to develop the beauty and dignity of the Catholic liturgy in an Anglican setting, and the first volume of Gueranger's book, published in 1840, gave him the opportunity for another lengthy article in *The British Critic*. The article is concerned with the importance of religious ceremonial, Oakeley intending to provide scriptural justification for liturgical formality in the face of an ostensible lack of authority for formal worship.

Oakeley began by defending Gueranger and other liturgical scholars against those who accused them of wasting time and energy in 'navigating their course among the shoals of Judaical formality'.[8] The prima facie evidence of scripture was against any kind of formal ceremonial in worship, and Oakeley was prepared 'to concede to the Calvinist, that, in his objection to . . . matters of external religion, he has the apparent evidence of scripture'.[9] But he countered this by allowing them the evidence only 'of its literal wording',[10] and he put the proposition that the strong words of Christ against the Pharisees (Matthew chapter 23 and Luke chapter 11) were not directed against outward religion as an accompaniment and expression of the spiritual mind, but as its substitute;[11] and he called for a 'closer and more thoughtful inspection' of scripture.[12] It was apparent, he argued, that the scriptural argument for an unformal and even anti-formal Christian Church was one that proved too much, and that every Church would run aground on the rocks of this argument, with the sole possible exception of the Quakers, though even the Quakerism of his own day had formal modes of speech and dress.[13] 'What then shall we do; include all, or exclude all . . . It seems plain enough, that, either the Church has authority in rites and ceremonies, or not'.[14]

Oakeley's answer was that of course the Church had authority, and that the Catholic Church and its liturgy were not to be compared with Pharisaical Judaism. 'Every religionist quarrels with the amount of forms which exceed his own practice; and naturally turns to a description of the Pharisees for an illustration of the evil he condemns'.[15] Obviously Catholic liturgy seemed to run counter to the letter of the New Testament, but was it a contravention of the spirit of Scripture? This was a quite different question from the charge of contradicting 'mere wording'.[16] Despite this superficial disagreement, there was no substantial inconsistency because the authority of scripture and the Church were equal. The Church was to be interpreted by the bible, and the bible by the Church, and when, to an individual, they appeared to be in conflict, then such an appearance of conflict was due to an error of judgement on the part of the individual.[17]

Oakeley observed that there were passages in epistles which were hardly explicable 'but upon the supposition, that the eucharistic ordinance was solemnised by the apostles themselves as a sacrificial act'.[18] Oakeley gives no list of the texts he has in mind, but quotes instead from the second part of Froude's *Remains*, which includes an essay on the Church in apostolic times. He adopted Froude's conclusion that either the pupils of the apostles had made innovations quite glaringly different from the practices of the apostles themselves; or that a liturgical system existed in the apostolic age in substance, though not in all its ceremonies.[19] Oakeley was not surprised that there were so few references to liturgy in the New Testament, since both the gospels and the epistles were not written to prescribe and enforce religious ritual. 'All that we can expect, if it existed in the days of the apostles, is, an occasional allusion to it in their epistles, as existing, and a plain acquiescence in it; and this much we find'.[20]

He quoted the famous passage from Saint Paul (1 Corinthians 10:16) adding, 'who will then say that other actions . . . may not have accompanied the celebration merely because Saint Paul does not happen to allude to them'.[21] R. W. Church describes Oakeley as the 'master of a facile and elegant pen', yet 'without much learning',[22] and it is painfully clear that Oakeley, despite a 'facile and elegant pen' was using scripture to confirm and sustain the practices of the Roman Catholic Church by a mixture of biblical fundamentalism and strained exegesis. The authoritative construction of a liturgy based on the slightest of references and the absence of any direct prohibition is an uncertain business. There is nothing wrong in his thinking, but his arguments are very much weaker than he himself supposes them to be. He challenged those who upheld the authority of scripture over tradition to justify their departure from the letter of scripture where it enjoined or recognised such actions as the washing of the feet of the disciples 'which seems to be enforced on Christians as plainly as words can speak';[23] the kiss of peace, the anointing of the sick, and the bowing of the knee at the name of Jesus. He added the slightly more doubtful examples of the burial of the bodies of martyrs under altars (Revelation 6:9), and the wearing of white vestments by the officiating ministers (Revelation 4:14). 'Although the superficial appearances of the New Testament are anti-liturgical, it seems no less certain, that to a closer and more faithful examination it discloses vestiges of the Church system, which, except upon the Catholic hypothesis, are, we will say, unsurmountable'.[24]

The Reformers inevitably came in for criticism, and Luther in particular, for urging the recitation of whole psalms and chapters from the bible, as involving too stiff and mechanical a view of services. 'One parable, or one miracle, or one short collection of precepts . . . is quite as much as the spiritual eye can take in at one view'.[25] In any case, the interpretation and use of the bible was a matter for the Church to deal with 'in such a way as the Church shall consider best for the expression of her own mind at the time'.[26]

Oakeley was not entirely happy with all the contents of Gueranger's book, and was slightly critical of Roman liturgies in one or two places. The reason may have had something to do with the fact that Dom Prosper Gueranger was an Ultramontanist. In his *Institutions liturgiques*, Gueranger laid down his basic conviction that liturgical uniformity was of the essence of Church unity, and that Gallicanism in liturgy led to Gallicanism in dogma and Gallicanism in Church politics. On these last two points Oakeley was in full agreement. 'We cordially go along with the author . . . in what we call his unnational spirit . . . National theories, even Gallican . . . appear to us to involve a subtle Erastianism'.[27] But he was less than happy with Gueranger's statement that Catholicism, in heart, in spirit and in liturgy, did not exist apart from visible communion with the see of St Peter; and where he described England as being as systematically rooted in Protestantism as

Zurich and Geneva; and where he took no more notice of *The Book of Common Prayer* than he did of the Confession of Augsburg.[28] Oakeley was too well aware of the diversity of practice within the Church of England. 'The varieties of practice in any single diocese, even those most vigilantly overlooked, surpass belief . . . If then uniformity be the symbol of unity, what, alas, must be the distractions of the Church of England'.[29] He fired two shots against the Roman practices but they were very small and half-hearted. Reading through the New Testament, he found that it discredited veneration of the Blessed Virgin Mary,[30] and he also commented on the severe paucity of scriptural readings in the Roman Breviary as 'something which savours of abuse'.[31]

Oakeley's experience with Gueranger's conviction that liturgical uniformity was one of the outward expressions of the unity of the Church with the see of Rome, is not unlike Newman's experience of reading Wiseman's article in *The Dublin Review* of July 1839, on the Donatist heresy. The difference between the two men lies in the fact that whereas Newman was an intellectual, capable of understanding and accepting a well-reasoned argument, even though it dealt a severe blow to his own beliefs, Oakeley was not. He was a good example of a man whose head was on many occasions ruled by his heart. With his heart set firmly in the direction of Rome, his mind was not to be moved or changed by argument. Since Gueranger had argued that uniformity would be the result and therefore the token of unity in the Spirit,[32] 'There seems to us but one way of meeting the difficulty of our position; and that is, not to keep the true standard out of sight, or endeavour to misrepresent the facts, as they exist among ourselves, into an apparent conformity with it, but to exhibit the glorious ideal at the risk of seeming visionary, and to expose the actual deviations from it, with the certainty of being thought treacherous'.[33]

Part of the ideal of which Oakeley wrote was the celebration of the eucharist, 'the glory and the sun of the liturgical system . . . to which all other parts of the divine office are introductory, or subservient'.[34] He listed the ways in which the Church of England fell far behind the Church of Rome in upholding the central place of the eucharist in the worship and life of the Christians. It had been displaced as the nucleus of worship; the sermon and not the sacrament was regarded as being the essence of divine worship, and therefore the 'daily bread' of the religious life had been replaced in the Protestant system by the 'husks of a mere capricious teaching'; the eucharist was not considered a necessary part of the service at the consecration of new church; and the altar had been eclipsed by the pulpit in many churches'.[35]

Oakeley defended the intricacy of rubrics and the elaborateness of religious ceremonial by likening them to the prodigality of care shown by the ardent lover to the object of his affections. 'How will he watch his expressions! How will he adopt the current forms of endearment? . . . How will he lavish his guineas by tens or hundreds, or even thousands, according to the length of his purse, on a bracelet, a few lace pocket handkerchiefs, a boudoir or a parterre . . . We hope the illustration is not unbecoming'.[36] The rite and ceremonies of the Church were not intrusive distractions but outward displays of truths. 'It is no mere accident of religion, it is of its substance; no adscititious ornament but a spontaneous and native development. Forms are the expression of the mind of the Spirit; rites are breathing words; ceremonies, the signs of momentous truths. In the majesty of her symbolical system, the Church stands out as the vestibule of heaven'.[37]

Oakeley's belief in the doctrine of transubstantiation is stated in *Bishop Jewel*, as well as his acceptance of the eucharist as a propitiatory sacrifice, and he was critical of the Reformation in so far as it had led to the discontinuation of a daily celebration of the eucharist 'the daily sacrifice, of which for fifteen hundred and more years the sanctuaries of Christendom had never once been unconscious'.[38] The use of the words 'solemnise' and 'celebrate' implied a 'mystery' and an 'oblation', and they had been superseded by those which 'import that man is the object, and intellectual illumination, the end, of divine worship'.[39] He dismissed the old High Church party, typified by Archbishop Laud who strongly enjoined bowing to the altar 'while at the same time entering protests . . . against the full and consistent view of the great doctrine, which gives to the altar its especial claim upon the homage of the Christian worshipper'.[40]

For all that Oakeley fussed about the presentation and practice of the liturgy in Margaret Chapel, and absorbed himself in the study of the subject, he had a right understanding of its place in Christian worship, and of the doctrines of which they were the outward expression, and he issued warnings against the misuse and abuse of ceremonial. He warned against 'taking up Catholicism as mere poetry or aesthetics . . . lest any should mistake taste for religion', and become too preoccupied with the 'fascinating tendencies of her symbolism'.[41] Outward forms could be dangerous until their proper nature was understood and their adoption became the outward expression of an inner life. 'They were signs of realities, and not mere securities for decency'.[42]

In his criticism of the 'theatrical' tendency in worship, the doing of such things merely for effect, Oakeley reserved his final words for an attack on a royal baptism which had recently occurred at Buckingham Palace.[43] 'We have seen, what we must confess, was to us a painful representation of a (so-called) "altar" erected at Buckingham Palace

... It was decorated ... or rather laden with plate (one article of which was a gold "salver"), illuminated by several candelabra, and embroidered with the sacred initials ... On a bracket some way up the wall was a bust, apparently of George IV, as of some tutelary saint, or rather presiding genius ... What has an altar to do with a christening anywhere; least of all in a drawing room? The covering ... is said to have become the perquisite of some official; and has probably by this time shared the fate of the splendid new gilt altar at which the marriage of our sovereign was celebrated, and been sold at auction'.[44] Had his earlier work and writings not done so, these comments would have halted Oakeley's chances of preferment in the Church of England.

Rites and Ceremonies is a sensible and well-written article, unlike the emotive and provocative Bishop Jewel. Dealing largely with the presentation of the liturgy, its sentiments were of a more personal concern and therefore less controversial than attacks on the English Reformation and the Reformers. There was no regurgitation of the angry protests that had greeted the publication of the July issue of the journal.

The respite did not last for long. A new storm erupted in October 1841 when an act of parliament laid plans for the creation of an Anglo-Prussian bishopric in Jerusalem. The genesis of this bizarre conception lay with King Frederick William IV of Prussia who, apparently, wished to give Protestants a recognised status in the Holy Land by sending a bishop who would take charge of all Anglicans, German Lutherans, and any other non-Roman and non-Greek Christians who cared to acknowledge his authority. Thus far there were few objections. But the details of the plan called for nominations to the bishopric to be made alternately by the English and Prussian governments, and the endowments of the bishopric were to come equally from the two countries. Each nominee would take his orders from that source, but he was to subscribe to the Confession of Augsburg and observe the order of the German Evangelical Lutheran Church, and he would be free to ordain Lutherans who accepted the Thirty-Nine Articles.

The first sign of opposition came from a leading article in *The Times* of 19 October 1841, which saw the new bishopric as a travesty of the rights of the Eastern Orthodox Church. But there was widespread support for the idea. Politicians saw it as a means of asserting an Anglo-German presence in an area where France and Russia had long enjoyed dominant influence. Evangelicals were delighted by this strengthening of links with Continental Protestants. The High Church party, though far from enthusiastic, discerned the possibility that it might lead to the introduction of episcopacy into the German Lutheran

Church. A number of serious bible students of millenarian tendencies saw it as a means of gathering the Jews to Protestant Christianity as part of the divine plan for the impending return of Christ.

The Tractarians alone regarded the scheme as an abomination. Their fundamental objection was that the plan implied a kinship between the Anglicans and Continental Protestants, which they firmly denounced. The plan for the bishopric assumed that there was very little difference between the two churches, and that the very inconsequential differences which did exist, could be resolved by simple subscription, either to the Thirty-Nine Articles by Lutherans, or to the Confession of Augsburg by Anglicans. Although a full scale Tractarian assault on the scheme was launched in November 1841, it was too late to prevent the consecration of the new bishop on 7 November. On 11 November Newman sent an official protest to the Bishop of Oxford and to the Archbishop of Canterbury deploring the scheme on the ground that Lutheranism and Calvinism were heresies repugnant to scripture, and that the Church of England was admitting such heretics to communion without them renouncing their errors. 'Here I am labouring with all my might to keep men from Rome and as if I had not enough trouble a new element of separation is introduced'.[45] 'If any such event should take place I shall not be able to keep a single man from Rome. They will all be trooping off sooner or later'.[46] Five weeks later Newman told a very different story to his sister.[47] 'Do not believe any absurd reports. They talk in the papers of secessions among us to Rome. Do not believe it. Not one will go'.[48]

The whole affair was deeply unsettling to Oakeley, one of the very group for whom Newman was 'labouring with all his might' to keep from seceding to Rome. The Jerusalem bishopric served to fan the flames of Oakeley's suspicion that, in spite of the efforts of Tract 90, the Church of England was not really as Catholic as he might have thought, especially when its bishops did something so obviously uncatholic. He gave the substance of his beliefs in a letter to Pusey, who had initially given his cautious approval to the Jerusalem scheme. Oakeley had accepted newspaper reports which stated that the King of Prussia wished to unite the Protestant churches of his kingdom in one national church, and had come to the Church of England, a sister Protestant body, to inject episcopalianism into the new church with a view of combining discordant elements, and securing peace and union among his subjects. This concept of a 'national church' was anathema to Oakeley who had attacked such national theories in *Rites and Ceremonies* as involving a 'subtle Erastianism'.[49] Here it was rearing its head in Continental Protestantism. 'The idea of a national Church in itself I cannot but regard as essentially uncatholic. The Catholic

Church, is not, as I believe, a collection of separate bodies forming an aggregate, of circles as in a river, touching one another, and forming a collection of circles, but one circle which has so entirely absorbed all others into itself that no trace of their independence remains'. The plan smacked of Erastianism, and to Oakeley, Erastianism was a form of antichrist. 'Did our church strongly uphold Catholic principles as well in her existing administration as in her formularies, then I would hope that good might come of anything she does, though ever I should have thought such proceedings as these had the appearance of doing good that evil might come'.[50]

The affair of the Jerusalem bishopric had unsettled Newman as much as it had unsettled Oakeley, and from that point, it marked the beginning of the end of his membership of the Church of England.[51] But there is no evidence that he was at all in sympathy with the position of Oakeley and Ward, since contemporary correspondence shows that he was highly suspicious of Oakeley's activities.

In the winter of 1841-2 there was a short exchange of letters on the subject of Oakeley and the work at Margaret Chapel, between Newman and his former pupil, Samuel Francis Wood. Wood had been called to the bar in 1835, and from about that time he had begun to worship regularly at Margaret Chapel. Henry Parry Liddon described Wood as 'a layman of saintly life whose early death [in 1843] was mourned by Pusey and Newman'.[52] In December 1841, Wood was less than happy with whatever Oakeley was doing at the Chapel and said as much to Newman. Newman wrote a very reassuring letter in reply. 'Oakeley told you what I thought generally for he came with a message from you. I do not at all like forcing the mind – and I recommended that you should join in such services as were pleasant to you. He seemed to think that they would not wish to adopt any in which you would not wish to join'.[53]

A further letter in January 1842 showed that Wood was increasingly disillusioned with Oakeley and Margaret Chapel, and was thinking of leaving. Newman did his best to dissuade him. 'I have been thinking over your leaving Margaret Street, and think you should not – that is, unless your continuing there grows very irksome to you. At the present time it is important for the sake of those who are, or who are likely to be there. It ever will be a very rare thing for a person to despair of our external state as you do, and yet to remain in it'.[54]

Whatever Oakeley was doing or saying at the chapel, Wood was unhappy to the point of deciding to leave. The last sentence of Newman's letter indicates that Wood was as unhappy about the state of the Church of England as Oakeley, yet had no intention of leaving it. Possibly Oakeley's continuous praise of Catholicism irritated

Wood, who found himself out of sympathy with Oakeley's opinions, and therefore in an uncomfortable position at the chapel. Newman urged Wood to remain at the chapel as a steadying influence. 'I think you can be of great use to other men in directing their thoughts to interior religion as a sufficient occupation to say the least . . . I would have you reflect whether it be not your duty at the present time, that which providence marks out for you . . . Ward you will often find at Oakeley's – and though he is not a man to be carried away, yet I feel sure you would do him good by developing his tendencies to quiet . . . it might be a soothing and tranquilizing duty . . . thus to employ . . . You are older than most of the persons likely to be there'.[55] If Newman hoped that Wood might have some soothing effect on the pugnacious Ward and the impulsive Oakeley, he was to be disappointed by the premature death of Wood fifteen months later at the age of thirty-three.

Mozley was still unhappy about Oakeley and Ward writing articles for *The British Critic*, and he suggested to Newman that if they were so dissatisfied with the present state of the Church of England, they might consider withdrawing from active participation in Church life, and set up an urban monastery or college, on the lines of those suggested by Froude. 'Froude's colleges for larger towns have only been talked of. Why should not those who are very dissatisfied and who despair of success – why should not Ward and Oakeley and others attempt such societies?'[56] Mozley was perhaps unaware or dismissive of the attempt by Oakeley to establish a collegiate monastic community in his house in Margaret Street which had begun a month or two earlier. He certainly knew nothing of the qualities required for a successful monastic life; Oakeley and Ward were not of the stuff of which monks are made.

At the beginning of December 1841 Oakeley was pressing Mozley for space for an article in the January 1842 issue of *The British Critic*, proposing a further piece on some aspect of worship and liturgy, such as eucharistic hymns. He was fully aware that it should be non-controversial. 'I am aware that it is undesirable at this moment to give people a handle against us; & this I would remember in writing. On the other hand should you be quite full, I will try something for a future number'.[57] The issue for January 1842 was already full, and Oakeley made no contribution either to that or to the April issue. Mozley was full of admiration for Oakeley's literary talent and single-mindedness, but found it worrying at the same time and believed, wrongly, that Oakeley was on the verge of becoming a Roman Catholic. 'I see in him a determination to commit us all to the very utmost. That he will go over to Rome very soon . . . I have not much doubt ... He prefers the Roman Communion and has got over the difficulties of the case ... I have been fifty times startled by passages in his articles for *The British Critic*, but I have always made it my rule to let everything pass that I thought could be defended whether I liked the first blush of it or not'.[58] Newman was in partial agreement, but not so certain that Oakeley would go to Rome independently. 'Oakeley I am suspicious of. I think at present he would do nothing without me ... Ward I see much of, Oakeley little. In confidence I tell you I have only lately been speaking to Ward about Oakeley'.[59]

The joint experiences of Newman, Mozley and Wood tend to suggest that Oakeley was striking an independent line, and was not so much in the shadow of Ward as some historians of the Oxford Movement have tended to see him. Bouyer, for example, describes Oakeley as 'a relatively colourless personality',[60] compared with the character and bombast of Ward. This is unfair to Oakeley who, while deferring to Newman and seeking his advice, was independent and critical enough to make up his own mind, and was certainly far from colourless.

Having nothing to do with the January and April 1842 issues of the *Critic*, Oakeley occupied himself with the idea of translating and publishing a collection of homilies for holy days by the early saints, and he sent his apologies to Mozley, telling him that he was 'almost knocked up with the work'.[61] The collection was published in June 1842 and prefaced by a publisher's 'Advertisement' written by Oakeley. Having disposed of the prima facie anti-formal texts of the New Testament in *Rites and Ceremonies*, he developed this by saying that the early saints displayed a continual deference to the authority of the Church in the interpretation of the biblical texts because it was 'the only security against error in the interpretation of the Written Word'.[62] In so doing, he almost ascribed to the homilies an authority greater than that of scripture itself. 'They manifest of penetration into the more recondite sense, and remoter bearings of the sacred text ... it also furnishes the glimpse of an absolutely unfathomable abyss below the depths which it actually discloses'.[63] The homilies were not simply the words of ordinary Christians, they were 'translations of the saintly mind'.[64]

Oakeley also noted that the Catholic Church in the days of Saint Ambrose wore, 'essentially, the same aspect as at this day'.[65] The early Fathers of the Church appealed to Oakeley because of their devotional teachings, which found a response in the strong streak of devotion that ran through his own nature. The unpolemical character of their homilies was more attractive than the decidedly polemical writings of the English Reformers. 'We seem to be placed . . . at the feet, not of this or that teacher, but of a holy conclave; wherein, though there are many voices, there is evidently but one mind'.[66]

Oakeley's next article for the *Critic* appeared in the issue for July 1842 under the title *What is meant by unprotestantizing?* It was a sequel to *Bishop Jewel*, and explained his intentions in calling for the unprotestantizing of the Church of England.[67] The phrase caused alarm to almost everyone for whom the Church of England was either Protestant, or it was not; and if it was not, then it was Catholic and a part of the Roman Catholic Church. Oakeley was working on the article by the end of April 1842[68] in response to a tract, critical of *Bishop Jewel*.[69] Newman took fright at the thought of more trouble and, without seeing it, supposed it to be an attack on Bird, rather than a defence of *Bishop Jewel*.[70] Oakeley was able to assure Mozley that it was nothing of the kind. 'I am . . . very anxious to explain my meaning in the passage he quotes . . . and hope also that those who like the Bishop of Oxford think us too hard on the Reformers might be better pleased with the explanation than with the article'.[71]

The article was finished in June 1842 and Oakeley posted it to Mozley saying, with surprising obstinacy that, firstly, he would only consent to minor alterations in its shape; secondly, he would not consent to the changing of any of its sentiments; and thirdly, that if it proved impossible to alter the article to their mutual satisfaction, then he would consider publishing it as it stood, 'on my own responsibility and perhaps with my own name'; though he agreed not to do this without first consulting Newman.[72]

The article did not, as it turned out, contain a polemical attack on Bird. Instead it was, at first, surprisingly moderate and well-balanced. Oakeley asserted that he would 'intrude upon the peace of the contented, and raise doubts in the minds of the uncomplaining' only for 'some very vital truth,' in this case, the unprotestantizing of the Church of England.[73] Until this took place, the Church would never regain 'its original power and hold upon the nation'.[74] Though he wanted to see 'a great change in the English Church', it need not necessarily be of nature and essence, or of formal system or doctrine, 'but in tone . . . the infusion into her system of a new spirit'.[75] This is a contradiction for Oakeley, who had already adopted the doctrine of transubstantiation, quite at variance with the Thirty-Nine Articles. He insisted that he had no intention of 'revolutionising the Church',[76] or of 'blowing up the Establishment'.[77] Thus far Oakeley appeared to be soothing and conciliatory, and much of this may be due to the adverse reaction to *Bishop Jewel*, as much as to Bird's tract. Everything has been shifted away from 'institution' and 'doctrine' to 'tone' and 'spirit', to ease the fears of his critics. Oakeley declared himself to be no revolutionary since such people applied themselves to the changing of institutions rather than the changing of men, and their first aim was to erect a system rather than to implant a spirit.[78] Unprotestantizing should not be seen as 'analogous to that of storming a height, cannonading a fortress, to be performed in military fashion, amid the cries of the victors and the vanquished',[79] because he understood Protestantism to be 'not so much a collection of doctrines constituting a protest against Rome, as a certain tone of mind, a certain general disposition'.[80] It is doubtful if the Reformers would have agreed with him on that point. He assured his readers that he envisaged no change in external constitution or essential doctrine; no reconstitution of formularies or service books; and no reunion with Rome under present circumstances; simply a change of opinion and feeling.[81] Furthermore, the Church of England was not going to unprotestantize at all 'unless the Church of England so wishes'.[82] What was needed was 'a kind of education to be going on in the country at large'.[83]

At first sight, all this talk of 'education', and changes of 'opinion' and 'feeling' does seem soothing and placatory, and so the article was intended to be. But Oakeley had not really changed, and occasional flashes of explicit belligerence are present, and in a style of challenge even more direct than that in *Bishop Jewel*. He maintained his charge that Protestantism was 'faithless, presumptuous and irrelevant', and 'the natural result of measuring religion by the reason and feelings of the individual'.[84] Again the gauntlet was thrown down, though more gently this time. 'Let the present be considered a war of opinion, and let it be conducted on both sides with the legitimate weapons of argument and persuasion . . . If they choose to consider that the advocates of Church opinions (i.e. the Tractarians) have something to say for themselves – well; if not, nothing more is to be said. And should the religion of the nation decide against them, they will have simply to retire from the field of controversy, and acknowledge their failure'.[85] 'So we may indulge the hope, that the present opposition to a revived Church system is one which will gradually yield to time, to habituation, to a maturer explanation of it on the one side, and a maturer appreciation of it on the other'.[86]

The degree of moderation and tolerance shown in the article did no good for Oakeley's reputation in the eyes of those who had already condemned his Romeward tendencies. Oakeley had called for reunion with Rome, and his statement that he did not see it occurring under present circumstances did not allay fears that he believed in it, wanted it and would work for it. Gladstone realised this in July 1842 when he made it his object to discover more about the beliefs and activities of the Romeward section. 'It is startling. They look not merely to the renewal of the Catholic idea within the pale of the Church of England but seem to consider the main condition of that development ... to be reunion with the Church of Rome ... They recognise, however, authority in the Church of England, and abide in her without love specifically fixed on her, to seek the fulfilment of this work of reunion. It is, for example ... the sole object of Oakeley's life'.[87]

In September 1842, Mozley himself came under strong criticism from his own diocesan, Bishop Denison of Salisbury.[88] Denison spoke harshly of *The British Critic*, describing it as sitting 'in the critic's chair placed somewhere in the vague region of an imaginary Catholicism'.[89] Newman advised Mozley to write or speak to the bishop as soon as possible, taking up his criticisms.[90] Mozley refused, on the ground that neither he nor the bishop could handle difficult interviews. 'He would be short and bluff, and so should I'.[91] Newman then counselled Mozley to resign, in the face of what amounted to a censure from his diocesan bishop. If he would not resign the editorial chair, then Oakeley and Ward must go. 'I think you must discharge Oakeley and Ward, and if you think so, I will take the responsibility. Depend on it, they cannot write without bringing in their notions'.[92] Considering the trouble he had had with the two men, Mozley was surprisingly loyal to his two contributors. 'I think there is no need to do anything at present about Oakeley and Ward. I wish them still to write for the B. C'.[93] Newman answered with a very equivocal letter. If the bishop of Salisbury could be pacified 'merely by excluding Oakeley and Ward from your pages, it is what I should most like you to do ... I so dislike row and agitation, constitutionally, that I should be glad if the Review could get more humdrum. I am sure our principles will spread eventually and they will spread better for going slow'. Then he continued by giving his support for the two men. 'I agree in the main with Ward and Oakeley, and at all events think they are doing a good work by breaking down prejudices etc., and if I do not write like them it is only because it is not my way. I could not say what I say without unreality or, sometimes, without offending my ideas or taste and propriety. But still I am sure they are doing good'.[94]

Newman's equivocal attitude to Oakeley and Ward at this stage is best explained by his dislike of 'row and agitation', of which there had been no shortage since Tract 90. He had distanced himself from the mainstream of Tractarian activity ten months earlier when he moved to Littlemore, living there in partial seclusion until he became a Roman Catholic in 1845. After the affair of the Jerusalem bishopric, he was beginning to grow weary of constant strife.

Mozley's attitude was, in some ways, equally equivocal. In January 1842 he complained to Newman that he was 'fifty times startled' by passages in Oakeley's articles, and that he was convinced that Oakeley was leading the movement to Rome. By September of the same year Mozley had adopted a new position of defending Oakeley and Ward against Newman's recommendation that they should cease to write for the *Critic*, or that Mozley himself should resign. Mozley refused to do either, which leads to the suspicion that he rather liked the situation. He was the rector of a small parish in the diocese of Salisbury, and might have ended his days as such. Now he found himself the centre of attention in a way that he had not been before, and he did not intend to let that go. Keble suspected as much. 'What will Mozley do? Will he follow Newman's example? I think not, for he likes the B. C. better than ever Newman did the tracts'.[95] With such feelings of importance, Mozley was not inclined to dismiss his two controversial contributors and let the journal become 'more humdrum' as Newman had suggested, with the consequent loss of interest and attention.

Newman attempted to continue the correspondence and offered some well-chosen words of advice to Mozley. 'You must look reality in the face. If the B. C. persists in its Romanism you will gradually have one indignant cry against it from all parts of the Church and you will lose your position'.[96] But Mozley stubbornly refused either to resign or to dismiss Oakeley and Ward, and in a state of exasperation, Newman washed his hands of the affair. 'Take what theory you please, but act upon it'.[97]

As indicated by his letter to Mozley of 26 September, Newman was not at all sure of his own position, and when Pusey pressed him for a statement of his standing in relation to Oakeley and Ward, he took refuge in further equivocation and uncertainty. 'I have never been myself pained at Ward's or Oakeley's writings, which I know you have been. As to my being entirely with Oakeley and Ward, I think my sympathies are entirely with them; but I really cannot determine whether my opinions are, I do not know the limit of my opinions . . . I have intended ever since the Bishop of Salisbury's Charge to take the first public opportunity which occurred of saying that I agreed with the substance of Ward and Oakeley's articles. I think either the whole of this or nothing should be told to Oakeley'.[98]

Oakeley discovered that changes were being proposed, or at least that Newman had made suggestions to Mozley, and he wrote to Newman urging him not to make any changes. The journal was 'doing vast good . . . and it comes from one of the Ladies in Waiting that Her Majesty is a regular, if not a docile, student of its pages . . . Its discouragement or changing hands would be a heavy blow and discouragement to Catholicism'.[99] This is hard to accept. Queen Victoria was notoriously low church in her religious views, and had a constitutional distrust of bishops to the point that she was more sympathetic to presbyterianism in matters of church government. Her religion was very simple, uncomplicated and untheological, and Oakeley's concept of an old English and non-Roman Catholicism would have quite eluded her reductionist ecclesiology.

Seeing the need to make some kind of response to Bishop Denison's criticisms, Mozley decided to write a review of Denison's *Charge* and insert it in the January 1843 issue. Unfortunately, although Mozley did write a review and showed it to Newman who gave it qualified approval,[100] he decided, for some reason, to abandon the piece and to ask Oakeley to write something in his place. It was a bad move. Oakeley used the opportunity not so much to review the Charge as to answer it and to provoke further opposition.

Instead of responding to Salisbury alone, the article took the form of a less personal review of the *Charges* of five bishops – Exeter, Salisbury, London, Llandaff and St Davids – during the year 1842.[101] 'The general tenor', began Oakeley, 'of the *Charges* delivered during the past year has been in a most unprecedented degree in favour of Catholic views'.[102] But this was not all, and he partially criticised the *Charges* for themselves being critical of articles that had appeared in the *Critic*. The Bishop of Salisbury's *Charge*, though unnamed, came in for particular attention, and Oakeley expressed his 'deep concern' that such a view had been taken. But he refused to give any undertaking that the journal would change its course as a result of such attacks. 'We feel sure, however, that neither is any specific defence of what is past expected from us, nor any definite undertaking for the future'.[103]

Oakeley deferred to the mixed character of the Church of England by virtue of the fact that whereas the rest of the world, with which the Church of England had communication to any important extent, was divided into two distinct portions – Protestant and Catholic – the Church of England itself included both Protestantism and Catholicism within itself. 'Mixed in the opinion of her members; mixed in her formularies, and mixed in her external bearings and foreign sympathies'.[104] The Church of England was continually being modified by these two elements within it. 'It is, in matter of fact, always in a state of change and transition. Thus it cannot be pretended that it is the same as it was left by the Reformers. It has undergone many fundamental alterations'.[105] The two forces of Catholicism and Protestantism had balanced each other, but now the issue of the Jerusalem bishopric had caused the church to launch in a Protestant direction. 'So great a development has there been this past year in the latter direction, that there is no small reason to apprehend that the Church of England is soon to become a member of an extensive Protestant confederacy ... It has no longer even the *vis inertiae* of the last century. If it is to be stationary any longer, it must be by the resolution of forces'.[106] And Oakeley returned to his familiar theme of the intrinsic evil of the Reformation, declaring its principles to be 'a most dangerous and delusive chimera. It betrays an evil original by a certain unstable, fleeting, receding and vanishing character'.[107]

He defended himself against the charge that he was introducing a new and foreign element into the Church by subjecting it to external judgement, seeing how far it measured up to its full Catholic potential by comparing it to Roman Catholicism. He declared himself unable to find any other guide by which to reconcile perplexing discrepancies in the Church of England 'without the adoption of a rule which, while it is in this particular branch of the Church, is also out of it, as being common to the whole body, viz. the rule of Catholicism, or universal consent'.[108]

After his comparatively conciliatory article explaining the 'unprotestantizing' of the Church of England, *Episcopal Charges* is much more a sequel, in sentiment, to *Bishop Jewel*, though far more warlike and provocative in character. The following question about the two systems, Catholic and Protestant, reads like a piece of apocalyptic. 'Two great systems are growing up into larger proportions and distincter outline: each aiming at the entire destruction of the other ... In England especially they are in a state of collision: they fight for the Anglican Communion; for the temporal influence of the British Empire; for our literature, our philosophy, our poetry, our education, for every city, town and village; for every body, soul and mind; for every day and hour; for every act and form of action; for every passing thought and feeling of our lives'.[109] Protestantism had 'wrested nearly all Scotland', it had 'generated a mass of schism within the Church of England ... it has so infected and enfeebled the English Church, that it can neither cast out this mass ... nor do anything effectual towards its purgation and cure, nor even arrest the gangrene which, from the intimate presence of so much corruption, is preying on the whole body of the Church, draining her vital powers ... and secretly cankering all that seemed to continue sound and pure'.[110]

If these passages are accurate expressions of Oakeley's thoughts, he had developed two distinct traits by the beginning of 1843. Firstly, he appeared to be labouring under the illusions that Catholicism, as represented by the Tractarians, enjoyed a wider and greater influence in the Church of England in 1843, than was really the case. For all his talk of the 'two great systems', Oakeley was writing only ten years after the Assize Sermon, and the Oxford Movement was still in its infancy. The great majority of members of the Church of England believed their Church and themselves to be Protestant to the core, and they could not follow the subtleties of Oakeley's mind in his drive towards a non-Roman and apparently hypothetical Catholicism, Bishop Denison was close to the truth when he spoke in his *Charge* of 'the vague region of an imaginary Catholicism'.[111] Elevating the whole Catholic against Protestant argument to the realms of an immediate and national struggle must have bewildered the average reader who would see it much as it reads today, as the product of a passionate but eccentric mind.

The second emerging trait is Oakeley's growing dislike of Protestantism. As late as April 1840, he was still speaking of 'the degenerate Church of Rome';[112] in July 1841 he spoke of the Roman Catholic Church as 'our Mother';[113] now he speaks of Protestantism as 'corruption . . . preying on the whole body of the Church', in terms reminiscent of a final struggle between good and evil. 'This Catholic system, with whatever faults and corruptions it may be overlaid here and there, yet has this immense note of truth and Divinity, that it does safely enshrine and keep what we consider essential, whereas our own actual system fails to do'.[113] He could not see how the Church of England could arrest the process of her own dissolution (which he believed to be approaching) without becoming more Catholic. Leaving her as she was 'does not answer against heresy'.[114] 'In each progressive peril that assails the most essential being and welfare of the Church of England, they who take their stand on the Catholic system will be found her truest and most constant defenders'.[115] Given these two traits in January 1843, it could only be a matter of time before Oakeley left the Church of England.

All the evidence points to an impulsiveness and lack of patience, and an inability to distinguish between reality and unreality, and between what was attainable and what was impossible, given the nature of the Church of his own day. He was straining at the leash held by more sober, more deliberate and more realistic Tractarians such as Newman and Pusey. His devotion to the Roman Catholic Church was developing at a much faster pace than theirs. As he moved onwards so he left the Church of England further and further behind and, inevitably, his impatience and intransigence increased.

His attraction was not primarily of the nature of intellectual assent to proven argument, but more of a gut feeling that it was somehow 'right'.

Oakeley had taken to Catholicism like a duck to water. Something in the outward expression of the Catholic faith satisfied a need within him, a need which the Church of England was increasingly unable to satisfy. The Roman Catholic Church was beginning to realise for him 'the impressive and consolatory idea of a visible Church'.[116] He had not yet identified the Church of his upbringing as being irredeemably and irreversibly Protestant, anymore than it was completely Catholic,[117] but he now saw it as a battleground between the two. The only question was, when and how would he decide that Protestantism had won, and that his own position within the Church of England was untenable. Oakeley had no definite intention of going at this time. He was not really a leader or a commander so much as a well-intentioned, impatient and slightly rebellious subordinate lieutenant; as Liddon said, 'urging the wheels of an unbalanced logic in the direction of Rome, although without as yet any definite idea of going thither'.[118] In the light of subsequent events, Newman's comment is the most prophetic: 'I think at present he would do nothing without me'.[119]

Chapter Seven

Closing the valve

THE END OF THE BRITISH CRITIC

Under no conceivable circumstances . . . can the tone adopted by The British Critic, since it passed from the editorship of Mr Newman in 1841, be excused. I confess my surprise that this periodical has so long been permitted to continue in the same course.
William Palmer

Following the long overdue suppression of several bishoprics of the Church of Ireland in 1833, the reforming Whig government of Earl Grey pressed ahead with further legislation to update the archaic geography of the dioceses of the Church of England, in an effort to respond to the problems created by the Industrial Revolution. The government proposed the creation of new sees based on the northern industrial cities of Manchester and Leeds, on the ground of the necessity of providing episcopal oversight for their rapidly increasing populations. But the creation of a new see was not a straightforward process. Objections were raised by radicals to the prospect of another two bishops in the House of Lords, yet the thought of a diocesan bishop outside the Lords was inconceivable, and the government was not prepared to set a precedent. The only practical solution was to amalgamate two existing sees at the same time as the creation of a new one, thereby keeping the number of bishops in the Lords at the same level. Accordingly, the dioceses of Bristol and Gloucester were merged to allow the creation of a new diocese of Ripon including the city of Leeds, from the archdiocese of York, The scheme of amalgamation was pushed through in 1836 with little fuss, but the creation of the see of Manchester met with stiff opposition. The sees selected for amalgamation were those of St Asaph and Bangor, in Wales. The plan was proposed under the Established Church Act of 1836, the

Crown being empowered to constitute the new diocese by Order in Council, which was issued on 12 December 1838. Nothing was in fact done for several years because of the combined opposition of angry Welshmen who demanded the retention of their bishops, and Manchester Dissenters who declared a new bishop to be a useless excrescence.[1]

The plan was reconsidered in the early 1840s by the government of Sir Robert Peel, and Oakeley took up the cause of the threatened Welsh sees and put pen to paper for *The British Critic*, in the issue for January 1843, with *Episcopal Charges*. It demonstrated that Oakeley had a very romantic view of life in the principality of Wales, 'whose charms ... are celebrated in every form of metre on the glossy surface of the album, and delineated in every variety of style on the tinted pages of the sketch book'.[2] He spoke of the Welsh treating their dead as 'the objects ... of much reverent and pious regard',[3] and he discerned in the affection with which the poor of Wales clung to these traditions as 'an evidence of religious-mindedness'.[4] The Welsh were a Catholic people; 'they beseem a land which was once the asylum of saints as well as the nursery of bards, and the school of heroes', whose mountain fastnesses formed 'the shelter and stronghold of the aboriginal faith of Britain'.[5] Oakeley had discovered, to his great delight, that while England was under the rule of Saxons, there was a flourishing and orthodox Welsh Church with an archbishop and seven bishops at its head'.[6] This double fascination, with the Welsh countryside and the ancient Celtic Church, quite blinded Oakeley to the realities of life in certain parts of Wales, particularly the large urban populations around the coal mining regions, and the growing employment of women and children in those mines.

Oakeley had a very meagre knowledge of Welsh life. His memoirs record only two visits to Wales, in 1808 and 1810,[7] the latter occasion including a visit to the house of his uncle, William Oakeley, at Tan-y-Bwlch in Merionethshire. Since his uncle died in 1811, and either he or his mother were ill in the summers of 1812, 1813 and 1814, before he went to school in 1815, the visit of 1810 may have been his last to the principality, though it is possible that he may have visited Monmouthshire during Charles Sumner's brief tenure of the diocese of Llandaff in 1826-7.[8] Childhood memories may lie behind his inexperienced and dreamy view of Wales and the life of its people; a view that probably knew nothing of life for the miners who worked in his uncle's slate mine.

Oakeley's article in protest against the suppression of a Welsh bishopric was published nearly ten years after Keble's Assize Sermon in protest against the suppression of Irish bishoprics, and he took up Keble's line that the Church was a divine society ordained of God, and therefore outside the jurisdiction of the state. Using an act of parliament to suppress what God's church had created was intrinsically wrong.[9] The act was 'both hateful and anti-Christ' because it involved 'the right of parliament not even constituted with any reference to the creed of its members, to meddle with divine institutions'.[10] On the question of the establishment of a bishopric at Manchester he was, at first, cautiously neutral. 'It is commonly supposed that a bishopric at Manchester is to be endowed out of the spoils of the Welsh Church. This is, as we believe, not a certain, though a probable contingency'.[11] But he went on to describe the robbing of Wales 'to save the pockets of the Liverpool and Manchester manufacturers, who, if they cared to have a bishop at all, might endow a see among them by means of a shilling subscription'.[12] The suppression of a see, quite apart from the expropriation of its revenue, was an evil, 'and evil must not be done that good may come of it'.[13] Even if the revenues of the suppressed sees were partly to be applied to a programme of church building in north Wales, 'they will surely receive a destination equally foreign to the intentions of the saints who founded the church in north Wales, and the kings and nobles who enriched it'.[14]

On the ground of pragmatism, Oakeley's arguments were unsustainable, in that he ignored the real need for a bishop in the growing industrial city of Manchester to co-ordinate the pastoral work of the church in that area. He shows no understanding of, or sympathy for, the difficult position of the government in its efforts to satisfy all interested parties, and he placed much emphasis on the proposed disendowment of the suppressed see, regarding its revenues as inalienable and guaranteed to that see in perpetuity. 'The funds would ... be employed upon objects to which they have been solemnly dedicated and no blessing ever will attend the disposal of ill-gotten wealth'.[15] He did raise the valid point that the bishop of the new united Welsh diocese would face increased transportation difficulties in attempting to cover an area of 3,520 miles. 'There are ... very few parts of the country which form the diocese of Bangor ... in which a carriage even with four horses can proceed at the rate of more than six miles an hour'.[16] It was, he urged, the duty of all clergy to voice their objections to the scheme 'which ... is undoubtedly an abstract sin'.[17]

The Sees of St Asaph and Bangor is worth mentioning because of what it reveals about Oakeley's unreal attitude towards a contemporary ecclesiastical problem, an attitude formed more by fascination for the ancient Celtic Church in Wales than by a pastoral concern for the industrial working classes of Manchester. Much of this is no doubt due to the Tractarian view of the divine right of the Church, but there is a hint of an upper-class contempt for the Manchester and Liverpool manufacturers; Oakeley was, after all, the son of a baronet. But his voice was only one among many, and when the see of Manchester was eventually established in 1847, the government decided to adopt the innovation of the junior diocesan bishop having no seat in the House of Lords, instead of suppressing or amalgamating sees.

As Oakeley's articles grew progressively more belligerent with the passage of time, so an angry discontent grew against *The British Critic*. One of the more notable complainants was William Palmer, Fellow of Worcester College, who had complained to Newman about the content of *Bishop Jewel* in July 1841. Palmer had sprung to the defence of Newman after the publication of Tract 90, but was horrified by *Bishop Jewel* and cancelled his subscription to the *Critic* in protest. The protest went unheeded, and Oakeley and Ward continued to contribute to the journal which went, in Palmer's opinion, from bad to worse during the two years of Mozley's editorship. 'I know men who admit the Papal supremacy and various doctrines and practices of Romanism . . . the Reformation was most terrible evil, and the Reformers must be painted in darkest colours . . . you will need no proof of the existence of a Romanizing party – a party which . . . is dissatisfied with the English Church, is in doubt whether it is lawful to remain with the English Church – and condemns our whole system'.[18] He complained bitterly to Pusey about what he saw as a situation where Tractarian principles were becoming inextricably mixed up with Romish tendencies, the latter continually developing and acquiring more and more adherents, 'and in time we should see such a storm raised as would crush all Church principles together in their excesses – expel all valuable principles and practices from the Church of England – and end in a far wider and more terrible schism'.[19]

Palmer went to see Newman and urged him to control Oakeley and Ward, showing him articles in the *Critic* 'which had latterly become most painful to Churchmen, abounding in what was utterly unfavourable to the Church of England, and favourable to that of Rome . . . I professed upon him the great offence such things had given, and urged his influence as editor to suppress such teaching in future'.[20] Newman replied with 'evident excitement' that he was no longer editor of the journal, and that since the heads, both of the university and of the church, had condemned him and succeeded in destroying his influence, they themselves 'would have to deal with younger men, whom it was not in his power to restrain', and he refused to interfere.[21] Palmer, as a resident Fellow of Worcester College, must have known that Newman was no longer editor of the *Critic*. Like many others, he saw Newman as the presiding intellectual genius of the movement, to whom all deferred, and who, by virtue of that fact, still exercised an amorphous suzerainty over editorial policy.

His picture of Newman is interesting. According to Palmer, Newman was in a state of 'evident excitement' (i.e. agitation), presumably because of the distraction of the timing of his resignation as Vicar of the Church of St Mary the Virgin. Newman was about to enter the last phase of his membership of the Church of England, and the activity of those individuals whom he had once sought to control was no longer his concern. If Palmer's account of their meeting is accepted, Newman displayed what can only be described as a fit of pique. Since the Church had 'destroyed' his influence and condemned him, by censuring Tract 90, they would now have to deal with Oakeley, Ward and the others in this rising and Romeward generation of Tractarians without the benefit of his help. Newman's attitude might almost be construed as bitter; by rejecting him, the Church of England was to get all that it deserved.

Confronted with Newman's resolve to do nothing, Palmer began to write his own protest against the Romeward Tractarians and their influence in the movement. It was published in September 1843 with the title *A narrative of events connected with the publication of the tracts for the times*. Though it was intended to be primarily a work of protest against Oakeley and Ward, it enjoys the distinction of being the first comprehensive account of the Catholic revival within the Church of England. The first part is a soberly objective account of the history of the birth of the movement in 1833 and 1834, with an occasional note of resentment, chiefly when his advice had not been sought, nor taken when offered. But on the subject of *The British Critic*, Palmer was harshly critical.

He praised Newman, Pusey and Keble as 'eminent and holy' men, and urged their disciples 'to use more gentleness, to cultivate a greater spirit of charity, patience, forbearance and tolerance'.[22] He avoids mentioning the names of Oakeley and Ward, but the references are unmistakable. In reviewing the history of the early Tracts, Palmer stated firmly that 'it was never their design to ... diminish in any degree the attachment of our people to the National Church ... to give countenance to superstitious or idolatrous practices; to subvert the principles of the English Reformation'.[23] 'The tracts and their writers were opposed to the Romish system'.[24] Yet within the preceding two or three years 'a new school' had made its appearance and led to hitherto loyal and contented members of the Church of England beginning to feel dissatisfied with the principles of that Church and to show hostility towards the Reformers. 'We have seen in the same quarter a spirit of – almost servility and adulation towards to Rome, an enthusiastic and exaggerated praise of its merits, an appeal to all deep feelings and sympathies in its favour, a tendency to look to Rome as the model and the standard of all that is beautiful and correct in art, all that is sublime in poetry, all that is elevated in devotion'.[25] In conversation, Palmer had heard 'remarks . . . indicating a disposition to acknowledge the supremacy of the see of Rome, to give way to all its claims, however extreme'.[26] Blame for the separation between England and Rome was laid at the door of the Church of England, quite openly and without apology. 'Her reformers are denounced in the most vehement terms. Every unjust insinuation, every hostile construction of their conduct is indulged in; no allowance is made for their difficulties, no attempt is made to estimate the amount of errors which they had to oppose'.[27]

These are clear references to Oakeley and his attacks on the Reformation, and Palmer admitted that 'the admission of such articles as that on "Bishop Jewell" . . . have compelled me to break silence'.[28] He was appalled by the tacit acceptance of the doctrine of purgatory in certain quarters, and the feeling that clerical celibacy and auricular confession were compulsory. 'Beside this, intimacies are formed with Romanists and visits are paid to Romish monasteries, colleges and houses of worship'.[29] He condemned Oakeley's theory of unprotestantizing the Church of England,[30] and his desire to see it 'recede from the principles of the Reformation'.[31] For two years or more *The British Critic* had been under the influence of those 'who are uncertain in their allegiance to the Church of England, and who cannot be considered friendly to her'.[32]

Palmer reviewed the years 1841–3 and the increasing influence of the Romeward section during that period, and put forward three possible explanations for the behaviour of Oakeley and Ward and their supporters. Firstly, he conceded that they might well have genuine doubts about the position of the Church of England. But if so, he could not conceive 'a greater pain' than to raise doubts in the minds of others where such doubts ought not to exist, only because of their own infirmity of judgement and want of knowledge. If they had such doubts, they were conscience bound 'to seek silently for the solution of those doubts; to cease from writing or speaking on subjects in which (their) opinions are unsettled'.[33] Secondly, they had satisfied themselves that it was a matter of duty to remain where they were and to propagate Tractarian principles from within the Church of England. But if so, then they had no right to excite doubt and dissatisfaction and encourage the temptation to secede. 'It is sinful even to contemplate the possibility'.[34] Thirdly, it was possible that they had convinced themselves that it was their duty to become Roman Catholics and were waiting only for the right moment openly to declare it. This was the view to which Palmer inclined although he made a rather hollow-sounding protest of refusing to believe that Oakeley could be guilty of such a heinous crime. The innuendo of his statements is an accusation that the two men constituted a papist fifth column within the Church of England, engaging in subversive tactics behind the lines. 'I will not believe that such disgraceful and detestable treachery and hypocrisy can exist in any one who has ever partaken of the sacramental privileges of the Church of England . . . I cannot for the moment entertain the notion of such revolting iniquity: – and yet it is impossible to offer any reasonable answer to those who suspect that there are individuals who remain within the Church of England only with a view to instil doctrines which would otherwise be without influence'.[35]

This last possibility, though Palmer obviously believed it, can be discounted at least as far as Oakeley is concerned. He was genuinely plagued by doubts about the status of the Church of England, but saw no further ahead than remaining within the Church and doing his best to spread Tractarian principles. He was simply not capable of the kind of duplicity with which Palmer charges him. Stealth, cunning and calculation were not Oakeley's way of saying and doing things. He was too open and too impulsive in his behaviour to play the role of a nominal member of the Church of England, in heart and mind a Roman Catholic merely biding his time.

Palmer hoped that he would be able, by exposing to public gaze the activities of the Romeward section, to precipitate a crisis and thereby drive a wedge between the two wings of the Tractarian movement, driving Oakeley and Ward out of the Church of England before they acquired too many supporters.[36] He had failed to gain any support from Newman before the publication of his book, and it was no more likely that he would gain support after publication. Newman dismissed Palmer's effort as 'moonshine',[37] and gave it no further attention.

The significant consequence of the publication of Palmer's tract was the demise of *The British Critic*, the mouthpiece of the Romeward section. Palmer had lambasted the journal saying that he expected to see a change in management. 'Under no conceivable circumstances . . . can the tone adopted by *The British Critic*, since it passed from the editorship of Mr Newman in 1841, be excused. I confess my surprise that this periodical has so long been permitted to continue in the same course'.[38]

In the wake of such damning criticism, there was little choice except to cease publication. Palmer was not the only interested party to object to the line of its contents. The hitherto neutral and aloof figure of Francis Rivington,[39] the publisher of the journal, told Mozley that the clear preference for Rome in so many recent articles could not be consistently expressed in a journal professing to be an organ of the Church of England.[40] 'Troubles were thickening around the firm, and the outlook ahead was of a stormy kind and threatened to involve the firm in most anxious considerations of an unavoidable kind. The writers ... were taking what were then considered more and more extreme views. Remonstrances poured in from all sides upon the Rivingtons, the circulation became considerably restricted'.[41]

The excuse needed to close the journal was found when Mozley submitted his resignation to Rivington in September 1843, and wrote to Newman and to various members of his family to the effect that he was thinking seriously of becoming a Roman Catholic.[42] On Newman's advice, he delayed taking the step, and it is doubtful if he ever seriously intended such a move. It seems to have been more of an alarm call than anything else. 'I believe I was seeking a rest. I was distracted and wearied with discussions above my measure, my faculties and my attainments. I disliked the tone of disputants, all the more because I easily fell into it myself. The Church of England was one vast arena of controversy'.[43] Mozley had reached the end of his tether. Quite apart from Palmer's stinging, if oblique, criticisms of his ability to edit the *Critic,* and the editorial workload, Mozley had other problems with which to contend. He had decided to provide his parish of Cholderton with a new church, the medieval church being too small and undistinguished. Raising money for the completion of the building was a constant worry, since the parish was not well endowed. It was the poorest living in the gift of Oriel College, and the population of the village was only 200, (it had risen to only 208 by 1935). Mozley had generously used almost all his private income and savings on the new building, and spent much of his time appealing for funds to complete the work. The stress of this major undertaking was increased by the fact that his wife had been seriously ill for much of 1843.[44]

Mozley went to see Rivington and told him of his wish to resign. Rivington was unprepared for such an event but showed nothing but kindness to the weary and harassed editor. 'His way of taking it then and long after deeply impressed me. There was not even a suspicion of reproof or complaint in his words or his looks; and he never made any allusion to my runaway horses, Ward and Oakeley, or to any of the articles, to which exception might justly have been taken'.[45]

Mozley's resignation was followed by a sequence of events now difficult to put into chronological order. The meeting between Mozley and Rivington had certainly taken place by 14 September 1843 and probably much earlier in that month. Afterwards Rivington wrote to Newman asking him to name a successor.[46] Newman declined for reasons which are best explained by his formal resignation of the parish of St Mary the Virgin a few days later, on 18 September. He had enough to occupy his mind without the problem of the editorship of the *Critic*. At some point during the month, but before the 16 September, Mozley's younger brother, James Bowling Mozley,[47] went to see Rivington to discuss the future of the journal intending, if the opportunity presented itself, to recommend the appointment of R. W. Church.[48] At this stage, Rivington had no thought of ceasing publication. 'He was very civil, even communicative on the subject of the B. C. [and] seemed less alarmed than I expected; inclined to keep up B. C. on its hitherto footing, only dropping Oakeley. But he did not give any opening of my talking of a successor . . . I suspect he took my visit as an offer of myself. This was my fear at first, but it could not be avoided'.[49] So Mozley departed with nothing accomplished. But the interesting point from his encounter with Rivington is that the proprietor regarded Oakeley as the most objectionable of the contributors and, with his exclusion, was prepared to see the journal continue, presumably with Ward, as before.

The October 1843 issue of *The British Critic* appeared as usual, and included an article by Oakeley on the innocuous subject of music.[50] The date of Rivington's decision to close the journal was probably somewhere in the first half of October 1843, after the appearance of the new issue, when some thought would need to be given to the content of the issue for January 1844. By 23 October 1843, Oakeley had heard, via reports from Oxford, that Rivington had taken the decision to close the journal, because he told Mozley that he was being pressed by his friends to take on the job of editor to save it from oblivion; and that if Rivington had objections to this arrangement, then he should be asked to sell his interest in the journal. In his memoirs, Oakeley declared that at the time he was indifferent to these efforts on his behalf. 'I confess that I have no very strong feelings in the matter, and if others had been of that opinion should willingly have seen the thing drop . . . I see no alternative about taking it if it is pressed upon me by others, though I will make no move'.[51] His candidacy was still being canvassed as a strong possibility on 14 November 1843 when James Hope,[52] a member of the congregation of Margaret Chapel wrote to Newman, 'The B. C. as far as I can tell will decidedly change its position under the new editorship'.[53]

Whether through his own genuine desire not to be involved, or because of the animosity of others, or a combination of both, Oakeley's candidacy had certainly been extinguished by 26 November 1843 when Pusey reported to Manning that he had found Oakeley in 'a very calm frame of mind, unwilling to act upon his own responsibility . . . and wishing to go on calmly in his own duties, abstaining from anything which may add to our confusion'. He had also found Oakeley to be quite philosophical about the fate of the *Critic*. 'I may say to you that he declined editing the B. C. when pressed by some friends; he thought Mozley's resignation of it seemed to have brought it to a natural close, and that he was following the guidance of God's providence, to allow it to expire'.[54]

At the same time as these complicated negotiations, William Palmer wrote to Rivington offering to launch a rival journal, if Rivington would agree to publish it.[55] Rivington agreed and suspended publication of the *Critic*, replacing it with a new journal styled *The English Review*. Despite the support of the High Church party who were offended by the Romanizing tendencies of the *Critic*, Palmer's new journal was not a great success and ceased publication in 1853. Palmer himself resigned in 1845 after a dispute with the editorial committee.[56]

If Palmer's aim was to precipitate a crisis and force the Romeward Tractarians out of the Church of England, then eventually he succeeded, though in a way he might not have expected. When the crisis came in the following year, it came from the voluble Ward rather than Oakeley, whose role throughout the proceedings surrounding the demise of the *Critic* was entirely passive. The closure of the *Critic* was, for Ward, like the closure of a safety valve through which he periodically let off steam. Sooner or later it would get out by another way and in a less controlled manner.

The period of crisis began in June 1844 when Ward published his enormous and rambling book *The Ideal of a Christian Church*. The consequences were considerable, both for Ward and for Oakeley, who loyally supported his friend throughout the arguments that followed. But until the appearance of Ward's book, Oakeley showed no interest in preparing a counter-blast against Palmer and greeted the demise of the *Critic* with supine acceptance. Despite Palmer's attacks, and considering that the journal had been the channel through which he had expressed the developing pattern of his thoughts over the preceding three and a half years, he remained surprisingly aloof from events surrounding the demise of *The British Critic*; but then other matters occupied his mind.

Chapter Eight

A widening mind

MISCELLANEOUS PROJECTS

Perhaps you may be able to form a better opinion how far out of London people would feel the object worth a great effort. Certainly looking to the way things have turned out around me, I do feel it very important.
Frederick Oakeley to John Henry Newman, 27 April 1842

I Margaret Chapel – the plans to build a new church 1842–1844

By the end of 1841, Oakeley had settled into a regular routine at Margaret Chapel. He had reordered the interior of the chapel to his satisfaction and the satisfaction of most of his congregation, and he had established the beginnings of a monastic community in his house across the street, and the plain little chapel was a flourishing centre of Tractarian worship in central London. But a cloud hung over its future, and in 1842, Oakeley began to think seriously about the long term future of the chapel. The freehold of the site was owned by the Crown, and the lease, still held by Henry Drummond, was due to expire in 1848. At that time the site would revert to the Crown.

It would have been possible to wait until the expiry date and then negotiate a renewal of the lease with the Crown, or negotiate the purchase of the freehold but, after consultation, Oakeley decided on a more ambitious scheme to secure the future of his work. He proposed to buy the remainder of the lease from Drummond, negotiate the purchase of the freehold, demolish the chapel and build a new church on the site. If this were not possible, he would seek the freehold of another site from the Crown. Robert Williams MP, a member of the congregation, had intimated that the government would look favourably on such requests. Buying the remainder of the lease from Drummond at a cost of £1,200 was not a problem. The difficult question, *'on which we shall be very glad of advice*',[1] was whether to build on the existing site, which could not hold a church or chapel seating more than 300 people, at a cost of £5,000; or, with the acquisition of additional ground, to build a larger church at a cost of £12,000. Oakeley was certain that he could raise £5,000 without difficulty, but the larger plan would require an appeal, and he asked for Newman's comments on the prospect. 'Perhaps you may be able to form a better opinion how far out of London people would feel the object worth a great effort. Certainly looking to the way things have turned out around me, I do feel it very important, but I cannot expect those who are not on the spot, and who have their own more immediate calls to feel it more than a secondary object'.[2]

Newman's reply has not survived, but Oakeley decided to press ahead with the scheme for a larger church and sent out a circular letter, dated the feast of St Barnabas (11 June) 1842, outlining his plans for the erection of 'a new, and more appropriate, Church', and establishing a fund 'which I hope may at no distant period, have accumulated sufficiently to allow of the commencement of the work'.[3] The new church would be 'suitable to its purpose', and the services would be on a 'secure, permanent and ecclesiastical footing'. Donations should be made unconditionally, and would be invested quarterly in Government Securities in the names of Oakeley and Edward Bellasis, the treasurer of the Fund. Quarterly collections at the chapel on Christmas Day (25 December), the Annunciation (25 March), the Nativity of St John the Baptist (24 June), and St Michael and All Angels (29 September), would be added as well.[4] A further source of income came from the proceeds of the sale of a small book of prayers, written by Oakeley and published in September 1842.[5]

At Oakeley's suggestion, Robert Williams wrote to Thomas Mozley, who was deemed to be something of an expert on church building, in view of the fact that he was building a new church for his own parish of Cholderton. Williams revealed that they were hoping to secure a new site on the corner of Margaret Street and Great Titchfield Street, 112ft x 60ft, for the erection of a church to seat 400–500 people. 'My first thought was to send you drawings of all the designs I have had in my head – many and various – as you may suppose – but, on the whole, I incline to ask you to consider the subject first without seeing our plans – and suggest the sort of church you should propose under the circumstances'.[6]

There is no surviving record of the fund at the time of Oakeley's departure in 1845, but no building work was started during his ministry. The finances of the chapel were in a parlous state in April 1843 when Oakeley asked Newman for help. It transpired that Robert Williams had, until then, generously paid the rent on the chapel and on Oakeley's house, amounting to £250 per annum. Williams was now 'too poor to go on with it ... In an extremity (he) would still come forward, but I do feel it a duty to relieve him considering all he has done'.[7] Oakeley avoided asking Newman for direct financial help but hoped that he would bring the plight of the chapel to the attention of others. In the meantime one of the quarterly collections for the new church would be put aside to pay the rent. Even this proved to be insufficient because by the summer of 1844, Oakeley was obliged 'to apply two of my collections for the new church to the purpose of the chapel'.[8]

With this fifty per cent reduction in annual income, the implementation of the plan to build a new church was inevitably deferred. Oakeley was ill for much of the summer of 1844, and the events from the autumn of that year onwards ensured that the new church received less and less attention, as it was quickly overtaken by more pressing matters.

With Edward Bellasis, Oakeley remained in theory a trustee of the funds raised for the construction of a new church until 30 September 1845, when he resigned and devolved sole responsibility for the fund on to Bellasis. His resignation was announced by means of a circular letter as from Balliol College to all those who had contributed to the fund. The circular was final and dismissive in its tone, and demonstrated that Oakeley had lost all interest in the project and did not imagine that the chapel would ever be rebuilt. 'I am no longer in a position to administer this trust in conformity to my original pledges, and feel myself precluded in conscience from being a party to its administration under the changes which have occurred ... You ought to be aware that, the object for which the Fund was collected having failed (at least in its entirety) it is the opinion of lawyers that you are at liberty to reclaim your contribution in the event of your being dissatisfied with the purpose to which it may be intended to apply the fund, so far as it may remain unreclaimed'.[9]

Despite his negative attitude, and unlike some of his other projects, the plan for a new church in Margaret Street did not disappear into oblivion. Oakeley had created a stronger congregation than he imagined; it did not disperse and the chapel did not close. The fund had been started and it continued under the management of Bellasis, and under Oakeley's successor, the new church began to rise and the plan was brought to completion. In 1847, after complicated negotiations with the government, the Duke of Portland, and others, the freehold site of Margaret Chapel was acquired for £9,000. The chapel was demolished in 1850, and for nine years the congregation worshipped in temporary chapels before the consecration of the new church in

1859. Richards fulfilled all Oakeley's plans except in the matter of the dedication. Oakeley had planned to dedicate the new church to the Blessed Virgin Mary. But in the years after his departure in 1845, it was decided that the dedication should be 'All Saints', on the ground that it would be easier to adorn the church with the figures of various saints than with illustrations of the history of one particular saint, and Oakeley's plan for a church to be known as 'St Mary's, Margaret Street', quietly disappeared.[10]

Whether Oakeley had any contact with Margaret Chapel after 1845 is unknown, but he may have passed along Margaret Street, if only from sheer curiosity to see it replaced by William Butterfield's All Saints' Church. He bore no ill-will to his successor, William Upton Richards, or his ministry at the new church, and the best indication of his kindness and generosity can be seen in the tribute that he paid to Upton Richards in 1855. 'The gentleman who succeeded me . . . and is still its minister, is person of the most unblemished life, the highest integrity, the most amiable disposition, and the purest intentions; and I have no doubt that good must come of the honest exertions of such a man'.[11]

II Lives of the English Saints 1843–1844

In the early months of 1843, Newman was directing his thoughts towards a new project, a series of biographies of the early English saints. The plan was initiated by Newman for the same reason that had given rise to Tract 90, the desire to attract the attention of the Romeward Tractarians to the Catholicity of the Church of England. The theory was to direct those of literary ability such as Oakeley, Faber and Dalgairns, to the Catholic past of the Church of England, thereby diverting their attention from the Church of Rome. 'I thought it would be useful . . . as giving them an interest in the English soil, and the English Church, and keeping them from seeking sympathy in Rome as she is'.[12] Newman believed that a study of the English Church in the Middle Ages and before would inspire a love of the national church and, at the same time, inject it with a Catholic tone, by reminding his wayward contemporaries that the Church of England of their own day enjoyed an essential and unbroken continuity with the pre-Reformation church. 'People shrink from Catholicity and think it implies a want of affection for our National Church. Well, then, merely remind them that you take the National Church, but only that you do not date it from the Reformation. In order to kindle love of the National Church, and yet to inculcate a Catholic tone, nothing else is necessary but to take our Church in the Middle Ages'.[13]

By the beginning of April 1843, Newman had compiled a list of saints whose lives he proposed to include in the series. It was to be a major undertaking, there being more than three hundred and ten saints or groups of saints on his list, and even this was not complete. The Cornish saints were omitted because there were too many of them, and other minor saints were excluded when next to nothing was known about them.[14] Newman began to hand out the titles to his friends, 'the majority (of whom) were of the party of the new Movement',[15] trying to match the character and life of the saint to the interests of the prospective author. He suggested Saint Boniface to J. W. Bowden, who was a 'Continentalist'; Saints Anselm and Lanfranc were given to R. W. Church, who had published an article on them in *The British Critic*. But Newman issued a warning. 'I mean the work to be historical and devotional, but not controversial. Doctrinal questions need not enter. As to miracles, I think they may be treated as matters of faith – credible according to their evidence'.[16]

Oakeley was given the task of writing a life of Saint Augustine, and warned Newman that there might well be a difference of opinion between them. He agreed to contribute to the series, and to help Newman in whatever way he could, seeing it as 'time well employed'. But there were bound to be problems over miracles. 'The only point about which I see any likelihood of difficulty is that of miracles which some of us, perhaps, might not treat in a way you would feel it well to recognise in a publication intended for all eyes'. He had talked over the matter with Ward, who thought it 'a nice plan'.[17] The problem with miracles was that Oakeley was inclined to accept them unquestioningly as literally true, whereas Newman had a tendency to be cautiously critical. Newman was not disposed to consider the potential difference of opinion to be worth a fight, and his final thoughts on the subject constitute a very shifty piece of thinking. 'If the alleged facts did not occur, they ought to have occurred (if I may so speak); they are such as might have occurred, under circumstances; and they belong to the parties to whom they are attributed potentially, if not actually; or the like of them did occur; or occurred to others similarly circumstanced, though not to those very persons'.[18]

Newman decided to offer the responsibility of publishing the series to the well-established and trustworthy figure of Francis Rivington. Rivington was pleased with the offer and thought that the series would be 'likely to be popular ... perhaps you could shortly send me a few lines in explanation of the plan of the "Lives" which might be useful as a sort of preliminary announcement'.[19] Rivington produced the first page of the prospectus at the beginning of August and sent it to Newman for approval. He did not envisage publication of the lives until the early months of 1844, and proposed delaying the general issue of the prospectus until the appearance of the next issue of *The British Critic* in October 1843.[20]

The various authors started work on their respective saints, and the project progressed steadily through the summer and autumn of 1843. George Tickell,[21] one of Oakeley's 'monks' at Margaret Street, eagerly accepted Newman's invitation to write the lives of Saint Elgiva, Saint Wulfhilda and Saint Edith,[22] though Oakeley felt that Tickell was too 'diffident' in putting his materials together.[23] He himself worked on the life of Saint Augustine with a fair amount of diligence, searching the shelves of the British Museum Reading Room, and going down to Thanet and Canterbury 'to pick up what I could'.[24]

The project began to run into trouble in November 1843 when Francis Rivington withdrew his agreement to publish the series. His withdrawal took place against the background of the closure of *The British Critic* and was not so surprising. Involvement with the Tractarian movement was not altogether to the commercial advantage of Rivington's. Newman was in a quandary. 'Rivington is looking over the sheets to decide whether he will take it or give it up . . . Between ourselves, [he] has read, has condemned, has given up the undertaking – and now I am quite at sea with a quantity of matter, part printed, part preparing, part promised . . . and I do not see but I must go on – though I suppose there will be some delay'.[25] In a less charitable tone, F. W. Faber,[26] who had been commissioned to write the lives of eight of the northern saints, told Newman that he was disappointed, 'but Rivington has once or twice behaved so scurrilly that I am not surprised'.[27]

The withdrawal of Rivington caused Newman to think of James Toovey, the publisher and bookseller, of 36 St James Street, London, as a possible successor. He consulted James Hope who could not supply any information about Toovey beyond saying that 'Oakeley knows all about him' and 'Gladstone spoke well of him to me one day'.[28] Oakeley loyally supported Toovey as a possible publisher for the series, though with slight exaggeration. 'Toovey is up to anything in the way of publishing – There is no fear of his drawing back'. But Oakeley immediately qualified this by referring to his 'want of capital which prevents him undertaking any responsibility in money arrangements'.[29] Toovey was most anxious for the job, 'if he can possibly feel himself warranted in a pecuniary point of view'.[30]

Even at this early stage, with the project still largely on the drawing board, Newman was beginning to have serious doubts about his own involvement. The first volume in the series, the *Life of St Stephen Harding*, by Dalgairns, appeared at the end of 1843. Pusey read it and declared that it would cause 'a sensation', and this threw Newman 'into great perplexity'. 'I wish I had something like a view of what was best to do about them'.[31] He corresponded with James Hope, who functioned as the legal adviser to the Tractarians and, a few weeks later, decided to withdraw his name from the planned series, 'You yourself . . . said "Delay the plan, for you will be putting yourself at the head of the extreme party – *The British Critic* having stopped": now, I am more than delaying, I am withdrawing my name. I am sure this is a great thing, even though my initials occurred to this or that life'.[32] Newman discarded the idea of producing a series of lives, and allowed each author to publish as and when he was ready, and he suggested to Oakeley that he might like to take over such remaining editorial work as there was likely to be.

Oakeley was not entirely happy with the prospect and tried to persuade Newman to retain some residual responsibility. 'It [should] . . . be made plain that the Lives are part of the plan which you generally approved, but were obliged from circumstances reluctantly to abandon'.[33] He used the argument that Toovey had 'misgivings about the sale of Lives, supposing that they should come to be generally disconnected, in public opinion, from your name and patronage'.[34] But Newman was determined to give up the day to day work on the series, and surrendered the task to Oakeley, 'which he kindly at once willingly assented to undertake'[35] on or about 22 January 1844. Despite Newman's comment to Toovey, Oakeley was reluctant to be seen publicly as the editor and insisted that his name should not 'be brought forward or in any way made public', and Toovey hoped that Newman would be 'as much as ever interested in the undertaking'.[36]

Newman agreed to forward to Oakeley any contributions that he received. Oakeley would make the final decision, and his judgement would be absolute. Nevertheless, Oakeley expressed the wish to be guided by Newman's opinions as to the whole project 'and to relieve you of all responsibility without publicly sustaining it myself'.[37] There is no obvious explanation for Oakeley's reluctance to accept public responsibility for the scheme. Perhaps his reputation as a 'Romeward' Tractarian made him nervous about its possible effect on the sale of the series. *The British Critic* had closed down only three months before, partly as the result of his articles. He may have thought himself unworthy to supplant his spiritual mentor in such a public way.

Toovey continued to correspond regularly with Newman on the smallest details of production, such as the price and the colour of the cover, until the end of March 1844. Newman may have also retained authority to decide who would write the lives of which saints, since

Oakeley asked on 20 March, through Toovey, to write the stories of the companions of Saint Augustine 'if they had not already been allocated'.[38] But Newman was anxious to extricate himself from further involvement and wrote to one correspondent who was worried about the reception of the series, 'Pray do what is most satisfactory to your judgement and feelings and whenever you come to a decision have the kindness to acquaint Mr Toovey with it, as I now have only an accidental connection with the undertaking myself'.[39]

Oakeley spent the early days of his editorship fussing about the colour and design of the cover. Toovey, probably at Oakeley's suggestion, had thought of asking Pugin to design the cover,[40] and suggested that it might be printed in red and white which 'would be serviceable and not expensive', rather than purple and gold which 'would perhaps look well, but would wear badly'.[41] However 'Mr Oakeley inclines to the more quiet colour of lilac, but thought that we could not do better than take Mr Pugin's advice'.[42]

With Newman's withdrawal from active editorial work, Oakeley was left in control of what remained of the project, supported by younger and more extreme enthusiasts such as Faber, Dalgairns,[43] Pattison,[44] and others, in effect the third generation of Tractarians; unfortunately they had difficulty in distinguishing fact from fiction and, as nominal editor, Newman's reputation as an historian suffered. His hope that the project would provide a diversion for his Romeward followers proved forlorn. Critics damned the series from the appearance of the first volume, the *Life of St Stephen Harding* by Dalgairns. It was held 'to be of such a character as to be inconsistent with its being given to the world by an Anglican publisher'.[45]

The irritation was not eased by succeeding volumes, and the most hostile reaction greeted the *Life of St Wilfrid* by Faber. 'In it the Catholic tendencies of the Tractarian school were developed with utmost freedom'.[46] It contained such controversial statements as, 'To look Romeward is a Catholic instinct, seemingly implanted in us for the safety of the faith';[47] 'a church without monasteries is a body with its right arm paralysed';[48] St Wilfrid 'materially aided the blessed work of riveting more tightly the happy chains which held England to St Peter's Chair';[49] and, 'Never was there upon earth a tribunal so august as that of Rome'.[50] But the fact remains that both Newman and Oakeley read and approved the *Life of St Wilfrid*, Newman certainly before it went to press, and probably Oakeley as well,[51] thereby associating themselves with Faber's views. When the *Life of St Stephen Harding* appeared at the end of 1843, it was prefaced by a statement from Newman announcing his decision to discontinue the series as originally envisaged. Partially completed

Lives would be published 'in similar form by their respective authors on their own responsibility'.[52] But this was not strictly followed since Newman was committed to follow through certain of the Lives. 'I had various engagements with friends for separate Lives remaining on my hands. I should like to have broken from them all, but there were some from which I could not'.[53]

Oakeley's role as editor of the series after Newman presents something of a mystery, since there is very little surviving correspondence beyond a few letters in January and February 1844 discussing Pugin's design for the colour of covers. It seems that his editorial contribution was minimal. He may have made changes to texts before sending them to Toovey, but this is unlikely since they were written by people with views very similar to his own. Any editorial role that he exercised would have ended with the onset of his illness in the summer of 1844 when he gave up work on everything, including his own *Life of St Augustine of Canterbury*. The Lives continued to appear regularly throughout 1844 and into the early months of 1845, notwithstanding Oakeley's illness, each probably being published on the responsibility of its author. Of the original list of three hundred and ten, only thirty-two Lives eventually appeared.

Oakeley's *Life of St Augustine of Canterbury* was published in two parts. The lack of corroborative correspondence, or a dated preface, prevents the assigning of precise dates to their appearance. But the first part (Chapters 1–13) was published between March and July 1844, and the second part (Chapters 14–20), towards the end of the year, probably in October or early November. The book runs to some 260 pages, of which approximately half deals with St Augustine, the rest being a general survey of Christianity in England before his arrival. None of the Lives, with the possible exception of that of St Neot by J. A. Froude, is an edifying production by the standards of critical scholarship[54] and Oakeley's work is no exception. To describe it as a piece of fictitious hagiography would be unjust. But all too often Oakeley displays an uncritical acceptance of events which among his contemporaries were treated with some dubiety. The eighteenth century had a healthy contempt for hagiography, and engendered a well-developed sense of critical history. Oakeley enjoined his readers to accept, for various reasons, even those reputed occurrences about which he himself had doubts. He referred to the legendary visits to England of St Peter, St Paul and St Joseph of Arimathaea, in AD 60, 62 and 63 respectively[55] and, while admitting that they could not be proved, he claimed that the traditions were far from worthless. He illustrated his point by reference to St George. 'Upon what evidence do we put faith in the existence of St

George the Patron of England? . . . the belief of prejudiced or credulous witnesses, the unwritten record of empty pageants and bauble decorations . . . a powerful array of suspicious legends and exploded acts. Yet, after all, what Catholic is there but would count it a profaneness to question the existence of St George?'[56] Oakeley accepted the story of the conversion of the legendary King Lucius in c. A.D.182,[57] quoting Bede as his authority, but admitting that the story of 'good King Lucius' was known 'from sources of greater or lesser authenticity'.[58] When Lucius' emissary arrived at Rome, he was greeted by the 'good Pope Elutherius' (175–89), who was 'in raptures of joy on receiving the message of the British King'.[59]

Oakeley admitted that here was 'a total dearth of trustworthy information'[60] between the death of Lucius and the martyrdom of Alban, but attempted to fill the gap by reliance on Bede and on the more untrustworthy historian, Gildas, for a history of the Celtic Church. With echoes of *The Sees of St Asaph and Bangor*, Wales caught Oakeley's attention, the fifth and sixth centuries being 'the golden age of the Welsh Church which was at that period both the fruitful mother of saints, and the vigorous defender of the faith against heresy'.[61] He described the calling of a synod at Brefi in c.560 by Saint David, and its 'orthodox decrees . . . the record of which has, however, entirely disappeared, with all the other documents of the time'.[62] In fact, the Synod was called by others and Saint David, a man of retiring disposition, was induced to attend only after pressure. Its 'orthodox decrees' enacted canons of discipline for the clergy and laity, not the suppression the Pelagian heresy as Oakeley supposed.

From these obscure stories, Oakeley moved to the historically reliable account of the sending of St Augustine by St Gregory at the end of the sixth century. Yet even here his sense of historicity lapses on occasions. He repeats the discredited 'angels not angles' story;[63] he prints a verbatim account of the initial interview between Augustine and King Ethelbert of Kent;[64] and gives a detailed description of the consecration of the font at St Martin's Church at Canterbury.[65] He also spent five pages describing the pallium and its origins and purpose.[66]

The advertisement gives no idea of Oakeley's thinking in writing the life of St Augustine, nor are there references in any contemporary correspondence to his intention. The nearest indication may be an obscure passage three-quarters of the way through the book, which might almost be autobiographical. 'In proportion as their eye is dulled to the claims of the outer, it is sharpened to behold the wonders of the inner world. Such Christians live and range in an element of their own. Their histories are accordingly almost like meditations; no wonder if to them, whose conversation is in the lower world, the records of their experience should be wearisome as the tale of dreamers, their chronicles of events read like fiction, their comments sound like the ravings of fanaticism'.[67]

Oakeley's treatment of the stories of Christianity in England before the arrival of Augustine are sufficient evidence against his ability as a critical historian, and his acceptance of the miracle stories shows the work to be designed for the edification of the faithful. There are references to Catholicism here and there. In the story of the healing of the blind beggar, Oakeley posed and answered the question of why such miracles should not be performed in his own day in the name of Jesus. 'Truly because we lack the conditions of its power – Catholic faith and Catholic sanctity'.[68] In answer to the question of whether such miracles ever in fact occurred, he requested the reader to 'suspend his judgement'. 'On this point we are warranted in being comparatively little solicitous; for that St Augustine of Canterbury worked miracles for the conversion of England is acknowledged even by many Protestants; and what precisely those miracles were is surely a secondary consideration'.[69] He defended even posthumous miracles attributed to the saint on the ground that the Church had always believed 'a singular virtue to reside in the bodies of saints', and that the account of the healing nature of the bones of Elisha (2 Kings 13:21) gave scriptural support for such belief.[70]

No-one would read the *Life of St Augustine of Canterbury* unless they wished to be edified. It is too uncritical to be treated as a serious and well-researched piece of scholarship aimed at uncovering the truth. But this was not Oakeley's intention, and if his indiscriminate use of historical resources and his fussy preoccupation with detail is discounted, and personal judgement is suspended as he asks, then it does read as a work of edification, remarkably free from the strident anti-Protestant statements which mark so much of his writing. Similarly, there is no adulation of Catholicism, though there is one ambiguous comment at the end of the book. 'What remains but . . . to trust that our Lord will turn a pitying eye on our much-loved England, and hear the prayers of her patrons and benefactors in her behalf that her children may once more "look unto the rock whence they were hewn, and to the hole of the pit whence they were digged" (Isaiah 51:1)'.[71] In Isaiah's prophecy, the Rock is God, but given Oakeley's thought, there is good reason to suppose that here Oakeley is using the text as an allusion to Rome. He had referred to Rome in *Bishop Jewel* as 'our Mother; to whom by the grace of God we owe it what we are what we are . . . may we never be provoked to forget her'.[72]

III Translation of the works of Saint Bernard 1843–1844

Oakeley's interest in the life and writings of Saint Bernard is first recorded in a letter to Thomas Mozley of 24 January 1843. He proposed to write a review of a new life of the saint for a future issue of *The British Critic*.[73] He also offered Mozley the alternative of an article on religious music; Mozley preferred this, and most of Oakeley's last articles for the journal are on this subject. His first serious proposal came in a letter to Pusey in December 1843. 'The other idea I sometimes indulge is a plan more magnificent and probably remote, but one which I sincerely hope will (come) some day or other'.[74] Oakeley felt that what he had seen and read of Saint Bernard's writings, particularly their richness and depth, would provide something from the Middle Ages to complement Pusey's plan for a Library of the Fathers. Saint Bernard's essential 'scripturalness' would commend his writings to 'religious people' and 'win over to the side of the Church warm-hearted persons who have been estranged from it by a fear of dryness and coldness'. Furthermore, Saint Bernard was 'more or less a favourite with some ultra-Protestants'.[75] If it proved practicable the scheme might be enlarged to include other saints from the Middle Ages such as Anselm, Bede and John Damascene. If not, 'a great deal might be done with St. Bernard alone'.[76]

On 9 January 1844, Oakeley had printed a prospectus of his proposed publication, and sent a copy to Newman. 'People seem to be taking to the idea – and one great advantage of the work, as of your Lives, will be that it will keep a number of persons permanently and usefully employed'.[77] Newman might have replied that he had hoped the *Lives of the English Saints* would keep Oakeley permanently and usefully employed.

The prospectus envisaged that the works of St Bernard would be published in four volumes, each one extending to some 650 pages, and being produced a rate of one volume every six months, at a cost of 18s per volume. If there were enough subscribers (750 were needed for the project to be viable), the first volume would appear at Michaelmas 1844, and the whole project would be completed in two years. Oakeley had a collaborator in the project in the shape of the Revd John S. Brewer, Classical Tutor at King's College, London, though it seems that it was Oakeley alone who promoted the scheme. In the words of the prospectus, the plan was 'to promote acquaintance with the writings of this great saint, and that in an unmutilated form. Any omission would seem to involve an expression of opinion, both upon the part excluded and the part retained; whereas the Editors' wish is, to keep clear of the exercise of private judgement altogether, and simply to exhibit the work as a fact in ecclesiastical literature'. As to the benefits of the project, the prospectus listed nine: a truer estimate of the theology of the church in the Middle Ages; an insight into the workings of the monastic system; an interpretation of the scripture, especially the book of psalms; deeper views of the bible 'than have been prevalent among ourselves', to release the stores of practical teaching and assistance in devotion which were to be found in Bernard's sermons; the extent and variety of society in the Middle Ages, as revealed by Bernard's letters; 'the display of such eminent Christian graces as those which the writings of Saint Bernard exhibit, in union with that deference to the Church and its Ordinances, their connexion with which ... has, from various causes, been not always so fully recognised as could be wished'; and generally, 'the opportunity of studying a saintly character in its manifold developments and complicated relations, as the teacher of the ignorant, the guide of the perplexed, the reprover of the erring; as a preacher, spiritual director, religious superior, citizen, friend, and lastly, in retirement and communion with God'.[78]

Oakeley asked Pusey for his help in December 1843, initially requesting him to look at Saint Bernard's expository writings 'e.g. the sermons on the canticles and the 91st Psalm'.[79] He was also hoping that Keble might help them with the translation.[80] The work was 'a formidable undertaking' as Oakeley described it to Gladstone, and he had gained 'a coadjutor who is well fitted to supply some of my own deficiencies'.[81]

Pusey was not entirely happy with every aspect of the plan, and raised objections to some of Saint Bernard's theological views. Oakeley suggested a compromise by confining the work, at first, to a biography of Bernard, followed by his letters, which were 'upon the events of the time rather than theological matters ... To the best of my belief there is not a single passage in the letters to which you would not cordially subscribe'.[82] But he was adamant that this was an interim arrangement. The publication of a biographical sketch, together with the letters, would fill two volumes and could be published separately, with the rest of the works 'to follow or not according to circumstances when these had appeared'.[83] It should not be seen as a substitute for the full project, 'but merely as a change in the mode of carrying it out; and with the intention of ultimately doing so to the full ... I cannot but hope good from bringing out the life of so great a saint'.[84]

Pusey was cautious about the plan and did not wish his name to be linked with the works of Saint Bernard in their entirety, a matter which had escaped Oakeley's notice. He knew that the appearance of Pusey's name on the list of subscribers would add considerable prestige to the project and encourage wider subscription, and was anxious to gain his approval and support. It had not occurred to him that Pusey might raise objections. 'I never anticipated an objection from any one of my friends ... If I had imagined an objection on your part, I think I should have paused before putting out the prospectus ... I proceeded unsuspiciously'.[85] Pusey objected to certain of the saint's writings, and was concerned that the use of his name as a subscriber to the publication might imply that he approved of them for devotional use. Oakeley assured Pusey that he had no wish to force particular devotions on any one who might take exception to them, and pointed to the fact that he had included a disclaimer in the prospectus. This had been inserted at the wish of the Bishop of London, who told him at the time of the publication of *Homilies for holy days and seasons*, that he seemed to be identifying himself with them. 'I was inclined to [Saint Bernard] in preference to any other medieval saint by considering the singular estimation in which he had been held in England'.[86]

Keble was as uneasy as Pusey about the plan, believing that minds would be better directed to the works of the Primitive Church for the time being. 'If the medieval system is really the intended development of primitive catholicity, is it not the most natural way for the English Church to recover it through primitive catholicity, instead of being urged directly to it; and therefore even on medieval principles are we not doing the best in confining ourselves for the present to those things in which the earlier Church is unquestionably with us'.[87]

The trio of disapproving voices was completed by Newman. As with Pusey, the substance of Newman's criticism is unknown. But he did reveal them to Oakeley, who thanked him and responded by saying that he did not feel that Newman's objections would apply to the biography and letters 'which form our immediate object'.[88] Keble wrote to Newman telling him of Pusey's unease, and provoked a forthright response. 'I wish I had any idea that Pusey's feeling was what you represent, since I would not have subscribed to it. As it is, my name, I believe, is in print. My opinion about the publication was not asked – and since I saw the prospectus, what I have said has been to throw cold water upon it'.[89]

That comment by Newman at the beginning of March 1844 is almost the last we hear of Oakeley's plan for a full scale work on the life and writings of Saint Bernard. During April 1844, he was incapacitated by a serious illness which forced him to take a long period of rest, initially away from Margaret Street, and later, across in Ireland. He had recovered some of his strength by the end of June, but was still weak and did not expect to return to work before November. 'And when I do take up my pen again for any matter which requires thought and application, then the 2nd Pt. of St Augustine of Canterbury, and the Life of St Bernard will have first claim on me'.[90]

The second part of the *Life of St Augustine of Canterbury* was published towards the end of 1844, but there are no further references to Saint Bernard after June 1844. As the prospectus had been printed and distributed, it is possible that the number of subscribers never reached the required figure of 750 to make the project viable, but the more likely explanation is that the project was overtaken by other events. Recovering from his illness, he set to work in the autumn of 1844 to finish his work on Saint Augustine, intending to begin work on Saint Bernard shortly afterwards. But in mid-December, the Vice-Chancellor of Oxford had announced the intention of the Heads of Houses to take proceedings against Ward over *The Ideal of a Christian Church*. Oakeley's decision to take the side of Ward and defend his friend, was inevitable, and all his plans for Saint Bernard were shelved until a more propitious time. It was not to come.

In addition to his co-translator, Oakeley was also assisted by Gladstone's brother-in-law, Lord Lyttleton. At the time of Lyttleton's suicide in 1876, Oakeley wrote to Gladstone expressing his sympathy. 'I well remember him in our Margaret Chapel days. He used to help me in a translation of St Bernard which I then thought of prosecuting, but which circumstances afterwards interrupted.[91]

IV Translating the Sarum Breviary 1843–1844

Of the miscellaneous projects with which Oakeley was involved in the years 1843–44, one was an idea long desired in Tractarian circles, to translate and publish the Sarum Breviary.

Newman had begun to use the Roman Breviary privately in about March 1836.[92] In June of that year he published Tract 75. *On the Roman breviary as embodying the substance of the devotional services of the church Catholic*, which went into a second edition the following year. After the death of his wife in May 1839, Pusey began to use the Sarum Breviary as a supplement to *The Book of Common Prayer*, but refrained from recommending its use to others. It was, besides, difficult to find a copy, because it had not been printed since the reign of Queen Mary I (1553–8), and the few surviving copies were held by cathedral and college libraries, and by the occasional book collector. Because of Tract 75, the Roman Breviary increased in popularity as a source of devotions, and Pusey felt that a new edition of the Sarum Breviary would be 'less likely to invite people to Rome, than the Roman'.[93] Newman was in favour, but Keble was cautious and, on reflection, Pusey hesitated and the project was abandoned.

But Pusey was not the only Tractarian to be interested in the project. Others included Samuel Francis Wood and Robert Williams, both members of Oakeley's congregation at Margaret Chapel. In July 1841, Newman told Keble that he had 'just stopped Robert Williams going on with the printing of the breviary. He would not print it without my countenance, and that I did not feel I could give'.[94] After Wood's death, in April 1843, his manuscripts passed into the possession of Williams, and both he and Oakeley began to consider the possibility of publication. Oakeley was confident of Pusey's support and told him that the only thing they lacked was money. 'I am sure you will not wish to do anything which might interfere with an object, which R. W. has laboured for several years'.[95]

Because of the lack of documentary material, it is difficult to trace the chronology and extent of Oakeley's involvement in the project. But it seems unlikely that it was either deep or extensive. Pusey exercised a superintending control over the project since Oakeley offered his services in the translation of some of the breviary hymns, 'as you were so good as to say that you would employ me in that delightful work'.[96] This was written in March 1844, and Oakeley's involvement ceased with the onset of his illness in April. Towards the end of June, Oakeley apologised to Pusey for not being well enough to be able to do any work on the breviary. 'I feel a little uneasy about the breviary because I do not expect to return to work before Nov. and then only if my recovery shd. have gone favourably'.[97]

The project lingered for some weeks, and Pusey was planning to start printing at the beginning of July.[98] Fragments of the breviary did appear in brown paper wrappers in Oxford shops, and were used in the private chapel at Littlemore, but the work was never finished, and the complete breviary was not published in the lifetime of either Pusey or Oakeley.

V Translation of St Bonaventure's Life of Christ 1844

Oakeley's first interest in the works of Saint Bonaventure, the thirteenth century Franciscan cardinal, philosopher and theologian, was his translation of Bonaventure's Passiontide hymn, 'In passione Domine' (In the Lord's atoning grief). It appeared in his *Devotions commemorative of the passion* published in 1842. It was included, with some alterations, in the first edition of *Hymns, ancient and modern*, published in 1861.[99]

At Lent 1844, Oakeley published a translation of Saint Bonaventure's *Life of our Lord and Saviour Jesus Christ*, a highly coloured and meditative account of the life of Christ. While intended as an aid to private devotion and meditation, it brought considerable criticism of Oakeley. He had added a lengthy introduction justifying, in the eyes of Protestants, the considerable areas of licence taken by Bonaventure in meditating on the life of Christ. The work provoked angry condemnation from J. C. Crosthwaite, rector of the parishes of St Mary at Hill and St Andrew Hubbard in the city of London. His criticisms were published in the *British Magazine*, a journal of which he was the editor between November 1844 and December 1845. They were collected and published under the title *Modern hagiology* in 1846. Crosthwaite's criticisms began with the assumption that because Oakeley defended Bonaventure's methods of meditation, he therefore believed everything written by the saint and therefore should take full responsibility for republishing a piece of literature that Crosthwaite himself found objectionable. By the spring of 1844, Oakeley had become a well-known and controversial Tractarian, and was more accessible a target than Bonaventure who had been dead for more than 500 years. Consequently Crosthwaite directed all his attacks at Oakeley and not at Bonaventure.

Bonaventure had coloured many of the stories of the life of Christ, such as the nativity and the temptations in the wilderness, by adding his own details, by filling in the backgrounds, and generally by producing greatly extended accounts of incidents given no more than one or two verses in the bible. Such writing, which might be classified as lying somewhere between vivid imagination and deep spiritual insight, was completely unacceptable to Crosthwaite, who dismissed it as worthless, and attacked the stories which Oakeley related and supported in the introduction.

Oakeley referred to and associated himself with Bonaventure's account of the birth of Christ, which portrayed the Blessed Virgin Mary kneeling before her infant child, and the infant smiling at her 'with a look of uninfantine intelligence'. Oakeley was firm in his defence. 'You cannot prove me wrong, nor suggest any alternative which is not equally unauthorised, and more improbable. And, at last, what great harm, though I be mistaken? I do no violence to the sacred text; I am guilty of no irreverence'.[100] Crosthwaite's reaction was predictable. 'Are such gross and disgusting liberties with the word of God innocent and allowable? Is the only record of that stupendous mystery on which the whole hope of human salvation depends, a subject on which an unchastised imagination, or a gross and vulgar taste, may lawfully disport itself'.[101] 'Because you cannot prove me wrong, I am at liberty to make whatever additions to the word of God appear to me not incongruous with the original stories of the Evangelists'.[102] 'Mr Oakeley . . . treats it as if no testimony or tradition was pretended. Nothing can be more worthy of notice than his question – "What great harm though I be mistaken?" As to lawfulness of such proceedings, it seems to be not worth considering. Providing he does not see any "great harm" done by such licentious abuse of his imagination, he is satisfied'.[103]

In his account of the temptations in the wilderness, Bonaventure devised what Oakeley thought to be a 'sweet conception',[104] about the brief reference to the angels who ministered to Christ after the departure of the devil. The angels had gone to the home of Mary and Joseph at Nazareth and collected 'a mess of pottage, which she had got ready for herself and St Joseph, and a piece of bread, with a linen cloth and other necessaries; perhaps, too, our Lady procured, if she could, a small fish or two'.[105] Oakeley declared that he had chosen this particular story from Bonventure's text 'because it is one of the strongest which occur in the following pages, of addition to Scripture, and presumes an interpretation of the sacred text for which our minds are, I think, not at once prepared'.[106] Crosthwaite, whose mind was totally unprepared, was roused to fury and denounced this as 'horrible impiety'[107] and a piece of 'profane fiction'.[108] 'Is it possible for any persons to allow their imaginations such unbridled licence for any length of time, and retain any distinct perception of what is true and what is fiction?'[109]

The legendary post-resurrection appearance of Christ to the Blessed Virgin Mary was supported by Oakeley. 'Nothing is contained in the gospel on his appearance to our Lady; but I mentioned it at first because the Church appears to hold it . . . How he appeared to his Mother is nowhere written; but pious belief is as I have related it'.[110] Crosthwaite's answer to this was that he could not conceive of anyone piously believing anything which 'rests on no testimony of God, but on his own fancy and invention'. There is no piety in believing the creations of one's own mind to be reality'.[111]

Oakeley defended his belief in the usefulness of such meditation on scriptural texts on five counts. Firstly, anyone who sought to bring the gospel events vividly into the mind's eye inevitably introduced as a matter of fact a variety of ideas besides the strict letter of the sacred text'.[112] Secondly, imagination was a 'divine gift' and should be used 'in bringing sacred scenes and incidents before the mind'[113] Thirdly, it was the method of scripture to teach by hints 'which are lost upon the thoughtless but eloquent to the wise'.[114] Fourthly, if imagination and meditation were discounted, then such stories might still be defended on the grounds of 'tradition, subsequent revelation or reasonable probability'.[115] Fifthly, the very indefinite nature of scripture was clearly designed to benefit meditation. 'It may be that minds so feeble and undiscriminating as ours, would have been unequal to the task of dwelling upon so tangled and delicate a theme as a certainty'.[116]

Crosthwaite was not so easily persuaded. To his mind, the whole object was 'to turn the history of our Blessed Redeemer into poetry and romance – a process which Mr Oakeley calls meditation'.[117] 'One would have thought the feelings of reverence, which his party have so long claimed to possess exclusively, would have made him withdraw his hand, when he was tempted to give to English readers a work which pretends to supply what God has thought proper to conceal'.[118]

It is difficult to take Crosthwaite seriously, in that his reactions were so unthoughtful, unconstructive, emotionally violent and essentially negative. But he was not alone, and his views were typical of the *sola scriptura* section of opinion that would have treated any imaginative meditation as an addition to the scriptural texts, and therefore as profane and worthless. In fact, his offended sensibilities compare poorly with the charm, fluency and elegance of Oakeley's writings. In all his righteous censoriousness, Crosthwaite made no attempt to understand the principles of meditation, or Bonaventure, who had a profound influence as a spiritual writer, and whose theology emphasised the mystical illumination that God sheds on the faithful Christian, or indeed Oakeley, himself on a journey of illuminaton, who was clearly entranced and uplifted by his discovery of Bonaventure's meditation on the life of Christ.

Chapter Nine

The gathering storm

THE 'TRIAL' IN THE SHELDONIAN THEATRE

*It seems to me as clear as noonday that I ought not to hang back and
leave Ward to sustain the whole brunt of the battle. I feel it generous to
him – due to myself – charitable to the members of convocation – to let the
world know that the same arrow which hits him grazes another . . . it is
fair and proper to let them know exactly what they are doing.*
Frederick Oakeley to Edward Pusey, 21 December 1844

When the second part of Oakeley's *Life of St Augustine of Canterbury*
appeared in the autumn of 1844, Oakeley prefaced the work with an
apology for its delayed appearance. 'Illness and other similar causes
have obliged him to delay the publication of the second part of this
Life very much indeed beyond the time at which he had hoped that it
might have appeared'.[1]

This is the only reference in Oakeley's printed works to his illness in
the summer of 1844. There is no record of the nature of his illness, but
it was severe enough for him to require holidays away from Margaret
Street, and a long period of rest. Oakeley described it as 'a serious
illness', and that it lasted for two months.[2] The onset was probably
around the end of April 1844, since he was able to tell Pusey at the end
of June that, although he had recovered from the illness, he was still
physically weak and did not anticipate returning to work before
November.[3] Prayers were still being said for him at Littlemore in the
middle of September.[4] Oakeley's illness may well have been physical;
it was said that the residents of the Margaret Street community had
carried their monastic austerities to such extremes that George Tickell
had fallen ill and was obliged to go abroad for his health;[5] it may well
be that Oakeley's illness was due to the same origins.

Whether the illness was physical, or whether he had a nervous breakdown is a matter for speculation, but part of its cause could well have been the sheer pressure of work. Writing the *Life of St Augustine of Canterbury*, trying to write a life of Saint Bernard, and translating his letters, involvement in translating the Sarum Breviary, quite apart from raising money to build the new church and trying to run the existing one, was a punishing workload. Apart from these concerns, he had to ward off periodic attacks from the hostile Bishop Blomfield who viewed Margaret Chapel, its minister and its congregation as a Tractarian nest in the heart of his diocese. Oakeley's relationship with Blomfield had been strained since the publication of *Sermons, preached chiefly in the Chapel Royal*, at Whitehall in the spring of 1839, and he had been a prominent Tractarian, notoriously prominent in the eyes of many, since the publication of *Bishop Jewel* in July 1841. Whether his illness was physical or mental, it can be assumed that by Easter [7 April] 1844, Frederick Oakeley was a tired man.

His illness was sufficiently debilitating to require a move from Margaret Street 'to the Regent's Park for a change of air'.[6] He was still there on 14 August when Newman and Ward came to visit him.[7] He was so ill and weak that he was not even interested in discussing matters of religion when visited by the Roman Catholic priest of St John's Wood, a growing and fashionable residential area on the northern side of the park. 'I declined to see him, as I thought he might wish to speak to me on the subject of religion upon which I did not then wish to be troubled'.[8] It is conceivable that Oakeley did not wish to speak to the man on the ground that he was a Roman Catholic priest, though this is unlikely in view of his visit to Oscott. A more satisfactory explanation would be that Oakeley had 'overdosed' on religion in general, and was mentally and physically exhausted.

When he had recovered enough to travel, he returned to Margaret Street briefly before going to Ireland to stay with his friend William Bence-Jones.[9] On his way, he passed through Cork, and spent a day there. He worshipped at the Church of Ireland Cathedral of St Fin Barre in the morning, and in the evening went to vespers at the local Roman Catholic church. He was there only for a short time before feelings of guilt overcame him. 'Before the psalms were over I was seized with a scruple of conscience and hastily left the church. I mention these facts to prove how little intention I then had of leaving the Church of England'.[10] But the practices of the Church of Ireland were not guaranteed to satisfy his ideals in the field of liturgy. 'The practical representation of protestantism in Ireland was not calculated to check my Catholic aspirations, while, on the other hand, I saw and heard enough of the love borne by the people to the old religion to satisfy me at once of its tenacity of their devotion'.[11]

While staying in Ireland, Oakeley's Catholic aspirations received something of a jolt when he read in the papers that George Tickell, one of his 'monks' at Margaret Street, had been received into the Roman Catholic Church. Tickell had also fallen ill by the imposed monastic austerities of the Margaret Street community, and went abroad to Belgium for a rest. There 'he fell in with some members of the Weld family, who convinced him that his position was an unsafe one, and he accordingly became Catholic. On his return to London, he burst into the room of his fellow 'monk' George Bridges saying "Bridges, this is all humbug. I have a cab at the door; come and be received into the Church". He was so changed that Mr Bridges scarcely knew him, and in a few days the friends were again united in one faith'.[12] Bridges and Tickell remained in the Roman Catholic Church until their deaths in 1899 and 1893 respectively, and both men became Jesuits.

Oakeley was 'affected and distressed' by this 'hasty and inconsiderate act'.[13] On his return to London, he wrote an article in the form of an imaginary letter to Tickell and sent it to the *English Churchman*, a journal of slightly anti-Tractarian tone founded in January 1843. It was published with a flourish of trumpets by the editor who entitled it *Reasons for not joining the Romish communion*. Oakeley wrote it on his own authority, and after some thought. He was back in London by 16 September when Newman stopped regular prayers for him at Littlemore because of his improved state of health,[14] and he stayed there with Newman 1–3 October. The letter appeared in the *English Churchman* on 29 November. Subsequent correspondence indicates that Newman knew nothing of the content of the letter until it appeared in print. After reading it, he wrote, 'I cannot think that Oakeley's arguments in the E. Ch. will stand'.[15]

The letter is a good example of the confused state of Oakeley's mind, a confusion brought about largely by Tickell's departure for Rome. For the preceding three years or more, Oakeley had barely concealed his admiration for the Roman Catholic Church, convincing many people in the process that he was not far off joining it. In the letter, he tries, not very convincingly, to say that he has no intention of joining that Church. He believed that converts to Rome were making a tremendous leap into a situation of which they were insufficiently informed, and might find themselves beset with difficulties and perplexities when it was too late to turn back. Throughout the letter he protested his loyalty to the Church of England, but his statements show evidence of much agonising. He admitted his love and veneration for Rome, and his longing for unity with her, and his arguments for remaining within the Church of England owe more to sentiment and emotion than to theology or ecclesiology. 'You ask me, why I do not at once join your Church . . . I cannot. I am, as at present, as incapable morally of such an act, as I am physically unequal to flying, or performing any feat of bodily strength above my powers'.[16]

Oakeley attempted to tackle the question of how far sacramental privileges were attainable in a Church that was out of communion with the great body of Christendom, and especially the Roman Catholic Church. Admitting that 'I have not got the learning of my own to discuss it', he referred to the view of Roman Catholic theologians that the state of the Church of England was anomalous, and 'that the same opinion seems to be gaining ground among the greatest divines of our own side'. Yet he regarded their arguments as 'somewhat dry and technical' and, moreover, the Roman Catholic Church had not pronounced against the Church of England with any final and distinct authority. 'Let the Holy See apply itself with its wonted vigour and profound spiritual sagacity to the wonderful and unprecedented fact . . . of whole nations professing Christianity, yet apart from the Chair of St. Peter . . . and a decision which should be founded on an inquiry so conducted would undoubtedly be entitled to the gravest consideration on the part of all those who bear in mind with what breathless expectation the formal acts of the Roman See have ever been awaited, and with what dutiful attention received by the Church at large'.[17] On reading this, Newman remarked, 'I shall be very surprised if the Bishop of L[ondon], likes to be told that O[akeley] considers that the pope has a prior claim on his obedience'.[18] If the letter was supposed to list reasons for not joining the Roman Catholic Church, then the sight of Oakeley waiting respectfully for the judgement of the Pope, on whether the Church of England was in full possession of sacramental privileges, must have caused confusion in the minds of many.

Oakeley then moved to the question of inherent sanctity in the Church. There was no need to leave the Church of England, he declared, because it was as holy as the Roman Catholic Church. 'Sanctity is a quality, not merely higher in degree, but higher in kind, than ordinary Christian goodness . . . our Church, however barren of this especial and choicest product in other times, has, within our experience at least, put forth essentially the same fruit as yours'.[19] Oakeley generously excused Roman theologians who had pronounced against the Church of England on the ground that 'they have absolutely no notion of the work which is carrying on within our Church', the work of sanctification. 'While this gracious and heavenly light encircles me, I cannot help its penetrating me; and that it keeps me where I am by a kind of holy spell'.[20]

The question of the sanctity of or within the Church of England was an issue that had much exercised the mind of Ward, for whom sanctity was the test of a true Church. A Church that produced saints was a true Church. 'We are reminded of the one ultimate aim presupposed in all real religion – personal sanctification and salvation'. The function of the Church 'consists simply and solely in the work of individual sanctification and salvation';[21] 'the training up of saints ... this is an office which an ideal church will prize and cherish'.[22] Ward's inability to find it to his satisfaction in the Church of England was the reason for his departure. As Ward's closest companion, Oakeley might be expected to follow the same line and, in the *Life of St Augustine of Canterbury*, he does. Asking why such miracles as were performed in the days of St Augustine not were performed in his own day, he concluded, 'Truly because we lack .. Catholic faith and Catholic sanctity'.[23] Yet in the letter he states that sanctity is to be found within the Church of England. 'This note of sanctity is one, which, from its very nature, will be indefinitely more arresting to ourselves than to those at a distance ... That saintly persons should leave our communion ... does not make it less remarkable that their saintliness has been produced and sustained so long within it'.[24]

Oakeley next called up the image of a person (and here there may be a hint of autobiography) who, in the event of serious illness, was ready to die calmly in the fold of the Church of England. 'Now such a person has, I think, good reason for humble trust that God would not leave him, in a matter directing his eternal welfare, under some grievous and perilous delusion'.[25]

He urged those who were tempted by Rome to think of the possible consequences of 'so awful and irretraceable a step', and obliquely warned his readers that the Roman Catholic Church in England might not be entirely to their liking. 'Am I at once prepared to fall in with the ways of English Roman Catholics?' How know I that national peculiarities, which have become part of my being, may not seriously sooner or later, clash with the feelings and habits of my new associates?' 'We seem to miss in the great body of English Roman Catholics, those especial qualities which we are accustomed to regard as the peculiar fruits of the Church – tranquil faith, high devotion, penetrating wisdom, shrinking humility, deep considerateness'.[26] This is an extraordinary piece of sniping at the Roman Catholic Church in England, and so entirely out of keeping with his professed love and veneration of Rome, so consistently expressed in the period up to the time of this letter that it would seem to owe more to the emotion of the moment, than to any systematic development of thought.

'Why should I leave my communion ... Why should I join the Roman Church? I have a place to fill, and work to do, in the Church of

England; with more privileges than I use and more happiness than I deserve. I have kind superiors, holy guides, a dutiful flock, edifying friends. Why should I, with no summons from without, and no motion from within, thanklessly and presumptuously ... cut the cords which fasten me to my present anchorage, to drift away, I know not whither, to strike, it may be, on some rock of doubt, or to be stranded on some island of desolation'.[27] The only explanation for this piece of nonsense is that Oakeley, deeply wounded by Tickell's 'desertion', is upbraiding him and describing himself and Margaret Chapel as Tickell should have seen them.

There are far too many emotions at work in this letter, and far too many statements that contradict feelings expressed elsewhere, for literal acceptance of its statements. Oakeley himself provides us with a clue in the 'advertisement' to the *Life of St Augustine of Canterbury*. The second part of the work was written after Oakeley returned from Ireland, and having heard the news of Tickell's departure and is probably contemporaneous (within a few weeks) of the letter to the *English Churchman*. After apologising for the delay in its appearance, he added that it had been written 'under circumstances of a public and private nature, more or less disadvantageous towards calm thought and continuous attention which are due to a subject so solemn as the life of a saint'.[28] Many years later and thinking back to the letter, he recalled writing it 'under some feeling of irritation' and that its tone was 'querulous'.[29]

Why should Tickell's departure have caused him so much irritation? Nothing much is known of the relationship between George Tickell and Frederick Oakeley, beyond the fact that Oakeley had met him at Oxford and invited him to live a semi-monastic existence at Margaret Street from the autumn of 1841. Tickell lived very much in Oakeley's shadow in the years 1841-4. Without knowing his motive, Tickell, apparently, behaved less than honourably and honestly in choosing to leave Margaret Street and the Church of England while his mentor was convalescing in Ireland. Leaving Oakeley to read about it in the newspapers was not the kindest way to break the news. This behaviour perhaps accounts for the querulous tone of the letter, but does not explain the many inconsistencies to be found there.

Six months earlier, Oakeley would not have dreamed of likening the Catholic Church to a 'rock of doubt' or an 'island of desolation'. At the end of his introduction to his translation of Bonaventure's *The Life of our Lord and Saviour Jesus Christ*, Oakeley had all but warned his readers that because of the distrustful attitude of the Church of England towards him. 'Our own Church, which we long to love with the most devout affection, and to confide in the most unreserved submission, will not allow us ... to trust her; and, without trust, are driven upon reposing their trust elsewhere than in the existing, energising system; whether in the idea of the ancient church, or in the living church as elsewhere manifested'.[30] There is no doubt that Oakeley still had a deep love and respect for Rome, despite describing the English Roman Catholic Church as 'that unsightly vortex',[31] and he called on those former members of the Church of England who had become members of the Roman Catholic Church to do everything in their power, by virtue of their past religious experience, towards the establishment of amicable relations between the two churches, as a prelude to 'hastening that external union which, so it could be effected without injury to conscience, most English churchmen would, I suppose, agree in desiring'.[32] Oakeley had lost none of his ardour for Rome, but the departure of Tickell had given him a severe jolt and temporarily thrown him off his equilibrium. If the letter to the *English Churchman* was intended to convince its readers of his loyalty to the Church of England, then its very weak arguments make it less than convincing. His declared but superficial loyalty, expressed in such tones of anguish, only thinly masks a yearning for Rome.

There is reason to suppose that Oakeley's anguish and irritation may well be due to envy. With his love of Rome and things Roman, the thought of his conversion must have passed across his mind on more than one occasion. Perhaps, in the eyes of Oakeley, Tickell took the step that Oakeley had considered taking himself. Tickell's departure for the Roman Catholic Church can be seen as the logical conclusion of Oakeley's writing and teaching over the previous three years. Tickell had followed the teaching of his friend and mentor, and taken the natural step.

One correspondent to the *English Churchman* was convinced that Oakeley would not be long in taking the same step, judging from the content of the letter. 'I must candidly confess that the melancholy and disparaging view which he there takes of our position as a Church is such as would drive me wholly to despair, if I could think it true view at all ... I could not remain in the Church of England for another day in peace if I could think that we are (as Mr Oakeley's letter assumes throughout) a body wholly exterior to the Catholic Church'. Using personal sanctity as a justification for the existence of the Church of England was 'to reduce the evidences of our being Christian to the very lowest point', and 'just the next thing, to quitting us altogether'.[33] 'All this beating about for reasons, and apologising, and shrinking and leaning hither and thither what does it look like, I ask, but a clearing of the ground, and choosing the foothold, before "the plunge" is taken?'[34]

A further letter appeared in the issue for 12 December supporting Oakeley, but although he defended the line he had taken, in a private letter to Pusey, Oakeley refused to take any further part in public debate. 'I no where deny the Catholicity of our Ch[urch], but waive the question – stating the undoubted anomaly, but leaving theologians to deal with it'. He was sure that many people had been 'calmed' by his letter which 'does not imply more than it expresses .. I do wish people had more of the spirit of confidence. I shall not for myself take any further notice of the matter in public'.[35]

The comment that Oakeley was only clearing the ground to choose a foothold before taking 'the plunge' was not far wide of the mark. Since the publication of 'Episcopal Charges of the past year' in *The British Critic* of January 1843, Oakeley had seen Catholicism and Protestantism as two great systems struggling for control of the Church of England, and his departure from the Church of his upbringing was only a matter of waiting until he had decided in his own mind that Protestantism had won, when his own position in the Church of England would become untenable. But this assumes that the Church of England was changing, or not changing, under the influence of the Tractarians, and that Oakeley himself was standing still. His thoughts were changing and developing as much as the Church around him. The departure of George Tickell in the autumn of 1844 was only a temporary aberration in his gradual alignment with Rome, which had begun three years earlier with Bishop Jewel. All that was needed was something to set the process moving again.

The required incident was provided by the publication of Ward's book, *The Ideal of a Christian Church* in June 1844. This six hundred page book was put together in the space of a few months, as a response to Palmer's *Narrative of Events*. Ward's main point was that the practice of the Church of England fell well short of the mark when tested against what Ward considered to be the ideal of a Christian Church, and the ideal that he portrayed bore a remarkable resemblance to the contemporary Roman Catholic Church. Two quotations from the work will suffice: 'We find – oh, most joyful, most wonderful, most unexpected sight! We find the whole cycle of Roman doctrine gradually possessing English churchmen'.[36] 'Three years have passed since I said plainly that in subscribing the Articles I renounce no one Roman doctrine'.[37]

Few historians of the Oxford Movement have had a good word to say about the book. 'Ponderous and unattractive . . . ill-arranged and rambling',[38] 'voluminous and ill-compiled',[39] 'ignorance of history' and 'reckless dogmatism',[40] 'long and dull',[41] 'enormous and disorderly',[42] are among the milder comments. At the extreme, the book has been described as, 'This formidable bundle of verbiage and vicious vituperation'.[43] It appeared at the beginning of the university's long vacation, and nothing much could be done throughout the summer months. But when the university reassembled in the autumn, the reaction was hostile, and Oakeley's foothold appeared in the form of three proposals by the Hebdomadal Board of the university.

The move was instigated by Dr Benjamin Symons, the evangelical warden of Wadham College, who was also vice-chancellor of the university. The Tractarians had foolishly tried to oppose his election as vice-chancellor, a post held for a short period and in rotation by the heads of the colleges. On 13 December, Symons announced that the board would propose three resolutions to the meeting of convocation scheduled for 13 February 1845. Firstly, that *The Ideal of a Christian Church* should be condemned; secondly, that Ward should be deprived of his degrees; and thirdly, that in future, the Thirty-Nine Articles should be accepted by members of the university in the sense intended by their original framers.

Oakeley's decision to stand by his old friend was inevitable. He was too closely linked with Ward to do otherwise, and he personally could see nothing wrong with the book. More than twenty years after its publication, he praised it for its careful study and calm deliberation. 'It was no impetuous flyleaf, no slashing pamphlet, no piquant article in a suspected review, but an obese octavo, extending to six hundred closely-printed pages, the writer of which must have found time to mitigate the ardour of the most infuriated spirit in the process of its composition . . . The great probability, however, is that comparatively few of the numbers who voted for its condemnation were at pains to read it throughout, so that its size, instead of securing it a patient reception, operated simply to its disadvantage'.[44]

Oakeley did not waver once in his support for Ward. 'Mr Ward had acted with such kindness and generosity towards me and had done me much signal service in clearing and maturing my religious opinions that I regarded it as a plain duty to stand by him in his contest with the university'.[45] Ward had sought 'to disengage the Anglican Communion from a share in the miserable work of the Reformation; to relieve it of many soul-destroying traditions; and to strengthen its position by seeking out points of association, and awakening hopes of reunion with the Catholic Church'.[46]

Oakeley decided to go into battle, for and on behalf of Ward, by opposing all three resolutions. Many of his Tractarian colleagues, Pusey among them, disapproved of Ward and his book, and were far more concerned with the third 'anti-Newman' resolution. It presented the prospect of a new and semi-official interpretation of the Articles which would become binding on members of the University. Oakeley rightly saw the third resolution as a renewed attack on the interpretation of the Articles as laid out in Tract 90 which he had so vigorously defended three years earlier. He was certain that the final battle between Catholic and Protestant within the Church of England was about to begin, and that now was the time to unfurl his own banner. 'The result of the Oxford proceedings will be awaited with intense anxiety. I feel it right to put out possibly in a few days that I cannot subscribe except in the sense for which Ward pleads. To myself the success of any of three propositions and not the last only, would be most exceedingly perplexing – and altogether I anticipate as near at hand some great struggle between feeling which is almost entirely one way and conscience, or faith, which often seems to point another'.[47]

On 21 December 1844, whatever doubts Oakeley may have had in the immediate aftermath of the announcement of the Board's proposed resolutions had dispersed, and he was in an excited state of mind. 'I am anything but downcast I assure you. I do not know why, but I am just now, in most excellent good heart – one varies so to be sure; but somehow everything looks bright and clear'.[48] He had resolved all doubts and was intent on action. 'It seems to me as clear as noonday that I ought not to hang back and leave Ward to sustain the whole brunt of the battle. I feel it generous to him – due to myself – charitable to the members of convocation – to let the world know that the same arrow which hits him grazes another . . . it is fair and proper to let them know exactly what they are doing'.[49]

Tract 90 had enabled Oakeley to subscribe to the Thirty-Nine Articles in a Catholic sense. Ward had accepted this view on the basis of the internal evidence of the articles themselves,[50] and Oakeley on historical evidence.[51] The third resolution, condemning a Catholic interpretation of the Thirty-Nine Articles, was the most serious of the three. But the first resolution, condemning *The Ideal of a Christian Church*, was as serious to Oakeley as the third was to every other Tractarian. Oakeley had moved to the position where the condemnation of Ward's book would mean a condemnation of his own beliefs. He accepted Ward's conclusion that all Roman doctrine could be held and believed by an individual who might still, in good conscience, subscribe the articles. This marked the parting of the ways between Oakeley and Pusey. 'You are, my dear P., differently (placed) from myself: you sign upon a different view; you (like J. H. N.) do think that the articles preclude some Roman doctrine. I wish to believe that they do not, because I think they were drawn up on a principle of latitude in respect of R. Catholics . . . I cannot bring myself to deny any Roman decision. Now it would plainly be a great relief to me if No. 1 were not to pass, because it wd. be like a public recognition of the latitude which I claim . . . If No. 1 passes . . . there wd. be like a public slur upon the principle upon which I subscribe'.[52] 'I do not at all say that I should feel the success of Nos. 1 + 2 a direct call to leave the university as the success of No. 3 wd. of course be: but I must not acquiesce in the feeling against Ward's view, but on the contrary try to stem it, seeing that it is not for his strength of language that he is to be condemned, but for his view of subscription, and this is the view on which I subscribe'.[53] Oakeley reported to Pusey that he had discussed the matter, and his own particular line, with Newman, 'who quite understands it; and thought that nothing but benefit to all sides could come of each acting as he feels best. J.H.N. did think that the success of 1 + 2 would be a difficulty to such as myself'.[54]

These letters from Oakeley to Pusey in December 1844 are remarkable for their frank and forthright tone. Oakeley's sense of the inevitability of the step he was about to take, and his understanding that he would find himself in a very isolated position in future, a position of his own adoption to ensure that nobody else could be hurt with this actions.

Oakeley's absolute integrity in the affair of Ward's book, and his determination to proceed along the course in which he believed, was put to Pusey in a rather moving letter dated Christmas Eve 1844. 'Nothing but an overpowering feeling upon the duty and necessity of clearing my name would lead me to take a step which I know is a risk .. I hope therefore that it is not from any merely chivalrous impulse that I act – the step is too important and the feeling is too serious – but on the contrary that by not acting I shd. be giving in to a cowardly and selfish inclination'.[55] Oakeley told Pusey that he had tried to separate his own position from those of others, in the hope 'that it will be only myself and my own cause that will suffer',[56] and in an admirable display of self-sacrifice, he hoped that his own comparative moderation and quietness might help dissolve much of the anger and hostility directed against Ward. 'I also very much hope that by saying what I am honestly able on the side of caution and conciliation, I shall anticipate some of those objections which a declaration necessarily strong might otherwise provoke. Ward and I say things in a different way, which is not saying that his way is wrong or mine right – but so it is . . . it is certainly the fact that some, however few, are more tolerant of my "excuses" than of his – while yet nothing of mine cd. have penetrated as his has done'.[57]

Also in December 1844, Oakeley had a short correspondence with Henry Edward Manning, Archdeacon of Chichester. Manning had strong Tractarian sympathies, but had objected to Tract 90, had no sympathy for Ward and his views, and proposed to abstain from voting on the first and second resolutions. This was unthinkable to Oakeley who believed that everybody ought to have an opinion 'about so remarkable a book as Ward's which is either most valuable, or most reprehensible'.[58] Oakeley told Manning of his two opposite principles theory. 'I fancy to see a definite line in our church on two opposite sides, but not on the space between. When, then, I find yourself ... expressing what I may call theological sympathy with me, I am led to fear some compromise'.[59] The evidence for Oakeley's honesty and integrity, committed in one direction as it was, comes in a passage later in the same letter to Manning. 'I have got hold of a notion ... of a "something" definite, consistent, most real, most influential, – a something which vindicates to itself my whole mind – colours all my views – regulates all my sympathies – determines all my movements – a something which ... would make all feeling enthusiastic, and all action energetic'.[60] 'The one course which I cannot appreciate is the neutral. I feel all that there is to be said for it; of the sense of dutifulness, moderation, charity, absti- nence from exciting circumstances; I feel (I think) the temptation on the other side, to restlessness ... presumption, meddling ... I must follow out my own line of argument with however few compan- ions'.[61] The arraignment of Ward was the final critical contest for which he had been waiting. It was the catalyst which enabled him to move further away from the shadow of Newman, Pusey and Ward, and into a greater prominence.

Manning found Oakeley's letter very persuasive, and admitted that it would 'help me enter into myself and to reconsider the grounds of my present convictions both in matters of judgement and practice',[62] though he did not accept that neutrality could be the result of 'indiffer- ence or want of intense feeling but from regard to truth and fact'.[63] He agreed with Oakeley that there were only two consistent and tenable positions, placing himself on the Catholic side, but he differed from Oakeley only 'as to the nature of the true Catholic principles'.[64] He could not bring himself to agree with Oakeley on the acceptance of all Roman doctrine, especially the necessity of communion with Rome, the theory of infallibility, and the 'worship' of the Blessed Virgin Mary 'as it is permitted and practised in that communion'.[65] 'The unprotes- tantizing of the English Church does not signify the Romanizing of it'.[66] This was evidence enough for Oakeley to report to Pusey that, 'Archdeacon Manning ... is wavering. I am not surprised'.[67]

Late in December 1844 (the preface in dated 23rd), Oakeley pub- lished a second edition of *The Subject of Tract XC*, which had first appeared in 1841. The text itself was essentially unrevised, but he added a new and topical preface. 'The aspect of affairs is changed; and accordingly, if the argument was worth anything when originally put forth, there seems every reason in the way of duty to individuals, and to the church of which I am a member, to repeat at what I feel a most eventful crisis, what was said originally under circumstances of comparative security'.[68]

Oakeley did not urge members of the university convocation to vote against resolutions 1 and 2, which he opposed on personal grounds, but on resolution 3, which had far wider implications. 'It is conceivable that many members of our church may object to the proposed restriction upon the sense of our articles (amounting, in fact to a new test, and that emanating from only one of the universities, without the previous sanction of the Church of England.)'[69] He assured his readers that he did not identify Ward's views with those of Tract 90, nor did he feel that a vote against the third resolution would carry publicly the implication of support for Ward.[70] They could safely vote against the third resolution without any anxiety that they might be seen as supporters for Ward. But he went further than the content of Tract 90 and used the preface as a means of expressing opinions which he freely admitted were his alone. 'The reflection and experience of the first three years which have elapsed since the publication of this essay have left me in full and confirmed possession of the opinion, that the view of the Thirty-Nine Articles for which I here plead, and upon which alone, I myself am able to subscribe them, is . . . consistent with the grammatical sense of their words'.[71] He reiterated his belief that he could hold 'all Roman Catholic doctrine, as distinct . . . from popular perversions of it, and . . . from the question of the papal jurisdiction',[72] while honestly subscribing the articles which had been framed in 'not a Catholic, nor a Protestant, but a vague, indecisive, and therefore comprehensive sense'.[73] 'Sufficiently Protestant in tone to satisfy the Reformers abroad, and sufficiently vague in expression to include the Catholics at home'.[74] He made the valid point that if the authorities of both university and Church allowed evangelicals to assent to the formularies of the Church of England, then 'these like myself are a fortiori at liberty to subscribe the articles in ours'.[75] The only difficulty that Oakeley had was not with those articles which concerned themselves with Roman doctrine or practices, but with those, such as articles 11, 12 and 13, dealing with justification and works, which 'appear to contravene the most elementary truths of all religion'.[76]

Oakeley's claim to hold, though not to teach, all Roman doctrine, which was to figure so prominently in the succeeding few months, is stated here for the first time. Although nominally an introduction to the

second edition of *The Subject of Tract XC*, it constitutes a manifesto of
Oakeley's position, brought about by a desire to make a public gesture
of loyalty to Ward. He did not feel himself justified in 'sheltering . . .
under the cover of supposed differences as to this matter of subscription from others who have been directly assailed',[77] and he threw down
the challenge in a statement which was as noble as it was foolish. 'I
have no wish to remain a member of the university, or a member of the
Church of England under false colours. I claim the right . . . of holding
(as distinct from teaching) all Roman doctrine, and that notwithstanding my subscription to the Thirty-Nine Articles. If this right be
questionable, I wish it to be discussed; if the question be determined in
the negative, whether by the university or by the Church of England
. . . I shall trust that I shall be prepared with my course'.[78] The
approaching crisis was 'the most momentous by far of any which has
arisen in our church since the Reformation',[79] and Oakeley was beginning to discern a providential plan in everything that had happened
since he made his personal commitment to the Tractarian movement.
He saw the forthcoming 'trial' of Ward as 'the ultimate issue of a series
of natural occurrences, and conscientious acts'.[80] Even Palmer's attack
on *The British Critic* was seen as a natural development from the last
issues of that journal, as Ward's *The Ideal of a Christian Church* was
from Palmer's *Narrative of Events*.[81] Oakeley was convinced that the
whole course of the Tractarian movement since the publication of Tract
1 in 1833 was nothing less than divine providence. The guiding hand of
Almighty God was behind every phase of the movement. 'Anything
more orderly, more unconstrained, less like precipitation on any side,
or politic manoeuvring, or party combination, or any of those accom-
plishments which imply a weak cause and denote a merely human
agency than the whole process of this wonderful reaction from the
publication of the first tract to the present developed state of the controversy, it is, I think, quite impossible to imagine . . . had it been of man,
it had come to naught long since'.[82]

Manning carefully read the second edition of *The Subject of Tract XC*
and wrote a lengthy letter to Oakeley attempting to disprove
his theory 'that Roman Catholics being and continuing such in doctrine
subscribed the Thirty-Nine Articles at the beginning of Queen
Elizabeth's reign',[83] This was a crucial point in Oakeley's historical
argument for the catholicity of the articles, and the basis of his claim
that it possible to hold all Roman doctrine and still subscribe the articles. Newman had argued in Tract 90 that it was possible to be a
Catholic without contravening the articles. Oakeley took this a stage
further and on the basis of very slender historical evidence, argued that
the articles had been framed with the deliberate intention of allowing

Roman Catholics to remain within the Church of England. Manning examined Oakeley's historical sources, which were no more than a few obscure references and comments by seventeenth century historians including Thomas Fuller (1608–61), Peter Heylyn (1600–62) and John Strype (1643–1737). Examining these references, Manning came to three conclusions and put them to Oakeley. Firstly, that Roman Catholics continued in the communion of the Church of England. Secondly, that they were harassed by the civil power, not for their religion but for their politics. Thirdly, that among those who held high ecclesiastical office in Queen Mary's reign were possibly some who subscribed in Queen Elizabeth's reign. 'I am not aware of any proof you have adduced which goes beyond these conclusions: which as it seems to me amount to no more than that these subscribers succumbed and complied with the Reformation. I can find no indication that Strype, Fuller or Heylyn understood or intended anything more than this'.[84] Manning produced additional evidence from the same historians to show that the non-complying Roman Catholics had been deprived in 1560, the year before the articles were proposed in convocation; and that since Roman Catholic colleges had been established abroad before 1571 for missionary work in England, the two churches were already in conflict on matters of doctrine. That there were those who held office in Queen Mary's reign and subscribed in Queen Elizabeth's, showed only that 'there was a large compliant body which yielded to the governing powers'.[85]

Oakeley thanked Manning for his letter 'which deserves my best attention and shall receive it with the least possible delay', regretting only that Manning had not published it. If his (Oakeley's) argument was unsound 'then I most sincerely wish it to be publicly exposed'.[86] Manning had easily demolished the rather flimsy basis of Oakeley's argument, and Oakeley was not in a position to dispute Manning's greater scholarship. He hedged a good deal saying that he had not got his books with him, and had 'only a very imperfect recollection of the proofs by which I satisfied myself at the time of the inquiry'.[87] Manning's objections 'evidently require to be very carefully considered'.[88] This sounds suspiciously as though Oakeley had found Manning's arguments to be incontrovertible but was unable to bring himself to admit the fact. After vaguely skirting around the issue, he produced what he hoped would be an unimpeachable fact in support of his case. He maintained his argument that the articles were framed with the intention of including Roman Catholics. 'If the articles were framed with a comprehensive object at all ... may they not have been meant to let in Roman Catholics? ... No one I suppose would deny that Abp Laud went further in Catholicism than Bp Ridley, the least Protestant of the Reformers. Do you not then prove too much in disproving that the inclusion of Roman Catholics was designed, for how then can you shew that it was intended to include such as Laud?'[89] Oakeley's sense of history has gone well astray here, unless he was clutching at straws. The Church of England was in a state of flux from the reign of King Henry VIII (1509–47) until the restoration of King Charles II in 1660, only settling down as an episcopal and established church in his reign. Laud typified the High Church party, but he was not in sympathy with Roman Catholics and cannot really be used as an example by Oakeley in defence of his claim.

Whatever Manning's arguments, and however authoritatively based they might be, nothing could shake Oakeley in his view that the Thirty-Nine Articles were compatible with all Roman doctrine, and he warned Manning that there were many 'who if the question of subscription in the Roman Catholic sense be determined in the negative, whether authoritatively or on grounds satisfactory to their own consciences, are prepared to part with the articles and not with Roman doctrine'.[90] Oakeley wrote of this group as though he were not a member of it, but there is no doubt that in January 1845 he considered himself among them. Manning obligingly reconsidered the matter to see if he could find any further evidence for Oakeley's claims, but without success. But in a gesture of humility he declared himself 'insufficiently versed in the history of the period'.[91] This was followed by an equally generous gesture from Oakeley who was prepared to admit that many of the Roman Catholics who subscribed the articles were 'low fellows'.[92]

Manning's thoughtful and polite response to *The Subject of Tract XC* was not matched by the pamphleteers who rushed into print denouncing Oakeley for his shortcomings. One critic described his tract as 'marked by meagre historical argument', though it showed 'infinite subtlety', and was 'perfectly frank'.[93] William Goode, Rector of the city of London Church of Saint Antholin, and later Dean of Ripon, was less kind. In a 191–page tract, he extended the arguments of Manning to show that Oakeley's position and argument were 'so utterly and manifestly untenable, that an argument for the purpose of opposing it seems almost like one for proving that two and two do not make five'.[94] Goode went to great lengths to demolish Oakeley's arguments that Anglican divines of former generations had accepted all Roman doctrine not withstanding their subscription of the articles. Oakeley had taken some trouble to dig up various seventeenth century divines, in particular Bishops Forbes, Andrewes and Montague, and Herbert Thorndike, who had held various 'high' doctrines of the Eucharist or the Church; and he quoted them as a precedent for his own new position. Goode denied that any divine of the Church of England could be found 'who publicly maintained without censure the view, that all Roman doctrine might be held consistently with subscription to the articles'.[95] Oakeley's claim was 'wholly unprecedented', and his 'attempts to make out anything like the shadow of a precedent for it were utterly fruitless'.[96] The condemnation of Roman errors by and in the articles was 'distinct and decisive' and the testimony of the divines of the Church of England to that fact 'overwhelming'.[97] Oakeley might well have produced three or four divines who subscribed the articles and taught certain Roman doctrines, but it was a long leap from these isolated and incomplete examples to the claim to hold all Roman doctrine. 'All manner of heresies might be defended in this way, for it is morally impossible that during a period of three centuries, the Church should be uniformly and ceaselessly preserved in such a state of purity that no errors could be found in the writings of her divines uncensured'.[98] Oakeley himself was indulging in 'evasion, equivocation, and misrepresentation';[99] and this was characteristic of the 'disingenuousness and Jesuitism'[100] of the Tractarian movement as a whole.

At the end of January 1845, Oakeley published an emotional little tract specifically directed at those members of convocation who, for whatever reason, had decided to take no part in the proceedings on 13 February. 'As I write at the last moment, I naturally write in a tone of apparent vehemence . . . when the fire has actually begun, and a crowd of people are seen standing with their arms folded, we cry out'.[101] 'All I desire is that you should ask yourselves as in the sight of God, whether you can justify the course which you purpose taking on the 13th'.[102] Ward was faced with a combined opposition of evangelicals, high churchmen and conservatives, and his case 'was not so powerful that it could do without support, nor so desperate that it was beyond help'.[103] But the balance or probability 'seems to incline rather to the losing side than the other'.[104] The propositions were so carefully worded as 'under cover of an attack upon an individual, to imply a reflection upon a certain mode of subscribing the articles'.[105] This would place in a very difficult position 'fifteen or twenty'[106] of his own friends and acquaintances, who were members of the university and shared Ward's views. 'Do you wish to force these persons out of the university and the Church of England?'[107] A number of opponents of Ward and Oakeley would have answered in the affirmative to this question, and Oakeley recognised this, at least implicitly, when he posed the question of whether it was right for such people to leave. But he carefully avoided the issue, and answered his own question by saying that he 'was really not prepared with an opinion'.[108] But he was sure that the adoption of neutrality or aloofness from the debate would leave Ward 'a prey to the combined fury of evangelicals, rationalists, indifferentists, and short-sighted churchmen'.[109] Those who proposed to adopt this course of non-involvement should realise that the propositions against Ward were measures 'which, though aimed at one whose work of character you possibly dislike, may affect others whose tone . . . you perhaps like better'.[110] Such people would be 'swept away, one by one, from university, Church of England, and all, if through your lukewarmness the Heads of Houses find now and hereafter that they have the majority of convocation on their side'.[111] If the vote went against Ward 'who knows where the Hebdomadal Board will proceed next'.[112]

Gladstone drafted a long letter to Oakeley, cautioning him that this latest publication would do much damage, but Oakeley would have none of it. 'People must begin to make up their minds upon many subjects which have never before taken a practical shape, and that calm forethought and decisive action (whatever way) are the best securities for a contented and thankful acceptance of the issues of conduct which are not in our hands. You will I know excuse this pompous enunciation of truisms'.[113]

Oakeley was right to worry about the formidable power of the Hebdomadal Board, but was inaccurate in thinking that the members had proceeded entirely on their own initiative. The Board had been 'earnestly exhorted'[114] to take action against Ward by Archbishop Whateley of Dublin.[115] R. W. Church, in his history of the Oxford Movement says that, 'as usual the Board entirely mistook the temper of the university, and by their violence and want of judgement turned the best chance they ever had, of carrying the university with them, into what their blunders really made an ignominious defeat'.[116] Their proposal to degrade Ward by stripping him of his degrees, instead of expelling him from the university, invited ridicule since it would leave him in the very contradictory position of being an undergraduate fellow. But it was the third resolution that aroused the most anger. 'The cry, almost the shriek, arose that it was a new test ... and a new test no one would have'.[117] Oakeley's old friend, Archibald Tait, now headmaster of Rugby School, published an indictment[118] of the third resolution. Oakeley, Ward and Tait had been fellows of Balliol together, and though they had long since parted company on the question of doctrine, especially at the time of Tract 90, they remained the best of friends. Tait took great exception to the proposed new test. 'There is no need of narrowing the limits of the Church of England because some amongst us wish to make it too wide'.[119] Pusey announced in an open letter that he would not under any circumstances take the new test.

On 22 January 1845, the Hebdomadal Board, realising that it had misjudged the general feelings of members of the university, withdrew the third resolution, only to issue on 25 January, a circular inviting signatures for a petition to the Board to propose a new third resolution, a censure of Tract 90. Some four to five hundred signatures were gathered within a few days and on 4 February, the Board, 'mad enough not to see, not merely the odiousness of the course, but the aggravated odiousness of hurry',[120] announced the new third resolution.

The great 'trial' of Ward was held on 13 February 1845 in the Sheldonian Theatre. The day was wet and snowing, but by 12 midday, some twelve hundred Masters of Arts with voting rights had crammed into the building. 'Instead of an imposing semicircle of placid dignitaries in rich academical costume, there appeared a forbidding phalanx of time-worn faces, flushed with excitement or wrinkled with discontent . . . their faces also bore the marks of sectarian bitterness or controversial anxiety, rather than that glow of festive joy . . . The weather was raw, the building was cold, and the whole appearance of the affair in the highest degree ungenial'.[121] Newman was absent, but Pusey, Manning, Gladstone, Tait and Hope were there. The fellows of Balliol stood together, unanimous in their support for Ward, and in a touching gesture of solidarity with his friend, next to Ward on the rostrum, stood Frederick Oakeley.

During the preliminary period before he was called to speak, Ward, in a remarkable display of nonchalance, was observed by those sitting behind him, reading love letters from his future wife'.[122] He was given leave to address convocation in English, and he spoke for more than an hour, with Oakeley at his side. There were no other speeches before the votes were taken. The first vote, condemning *The Ideal of a Christian Church*, was carried by 777 votes to 386.[123] The second resolution, to deprive Ward of his degrees, was carried by the much smaller margin of 569 votes to 511. When the vice-chancellor rose to put the third resolution, the university proctors, H. P. Guillemard of Trinity College, and R. W. Church of Balliol College, exercised their right of veto, and no vote was taken. Church had no regrets about their decision. 'The university has committed itself to measures which, whatever Ward has said, are flagrantly disproportionate to his offence . . . The only thing to relieve the day has been the extreme satisfaction I had in helping to veto the third iniquitous measure against Newman. It was worthwhile being proctor to have had the unmixed pleasure of doing this'.[124]

The proctors held office for one year only, and Guillemard and Church were almost at the end of their term of office. With the

installation of their successors, attempts were made to revive the resolution and submit it to another meeting of convocation, but this time
wisdom prevailed on the Hebdomadal Board. 'This was the last act of
a long and deliberately pursued course of conduct; and if it was the last,
it was because it was the upshot and climax, and neither the university
nor anyone else would endure that it should go on any longer'.[125]

There the matter might have ended. Newman was living quietly at
Littlemore, pursuing his own theological development away from the
hectic activity of the city. He was not present at the Sheldonian Theatre
for the votes, though he subsequently wrote to Guillemard and Church
thanking them for their action. Pusey had achieved his desire to see off
the third resolution, believing that an official condemnation of Tract 90
would precipitate Newman's secession. He suggested to Gladstone that
he might like to use his influence in asking the Archbishop of
Canterbury to dissuade the Board from any further action. 'There
seems a general impression that the Heads are becoming more pacific
and that a renewed requisition against us will be a failure ... Your
communications with the Board and your name have done us good
service'.[126] Gladstone was similarly anxious for peace and quiet. 'I
concur with my whole heart and soul in the desire for repose: and I
fully believe that the gift of an interval for reflection is that which
would be of all gifts the most precious to us all, which could restore the
faculty of deliberation now almost lost in storms'.[127]

Gladstone's hope for a period of quiet was not to be realised.
Oakeley had firmly nailed his colours to the mast of Ward, and for
him, unlike most other Tractarians, the defeat of the third resolution
was not enough. The condemnation of Ward deeply affected Oakeley
who resolved, as he had said to Pusey on 21 December 1844, 'to let
the world know that the same arrow which hits Ward grazes another
... it is fair and proper to let them know exactly what they are
doing'.[128]

Chapter Ten

Throwing down the gauntlet

FREDERICK OAKELEY V. THE BISHOP OF LONDON

After the fullest and most careful consideration of your recently
published Letter, and of the statements which you made to me yester-
day; I am forced to the painful conclusion that it is not consistent with
my duty to sanction any longer your officiating in my diocese.
Charles James Blomfield to Frederick Oakeley, 19 February 1845

Oakeley was not slow to act, as a member of his congregation remembered many years later. 'We saw Mr Oakeley return to Margaret Street,
knowing that there was thunder in the air'.[1] While Ward's other friends
and colleagues were commiserating with him in his state of degradation,
Oakeley had taken on the role of Elisha and cast around his own shoulders the mantle of Elijah laid down by Ward. In the twenty-four hours
following the events in the Sheldonian Theatre, Oakeley wrote and
published an open letter to the vice-chancellor of the university, 'not
precipitately, nor on the spur of the moment, but undoubtedly after a
day of the most absorbing interest, and in the midst of a most exciting
confusion'.[2] The letter was written with a view of 'clearing my position
with the university',[3] and was certainly precipitate. Oakeley reminded
the vice-chancellor that he had sent him a copy of *The Subject of Tract
XC* some six weeks previously, stating his claims contained therein to
hold though not to teach all Roman doctrine, 'and here, with the same
deliberation and distinction, I again appropriate and repeat them'.[4]

In condemning *The Ideal of a Christian Church*, Oakeley declared
that convocation had condemned 'a statement on subscription, tanta-
mount in substance to the above',[5] and he felt impelled clearly to
reassert his attitude to the vote, and his own claim on subscription.
The vote had been a blanket condemnation of the whole book, but
since only certain extracts from the book had been formally read out

to convocation, Oakeley took the negative vote to be no more than the expression of 'a certain opinion upon a series of extracts'[6] from the book. These extracts comprised a variety of statements which Oakeley felt no need either to affirm or to deny except on the single question of subscription to the Thirty-Nine Articles. On this ground he took his stand, and by a twisted piece of casuistry, he managed to demonstrate that convocation had not really condemned this view of subscription at all. The condemnation of Ward's statement of subscription was only part of a common condemnation of a variety of extracts. In the minds of the proposers and supporters of the propositions, were all the extracts considered to be at variance with the good faith of the author's subscription, or only some of them, and if only some, then which ones? Convocation had condemned Ward's manner of subscription only in relation to certain selected passages. Oakeley neither claimed nor disclaimed to hold the other sentiments expressed in these passages, and separated in his own mind, the question of subscription from everything else. Convocation had not, in fact, condemned anything. It had merely expressed an opinion. He had received the Articles at the hands of the university which was 'no more than an organ and representative of the Church of England'.[7] Since the Church of England had 'no where declared against the sense in which I claim to subscribe to them, I accept them under no other limitations than those which are imposed by my own conscientious belief of their grammatical meaning, and the intention with which they were at first put out, and are now proposed to me by the church of which I am a member'.[8]

He then issued a challenge which the vice-chancellor could not afford to ignore. 'If, in the judgement of the Board over which you preside and of the house of convocation, I have rendered myself liable to penalty by the declarations above cited, I am anxious "not to shelter myself (as I say in my pamphlet) under the cover of supposed differences as to this matter of subscription from others who have been directly assailed".'[9] If no action was taken by the university after such a plain and public declaration, 'I shall regard such acquiescence as equivalent to an admission on my part of the academical authorities that my own subscription to the Thirty-Nine Articles is not at variance with good faith'.[10]

Oakeley had thrown down his gauntlet, and challenged the vice-chancellor to do his worst. The reaction to the letter was a mixture of anger, anxiety, astonishment and sympathy, all overlaying a feeling that perhaps it was not all together surprising considering Oakeley's loyalty to his friend – and his propensity for making bold gestures and statements. Newman asked Ward to convey his kind regards to

Oakeley. 'I feel very much for him just now – but I have little or nothing which could be put into words'.[11] Keble described Oakeley's letter as 'imprudent' and 'unnecessarily frank'.[12] Gladstone was most hurt by the move since he had thought that Oakeley was the kind of person who, though of extreme opinions, was capable of containing them out of gentleness and consideration for the peace of the Church. 'Yet he has just published, as I perceive with great pain, a challenge to the academical authorities, founded on the votes against Mr Ward'.[13] Gladstone had just witnessed the disintegration of his hopes for a period of peace and quiet. The *English Churchman* described the letter as 'aggravating'. 'Mr Oakeley ... invokes fresh penal measures on himself, informing the academical authorities that he shall regard their omission to prosecute as an admission of principle which nobody doubts it was the object of this later vote most strongly to disclaim. The proceedings appear to us unreal; for no man, merely by saying so, can really impose a construction upon another's silence; and unwise, as provoking enemies to fresh violence, and irritating friends by appearing to seek a quarrel'.[14]

All that could be done now was to wait and see how the Hebdomadal Board would respond. Any moves against Oakeley would be on foundations less secure than those against Ward. There could be no question of reintroducing the third proposition which had been vetoed with relish by the proctors amid scenes of evident rejoicing, and using that as a move against Oakeley. Oakeley had written no great work such as *The Ideal of a Christian Church* which could be examined in detail and condemned. One brief letter to the vice-chancellor was insufficient ground for the university to recall convocation and use it to censure Oakeley. Besides, Oakeley was not in the same position of subordination as Ward, who was a resident teaching Fellow. Oakeley, although still a Fellow of Balliol, and retaining his rooms in college, was resident in London for most of the year. It was difficult to see what disciplinary or punitive measures could successfully be taken against him. The second proposition, to deprive the bombastic Ward of his degrees, had passed by the slender majority of only fifty-eight votes. A similar vote against the kind and gentle figure of Frederick Oakeley, on less certain ground, was less likely to succeed. Could the vice-chancellor and the board really risk another emotional and divisive storm in the Sheldonian Theatre so soon after the last, and with the possibility of being defeated on the final vote? Yet if they took no action, as Oakeley had stated, such a course could well be taken as a sign of acquiescence in the manner of his subscription.

Oakeley himself thought it 'very improbable that the university would strike a second blow in the same direction',[15] and its refusal to act 'would reflect the character of self-stultification upon its former proceeding',[16] Clearly the board had to do something or it would be seen as making a humiliating climb down by their inaction.

In the light of subsequent developments, Oakeley believed that the board, desiring to do something, yet not anxious to become closely involved, resolved to hand the matter over to the Bishop of London; their excuse being that Oakeley was resident in London, not in Oxford, and therefore that the onus to take action rested with the Bishop of London'.[17] Bishop Charles James Blomfield himself contradicted this on 4 March 1845, when he issued a formal statement from London House stating that there was 'no foundation for the report that the bishop has received a communication from the Vice-Chancellor of Oxford on the subject of the letter addressed to the vice-chancellor by Mr Oakeley'.[18] Either Oakeley was mistaken, or Blomfield was lying, but it is now impossible to discover who is telling the truth. There is nothing in the minutes of the meeting of the Hebdomadal Board, or in any correspondence in the university archives to justify Oakeley's contention. But since the official records are so sparse, it cannot be stated categorically that no decision was made in university circles to hand the matter over to the bishop of London. It may be that the Hebdomadal Board did urge Bishop Blomfield to act, but that the bishop did not wish to be seen to be exercising his authority at the behest of the university. A more likely explanation is that he did not wish to take any action at all, and when forced to some days later, by further developments, wished to conceal the fact that he had initially refrained from taking action. Oakeley believed this last possibility to be the truth; that the bishop had initially declined to take action because 'if I were not amenable to the authority of the university so neither was I to that of my diocesan'.[19] Again, according to Oakeley, Blomfield passed the matter back to the university with the excuse that although Oakeley was resident in London, the letter had been published in Oxford and addressed to the vice-chancellor, and not in the diocese of London. Therefore the matter did not fall within his jurisdiction.[20] This is not entirely accurate since the letter, published in Oxford on Friday 14 February, was also published in London on Saturday 15 February.

On Monday 17 February, Oakeley received a note summoning him to appear at London House in St James's Square for a meeting with the bishop on the morning of Tuesday 18 February. At their meeting, Blomfield told Oakeley that he had received no communication from Oxford,[21] but that he took a serious view of the affair, and appears to have indicated that he would have to take some kind of action'.[22] Oakeley replied by putting up a strong defence of his letter to the vice-chancellor. The two men parted on kindly terms, and Oakeley left the meeting believing that Blomfield had not decided on any specific course of action, and he promised the bishop that he would keep their discussion secret'.[23] 'I had thus a fair chance of getting clear off between two fierce but innocuous fires. but my good angel, or as my friends would rather have said, my evil genius, prompted me to take a course of action which brought me at once within the power of my diocesan'.[24]

Almost as soon as he returned to Margaret Street, Oakeley started work on an open letter to Blomfield, expanding his open letter to the vice-chancellor, and adding new material here and there, in an attempt to soothe the bishop. He spent twenty-four hours working on the pamphlet, sending it to a printer on the afternoon of Wednesday 19 February. About two hours after the printer had received it, Oakeley received a request from the bishop to resign his licence immediately. Either Oakeley had completely misread the bishop's intentions, of Blomfield had got wind of the fact that Oakeley was to issue a new challenge.

The mystery is why Oakeley should promise to keep the whole matter out of the public gaze, and then immediately start work on a public letter; it seems as though he wanted a public fight, and conducting a debate with his diocesan bishop by means of the printing press was a sure guarantee that he would get what he wanted. If the university would not respond to a fairly mild letter, then his position must be stated with greater clarity and firmness to his diocesan bishop. The result was that Blomfield was manoeuvred into a position in which he had little choice but to respond to an open, longer and more controversial letter, addressed to himself, but for public consumption.

Oakeley reiterated his belief that if no course of action were taken against him, he would be justified in maintaining his position 'without even the suspicion of dishonesty and disingenuousness',[25] and thus far the Hebdomadal Board had taken no action against him. He felt obliged to issue a formal statement addressed to the bishop, because he ministered in Blomfield's diocese, and held the bishop's licence to do so, and he wished to clear the bishop's mind of 'the suspicion of wantonness or undutifulness',[26] by explaining his position. This, of course, he could have done by means of a private and confidential letter. He had never taught Roman doctrine 'in my public ministrations',[27] and he had no intention of doing so. 'My flock never so much as hear a (characteristically) Roman doctrine from my lips ... I very much doubt whether twenty members of my congregation or one poor person in my district (except Roman Catholics) know even what Roman Catholic doctrine is'.[28] Oakeley declared that he had always refrained from any course of teaching which might offend his incumbent,[29] and he had never sought to convert anyone to the Roman Catholic Church. 'If I see anyone disposed to join the Church of Rome, my arguments with such a one are always in arrest generally even in contravention of that step'.[30] But his public declaration now precluded him from preaching against Roman doctrine, and if he was under any obligation to do so, 'then I freely admit that I do not fulfil these obligations'.[31]

Oakeley touched briefly on church history in support of this, by saying that he believed the articles to be, if not in harmony, at least not in discordance, with the decisions of the Council of Trent,[32] and he was not surprised that the efforts of Tract 90 'to bring the Thirty-Nine Articles into somewhat of harmony with the decisions of the church universal'[33] had been greeted with enthusiasm. He warned against 'the exceeding dangers of a slothful and grovelling acquiescence in our actual position, and of an attempt to sustain ourselves in it at whatever sacrifice of consistency and acute conscientiousness'.

There is one reference to Oakeley's dissatisfaction with the Church of England, and it deals with the mode of interpretation of the Thirty-Nine Articles. Although he was quite convinced that the vagueness of the articles was intended to allow for the inclusion of Roman Catholics and therefore did not prohibit the holding of all Roman doctrine, he had begun to realise that this vagueness could accommodate other extremes of belief, and that nobody in the Church of England was empowered to make any authoritative pronouncement on just how wide the articles were intended to be. It was the first indication of his worry about the lack of coherence and authority in the Church. 'All I suppose will agree that the articles have a meaning; and yet they are actually subscribed in almost every conceivable variety of sense'.[35] 'Some authoritative imposer and interpreter of the articles surely there must be in our Church. Yet it seems easier to say where that authority does not, than where it does, reside'.[36]

Justifying his work at Margaret Chapel which, he said, had always been performed with due regard for the feelings of the bishop, Oakeley summed up his feelings that the Church of England was 'on the very brink of a momentous, though it may not be a sudden and conspicuous, crisis . . . it is of the nature of what is commonly called a 'presentiment', and therefore incapable of being colourably substantiated'.[37] The recent events at Oxford were not among the most alarming signs of the times because the decisions of Convocation 'are now generally admitted to be quite devoid of any other weight than that which they may possess, as declaring of opinion, on the part of a respectable but motley body of voters'.[38] 'The university of Oxford has entered upon a course of aggression; let it find some way of following up its step with safety, or retracting it with credit'.[39] The affair at Oxford did not worry Oakeley. He was more concerned with the involvement of what he called the 'authorities' of the Church of England on the side of the university, which would render the situation personally more difficult. Then came the explicit appeal to Blomfield. 'Pause, my lord, I implore you, pause, before you snap one binding tie, break up one compact system, dislodge one needful element, in the existing Church of England. It subsists by a balance; it is kept in its orbit through the operation of rival and conflicting influences. If we tamper with a body of such delicate structure and such heterogeneous materials . . . my own deep and deliberate apprehension is that it will break up, and its dissociated parts fly away in obedience to some powerful attraction . . . My lord, I will say no more, and perhaps, already, I have said more than my relative situation warrants'.[40]

A reading of *A letter to the Lord Bishop of London* leads the reader to agree with Oakeley; he had said far too much. If he felt as strongly as he seems to have done, then a letter containing these sentiments would have been better hand-written and marked 'private and confidential' than what amounts to a published personal manifesto. Had he used that procedure, or better still done nothing at all, he had a very good chance of avoiding any penalty either from the university of from the bishop of London. But he persisted in drawing attention to himself by publishing this letter to Blomfield and personally haranguing the bishop at the end of it. His behaviour was quite reckless to anyone with a sense of caution and deliberation. But caution and deliberation were not Oakeley's ways of working. His openness about the development of his own opinions was innocent to the point of naïvety; almost with the assumption that no one would condemn him for being honest about the struggles that were taking place in his own mind. Innocence is one strand; recklessness is the other, and here we see the influence of Ward. The two men had been close friends for about six years. Ward was a noisy and vibrant individual who aroused strong emotions, either one way or another, in everyone who met him. Ward's method of propagating the Catholic faith within the Church of England was to shout his latest conclusions from the housetops, a habit which Oakeley acquired, starting with the publication of *Bishop Jewel* in July 1841. In publishing *A letter to the Lord Bishop of London*, Oakeley had forced Blomfield's hand. He had stated his position and publicly requested that the bishop do nothing about it for fear of disturbing the equilibrium of the Church of England. To Blomfield, it was Oakeley who had disturbed the equilibrium of the Church of England since 1841; and there was nothing he could do except take action, and swiftly.

On Wednesday 19 February, two hours after Oakeley had sent *A letter to the Lord Bishop of London* to the printer, without sending a copy to the bishop, Blomfield sent a message to Oakeley asking him to resign his licence immediately. According to Oakeley's account of the day, Blomfield's message made no reference to the impending open letter addressed to himself, referring only to the letter addressed to the vice-chancellor, and to their conversation on Tuesday 18 February. It is possible, though it cannot be proved, that somehow Blomfield discovered the contents of Oakeley's forthcoming letter before it went to press and decided to use the maximum penalty at his disposal. The other possibility is that further pressure had come from Oxford in the twenty-four hours following the bishop's meeting with Oakeley. According to Oakeley, the two men had parted on kindly terms, Oakeley leaving with the impression that the bishop had not decided on any definite course of action. Something caused Blomfield to impose the ultimate penalty on Oakeley. His letter conveys a note of personal sadness and reluctance at having to take such a decision. 'After the fullest and most careful consideration of your recently published Letter, and of the statements which you made to me yesterday; I am forced to the painful conclusion that it is not consistent with my duty to sanction any longer your officiating in my diocese'.[41] Blomfield told Oakeley that he could not express 'how deeply I am grieved 'at being compelled to take such a step . . . and to lose for a portion of my diocese, the benefit which would result from piety and zeal and talent such as yours, if employed in driving away, instead of upholding erroneous and strange doctrine'.[42] Blomfield added his personal hope that Oakeley would be guided by the Holy Spirit and soon come to see his 'dangerous error', with the implication that the door was being left open for him to retract his statements, and remain in position at Margaret Chapel.

Oakeley asked for five days in which to consider his position, offering in the meantime to abstain from officiating in the chapel.[43] The bishop agreed to wait until Tuesday 25 February for a final answer.[44] During the following days, Oakeley took advice from his friends on how to proceed. Gladstone offered to go and see Blomfield, if he could take with him an assurance from Oakeley that he would withdraw his letter to the vice-chancellor, though not *A letter to the Lord Bishop of London*, of which no mention was to be made. Oakeley asked him to wait since others among his friends had told him that the bishop might be persuaded to withdraw his request without Oakeley's withdrawal of the letter to the vice-chancellor. 'I am most unwilling to write again to the vice-chancellor . . .

Therefore, supposing you not to feel you could use the *other* arguments with the bishop, it might better if you would defer your visit to him to a later day to give time for different negotiations'.[45]

By Friday 21 February, after a conversation with Gladstone, Oakeley had come to 'the full and deliberate conviction that I ought not under any circumstances to withdraw or modify my letter to the vice-chancellor which was indeed . . . so carefully worded that I was unwilling to suppose it likely I could be so duty bound to retract it and yet . . . you . . . certainly induced me for a while to waver'.[46] On the evening of the same day, Gladstone talked to Edward Bellasis, and proposed sending a personal letter to Blomfield, with a copy to Oakeley. Bellasis advised against letting Oakeley know what was intended because 'he wishes not to be cognisant of it (i.e. the help of his friends) at present, so far as relates to any communication with the bishop'.[47]

Gladstone wrote to Blomfield on Monday 24 February, the day before Oakeley was due to give a final answer to the bishop. Prudently, he made no attempt to support Oakeley's claim to hold all Roman doctrine, concentrating entirely on his spiritual and pastoral gifts. 'I can scarcely exaggerate the debt which seems to me to be due to Mr Oakeley as a restorer of the inward life and spirit of divine worship among us . . . Mr Oakeley's personal character, and the tone which has been imparted to the administration of divine ordinances in the chapel, and the hold he has established by these means upon the respect, gratitude, and attachment, of many persons not agreeing in his views of Roman doctrine, appear to me to form a subject so real and important . . . that it ought to be placed separately before your lordship as one at least among many elements of the case'.[48]

Support him as his friends might against the bishop, most of them, like Gladstone, were not prepared to support his position on Roman doctrine. In a long and rather sad letter to Pusey, Oakeley showed his sorrow at having to stand alone on his cherished belief. 'It is no small addition to so heavy a blow as that which awaits me, that none of my friends should have expressed themselves strongly upon the act which is the alleged and ostensible reason for it'.[49] In a fit of despair, Oakeley took the view that there was no chance of saving Margaret Chapel, and ascribed the origin of the movement against it, not to Blomfield, but to the machinations of George Chandler, the rector of the parish. This cannot be proved or disproved, since Chandler's personal papers have not survived. H. P. Liddon, Pusey's biographer, was certain that Blomfield acted at Chandler's behest,[50] but there is slight evidence that Chandler had some sympathy for Oakeley, and may have written an obliquely supportive letter to Blomfield. 'I thank you for sending me the copy of your correspon-

dent's letter. It has not at all affected my views of the question . . .
My course is clear, though painful, I lament that it has been forced
upon me by Mr Oakeley's public declaration'.[51] As Dean of
Chichester, Chandler was a close acquaintance of Manning, and
did his best to influence and guide the anti-Tractarian Bishop
Shuttleworth of Chichester towards seeing Manning in a more
favourable light. Chandler adopted a cautious attitude towards the
Tractarians, but took a keen interest in the work of the Cambridge
Camden Society. He became vice-president of its successor, the
Ecclesiological Society, at its inaugural meeting held in the All Souls
schoolroom.[52] He had been present at the trial of Ward in the
Sheldonian Theatre, and was the first to shake hands with the proctors after their veto of the third proposition.[53] S. F. Wood described
him as 'your round-headed little dean, rubbing his hands pleasantly,
promises everything, but does nothing'.[54] In his conversations with
the bishop, Oakeley claimed that Blomfield had told him that he was
not acting in response to a request from the vice-chancellor, and had
no wish to take action'.[55] He accepted this and took the line that the
bishop had been put up to it by others; thereafter Chandler became
the sinister figure behind the campaign against him.

The theme running through this flurry of correspondence in the
few days after the trial of Ward, is Oakeley's letter to the vice-chancellor. Both Gladstone and Pusey urged Oakeley to modify or better
still withdraw the letter. It had started the trouble, and if Oakeley
made a public retraction, the situation would not get any worse and
the status quo might be restored. Presumably they worked on the
assumption that the withdrawal of the letter to the vice-chancellor
would imply a withdrawal of the letter to the bishop, and a separate
retraction of that letter would be unnecessary. But Oakeley was in no
mood to compromise. He had decided that '*under no circumstances
whatever*'[56] would he withdraw either letter, and he was sure that he
was pursuing the right course. 'Every day, nay every hour adds to
the comfort and clearness of view with which I have been so wonderfully blessed . . . I am not more overpoweringly satisfied that things
are critical than I am also satisfied that the position I am "in" is
right, and even a hopeful one, even upon these principles of duty to
our own Church which it really must be plain that I recognise and
cling to'.[57] Unfortunately, Oakeley's opponents were not quite so
sure that this was what he was doing. He indignantly denied that he
had any intention of becoming a Roman Catholic, but revealed that
the departure of George Tickell had tempted him to follow, a temptation
he had resisted at the expense of his own peace of mind. 'Can it
be supposed by anyone who knows the circumstances that the rupture

of the tie with my dear Tickell can [be] otherwise than a strong temptation? Has it been a small trial to have been receiving the most
affectionate yet the most urgent letters from him these three months,
and to have to answer these letters only by maintaining firmly . . . my
actual position? Has my [time] at Margaret Chapel been ever affected
by the circumstances of losing the very flower and hope of my flock
in him? . . . Of course I cannot say all this to the public; it would be
simply be misconstrued.[58]

This is almost the only glimpse that Oakeley allows the outside into
the relationships that existed in the small community in Margaret
Street. It goes a long way towards explaining the agonising so evident
in *Reasons for not joining the Romish communion*, and reinforces the
view that Oakeley's attachment to the Church of England, even at
this late stage, was still firm and sincere. Those who accused him of
waiting only for the right moment to take the step that, mentally and
theologically, he had already taken, were doing him an injustice.
There was a small egotistical streak in Oakeley that was affronted
by Tickell's precipitate action, and Oakeley told Pusey that those
who attacked his letter to the vice-chancellor failed to realise 'that I
myself am, from circumstances, a *very* essential part of the situation
here', or 'the consequences of my being divested of all the work, and
prospect of work in the Church of England'.[59]

The lack of support for his distinctive position on subscription
caused Oakeley a certain amount of depression in the days following
the publication of his letters to the vice-chancellor and the bishop,
and he used Pusey almost as a confessor, to take the weight of events
off his own mind. 'I am moaning on all about myself. Do not
answer, please, but think over what I say and never mind expressing
agreement or disagreement'.[60] On Monday 24 February, the day
before he was due to send his final answer to the bishop, Oakeley
wrote to Pusey again, stating that he was now absolutely sure that
Chandler was intent on seeing the destruction of Margaret Chapel as
a centre of worship within his parish. Blomfield was entirely innocent
of any responsibility for the course of action he had apparently initiated, being guided instead by the sinister influence of the Dean of
Chichester. 'It appears that, while the dean has been giving me
complimentary assurances, my position here has been hanging by a
thread since last autumn . . . And now my conviction is that the
B[ishop] will and must give way, unless the D[ean] keeps him up to
it, and threatens (which I think is not unlikely) to resign if I am not
ousted'.[61]

The truth of this must be a matter for speculation. Oakeley admitted,
rather darkly, that he could not give any reasons for this suspicion, and

asked Pusey to take it on trust. 'I speak of *impressions* only'.[62] He told Pusey of his intention to publish another open letter to the bishop, 'which *I have no doubt will move him*',[63] and then painted a most uncharacteristic picture of Blomfield. 'He trembles and seems confused when the subject of M[argaret] C[hapel] is broached; he is fearful it will break up (he told me) and he finds the case of W. B. Noel[64] an insurmountable difficulty. He told me Margaret Chapel was getting too strong for him through the affections of the people, and must be broken up, now, or never'.[65] Blomfield was something of a waverer, both in churchmanship and politics, but Oakeley's description portrays the bishop as a man who has almost lost his nerve and control of the situation.

Oakeley urged Pusey to gather together a sufficient number of friends and supporters who would jointly voice their support for him to the bishop. Chandler should be ignored and circumvented, '(*for we must not treat the dean*, you know, *as* the mover). I doubt not it would tell powerfully'.[66] More importantly, exertions should be made for Oakeley himself and not solely for Margaret Chapel. Chandler was spreading the rumour that if Oakeley were removed, Margaret Chapel could continue under William Upton Richards, Oakeley's assistant, or under someone else. Oakeley regarded this as a ploy by Chandler to separate him from the support of his congregation. His ultimate aim, so Oakeley believed, was to suppress the chapel as an independent sphere of activity within his parish. 'The dean's idea is to prevent a *crash*, but to let it drop by degrees and melt into the parochial system'.[67]

Pusey took these accusations seriously and asked Chandler whether he was in a position to stop the proceedings before they reached a point of no return. Chandler replied that he was 'deeply, deeply grieved about the affair of Oakeley. And you may depend upon it that whatever is in my *power* to avert, or to stem, the consequences shall be done'.[68] He denied being anxious to bring the matter to a crisis, though he was sure a crisis would come as a result of the letter to the vice-chancellor which was 'ill-advised, and, in my opinion, uncalled-for'.[69] He had no power to intervene on Oakeley's behalf and was distressed to find 'by many applications that are made to me, that I am supposed to have more authority in this question than I really [have]'.[70]

Oakeley was now sure that his letter to the vice-chancellor was no longer the prime object under attack. The future of Margaret Chapel was all important, and it was under serious attack. Oakeley was determined to defend it at all costs. Divine providence and a personal resolve to fight with or without help, were Oakeley's standards, combined with the belief that he was heading for symbolic and heroic martyrdom. 'If I am sacrificed, the great points are gained . . . If I sink tomorrow, feeling has yet been rallied round me in a way which must do good. *But I shall not sink*, if people elsewhere will give me a helping hand as they are doing here'.[71]

Apart from the help of Pusey and Gladstone, the entire congregation of the chapel presented an address to the bishop in support of their priest, pointing out that Oakeley, 'partly by the mode of conducting the services, partly by the uncontroversial and practical tone of his teaching, and partly by his kindness and sympathy . . . has collected around him a body of persons of various grades of opinion, who all hold him in high estimation . . . we have never heard any doctrines inculcated which we have any reason to believe your lordship would have disapproved, and that we thoroughly believe that the influence exercised by Mr Oakeley . . . has always been exercised for good, and in restraining from extreme conclusions'. His departure would 'have very injurious effect' and 'produce the utmost distress and perplexity'; and the discontinuance of the chapel services in their present form 'will be a serious privation to us all'.[72]

Either on Monday 24 February or on Tuesday 25 February,[73] Oakeley printed a second open letter to the bishop. The words 'NOT PUBLISHED' appear at the foot of the title page, suggesting that it might not have been so widely distributed as the first letter. Poor Oakeley should have learned, especially at such a sensitive time with his future in the diocese of London in the balance, that conducting correspondence with his diocesan bishop, by way of the printing press and the public, was not a course of action guaranteed to produce the desired result; it could only compound his errors in the eyes of the bishop. Nevertheless, according to Oakeley, the bishop had been equally guilt of indiscretion, and he began *A second letter to the Lord Bishop of London* by accusing Blomfield of gossiping about his decision to revoke Oakeley's licence, and using this as 'abundant justification of this second public appeal to you'.[74]

Oakeley admitted Blomfield's canonical right to terminate his connection with the diocese of London, simply by revoking his licence. As a priest in charge of a proprietary chapel, Oakeley had none of the security enjoyed by an incumbent. He held his position by licence from the bishop which could be withdrawn at any time, without notice. But Oakeley was determined to go on the offensive by challenging Blomfield's decision. What did the bishop think that he was trying to achieve? Was he trying to remove him solely for contumacy? Was he trying to make a statement about the tenability of Oakeley's position within the Church of England in respect of his subscription to the articles? Oakeley reminded the bishop that he was also a prebendary of Lichfield Cathedral, and 'my connection with the chapter of Lichfield is of a less easily dissoluble nature'.[75] If he were to be forced out of the diocese of London, 'it would be competent to me to carry on the question into a new sphere, with a view to its being eventually determined before some competent tribunal, in which its merits would not be summarily disposed of, but discussed with a full regard to the various theological and historical bearings of a very complicated, as well as most important subject'.[76] He did not wish to pursue this course but reminded the bishop that it was open to him. 'My lord, my natural temper is not towards strife, but towards submission'.[77] Perhaps in quieter times this was true, but given the turmoil of February 1845, it has a hollow sound.

Oakeley's second point about the tenability of his position being determined by some competent tribunal was valid, considering that Blomfield had given no reason for revoking his licence. If Blomfield was, by implication, punishing Oakeley for his position on subscription to the articles, then he should say so, and action should be taken against other 'extreme' priests in the diocese, notably W. B. Noel. If Oakeley was to be punished then the bishop would be less than just if he failed to take commensurate action against Noel. Among those who warned Blomfield to pursue a visibly impartial course was Sir John Coleridge[78] who 'told him plainly that although he did not agree with Oakeley, yet that an interference with an extreme person on one side, without interfering with extreme persons on the other, was a position he could not support; that if Oakeley went, Baptist Noel . . . must go likewise'.[79]

Oakeley does not mention Noel by name, but he was a well-known figure in London at the time, and he is probably the person that Oakeley is referring to in the following passage. 'I know that I am what is called an 'extreme person' myself and that distinguished clergyman is also a very extreme person in the opposite direction. I have no doubt that distinguished clergyman considers that such as myself hold most dangerous and anti-Christian doctrine; and this is just what I feel of him and his friends'.[80] If something was to be removed from one end, then something would have to be removed from the other to restore the equilibrium.[81]

Oakeley suggested to Blomfield that there was cogent argument for maintaining the status quo at Margaret Chapel, namely the steady restraining influence it exercised on those who might be persuaded to go to Rome. The chapel and its ministry had become indispensable to a large number of people, and should it be changed in any way, or even closed, there would be 'an immediate movement into the Church of

Rome'.[82] Oakeley quoted three letters from members of his congregation who were distraught at the prospect of losing the chapel.[83] 'I care not how efficient might be the ministrations my successor, and I can conceive that they might be highly efficient; still, no matter how worthy the successor, and how unworthy the predecessor, down, as I much fear, the chapel will go'.[84] The catholic practices would be discontinued one by one, in response to the further demands of those who had clamoured for Oakeley's dismissal, and before long it would dwindle away to nothing. Oakeley added, in a somewhat threatening tone, that even if he were to be dismissed, 'I have no present intention of leaving London, and should so remain in the immediate neighbourhood of the chapel . . . A more unhappy position for my successor I can hardly imagine'.[85]

After a review of the events of the days since Ward's trial on 13 February, Oakeley concluded that he could not, under existing circumstances, voluntarily resign his licence, since it would be understood, wrongly, to imply an acknowledgement of error. 'My lord, it is absolutely necessary, for the sake of my position in the Church of England, that the termination of my connection with this diocese should be your lordship's spontaneous act'.[86] He urged the bishop to take 'a somewhat fuller consideration of my case', since he [Blomfield] was about to perform an act 'which will damage my character as a clergyman of the Church of England for ever'.[87] The bishop had give no full explanation of why he was revoking Oakeley's licence, beyond a reference to the letter to the vice-chancellor, and though a formal explanation was not necessary, he could not conceive that the bishop would refuse his request.[88]

The bishop had taken an important decision, and Oakeley produced a lucid argument to demonstrate that Blomfield was on very uncertain ground. In fact the argument is so well-presented as to make one wonder if it originated not with Oakeley, but with Bellasis, Hope, Coleridge and other Tractarian lawyers in London. The argument runs as follows. By revoking Oakeley's licence to officiate in the diocese of London, Blomfield, by implication, was stating that Oakeley was guilty of a serious misdemeanour. Was this misdemeanour Oakeley's claim to hold all Roman doctrine while subscribing the Articles? If it was, then was Blomfield claiming, as only one bishop among many, the right to pass judgement on such a claim, and rule it inadmissible? If he was, then was he quite sure that he sufficient authority so to rule? If the bishop was not making such a claim, could he then say 'who is the formal imposer and interpreter of the Thirty-Nine Articles? Or whether there be any such imposer or interpreter, or any authorised sense in which they are to be subscribed?'[89] The thrust of the argument was that Blomfield was taking great responsibility on his own shoulders, and it might be better for him to delay acting until he could do so in concert with his fellow bishops, 'and especially not without the concurrence of his grace the archbishop of Canterbury.[90] The bishop would also be well-advised to ascertain the feelings of the dean and chapter of Lichfield Cathedral.

If Blomfield was in any doubt as to Oakeley's position, the latter obligingly repeated his ground of subscription, with a clear indication that even as he wrote, his stand was changing. Hitherto, Oakeley had stated his firm belief, without qualification, that subscription was compatible with holding all Roman doctrine. In his repeated assertion of this claim, he added that the articles 'are just, and only just, capable of being honestly subscribed in such a sense as not necessarily to exclude any formal decision of the western church', and that they did not require the renunciation 'of any one of those formal decisions'.[91]

Oakeley claimed that everything he had written in *A second letter to the Lord Bishop of London* was included entirely on his own authority. He had studiously avoided showing it to any of his friends because 'they would have advised me to leave out many things as injudicious and impolitic'.[92] But he had decided to include everything in an effort to enable Blomfield to understand him, and Oakeley's final words have a rather pathetic ring to them. 'My lord, I have been most open with you; and now you know the worst of me . . . But, my lord, most honestly, I do not want to gain an end; I want that your lordship should understand me, and do what is right. I do not think your lordship ever has understood me; and, now if you do not, it will be no fault of mine'.[93]

On Tuesday 25 February, the day on which the final answer was due, Oakeley sent his message to Blomfield couched in language which indicates that the bishop had seen the second open letter and was being asked to consider it as fresh evidence for delaying or changing his plan. In view of the many testimonies 'which I understand that some of my kind friends have tendered to your lordship, (quite independently of myself)', Oakeley would delay a formal reply to the bishop's original request until late that same evening, 'with a view of enabling your lordship to express in the meantime whether, on the whole, and under existing circumstances, your lordship still feels yourself in duty bound to request its immediate restoration into your hands'.[94] With those words, the initiative was passed back to Blomfield.

Chapter Eleven

The last affray

THE TRIAL IN THE COURT OF ARCHES

I said that I thought he ought to face the question whether he had
not a moral conviction that he should join the Church of Rome –
that from what I heard him say, I doubted whether there was any
prospect of such an event when he let the suit begin – but that his
state of mind seemed different now – and that it affected as I
thought, the question of a suit.
John Henry Newman to Beresford Hope, 14 May 1845

Blomfield was now in a difficult position. He had decided to take
action against Oakeley by revoking his licence. This may or may not
have been done at the request of the Vice-Chancellor of Oxford, but
that letter was past; *A letter to the Lord Bishop of London* had given
Blomfield whatever further excuse he might have needed to discipline
this wayward Tractarian in the heart of his diocese. By action and by
word, Oakeley had pushed Blomfield to a point where the bishop had
to respond to such a vigorous and public challenge, polite though it
was. Oakeley's frankness and honesty would have been highly
commendable in many other situations. But at this crucial time, it
was to cause his downfall.

Oakeley had delivered two public challenges to Blomfield who now
had little option but to respond. If he remained silent, he would lose
stature and credibility both in his diocese and in the wider church.
But *A letter to the Lord Bishop of London* had created a difficult situation. It put forward a clever argument which cast strong doubts on
Blomfield's ability to act. Could the bishop revoke a licence without
giving any reason? If not, then what was that reason? Blomfield had
mentioned only the letter to the vice-chancellor, without elucidation.
Was Blomfield making a judgement about Oakeley's method of

subscription? Did he have sufficient authority, as one bishop among many, formally to condemn Oakeley by revoking his licence? Would that judgement by one bishop have universal application throughout the Church of England? Something had to be done, but what?

Blomfield sought the advice of Stephen Lushington,[1] an eminent ecclesiastical lawyer. Lushington replied that it was indeed a difficult problem. The validity of Oakeley's subscription turned 'in a great measure upon historical considerations', and was so doubtful that he advised Blomfield not to proceed against Oakeley'.[2]

On Wednesday 26 February, Blomfield informed Oakeley that he was no longer sure that the simple revocation of a licence was the proper mode of proceeding under the circumstances, 'or whether a different course should be pursued'.[3] As the matter might take some while to sort out, he would not object to Oakeley resuming his ministrations at the chapel on an interim basis, 'with a distinct understanding that it is to be considered as a provisional arrangement; to continue till I shall have decided upon the steps to be taken in the matter'.[4] Blomfield also required an undertaking from Oakeley that he would not teach or preach 'any of those doctrines which are considered to be peculiar to the Church of Rome, as distinguished from the Church of England'.[5]

It was an apparent victory. Oakeley's immediate friends were jubilant,[6] as was Oakeley himself, though in a slightly more restrained manner. He told Gladstone that 'great things had been won in the struggle for the mind of the Church of England'.[7] He had had a private conversation with Blomfield (possibly on Wednesday 26 February), and, said Oakeley, if he had been at liberty to mention their discussions, 'I could give you all far more hope and confidence than he authorises me by his letter'.[8] Both hope and confidence proved to be short-lived illusions, and the apparent victory proved to be no more than a brief remission.

Newman had kept aloof from events since the trial of Ward in the Sheldonian Theatre, but he was pleased by this turn of events, both for Oakeley and for the sake of his congregation at Margaret Chapel. But however pleased he might be, he kept a firm distance from Oakeley's interpretation of the Thirty-Nine Articles, regarding it as completely untenable and refusing to be associated with it. 'To say that all Roman doctrine is compatible with our articles is to me a paradox to which not even the Bishop of London can give currency'.[9] Letters passed between Oakeley and Newman at a fast and frequent level during the period February-October 1845, and there are many references in Newman's papers to letters which no longer exist. But enough survives to enable the construction of a picture of relations between the two men in that eventful year.

Oakeley paid several visits to Littlemore, but Newman was careful to maintain a detached position, observing from the sidelines and helping only when asked, and then only in a limited way, as he wrote to Keble. 'This affair did not annoy me at all. I took no sort of interest in it. I could not, with such real subjects of pain already on my mind'.[10] He revealed that Oakeley had been depressed by the criticisms of some of his friends, including Keble himself. 'Oakeley has been somewhat downcast by opinions, among others I suppose of yourself, against his letter to the bishop. I suppose no one but himself is a judge quite under his feelings and views, for they are so much his own'.[11] Keble agreed: 'I wonder that a person of Oakeley's experience should be so much hurt and astonished at not carrying everyone along with him in so very delicate and critical a move. He writes as if one blamed his motives or as if it were inexcusable to question his judgement'.[12]

Relations between Pusey and Oakeley went through a difficult phase after 25 February. Pusey, probably provoked by Oakeley's letters to the Bishop of London, wrote to him in terms that were severely critical judging from the answering letters of Oakeley and Ward. Oakeley was so upset by Pusey's letter, that he asked Ward to answer it immediately, and deferred his own reply until the following day. Ward explained to Pusey that Oakeley was 'very much engrossed just now with occupation connected with the greatest crisis in his life'.[13] He told Pusey that Oakeley's two letters to the Bishop of London were 'the most powerful works he has ever written'.[14] 'It has been a matter of daily increasing astonishment with me how well and quietly he has done it and how wonderfully his powers seem to have risen under the pressure of circumstances'.[15] Pusey's letter had caused Oakeley 'the greatest pain' and 'he particularly desires me to say that he cannot, after it, feel at present so much disposed as he was to write openly to you and ask your advice . . . when beset by public troubles'.[16]

That was all that Oakeley had asked Ward to write, but Ward was Ward, and he would happily use several paragraphs where one would be sufficient. Loyalty to Oakeley was his guiding factor, and he condemned Pusey for failing to understand the personal pressures under which Oakeley was labouring in an effort to preserve his work at Margaret Chapel. 'If you were on the spot, you could have had an idea of the *anguish* of mind which has been caused in the minds of many gentle and humble souls at the idea of leaving M[argaret] C[hapel]'.[17] Ward continued, pointlessly, by painting an emotional and silly picture of many female members of Oakeley's congregation swooning at the thought of him being forced to leave the chapel, or the chapel closing, or both. One of them, according to Ward, was in such a state of health that 'the result of this business may make to her the difference of living and dying'. Ward then continued by citing his fiancée, Frances Mary Wingfield, 'who considers Oakeley to have been by far her greatest benefactor in the whole world'. He continued by rebuking Pusey for his ill-considered timing. 'In justice to [Oakeley], I ought to say that as far as such a one as myself can judge on such a matter, he seems to me perfectly *wonderful* as to the sweetness and equableness of temper with which he has taken the whole business. His nights at present are perfectly tranquil, while he works most energetically the whole day. He thinks of going for a few weeks into the country in search of repose, which he so much needs. Perhaps you would kindly *reserve* any comment you may have to make until that period has elapsed, as any additional trial, not absolutely necessary, must be so prejudicial'.[18]

Pusey had told Oakeley that he regarded his claim not to teach Roman doctrine from the pulpit as of no great significance, since he taught it everywhere else. Ward replied to this accusation with a degree of ambiguity. 'He avows that he holds it, and there he leaves it. All his practical works display an anxious desire to accommodate the task to the existing attainments of his readers'.[19] As to the reasons which had induced both him and Oakeley to make plain and bold statements of their beliefs, 'we could not be easy in our experience if we subscribe them without publicly proclaiming the sense in which we subscribe them'.[20] As Oakeley was very tired by the events of the last week, he was thinking of going to the country for a few days. 'Perhaps you would kindly reserve any comment you may have to make until that period has elapsed'.[21] Oakeley had not gone to the country before, the next day, he himself wrote to Pusey explaining that he had asked Ward to write in his stead because he would have written 'briefly' and 'impetuously. 'The more I consider the fact of your letter, the more I feel that I hope you would another time reconsider the question of writing such a one under the circumstances . . . Could anything depress me . . . it would be the impression of your dissatisfaction with my various proceedings'.[22]

Oakeley sent a rather sharp letter to the *English Churchman* on 26 February, lamenting the fact that so many of his friends at Oxford had expressed their disapproval of his action. 'I cannot but feel, that very many of those for whose aid I might have looked have, to all appearance, permitted their sympathies to be in some degree weakened . . . by their dissatisfaction at my proceeding'.[23] As someone who had exposed himself to severe risk on a matter of conscience, he felt that he deserved 'forbearance at least, if not . . . zealous sympathy'.[24] He admitted that his actions had stirred up considerable trouble, not only for himself but in a wider field, but urged his readers to remember that 'because certain actions issue in temporary mischief, it does not therefore follow that they may not issue in ulterior good'.[25] Oakeley was beginning to see himself as a symbolic martyr and confessor, and such an end could only be a blessing for the church. 'We hear, I think, too much of these words "impolitic" and "injudicious".'[26]

On Thursday 27 February, Oakeley was convinced that Blomfield would take no proceedings against him. The struggle was over and a great victory had been won for the catholic cause, and he relished each moment of the struggle. 'I would not have lost this last week for anything'.[27] Although the bishop had used the words 'interim' and 'provisional' in his letter,[28] Oakeley, not for the first time, had left Blomfield's presence, thinking that the bishop was more favourably disposed towards him than events subsequently proved. 'Were I at liberty to mention the result of a private conversation I could give you all far more hope and confidence than he authorises me by his letter. And could I impart my own private impressions, I would say that great things had been won in the struggle for the mind of the Church of England'.[29] There are two possible explanations for this delusory euphoria, which was to be dashed within a few days. Either Blomfield had misled Oakeley, or Oakeley had misread Blomfield. Oakeley was an open and honest individual and incapable of duplicity, but he was a shade too open and enthusiastic, and might have read more into Blomfield's friendliness than he should have done. He does use the words 'private impressions', and there is no doubting the cautionary note sounded in the bishop's official letter on Wednesday 26 February.

The situation was made more difficult by the fact that Oakeley had suddenly become newsworthy, and accounts of his activities began to appear in the columns of *The Times*. On Friday 28 February, the newspaper announced, in a rather pompous tone, that Oakeley, 'who has made himself so notorious by his Romanist publications, and by a later defiance to his diocesan, has at length been suspended'.[30] The blatant inaccuracy of this statement irritated Oakeley who replied that he had not been suspended, that his ministry continued with the sanction of the bishop; and that he could not be answerable for any other items of news other than those that he expressly authorised'.[31] He made no mention of the bishop's decision to allow his ministry to continue only on a provisional basis. Blomfield was annoyed by this statement, which he correctly supposed left the reader with the impression that the bishop had decided to take no action against

Oakeley. He issued a statement to *The Times* saying that Oakeley continued in his ministry at Margaret Chapel only 'till the Bishop shall have obtained the opinion of his legal advisers as to the proper course of proceeding in so grave a case'.[32]

The *English Churchman* considered that no legal proceedings would be forthcoming because the ecclesiastical courts were likely to decide against the bishop.[33] At that time, the paper took a moderate position and had no sympathy either with Oakeley or W. B. Noel in their doctrinal beliefs. But it adopted the view that Oakeley was being made a victim to appease the wrath of the Vice-Chancellor of the University of Oxford, and credit should be given to Blomfield for taking Lushington's advice that the simple revocation of Oakeley's licence was unwise. In doing this, Blomfield was 'refusing to allow himself to be made the tool of the Heads of Houses in Oxford, and the executioner of mere popular malevolence'.[34] Lushington's advice implicitly condemned the proceedings against Ward, proving that the university had committed itself 'to a different construction of a clergyman's duties and responsibilities than what the Church, whose servant she professes to be, has actually laid upon him'.[35] As to those who clamoured for Oakeley's dismissal, 'when we see an attempt made, by those who we believe to be, as regard their pastoral ministrations, far superior in sound churchmanship to their persecutors, we will do our utmost to oppose such procceedings'.[36]

By the 3 March Blomfield had decided that something had to be done as he reported to the Bishop of Gibraltar. 'Mr Oakeley's barefaced avowal that he holds, as distinct from teaching 'all Roman doctrine', has made it absolutely necessary for me to take some decided step. The precise form of providing against him is not yet determined upon. In a matter of such grave importance, I have deemed it right to proceed cautiously and regularly; and I have requested Dr Lushington's advice as to the course most proper . . . I expect that he will pass over to the enemy camp, taking a certain number of his congregation with him, and that this will be the signal for Newman's open defection. It is however possible, that they may set up an Episcopal Church not in connexion with the state, if they get a bishop from Scotland, or America, but I hope that neither of the Churches in those countries will abet so schismatic a proceeding'.[37]

By 10 March, the bishop had decided to institute formal legal proceedings against Oakeley. If the verdict of a court of law was the only way that he could justifiably be removed from Margaret Chapel, then to the courts he would go. Blomfield's decision was no doubt taken on careful legal advice, but it must have been exacerbated by Oakeley's correspondence with the newspapers. Such letters 'have been calculated that produce, and have in fact produced, an impression that I had relinquished all intention of proceeding against you'.[38]

Proceedings were not formally opened until 8 April, but Blomfield had told Oakeley of his intentions by 10 March, because on that day, a circular letter was issued, appealing for funds to help with the legal costs of the case. It was put out in the name of a committee formed by James Hope and consisting of himself, with Edward Bellasis, Edward Badeley[39] and John Chambers.[40] Hope appears to have done his best to help Oakeley, but was not whole-hearted in his efforts. When he sent a copy of the circular letter to Gladstone, he told him that he was anxious that, as the case might throw light on (unspecified) collateral points, it should be well-conducted. He was also anxious that Oakeley receive a fair trial, but of the outcome he was not hopeful. 'This looks like the beginning of the end'.[41]

Gladstone declined to contribute to the fund for Oakeley's defence, telling Hope that he would give the reasons at a later date'.[42] The reasons are probably those that he gave to Manning when he told him that Oakeley had 'sadly complicated these vexed affairs', and that he was 'painfully impressed with the belief that Oakeley had nothing like a measured theological view of the case'. Furthermore, he was becoming 'more tenacious' and 'evidently wedded in heart to this controversy of his own – a bad sign for our peace'.[43]

Hope was not helped by Oakeley, who was inclined to let the case go by default, partly because he felt that whatever defence was put up, the bishop would win, and partly because he 'disliked a subject like the Blessed Sacrament to banded about by lawyers'.[44] Hope urged Oakeley to place himself in the hands of competent legal advisers and, if he lost in the Court of Arches, to appeal to the House of Lords; he need have no fear about expenses, since they would take care of that for him. But Hope did cautiously raise the possibility that Oakeley might become a Roman Catholic in the near future, 'and if that is the case, it is useless to proceed'.[45]

At first, Oakeley decided to follow Hope's advice and contest the case with the aid of professional counsel, and he asked Newman for a short list of books that would bear out the claims of Tract 90. 'I mean such books as you refer lawyers to ... They must not be too many or too hard'.[46] He was initially confident about the prospect of a fight, hoping that the influence of his elder brother Herbert, now Archdeacon of Colchester, might avert the case.[47] But his hopes were dashed by the premature death of Sir Herbert Oakeley on 27 March.

The machinery of the ecclesiastical legal system moved slowly through March, April and May, towards a climax in June. Oakeley was prosecuted under the provisions of the Church Discipline Act of

1840. The act empowered a bishop, in cases of alleged non-criminal offences, to set up a commission of inquiry, which should institute a preliminary investigation to decide whether or not there was a prima facie case. Alternatively, the bishop could transmit these preliminary investigations, by Letters of Request, to the provincial court which, in the province of Canterbury, was the Court of Arches.

Blomfield chose the latter course and issued his Letters of Request on 8 April. Oakeley was charged with an offence against ecclesiastical law by writing and publishing *A letter to the Lord Bishop of London* on 19 February, 'in which said pamphlet or letter, doctrines are openly maintained and affirmed directly contrary or repugnant to the true, usual, literal meaning of the Articles of Religion'.[48] Oakeley was summoned to appear and answer this charge 'touching and concerning his soul's health' for 'the lawful correction and reformation of his manners and excesses'.[49] With such a carefully worded accusation, Oakeley had little chance of winning the case. Holding all Roman doctrine could not stand against the 'true, usual, literal' meaning of the articles. If he were to win on some points, he would be caught on others. As Newman observed, 'it does not state any specific false doctrine, but accuses him generally of Romanism'.[50]

Preliminary hearings were held on 15 and 22 April to allow the presentation of supportive evidence by counsel, with a final session on 4 May at which both proctors summed up their cases and presented a 'prayer' of petition. The bishop's proctor urged that Oakeley should be 'duly punished and corrected, according to the exigency of the law'. and Oakeley's proctor 'prayed' that his client be dismissed from all further observance of justice in this suit'.[51]

Oakeley may have been present at the first session on 15 April, because he had doubts about his future by 17 April when he talked of going to Littlemore 'if cast out' of Margaret Street,[52] and during late April and May he spent much time at the village in conversation with Newman. He arrived at Littlemore on Saturday 26 April and stayed at the house of a Miss Giles until Friday 2 May. Newman talked to him on the evening of Sunday 27 April, and feared that his departure to Rome would not be long in coming, a feeling which was shared by his close acquaintance, Ambrose St John.[53] 'St John says what cannot be doubted, that he is going very fast . . . If one did not too well fear it was one's own doing, it would be a comfort, as being a confirmation to hear of such things'.[54]

Having returned to London to do duty at Margaret Chapel on Sunday 4 May, Oakeley returned to the house of Miss Giles at Littlemore on the evening of Monday 5 May, staying until Thursday 15 May. He talked to Newman on several occasions and they dined together at least five times. The situation was rendered personally difficult for Oakeley by the presence of none other than George Tickell, who had caused Oakeley so much grief in the autumn of 1844. Tickell stayed at Littlemore for a few days in the week beginning Monday 5 May, and dined with Oakeley and Newman on Thursday and Friday of that week. What passed between the three men will forever remain a secret, but their conversations must have influenced the impressionable Oakeley. Newman, moving quietly, intellectually and deliberately in the direction of Rome. Tickell, the recent and enthusiastic convert, who had bombarded Oakeley with letters urging him to make the same move. Oakeley himself, in a state of turmoil, faced with the probability of losing Margaret Chapel and all his work there, and wondering what to do and where to go.

Newman has left two brief glimpses of that week at Littlemore. After dinner on Friday 9 May, Newman left St John, Tickell and Oakeley, to write a letter, but he could hear Ambrose St John 'talking in a most edifying way to Tickell about the scarlet, and the white and gold, robes of the Archbishop of Malines'.[55] The other glimpse says much about the level of pressure that Oakeley probably had to endure from Tickell. On the day of his arrival at Littlemore, Tickell began his stay by trying to convert Newman. But Newman was not to be moved by the young enthusiast. 'I have kept my gun cocked and loaded, intending to discharge upon him if he made a second attempt, but he has kept the peace'.[56]

Tickell left Littlemore on Saturday 10 May, but Oakeley stayed on. On Tuesday 13 May, James Hope, leader of the group of lawyers defending Oakeley's cause, arrived at Littlemore to see Newman. He asked for Newman's help and advice with Oakeley, which raises the possibility that Oakeley had gone to Littlemore to live in self-imposed exile, refusing to take any active role in the continuing legal process, and leaving his friends to bear the brunt of the fight. That same evening, Newman had a long talk with Oakeley and conveyed his impressions in a letter to Hope the next day. The letter reveals that Oakeley was in a dilemma and had sought refuge at Littlemore, not knowing which way to go. 'I said that I thought he ought to face the question whether he had not a moral conviction that he *should* join the Church of Rome – that from what I heard him say, I doubted whether there was any prospect of such an event when he let the suit begin – but that his state of mind seemed different now – and that it affected as I thought, the question of a suit'.[57] Oakeley avoided this thrust by replying that he was certain that the case would be decided in his favour on technicalities, and, therefore, whether he went to Rome or not was immaterial. Newman could have repeated at this

point what Hope had said to him, namely that Oakeley's departure for Rome after an acquittal 'would have a very bad effect on
the Anglo-Catholic cause . . . and be a disadvantage to it in public
opinion and with the bishops'.[58]

Newman warned Oakeley that he did not think the case could be won
on technicalities. Since Oakeley's lawyers were asking for sources to
support his claim on Roman doctrine, it was beginning to look as though
a major fight was in prospect. If the arguments moved into questions of
doctrine, 'I thought his was a bad case to try it upon; that his view was
an extreme one'.[59] Many people were spending time and money in an
effort to save Oakeley in the Court of Arches. It was a considerable risk
to take on a case such as Oakeley's. 'Therefore I said . . . what is there
that *calls for* that risk. If its favourable issue will have the effect of
keeping you in the Church of England, this is the reason for it – but if it
will produce no great effect one way or the other, whether you succeed
or not, the risk is for nothing. You have then to make up your mind how
you feel towards the Church of England'.[60] Newman then delivered his
parting shot by firmly distancing himself from Oakeley's belief that all
Roman doctrine could be held by a conscientious Anglican. 'I have
always and everywhere resisted it'.[61]

Hope had asked Newman to secure an undertaking from Oakeley that
the success or failure of the case would mean the difference between his
staying in or leaving the Church of England. The committee of lawyers
was not prepared to fight on such an extreme position unless it was with
the object of keeping Oakeley in the Church of England. Oakeley was
unable to give the undertaking.[62]

Oakeley left Littlemore for London on Thursday 15 May, leaving
Newman in a quandary. Whether Newman advised Hope and his friends
to continue the case or to withdraw from it, there was a strong possibility that Oakeley would become a Roman Catholic sooner or later. 'Now
what shall I advise them to do? The said Oakeley . . . is as near the
Church of Rome as is possible for a stranger to the said Church to be'.[63]
Ambrose St John warned Newman that if the case was dropped Oakeley
would have to give up the chapel in obedience to Blomfield's original
request that he surrender his licence, and after that, 'he will go over at
once'.[64]

When he arrived back in London, Oakeley discussed the matter
with his advisers, and they jointly decided that even if he was planing
to resign the chapel, he should wait until after the judgement of the
Court of Arches. An immediate resignation would be a greater blow
or discouragement to the Tractarians than an adverse decision of the
Court.[65] Oakeley was undecided. 'I feel that I ought to have no
opinion of my own in this matter, and although I am very anxious to

be relieved of all further anxiety, yet I do not think that I ought to have any opinion against the wishes of others'.[66]

Oakeley was clearly in conflict with his legal advisers, he desiring to resign his licence immediately, they wishing to see the case through to its conclusion. Oakeley sought Newman's advice, and several letters passed back and forth between London and Littlemore in the period 20–28 May. Finally Oakeley asked Newman for a clear decision of whether he should go on or not.[67] When he had begun the case it was with the understanding, which had been accepted by his friends, that he would not be bound thereby to any particular course of action however the case might turn out. But now, with the possibility of defeat turning into a probability, he could not see any point in continuing.[68]

Oakeley had taken to heart everything that Newman had told him on the evening of Tuesday 13 May, and spent the succeeding two weeks agonising about what to do. Newman himself was convinced that the risk of failure was great, 'from the *extreme* character of those opinions which he has to defend; and very serious, considering what interests would suffer if he was unsuccessful'.[69] He circumvented Oakeley and wrote directly to Edward Bellasis, recommending that the case should be dropped, not only to avoid any serious after effects, but also because it was not worth the effort, because he was sure that Oakeley would become a Roman Catholic before too long. 'I am morally certain that he will join the Church of Rome sooner or later, but, I think in not a very long time. Whether he succeeds in the Court of Arches on technical grounds, or is cast on doctrinal, or succeeds on technical or doctrinal grounds in the Privy Council, this is the upshot of it – perhaps, for what one knows, while the cause is still pending, if the law is as slow as often it is . . . considering this moral certainty . . . it seems to me . . . inexpedient to go on'.[70]

Bellasis told Newman that he was aware of Oakeley's state of mind, but he and the rest of the group of lawyers thought that the least of all possible evils was to let the case proceed, even with the contingency of Oakeley's resignation.[71] This knowledge reassured Newman and cleared away all difficulties from his mind. 'I shall write therefore to advise him to let matters take their course, and give himself no more thought about it'.[72] But the delay in hearing from Newman was more than Oakeley could stand and, as Newman was writing to Bellasis on Tuesday 3 June, Oakeley wrote to Blomfield on the same day, resigning his licence.

The letter naturally made no reference to the Roman Catholic Church, but Oakeley frankly admitted that the circumstances of the preceding few months 'have forced upon me a painful but overpowering impression of the difficulties which actually beset my position and my path as a clergyman in the Church of England. And many of these difficulties are of a kind which even the termination in my favour of the suit . . . would not serve to remove'.[73] Obliquely, he quoted only one difficulty, that the Court of Arches was unlikely to make a formal settlement of the question on which Oakeley had asked Blomfield to make an authoritative judgement – the claim to hold all Roman doctrine. 'The prosecution of the cause under these circumstances could be productive of no advantage to the Church of England sufficient to counterbalance the excitement of the mischief attending it'.[74] Accordingly, he informed Blomfield that he resigned his licence, and declined to defend himself before the Court of Arches.

Newman was surprised, especially since Oakeley had charged him with delay, and given that as the reason for his sudden action. 'I am very sorry he has acted without the advice of his London friends. All along I have urged him to do so. Such is his state of mind just now, that I shall not tell him I am sorry – but only say I did not delay'.[75]

The *English Churchman* printed Oakeley's letter of resignation in full, accompanied by a surprisingly supportive editorial that accused Blomfield of vacillation. The bishop had originally asked Oakeley to resign his licence on the content of his letter to the vice-chancellor, yet when the case began in the Court of Arches, the charge had been shifted to *A letter to the Lord Bishop of London*. 'We cannot help thinking . . . that, as the suit was expressly instituted in order to settle a question which had arisen before Mr Oakeley's letter to the bishop, that letter ought not to have been set forth in the articles [charges] at all, much less to have been the sole foundation of them'.[76] The paper reasserted its view that Oakeley was not guilty of nearly so serious a misdemeanour as B. W. Noel at St John's Chapel, Bedford Row. 'Mr Noel's is by far the worst of the two, for while he practically and openly offends, Mr Oakeley merely propounds a theory'.[77] The editorial concluded with a tribute to Oakeley's work. 'We deeply regret that the solid advantages of the beautiful and unique services of Margaret Chapel should be sacrificed for objects, so utterly valueless . . . And even now, we would fain hope, although against hope, that some way may be found by which the pastor may be saved to the flock and they from being scattered abroad; for it is in truth a "beautiful flock".'[78]

The Times was less charitable, describing Oakeley's claim as a 'startling and tortuous exposition of faith'. and Oakeley himself as 'the Romanist teacher in the guise of the Anglican minister'.[79] This was both inaccurate and unfair, since Oakeley vigorously denied teaching Roman doctrine. The emotional tone of the paper's article continued with a demand that Oakeley should be stripped of his fellowship of Balliol. 'Is he ... to pursue at Oxford with those who are to teach others, the treacherous career which he has been compelled to relinquish at St Margaret's (*sic*)? We trust not. Some means, it is to be hoped, will be found to rescue Balliol from such a predicament, and arrest the infection of any pestilent doctrine that many be threatened by the volunteer associate of Mr Ward's culpability'.[80]

Any hope that Oakeley might have had of ending the crisis by resigning his licence to Blomfield and thereby putting a stop to the court case and relieving 'those embarrassments which have arisen out of my connection with your lordship's diocese',[81] were dashed when Blomfield declared, through this proctor in the Court of Arches, that he intended to persevere with the case, and declined to accept the proffered resignation'.[82] There was probably nothing else he could do; it is difficult to halt legal proceedings after they have commenced. Oakeley maintained his position and declined either to appear before the Court or to be represented by counsel.

The Court of Arches is the chief court of the Archbishop of Canterbury. Its name derives from the original meeting place of the court, the parish church of St Mary-le-Bow, otherwise called Sancta Maria de Arcubus, which was destroyed in the Great Fire of 1666. The court was then moved to the rebuilt hall of the advocates at Doctors Commons in Knightrider Street, a small street connecting Godliman Street and Peter's Hill, on the south side of St Paul's Churchyard. Doctors Commons (officially the College of Advocates and Doctors of Law) contained both the ecclesiastical and the admiralty courts, together with the advocates practising there. These advocates were a wholly separate body from barristers, and were required to hold doctorates in civil law from either Oxford of Cambridge before being admitted to practice in the Court of Arches. The Dean of the Arches was ex officio president of the college. With the passing of various legal reforms in the years 1857–9, the college ceased to function, and the buildings were demolished in 1867'.[83]

The case against Oakeley opened on Tuesday 9 June 1845. Oakeley, true to his word, did not appear, nor was he represented by counsel. The *English Churchman* reported this as a possible explanation for the fact that the Court was 'very thinly attended'.[84] Among those present was George Chandler, Rector of All Souls', Langham Place; James Endell Tyler, Rector of the neighbouring parish of Saint Giles-in-the-Fields; William Goode, Rector of St Antholin in the city of London and author of *Tract XC historically refuted*; and William Upton Richards, Oakeley's assistant at Margaret Chapel. Sir Herbert Jenner Fust[85] presided as Dean of the Arches, and the Queen's Advocate, Dr John

Dodson[86] appeared for the bishop. Fust enquired whether anyone appeared for Oakeley, and was informed by Oakeley's proctor that he had received no orders to instruct counsel.

Dodson opened the hearing by reading certain parts of the articles (charges) against Oakeley, including several passages from *A letter to the Lord Bishop of London*, from which it was quite clear, he argued, that Oakeley claimed to hold, and acknowledged that he did hold, all Roman doctrine. Dodson then read extracts from various divines 'to show the repugnancy which was considered to exist at the time of framing the Thirty-Nine Articles between the doctrines of the reformed church and that of Rome'.[87] Dodson quoted heavily from the articles and from the decrees of the Council of Trent, to show that the two were completely irreconcilable in doctrine. Dodson argued that Oakeley had failed to obey the injunction contained in the preface to the articles 'that no man hereafter shall either print or preach, to draw the articles aside in any way, but shall submit to it in the plain and full meaning thereof, and shall not put his own sense or comment to the meaning of the Article, but shall take it in the literal and grammatical sense'.[88] A conversation then took place between Fust and Dodson as to what the court was actually being asked to do. Was Dodson calling upon the court to request Oakeley to recant? 'Dr Dodson seemed somewhat puzzled by this question, and replied that he did not apprehend that it was intended 'to go as far as that', but that the court should punish Mr Oakeley, as it should consider that his offence deserved'.[89] After seeking clarification on a number of details, Fust concluded by announcing that he would take some time to consider his judgement, and expressed his regret that he would have to come to a decision without the benefit of an argument on behalf of Oakeley'.[90]

There are very few references to Oakeley's activities during the twenty-eight days between the opening of the case on Monday 9 June, and the delivery of judgement on Monday 30 June. Newman recorded that Oakeley 'came suddenly'[91] to Littlemore on the evening of Friday 6 June, only to leave again the following day. He did not go there again until Saturday 28 June. It appears that he ministered quietly to a supportive though anxious congregation, waiting for the judgement of the court. He made only one public statement of his position, published in the form of a letter to a friend, on Wednesday 25 June.

The 'advertisement' or preface has an air of resignation to the inevitability of what was about to happen. It takes the form of Oakeley writing in the third person, presenting his friends with an apology for the course he had pursued. He felt that an explanation was due to those 'kind friends and generous benefactors with whose feelings he may seem to have trifled' on a subject which they may have thought to be 'mere theory' or 'pure conceit'.[92] He hoped that his friends would wish and pray that every step of his future life would be 'under as large a vouchsafement of light as that which for nearly six favoured years has seemed to shine about his path at Margaret Chapel', in a career 'which is now drawing to an end'.[93]

The pamphlet displays a superficial contradiction in Oakeley's thinking, but it is only superficial. Oakeley informed his readers that he had no intention of leaving the Church of England. 'There I will, by his help, abide while I may. I have a place to fill and a work to do. I will not be the person to cut the knot'.[94] But all this has an air of unreality. What was Oakeley's conception of his 'place' and his 'work'? He had voluntarily resigned his licence, which, though Blomfield had refused to accept it, would be revoked after the expected unfavourable decision of the Court of Arches. This would deprive him of his one important sphere of work – Margaret Chapel – but there was every possibility that his prebendal stall at Lichfield would go as well. It could not be counted inviolable after a formal condemnation by the provincial court of Canterbury. Oakeley no longer had 'a place to fill'. 'I will not be the person to cut the knot'. What does this mean? His position in the diocese of London? He had already offered Blomfield his resignation. His membership of the Church of England? A decision to terminate that connection would be his alone. Oakeley was manoeuvring himself into a position where he could charge his critics with forcing him out of his Church and his job, he being completely innocent of any charge, or of responsibility for his own actions. This is no more than another example of a streak in his character which, according to circumstances, might be described as naïve.

The rest of the letter shows that Oakeley was moving further and further away from the Church of England, and that the knot which tied him to it, had all the substance of an illusion. Oakeley was the one who was cutting the knot, except that there was very little of the knot left to cut. Statements in *The claim "to hold as distinct from teaching", explained, in a letter to a friend* indicate that his preoccupation was the nature of authority in the Church of England. He had first raised this in *A second letter to the Lord Bishop of London*, challenging Blomfield to say who was the official interpreter of the Thirty-Nine Articles. Since Blomfield had failed to furnish a reply, merely referring the matter to the Court of Arches, Oakeley had come to a natural conclusion. 'It is Rome alone which seems to me to propose doctrines on the authority of the Church; as soon as I leave this firm basis, I get adrift, and am thrown in one way or another upon private judgement, private views of scripture, or of antiquity, or of both. If our Lord has left a church on earth, that church must be ... the authorised expositress of the word; and I see no church but the Roman which even claims to fulfil this office for the Christian world'.[95]

Oakeley repeated his statement that he would not teach Roman doctrine but, whereas he had stated in *A letter to the Lord Bishop of London* that he would not do so because of 'a special obligation to my kind superior the Dean of Chichester; I regard it as a condition of my relation to him ... to abstain from any course which I know might be displeasing to him'[96] he states, in *The claim "to hold as distinct from teaching", explained, in a letter to a friend*, that he had an undoubted right to teach them, and forbore to do so on his own authority, not through courtesy to Chandler. 'I do not ... deny my right to teach ... I waive it ... because I am not so disposed to act'.[97] This raises the question of how much longer he would have been content merely to hold Roman doctrine without teaching it. 'How can a person make up his mind to withhold from the flock what he knows to be important'.[98]

Oakeley then proceeded to some typically sweeping generalisations about unspecified areas of doctrine. Much Roman doctrine, he declared, was identical with Anglican doctrine, and there was a broad distinction between theological principles and theological dogmas. 'There are certain principles upon which all true churchmen are agreed. These principles consistently carried out will issue in Roman doctrine, and that certain dogmas are but accurate and formal enunciation of them. I am debarred from putting these principles in their dogmatic shape by moral obligation to the Church of England – but those obligations required me to inculcate the principles'.[99] Oakeley had a tendency to make these significant statements, without explaining what he means. He does not specify what principles or dogmas he has in mind, though presumably infallible revelation is at the base, or the process whereby the carrying out of a general theological principle can find its formal expression in Roman doctrine.

The pamphlet appeared on Wednesday 25 June, and judgement was due to be pronounced on Monday 30 June. Was it possible by such timing that Oakeley hoped to influence Fust's judgement? This was unlikely; one would expect to see some conciliatory gesture, evidence of a willingness to climb down. There is no such evidence. The flags flown in *The claim "to hold as distinct from teaching", explained, in a letter to a friend*, are as provocative and antagonistic as any of his previous writings. Oakeley appears to have thought that there was an even chance that the decision might go either way. But this was no longer of any concern to him. 'I am going to be out of the way of the Court of Arches on Monday; but I shall keep myself ready to return at Hope's bidding in case I can be of used towards mitigating the decision if adverse, or turning it to account if favourable. Hope thinks it might conceivably be right for me to defer my resignation for a few days. And to this extent I am at the service of those who are interested in the cause. I had thought of continuing to make London my headquarters at present'.[100]

On Saturday 28 June, he went to Littlemore, 'to be near Newman',[101] and stayed there until Monday 30 June to await the judgement of the court. He was away from Margaret Chapel on Sunday 29 June and, in a gesture of doing what he could to help, even though Oakeley's actions had led to a certain estrangement between them, Pusey travelled to London that weekend and preached to the distressed congregation of Margaret Chapel. The sermon was dedicated as follows. 'To the congregation of Margaret Chapel, with whom he has often in common worshipped, to whom he has, from time to time, with joy ministered, and with them in their devout services, found rest and joy, this sermon, preached by God's mercy, to remove anxieties, on a day of gladness, and the eve of heavy sorrow, is inscribed, with the affectionate prayer, that the God of all comfort will, in our comon sorrow, comfort them, and himself, the teacher and guide of all, replace the guidance and teaching of which in his inscrutable providence he has permitted them to be deprived'.[102]

The inevitable judgement was delivered by Sir Herbert Fust on Monday 30 June. Without any counsel to defend Oakeley's position, the hearings turned into a dialogue between judge and prosecution. Fust would ask for clarification of a certain point and Dodson would supply it. The Dean of the Arches did his best to play the role of the impartial judge but, as he said, in the absence of a defence counsel, the sole defence was the content of *A letter to the Lord Bishop of London*, upon which the charges were also based. 'He could not travel out of that letter for any explanation that might be offered of its contents . . . If any explanation could have been given beyond the letter itself, the court would have been ready to hear it; but Mr Oakeley . . . had not thought proper to make any defence at all . . . If this course of proceeding caused the court to put a construction upon the words of the letter which they were not intended to hear, the court might regret, but could not help it'.[103]

Since Oakeley had been tried under general law, the nature of the punishment was left to the discretion of the court. The court was bound by no rules and could have imposed a much higher penalty than suspension. But Oakeley, without any defence, inevitably stood condemned since he had publicly proclaimed 'without reservation, qualificatiop from falling into the same errors into which Mr Oakeley has suffered himself to be led'.[105]

The judgement was clear. The defendant 'hath offended against the laws, statutes, constitutions and canons ecclesiastical of this realm and the licence granted to him ... be revoked, and that he ... be suspended from all discharge and function of his clerical office and the execution thereof', to continue in force 'until he ... shall appear and retract his errors'.[106] 'I must also condemn Mr Oakeley, as a matter of course, in the costs occasioned by these proceedings, and I direct that notice of this sentence be published in the usual manner at the Chapel in Margaret Street, on Sunday next the sixth day of July'.[107]

Chapter Twelve

Wanderings in the wilderness

FROM LONDON TO LITTLEMORE

I get very nervous sometimes and want someone to talk to; but
perhaps it is as well one has to get right by oneself . . . I wish you
would write me a nice letter however short; I get hardly any but
letters of business or rowings; and I am quite down-hearted at times
. . . I hope all goes on well with me.
Oakeley to ? (the letter begins 'My dear John'), 7 October 1845

Since he had refused to take any part in the proceedings before the Court of Arches, Oakeley had nobody but himself to blame for its eventual outcome. But in view of everything he had said and written, it is unlikely that he would have won the case even if he had contested it. Instead, he interpreted the episode in a such a way that he was able to prove to himself that he was quite guiltless, having no responsibility for anything. The Dean of the Arches was guilty of serious legal misconduct, and the whole case was a travesty of justice. He could not even bring himself to read 'the sickening details'[1] of the case.

In Oakeley's view, Fust was guilty of judging an undefended case; of taking a publication to pieces and putting his own construction upon its meaning; and 'to give sentence upon such private and undisputed construction'.[2] 'I suspect that such a proceeding is against all law and justice'.[3] This statement shows the inadequacy of Oakeley's knowledge of the law; it did not occur to him that legal proceedings had been started, and that Fust had no option but to continue them to the end as long as the prosecution wished to continue them. Oakeley thought the judgement itself absurd because it limited his punishment to the power of officiating, even though he had not been charged with teaching (alleged) error. 'He is suspended from that particular function which he is not charged with having abused'.[4] In a rather strained view of the judgement, he believed that, though it was personally serious, it did not call into question the right of a person who claimed to hold all Roman doctrine to retain his benefice, because he had not been deprived of his position, but merely 'suspended'.[5]

This was a game of semantics. There is a valid distinction between 'deprivation' and 'suspension' but, in Oakeley's case, it is irrelevant, since he was not a beneficed clergyman and therefore had nothing of which to be deprived; his licence was simply 'revoked'. Deprived or suspended, the effect was the same. He was forbidden to officiate as a priest 'until he . . . shall appear and retract his errors'.[6]

Oakeley was now in an isolated and unenviable position. He regarded the retraction of his 'errors' as 'a simple impossibility',[7] because to him they were not errors; but the alternative prospects were not promising. He was forty-two years old and, by legal sentence, 'cut off from every occupation to which I was naturally inclined'.[8] He had no private means. He could not very well retain the Balliol fellowship for long since it had clerical duties attached to it, though it might have been legally possible. 'I had long determined against marrying and had no taste whatever for rural employments'.[9] The choice lay between remaining in lay communion with the Church of England, or secession to Rome.

It should be noted that beyond one or two fleeting references, the only detailed information about Oakeley's life in the summer months of 1845, comes from his own unpublished autobiographical writings, and they betray attitudes and opinions that he is unlikely to have held in 1845, other than in nascent form. For example, he admitted that the course he had followed had included many faults: 'I am not conscious of ever having had any other object that that of doing my best to serve the Church of which I was a member by endeavouring to bring her back into union with the Church Catholic from which I felt . . . that she had been most unnaturally severed. What I regarded as my duty to believe I regarded also as my duty to avow'.[10] This is not entirely true. Much of that which Oakeley accomplished, especially in the field of liturgy, was designed to bring a great beauty and sense of devotion into Anglican worship, and much of his effort derived from his admiration for the Roman Catholic Church. But there is no evidence that he actively sought or worked for a visible union between the Churches of Rome and Canterbury. he loved the Roman Catholic Church and held all her doctrines, but it was an emotional attraction based more on liturgy and devotion, and latterly on authority, than on an intellectual assent to doctrine. There is no evidence to show that Oakeley was an early, if eccentric, pioneer of Christian unity. If he was, then his methods were insufficiently cautious to produce the desired effect.

Barred from officiating as an Anglican priest anywhere in the province of Canterbury, Oakeley's interests moved ever further towards the Roman Catholic Church. He developed an existing friendship with two Roman Catholic priests in the weeks following the judgement. One was Fr Robert Whittey, of St Edmund's College, Ware, who later became vicar-general of Cardinal Wiseman; the other was the Abbé Boucqueau, chaplain to a convent in Brussels. Whittey had made the acquaintance of Oakeley as a result of an article on auricular confession which was published in *The British Critic* in April 1843. Whittey presuming that Newman was the author, wrote to him, and was put in touch with Oakeley. The two men became friends and, with Boucqueau, helped Oakeley during the summer of 1845. 'The former gave me much valuable information on the system of education pursued in Catholic colleges . . . The latter, although at the time when I knew him the chaplain of a convent, was intimately acquainted with the routine of parochial work, and greatly interested me by his accounts of the laborious and self-denying devotion of the Belgian clergy'.[11] This point about Catholic colleges is not conclusive evidence that Oakeley was thinking about the Catholic priesthood, but may be an early indication that thoughts of a future career were passing through his mind. But by the middle of September, he had decided that priesthood in the Roman Catholic Church was God's will for him.[12]

There are other brief glimpses of his wanderings during those few weeks in July and August 1845. A stay in Berkshire brought an invitation from the incumbent of a nearby parish to read prayers in his church. 'I was obliged to remind him that my time for such duties was at an end'.[13] He also paid a visit to Highclere, the scene of a more tranquil part of his life, twenty-five years earlier, with its happy memories of Charles and Jennie Sumner. A sermon published in 1851 seems to contain a passage which reflects his memories of those weeks in the summer of 1845. 'The recollections of childhood, and boyhood, and youth, which came crowding in on the mind in the last great conflict, – on minds which seemed to weary and too feeble to offer resistance – the sound of the village bell, the fragrance of the pastoral garden, the memory of the parents' love, the thoughts of the dying and the dead – why did they not prevail against the still voice of conscience, and the beckoning of the unseen hand'.[14]

The inevitable step was not long in coming; Oakeley could not remain in the wilderness for ever. After a period of wandering, he went to live permanently at Littlemore from the beginning of September.[15] There, the mind and presence of John Henry Newman worked its effect on the vacuum that was Frederick Oakeley. 'It was well known that he was anxious to prevent others from looking upon his example as a precedent, but it was unavoidable that his loss of confidence in the Church of England should exercise a powerful influence on those who had so long looked to him as a guide'.[16] Oakeley was ready to admit the inadequacy of his own learning, and the fact that he was guided in his development by Newman. 'I for one have not the learning necessary to determine for myself the question of our position as a Church, but I do find an inward response to the doctrine which comes to me from Newman's authority'.[17] If the Church of England was the Catholic Church in England (or at least a part of it) 'no one ought to move, not Newman more than another. If it be right for him to go on the supposition of the negative of that hypothesis, it is also right for others to go, who . . . take his view upon trust'.[18]

Pusey, though he may have known in his heart that Newman's conversion was inevitable, was always the last to admit the possibility of anyone leaving the Church of England for the Roman Catholic Church, and he tried hard throughout September to keep Oakeley from leaving. But it seems that he had lost the battle by 18 September, because of a statement by Oakeley (which is open to interpretation) that by that date, he had decided that his future lay as a Roman Catholic priest. 'I mean only that it may be, and as far as I can see, is, God's will that I should be where I can devote myself actively as a clergyman to the services of the Church and the maintenance of the faith, which under circumstances in the Church of England I cannot do without disobedience . . . I trust that I shall not go seriously astray in this great question'.[19]

Since active service in the Church of England was now denied him, there was only one alternative. Time and time again, Oakeley acquits himself of all responsibility for the course of his life at this time and ascribes it to a form of divine providence. He indignantly denied to Pusey that he had acted with any precipitness. 'I was anything but eager to catch at some excuse for giving up duty'.[20] He had offered the resignation of his licence 'mainly as an act of consideration towards the Church of England'.[21] Fust's judgement was 'no necessary consequence of my own acts'.[22] The experience of the proceedings had been 'unspeakably distressing' and he had deferred consideration of his future 'until the effect of that shock had quite subsided'.[23]

Pusey's efforts were in vain, and during his remaining weeks in the Church of England, Oakeley gradually divested himself of beliefs that he had once held so dear. His cherished belief that the Thirty-Nine Articles were deliberately drawn up with the intention of including Roman Catholics had been challenged by Manning and others at the beginning of the year. Oakeley admitted that Manning's arguments required 'to be carefully considered',[24] but warned him at the same time that he was prepared to give up the articles rather than Roman doctrine, if his theory was disproved.[25] Now he was prepared to concede that 'it would not be well to overlook the fact that the historical view . . . has been met and contradicted'.[26] In any case, the judgement of the Court of Arches had 'thrown it into the shade'.[27]

Oakeley's unique claim to hold all Roman doctrine without teaching it, could not long survive the Court's verdict, since he had now no place from which to teach anything at all. Pusey had offered to write to the *English Churchman* defending Oakeley against the verdict.[28] He tried to find loopholes through which Oakeley could be exonerated, his basic premise being that since the case was undefended, Fust had made serious errors of judgement in interpreting Oakeley's beliefs. If Pusey hoped that this procedure might keep Oakeley within the Church of England, then he was to be disappointed. Oakeley responded to his suggestions with a mixture of resolution, resignation and indifference. He did not think that anything could be made of his claim to hold without teaching. 'I explain myself as to mean not necessarily renouncing any formal decision of Western Christendom which is certainly putting my claim at the lowest'.[29] Pusey suggested that they try to make something of the phrase 'all Roman doctrine'. But Oakeley dismissed this idea saying that he had specified 'theological decisions' in *A letter to the Lord Bishop of London*, and the judge had understood him in that sense'.[30] Even if reversal of the judgement could be secured, Oakeley believed that events had gone too far, and were he enabled to officiate again in the Church of England, the inference would be drawn that he had surrendered at least something of that for which he had contended'.[31] The judgement of the court, he concluded, was 'powerful and stringent . . . it includes a palpable effect and a sweeping penalty which might be quoted to prove the undoubted authority of the Court which had pronounced it'.[32]

Oakeley had kept in touch with Newman and his companions at Littlemore since he had moved there at the beginning of September. He began by staying with his old friend W. G. Ward and his new wife at their cottage at Rose Hill.[33] Not long afterwards, the Wards were received into the Roman Catholic Church at the Jesuit Church at Bolton Street in London. There is no reference to this event in any of Oakeley's writings in or about the year 1845, which leads to the supposition that his lack of emotion was due to the fact that he was on the verge of taking the same step. It is likely that he moved to lodgings in Littlemore itself some time after Ward's conversion in September. He was certainly living there on Friday 3 October when J. B. Dalgairns came to see him that morning.[34] Dalgairns was in a state of happy excitement due to the fact that he himself had been received into the Roman Catholic Church a few days before.[35] He was only twenty-six years old, and one of the younger members of the Newman household. Dalgairns had been spurred on to make the move by the prospect of the arrival of his parents in Littlemore on Wednesday 1 October. They were opposed to the move, and Dalgairns had decided that he could wait no longer, and would have to make the move before their arrival. He was not alone; Ambrose St John, Newman's closest confidant since the death of Hurrell Froude, was received on Thursday 2 October.[36] Newman's monastery at Littlemore was beginning to disintegrate.

It was against such a background that Oakeley dined with Newman on the evening of Sunday 5 October. Neither of them has left an account of that evening, but it took place only three days before Newman was himself received into the Roman Catholic Church. It is almost certain that Newman told Oakeley nothing of his thoughts. His attitude to Oakeley was always characterised by caution and suspicion. He would have disclosed nothing to Oakeley, even if he was sure of the decision he was about to make. He had resigned his fellowship of Oriel College on Friday 3 October, telling his friends that 'anything may happen to me any day'.[37] He was unsure of the date of his reception, and may have told Oakeley such. But by Tuesday 7 October, Oakeley was in a sad and pitiable state. Conversations with Newman over dinner had done nothing to calm his increasing perplexity.

Poor Oakeley was very much on the fringe of the Littlemore circle and had no clear picture of what was happening. He was 'quite taken by surprise'[38] by the news of Dalgairns' conversion, and over the next few days he was in a state of bewildered loneliness. 'I am not in the secret of their goings on; and now one ceases to be taken by surprise whatever comes about. A great change has taken place in the appearance of things at the house since Dalgairns' return, and one cannot but suppose that it is the harbinger of still greater change. I get very nervous sometimes and want someone to talk to; but perhaps it is as well one has to get right by oneself . . . I wish you would write me a nice letter however short; I get hardly any but letters of business or rowings; and I am quite down-hearted at times . . . I hope all goes on well with me'.[39]

For the first time since the summer of 1841, Oakeley did not know what to do or where to go. For five years he and Ward had led the younger group of Romeward Tractarians and now he found himself overtaken by events. Many years later he recalled Wednesday 8 October, the day of Newman's conversion, as one of pouring rain. Few people were aware of what was happening, Newman wishing to be received quietly and without publicity. Oakeley was not aware that anything had happened until a day or two later. He had been in the habit of attending the recitation of the Office in the small oratory at the monastery. After Newman's reception he noticed two changes. Firstly, Newman and his companions began to pronounce the Latin in an Italian way; and secondly, the antiphons of the Blessed Virgin Mary, hitherto omitted, were now included at the end of Lauds and Compline.[40]

With the reception of Newman, Oakeley's move in the same direction could not be far away. But, rather surprisingly, it was not as soon as might have been expected. Three weeks elapsed before, on Wednesday 29 October, he took the step that his friends and enemies had long predicted. This seems a curious delay, remembering all that he had said and written over the preceding five years. Nearly all his close friends in the Tractarian fold had become Roman Catholics, and Oakeley could have been expected to join them almost immediately.

According to Oakeley himself, the delay was due to his desire for a period of time to reconsider a decision that he had already made, to become a Roman Catholic. 'I could not but feel that my way to it had been providentially cleared'.[41] Both his parents, who would have strongly objected to such a move, were dead. Four of his five brothers were also now dead, and among his sisters there was only one who would feel the move as an acute personal sorrow. To one of his friends he wrote: 'I am sure these times must be extremely painful to you, and wish I could give you any comfort; but the comfort you would value, of knowing that your friends are likely to stay with you, I do not think I can honestly give you'.[42]

He was not concerned about his fellowship of Balliol since that would cease on his becoming a Roman Catholic, but the resignation of his prebendal stall at Lichfield caused deep sadness. 'Lichfield Cathedral was so blended with the memory of my earlier years that I could not sever myself from it without feeling a special regret'.[43] His letter of resignation to Bishop Lonsdale[44] was answered by one of kindness, the bishop telling Oakeley how much he lamented the proceedings in the Court of Arches.

Until the day of his reception, Oakeley always believed that he had acted out of loyalty to the Church of England; that all his actions were consistent with such loyalty; and that the authorities of that church would regret the action they had taken against him. 'I can truly say that my affections were centred in Margaret Chapel, *not* in anything extraneous; and that things extraneous *did* but minister towards that attachment. The authorities have snapped a principal spring in the machinery of our system; and my own expectation is that it will go to pieces'.[45]

On Friday 24 October, Oakeley wrote to Newman saying that

he had 'come to the resolution to seek admission into the Catholic Church, and have no longer any difficulty but in the arrangement of the details'.[46] He accompanied his letter with a pamphlet entitled, *A letter on submitting to the Catholic Church*, written the previous day, which he proposed to publish. The letter functioned as his apologia for the step he was about to take, and gives his basic reason for leaving the Church of England. 'I refer to the offices of authoritative teaching, and definite and final direction, together with the satisfaction of all those especial . . . Christian instincts which the Church Catholic is undoubtedly meant to satisfy . . . such, for instance, as filial and brotherly affection'.[47]

This is a good illustration of the general tone of the letter which is a mixture of reason, direct providence, and bitterness. Oakeley gave the following reasons for leaving the Church of England. Firstly, the interpretation of Holy Scripture was, in the Church of England, left to private judgement. 'This, I believe to be the very straight road to heresy; and which in the Anglican Communion, actually issues in a countless variety of discordant and even contradictory exhibitions of the truth'.[48] Oakeley had moved a long way since 1835 when he had declared the Thirty-Nine Articles to be 'the Church of England's official interpretation of Scriptural truth'.[49] Secondly, the Church of England had 'no recognised system of moral theology, according to which, those who undertake . . . the direction of souls, are bound to shape their instructions. All is accidental, capricious and vague'.[50] Additionally, there was no recognised system of practical sacramental confession.[51] Thirdly, the Roman Catholic Church 'plainly corresponds with that type of the Catholic Church which is deeply and habitually impressed upon my whole moral and spiritual nature'.[52]

The letter also contains a good deal of more or less open bitterness. Oakeley had gone through several emotional storms since February 1845, culminating in the loss of his work at Margaret Chapel, and he looked back in anger on these events which had driven him (in his opinion) out of the Church of England. He came close to calling his condemnation and disqualification by the Court of Arches a conspiracy. 'If the object of authorities has been to take from me the means . . . of all [direct] religious influence . . . I acknowledge that the course has been most successful. I have no resource left me but to take to farming, or cultivate general literature – neither of which happens to be my turn'.[53] Despite the anomalies of the Church of England 'as an adequate object of loyalty and affection, I not only clung to her but gave myself up to her without examining the question of her historical claims upon my acceptance'.[54] He criticised the bishops for their complete lack of simplicity, sensitivity, sincerity and gentleness, and accused the Church of England of being 'the chief agent' of infiltrating sorrow.[55] It bore no relation whatever to its call to be the bride of Christ in terms of brotherly love. 'Heart burnings and bickerings alas! I fear . . . are to be found everywhere'.[56]

Oakeley was unrepentant for what he had tried to do. He was sure that all his behaviour had been consistent with the duty of a loyal member of the Church of England, and he believed that his loyalty had been 'very materially underrated'.[57] Though at Margaret Chapel he had engaged in an experiment which, as far as he knew, had no precedent. 'I never acted otherwise than with a direct eye to the provisions of my own communion . . . nor even consciously transgressed the order of my bishop'.[58] 'To bring my own Church into the utmost possible sympathy and harmony with the Roman, while at the same time scrupulously observant of her own express injunctions of authority . . . this was my idea of finest loyalty to the Church of England'.[59]

While this is true, some account needs to be taken of the feelings of the other side. Oakeley was stretching the latitude of the Church of England, both in doctrine and liturgy, to a point that was theoretically allowable, and therefore it could be argued that he was consistently loyal. He promptly obeyed Bishop Blomfield's requests in liturgical matters, and respected his ecclesiastical superiors. But he could not understand or cope with contemporary reactions. Candles, surplices, choirs and Gregorian chant, were novel and contentious elements in Anglican worship in the early nineteenth century. Oakeley might regard them as adjuncts that significantly improved the quality of the liturgy, but the Church of England was simply not used to such things. Three centuries of anti-Roman prejudice, inflamed by memories of Guy Fawkes and the Popish Plot, were part of the common folklore of England, and could not be erased overnight. The sixteenth century Reformation was too deeply ingrained into English national consciousness to be lightly attacked as a source of evil. Oakeley's assumption that there was an 'essential congeniality'[60] between the Church of England and the Roman Catholic Church was a standard claim of Tractarianism, and one which was embraced by increasing numbers of clergy and laity as the century progressed, but in 1845, most Englishmen found it hard to accept.

His final conclusion was that his effort 'to infuse the Roman spirit into the Anglican body',[61] was impossible to accomplish given the existing situation, and the only sensible course was to abandon the struggle. The attempt was compared to 'putting new wine into old vessels, the effect of which must be to mar the vessel and spill the wine – to dissipate the Catholic introduction and shiver the Anglican receptacle. But I cannot go so far as to regret that the experiment has been tried'.[62]

The day fixed for Oakeley's reception into the Roman Catholic Church was Wednesday 29 October, and the place was to be the little Roman Catholic chapel at St Clements, near Oxford; he was received by Fr Robert Newsham, the parish priest.[63] Oakeley had expressed a desire to be received 'in the most private manner possible',[64] but found, to his great discomfort, that the old priest had made arrangements to receive him with some ceremony, and in the presence of | the congregation.[65] He went through the ceremony with considerable feelings of emotion 'which it is happily as difficult as it would be undesirable to describe'.[66]

When the ordeal was over, 'I hastily left the chapel and pursued my way alone to my lodgings at Littlemore where I gave myself up to reflections'.[67] If he had hoped to be left alone in peace for any length of time, such hopes were quickly dashed. No sooner had he returned to his lodgings than a knock at the door announced the arrival of an emissary from Balliol College, bearing a form for Oakeley to sign, by which he would resign his fellowship. 'I obeyed the mandate without a moment's hesitation'.[68]

Towards the end of the day, Oakeley went over to the chapel of the monastery and joined Newman and his companions who were preparing to say the Office. Although it was customary to keep silence afterwards, Oakeley confessed to being 'a little disappointed'[69] that no one said anything to him afterwards, let alone offered him congratulations. 'I went back to my lodgings and retired to rest after what was incomparably the most trying day of my life'.[70]

Chapter Thirteen

A seminal role

FREDERICK OAKELEY AND THE OXFORD MOVEMENT

Mr Oakeley was, perhaps, the first to realise the capacities of the Anglican ritual for impressive devotional use, and his services, in spite of the disadvantages of time, and also of his chapel, are still remembered by some as having realised for them in a way never since surpassed, the secrets and consolations of the worship of the Church.
R. W. Church

When Newman published his *Apologia pro vita sua* in 1864, he spoke of 'a new school of thought arising in the Oxford Movement during the period 1839–41, which swept aside the original party of the movement, and took its place. The most prominent person in it was a man of elegant genius, of classical mind, of rare talent in literary composition – Mr Oakeley'.[1] In making this statement, Newman ignores, for reasons best known to himself, Oakeley's close friendship with William George Ward. The earliest chroniclers of the Oxford Movement, especially Thomas Mozley (1882), Wilfrid Ward (1889) and Richard Church (1891), and other contemporaries of Oakeley, such as Tait and Gladstone, speak of Oakeley and Ward as close, almost inseparable, companions and friends. Ward and Oakeley are generally linked together in any references to this second generation of Tractarians. Ward is the more well-known of the two, chiefly through his unreadable and almost forgotten *Ideal of a Christian Church*, and the subsequent events in the Sheldonian Theatre on 14 February 1845. Only fleeting references are made to Oakeley and his role in the Oxford Movement. The article on Bishop Jewel, the trial in the Court of Arches and Margaret Chapel, are the usual topics. This ignorance of Oakeley is continued by later historians of the movement, who have made little attempt to assess his contribution, preferring to concentrate upon the apparently more interesting figure of Ward. The most unfair comment is the description of Oakeley as 'a relatively colourless personality'.[2]

Beside the colourful figure of Ward, this description of Oakeley is understandable but unfortunate, because Oakeley's significance has been completely obscured by Ward. The extent of the friendship between Ward and Oakeley is now impossible to determine with accuracy, because of a total lack of surviving correspondence between the two men for the period in question. That they enjoyed a close friendship, at least until 1845, is unquestionable because of the testimony of those who knew them. Mozley described them as 'as different as can well be imagined, but somehow as much associated as Castor and Pollux, Damon and Pythias, or any other two inseparable pairs'.[3] Wilfrid Ward quotes a description of their friendship as 'the more remarkable from their difference of manner and gifts'.[4] W. G. Ward himself referred to his friendship with Oakeley during their Anglican days as 'especially intimate'.[5] Wilfrid Ward felt that his father had been 'to a great extent' the guiding force in Oakeley's life.[6] He preached frequently at Margaret Chapel, and 'all the arrangements at Margaret Street were submitted to Mr Ward's approval down to the smallest details . . . Oakeley, moreover, adopted to the full the theological principles which Ward developed'.[7] When Ward was seriously ill in 1843 or 1844, his doctors indicated that he might not survive. Ward told Oakeley that he might not survive the year, and the latter replied. 'Do not say that . If you were to die, the sun of my life would be extinguished'.[8] Wilfrid Ward, stated that his father and Oakeley saw less of each other and were less intimate after they were received into the Roman Catholic Church, and ascribed this to the authority of the church and their geographically divergent paths. Though there is an element of truth in this, Ward's marriage to Frances Mary Wingfield on 31 March 1845 would have introduced an additional note of separation.

Newman's relationship with Oakeley was quite different from that of Ward. His reputation has been enhanced by a series of near hagiographical writings in the years since his death, to the point where his faults had been extinguished, or at least obscured, by a cloud of devotion to his considerable genius. But there is sufficient evidence to show that Newman possessed a good deal of intellectual arrogance, and sometimes displayed impatience with those whose abilities were not commensurate with his own. Certain members of his own family found Newman to be something of trial, and one of his sisters once remarked that 'to become his friend, the essential condition is that you see everything along his lines, and accept him as your leader'.[9] Certainly Oakeley caused Newman a good deal of annoyance by his independent behaviour, but it needs to be said that Newman was not over-helpful to the developing Oakeley. He had less than a high regard for the content of Oakeley's writings, although evidently he admired their style, and kept him at a distance, despite their early acquaintance in the dining club of 1829–33. Even through the crises of 1845, Newman was coldly objective about Oakeley's continued membership of the Church of England, despite the fact that Oakeley admired and respected him and often sought his help and advice. R. W. Church's description of Oakeley as 'a man who followed a trusted leader with chivalrous boldness, and was not afraid of strengthening his statements',[10] is a perfect description of the relationship between Newman's Tract 90, and Oakeley's *The Subject of Tract XC*, the latter embellishing the former.

Newman was either unable or unwilling to control the zealous group of Romeward Tractarians, led by Oakeley and Ward, partly due to the uncertainty of his own position. The efforts of Nicholas Wiseman in *The Dublin Review* from 1836 onwards, to undermine the Tractarian belief in the catholicity of the Church of England, had badly shaken Newman's faith in the Church of England, and he ascribes his failure to control Oakeley and Ward to this reason. 'Nothing was clearer concerning them, than that they needed to be kept in order ... I was just the person above all others, who could not undertake it ... I had an intense sympathy in their object and in the direction of their path'.[11] Newman admitted in his *Apologia* that he had known Oakeley long before the Assize Sermon, and attributed Oakeley's development to his association with a group of 'eager, acute, resolute minds'.[12] Whether Newman's lack of control over Oakeley was due to his own preoccupation with other matters, or to a simple inability to control the irrepressible and young Romeward Tractarians, or to a basic sympathy with their beliefs, it gave Ward a much greater influence in the life of Oakeley than he might otherwise have had. Newman had a magnetic attractiveness, and Oakeley was only one of many people to fall under his spell. If he caused Newman any difficulty or embarrassment, then the fault lay partly with Newman who, through his lack of interest and concern, for whatever reason, created a vacuum that was filled by Ward.

Oakeley's critical attitude towards the sixteenth century Reformation, especially his attacks on Bishop Jewel, were an important part of his contribution towards the development of the Oxford Movement, whatever may be said about accuracy or historicity. Mozley was convinced that Oakeley's essay on reformation doctrine, that won him the Ellerton Theological Prize in 1827, did something to form this attitude. In the same year, Oakeley attended the lectures of Bishop Lloyd, who taught his students to regard the pre-Reformation and post-Reformation English Church as a continuous body. Thereby he created a sympathetic disposition in Oakeley towards Catholicism, six years before the start of the Oxford Movement. Newman thought that Oakeley, whom he knew at that time, was broadly in sympathy with the Oriel party of 1826–33.[13] But Oakeley then drifted into a evangelical phase from about the beginning of 1831, until 1835, and missed out on the sense of purpose and excitement of the earliest years of the *Tracts for the times*, as they began to appear from September 1833. Consequently, he joined the movement as part of a second-generation influx, although he was about the same age as Newman, with all the enthusiasm of a convert. Additionally, he was under the influence of the bombastic Ward from about 1834, although Ward did not embrace Tractarianism until late in 1838. This accounts for Oakeley's often contradictory attitude towards the Church of England in the mid-1830s, the period immediately preceding his commitment to Tractarianism early in 1839; the period when the influence of Tait was declining as that of Ward was growing.

The publication of Froude's *Remains* appears to have had a decisive effect on Oakeley's development. The first two volumes appeared in 1838 and a further two in 1839. Oakeley attributed his hostile attitude to the reformation, to the opinions he had absorbed from the *Remains*, and the shadowy influence of Froude on Oakeley, as on the other 'eager, acute, resolute' minds of the second generation of Tractarians should not be underestimated. There is evidence in *Bishop Jewel* to indicate that Oakeley saw himself at the literary heir of Froude, intending to pick up the pen laid down by Froude on his death in 1836. The two men were well-acquainted, at least from 1826, until Froude went abroad in 1832, though they were not then of the same theological mind. Oakeley declared that his beliefs and attitudes had been shaped by the reading of the *Remains*, and there are many similarities between the two men. Their extreme dislike of the Reformation is the most notable example. Froude had harsh criticism for Bishop Jewel,[14] and even Keble had changed his opinions and views on the reformers under the influence of Froude. Oakeley's attempt to set up a semi-monastic foundation in Margaret Street possibly derives from Froude's plans for colleges of priests in towns, or urban monasteries. Like Froude, Oakeley was accused of 'Romanising' and, as it was probably untrue of Froude, so it was untrue of Oakeley. A genuine desire to realise the full potential of the Anglican liturgy, 'to give that system all the advantages of which it seemed capable',[15] was not the same as a desire to 'Romanise' the Church of England; actively to propagate the doctrines of the Roman Catholic Church within the Church of England. Froude and Oakeley shared a dislike of Erastianism, a dislike first mentioned by Oakeley in

The Church Service, and developed in *Rites and Ceremonies*. The furore surrounding the appearance of *Bishop Jewel* mirrors a similar reaction when the first two volumes of the *Remains* appeared. But *Bishop Jewel* split Oakeley and Ward from Newman and Pusey, and was the first important declaration of the beliefs and aspirations of that group. 'His article on "Jewel" was more than anything else a landmark in the progress of Roman ideas'.[16] It may be thought surprising that Newman failed to see Oakeley as the person who continued and developed the work of Froude, but then Oakeley was Oakeley and, for Newman, no one could fill the place of the 'bright and beautiful' Froude.[17]

Perhaps Oakeley was a quieter and gentler version of the visionary Froude, but their zealous impetuosity was the same. Frederic Blachford's comment about Froude can so aptly be applied to Oakeley. 'He was not . . . a theologian, but he was as jealous for orthodoxy as if he were'.[18] It has been suggested that Froude represents the heroic, chivalric and self-sacrificing aspect of the Oxford Movement.[19] All those qualities are to be seen in Frederick Oakeley.

Oakeley was not a theologian and had little real grasp of the subject. In 1834, Newman had declared him to be 'most miserably deficient'[20] in divinity. So far as can be judged from his *Life of Saint Augustine of Canterbury*, his knowledge of the history of the Welsh Celtic Church, and his 'historical view' of the formulation of the Thirty-Nine Articles, he did not have much sense of historicity. Mozley found him 'avowedly sentimental rather than decisive in his religious views'.[21] 'His sentimental nature disposed him to reject the violence of logical or rather mathematical arguments'.[22] Isaac Williams thought Oakeley's abilities were 'rather showy, from an elegant and pleasing style, than either acute or deep'.[23] R. W. Church described him as a man 'without much learning'[24] 'whose quality and craving was refinement, not strength, or exactness of ascertained truth, or originality of any kind, but the grace and beauty of finish',[25] a point borne out by Oakeley's deep concern for liturgy and music. Gladstone echoed this, believing that Oakeley had a 'peculiar gift of discernment and feeling as to the nature of divine service'.[26] Oakeley's great strength was liturgy, and in this field he was a pioneer, and probably unsurpassed in his efforts to restore beauty, dignity and harmony to the barren services of the Church of England in 1839. He himself described his work at Margaret Chapel as 'a collateral, and yet independent, effort,[27] to the work being done at Oxford. Even the anti-Tractarian *English Churchman* described the services at Margaret Chapel as 'beautiful and unique'.[28] After Oakeley's arrival at Margaret Chapel in the spring of 1839, the Oxford Movement took on the appearance of two movements; one at Oxford concerned with doctrine, the other at London concerned with liturgy, and the work being done at the chapel was viewed as without parallel in importance. 'Elsewhere in London one might hear faint echoes of the distant fray, but to be at Margaret Street was to be with the vanguard of the advancing host'.[29] R. W. Church comes close to the best assessment of Oakeley and his work at the chapel. 'Mr Oakeley was, perhaps, the first to realise the capacities of the Anglican ritual for impressive devotional use, and his services, in spite of the disadvantages of time, and also of his chapel, are still remembered by some as having realised for them in a way never since surpassed, the secrets and consolations of the worship of the Church'.[30]

Oakeley should best be remembered a pioneer of liturgical and musical development. His steps were halting and modest by later standards, but he began a great work and was a man far ahead of his time. His work did not die with his departure from Margaret Chapel in 1845 for two reasons. Firstly, he had begun the idea and the fund for building a new church, and this was continued and brought to fruition by his assistant and successor, William Upton Richards. Secondly, Oakeley so engendered a spirit and an atmosphere of tenacity and unanimity among the congregation that they rallied together after his departure and ensured the building of All Saints Church, Margaret Street. Upton Richards disliked the chapel as much as Oakeley had done, and was determined to see Oakeley's scheme completed. The newly-formed Ecclesiological Society wished to build a 'model' church, and the two schemes were amalgamated.

Oakeley had a strong desire to upgrade the external appearance of divine worship and its setting, and a good sense of the beauty of liturgy and music. The origins of this concern for the beauty of devotion can be discerned in his childhood memories of Lichfield Cathedral, the lectures of Bishop Lloyd on Catholic liturgies, his favourable impressions of continental Catholicism, and even his mother's artistic talents. In his work at Margaret Chapel, modest though it was, he began the liturgical and choral aspects of the Oxford Movement, thereby prefiguring the work of the ritualists later in the nineteenth century.

None of this could have occurred without Oakeley's essential quality of devotion. For all that he could be inaccurate and extreme in his writings, Frederick Oakeley was a devout priest, and his devotion was accompanied by a shy, kind and gentle nature. Ward, Tait, Mozley and Church all testify to this. Tait spoke of him as 'my kind helper'.[31] 'It would indeed be disgraceful in me, if I could ever forget all that Oakeley did for me, when I first came up as a raw young Scotchman, and with scarcely a friend, to Oxford; he was quite a father to me'.[32] A year after Oakeley's death in 1880, W. G. Ward remembered that there were 'few who exceed him in humility, simplicity, unselfishness, unworldliness

... From the first he was just what his friends remember him to have been at the last: so full of public spirit and so devoted to public objects that the remembrance of self seemed to have no place in his thought'.[33] Mozley recalled him as 'singularly gentle, modest and humble-minded'.[34] Church found him to be 'always kindly, patient and gentle'.[35] Another remembered him as 'distrait, quiet and silent' with a 'shy and reticent demeanour'.[36] Dean Edward Meyrick Goulburn of Norwich called him 'good cultivated little Mr Oakeley'.[37]

Oakeley's inherent strengths ought not to be overlooked. 'Short in stature and halting in his gait, with a rough shock head and features deeply lined, and so short-sighted that to read he was forced to hold book or manuscript close to his eyes',[38] Oakeley was not a physically impressive figure. But he more than compensated for this by an ability to inspire, almost to mesmerise, those who listened to him. 'His first word arrested the attention, and the fascination increased with every sentence that he uttered. His sincerity was so evident – however bold and startling might be his ideas, it was so clear that he was determined to follow them without dread of the consequences whithersoever they might logically lead – his reasoning so lucid and choice of language so exquisite – that when his sharp metallic voice ceased to be heard, no syllable that had fallen from his lips seemed to have been lost, but all remained clearly fixed upon the mind for future meditation'.[39]

Chapter Fourteen

Ware, Southwark and Islington

THE CONTENTED YEARS

*Among the earthly consolations of my later life is the assurance that I
have a place in the hearts of those old friends who have always a
place in mine.*
Frederick Oakeley to Archibald Tait, 8 June 1872

On 29 October 1845, Frederick Oakeley made the decision that
marked a radical change of direction for the remaining thirty-four
years of his life. The Frederick Oakeley of Shrewsbury, of Lichfield,
of Highclere, of Balliol, and of Margaret Street, was subsumed,
though not, as it transpired, obliterated, within a new 'converted'
Oakeley who emerged from the crucible of the intellectual and liturgical debate of the Oxford Movement, to take his place securely
within the fold of the Roman Catholic Church. Can the remainder of
his life be summarised by the sub-title 'the contented years'? Was the
period 1845–80 one of continuous contentment? Did he ever regret
his decision to leave the Church of England? Did he live to rue the
day that he departed from the church of his upbringing? Did he ever
regret his conversion to the Roman Catholic Church? If 29 October
1845 is accepted as the date that conveniently bisects the life of
Frederick Oakeley, and certainly the date that ended the storms and
passions of his involvement with the Oxford Movement, what were
the experiences of his 'post-conversion' life? This chapter attempts to
answer these questions by examining the concluding phase of the life
of Frederick Oakeley.

A study of his later years is hampered by the comparative paucity of
primary material about his life after 1845. There is a great deal of autobiographical information about his Anglican years, and not only because

of the large number of surviving letters that he addressed to Newman and Pusey. In 1855 and again 1865, Oakeley felt able to look back to his years in the Church of England, and to reminisce about his last turbulent years as a disciple of the Oxford Movement, though from the standpoint of the convert who viewed that movement as a transitional phase between the Church of England and the Roman Catholic Church. The Oxford Movement emerges from his writings as one that was misguided in its aims and objectives and whose truest adherents eventually came to the realisation that their future lay in the 'true' church. In 1855, having founded the 'Islington Popular Catholic Club' for his congregation, he addressed four lectures to its members. Lectures 2 and 4 were entitled respectively, *Personal reminiscences of the 'Oxford Movement'* and *The Catholic Church before and after conversion*. In 1863 and 1864 he wrote four articles, published in volume 53 of the *Dublin Review*, and re-issued in 1865 under the title, *Historical notes on the Tractarian Movement 1833–1845*.

Oakeley never seems to have been embarrassed in talking about his Anglican past, and he reminisced about his experiences in those years with a gentle detachment that sometimes betrayed evidence of memories of a wearying struggle, but was never infused with antipathy. There had to be a discernible distance between his old life and his new life, to justify the move from one church to the other, and he was occasionally mildly critical of the 'errors' of the Church of England but, unlike some converts, he never displayed hostility to the church that he had left, or to those of his friends who had remained within it, and he deplored the fact that such an attitude should exist among his fellow converts. 'I deeply regret that the language even of apparent unkindness should ever have been used on our own side in speaking of those with whom we were once connected'.[1] His reminiscences of his Oxford Movement years were factual and affectionate, and written, as he said, 'with the view of helping to keep alive the memory of an important crisis in the ecclesiastical annals of this country'.[2]

Although he spoke with affection of his pre-1845 life as a Tractarian, he was, for some years at least, critical of the ritualism that emerged in the Church of England from the 1850s onwards, all of it being so far beyond the modest liturgical developments that he had introduced at Margaret Chapel. He regarded the Oxford Movement as dead and buried, its work as finished, and its effects on the Church of England as minimal. In 1865, twenty years after leaving the Church of England, he felt able to write: 'The spirit of Tractarianism has vanished, and its object in aiming at the elevation of the National Church as a teacher has been entirely and conspicuously defeated. Nor is it of any avail to answer that Anglican clergymen can do with impunity what years ago was found to be impracticable – that they can burn candles by daylight, wear chasubles, start confraternities, order processions, and the like. For surely such practices, where they do not express a generally received doctrine, or harmonise naturally with the system in which they are found, are more likely to bring disrespect upon religion than to serve its best interests. They are parts of a great whole, and when torn from their place in it, become at best but the tokens of eccentricity, and very probably also the occasions of a serious delusion'.[3] This view is not surprising and need not be taken seriously; he was an external observer of a movement in which he had no part, and his denial of the worth of ritualism was a wilful refusal to accept it as a logical development of Tractarianism, and, most obviously, that he himself was, arguably, the first ritualist. His views changed with the passing of time, and his last article, published in 1879 a few months before his death, showed a belief that the Tractarian movement had 'succeeded' and a much more favourable attitude towards the results of the ritual movement in the Church of England.

Oakeley's *Personal reminiscences* of 1855 and the *Historical notes* of 1865, which coincided with the tenth and twentieth anniversaries of his conversion, both cease with that event. The other definitely autobiographical work that covers the pre-1845 period, is a group of unpublished manuscripts now in the library of Balliol College, deposited there in 1946 by Oakeley's great nephew, Major Edward Francis Oakeley (1870–1954). The manuscript is in three sections. The first, entitled *The story of my life*, is of uncertain date, but covers the period of Oakeley's life from his earliest childhood memories until his election as Chaplain Fellow of Balliol in 1827. Two shorter sketches, one written in the first person singular and entitled *Canon Oakeley's memoirs*, the other in the third person, were both written about 1879 not long before his death; they contain a much abbreviated account of his childhood and early adult life, concentrating on his religious development after 1827. Both documents finish about the time of his conversion, and may have been left unfinished because of his death in January 1880. There is evidence that Oakeley had drafted a preliminary sketch for an autobiography in August 1874, but which of these documents it might have been is open to question. 'I thank you for the interest you have in my personal history', he wrote, 'but I must ask you not to think of publishing any other biographical memoir of me other than the one I gave you . . . I could easily make it more complete, if you like to let me have it again'.[4]

There is very little material about his years from 1845–50, but another manuscript covers the first eighteen years of Oakeley's ministry as Roman Catholic parish priest in Islington. Entitled *History of St*

John's Church since 1850, it was written by Oakeley in February 1868, in his typically elegant style; it was never published, and was not discovered until several decades after his death. Although principally a history of his work at St John's Church, the last thirty years of Oakeley's life were intimately bound up with the life of that church, and his trials and tribulations emerge in much the same way, though not to the same depth, as those he endured at Margaret Chapel. But it is primarily a history of his work at St John's and contains none of the theological development of *The story of my life* or *Canon Oakeley's memoirs*.

It is almost as though Oakeley himself felt that his religious development was complete; that there was nothing of consequence to say after 1845; and that he deemed it more important for his readers to know where he had travelled from, why he had travelled to where he was, and to travel with him along that same route. Like many before and after him, he wrote eloquently and with great interest and a sense of immediacy about his earliest and formative years, but a sense of passivity and contentment marked his Islington years, which were occupied by rhythm and routine and the mostly unspectacular daily tasks of a Roman Catholic parish priest, although admittedly with the occasional foray into controversy. It can be concluded that Oakeley himself felt that there was little of note that he wished to record about his post-1845 life. This is something of a pity, because there are many fascinating vignettes of his Roman Catholic years, provided by his contemporaries, not least in the way that he maintained contact with many of his friends in the Church of England. Gladstone in particular was a regular correspondent, the two men having known each other since before 1838, and they often exchanged copies of their latest publications. But the most remarkable of friendships was that between Oakeley and Archibald Tait, who kept in touch and retained an affection for each other, even after the latter had become Archbishop of Canterbury in 1868. 'The parting of friends' was not a relevant description of the relationship between Oakeley and Tait after 1845, and after a few years of distance, the maintenance of their friendship became a priority that the divergence of their doctrinal paths never erased.

The arrival of Newman and Oakeley and all the other 'Oxford' converts of 1845 was trumpeted by the *Dublin Review*, which treated Oakeley's work at Margaret Street almost as a wasted effort that should never have been attempted. 'Mr Oakeley's perseverance in such duties (too long, though it were, for his own welfare and peace of mind, since it undoubtedly obstructed his recourse to the centre of unity and the fountain of all true blessing) will seem to stronger persons a stronger proof of his devotion to [the Church of England] than passing expressions of misgiving are a disproof of it . . . These men [Ward and Oakeley] did on the whole try to carry out Catholic principles in the Anglican Church, and were absolutely and hopelessly foiled in the attempt. They overcharged the vessel and she sank under the load. Their common object was to Catholicise their Church, though they set about it in different ways . . . And where do they now find themselves? . . . In pure, ultramontane, genuine, Roman, Catholicism'.[5] The article, entitled 'The recent conversions', was printed in the *Dublin Review* in 1846 and is thought to be the work of Oakeley himself, although with revisions by Bishop Nicholas Wiseman, Vicar Apostolic of the London District.

With Newman and Ambrose St John, Oakeley was confirmed by Wiseman in Pugin's Gothic chapel at Oscott College on Saturday 1 November 1845. Afterwards he went back to London to clear his house in Margaret Street, before going to stay with a friend at Newbury. From there he went to Littlemore for a short period, before moving to temporary lodgings in Oxford. He was destined for the priesthood, but was indecisive about the choice of seminary. First thinking of Oscott, he later changed his mind, and on 22 January 1846 he went to St Edmund's College at Ware in Hertfordshire, to begin his training.

The choice of Ware was unusual in that most of the converts of 1845 preferred Oscott, and this was Oakeley's first choice as Newman noted. 'Oakeley has settled at St Edmund's, meaning to be at Oscott till over Christmas . . . Dr Wiseman has been most singularly kind about it, showing no suspicion at all though Oakeley changed his mind about Oscott'.[6] Oakeley appears to have chosen Ware partly because of his friendship with the Irish-born Vice-Rector, Dr Robert Whitty, whom Newman described as 'a very simple, warm-hearted, reflecting person'.[7] Among Oakeley's many articles for the *British Critic* was one published in 1843, entitled *Sacramental Confession*. Whitty read the article and admired it, and met Oakeley at the time of publication to discuss the points that it raised. Another reason for going to Ware was the presence of William George Ward. Oakeley and Ward had visited the college in their Anglican days, and there were those still alive in the 1890s, who could recall the interest that it aroused at the time. 'Many still alive remember the feeling of curiosity with which their arrival was watched by the students and professors. They came one afternoon, together with Mr George Tickell, also one of the Tractarians, and spent several hours at the college'.[8]

As a married man, Ward was barred from ordination as a Catholic priest, but he delighted in the atmosphere of Ware, and by arrangement with the college, he had a small house (which later became a preparatory school) designed by Pugin, built in the seminary grounds. Oakeley loved Ware as much as did Ward. 'There is a quietness about this place which makes it very delightful. The Church services too, though under great disadvantage, are exceedingly solemn and pleasing. A beautiful new chapel is building under Pugin, to which the students are looking forward with great expectation. They are great musicians, almost entirely self-taught, and conduct the whole musical service and very beautifully'.[9]

Fr William Dolan, a student at Ware at the time, remembered that Oakeley initially did not create a favourable impression on his fellow students. For all that Oakeley had been straining towards Rome in the few years prior to his conversion, his arrival at Ware soon exposed lacunae in his knowledge and understanding of that church. 'We had heard so much of the Oxford converts and of the ritual of the 'Tractarians' that we expected to find Mr Oakeley fall in at once with the ordinary routine of our services. We were, therefore, rather surprised when we found him more or less bewildered by the whole thing. He made one or two curious mistakes, which we were not slow to notice and to make fun of. For example, the first time that he saw a High Mass, when the Priest, Deacon and Subdeacon said the Confiteor in turns, he thought they were disputing with each other as to what should be done next, and as to the proper rubrics. Again, the first week that he was at the college, he caused great amusement when, on finding a boy 'kneeling on a gallery', and being told that it was a 'penance', he accepted this as meaning a Sacramental Penance, and thought that the boy must have been confessing some very grievous sin. When we got to know him, we soon forgot these little mistakes. He mixed with us all as if he was one of ourselves, and became a leading spirit in the house. At one time he created quite an enthusiasm for ecclesiastical functions and ceremonies, and we found him so unassuming and at the same time so thorough and genuine that we learnt to respect him very highly, and were always ready to take up anything that he might propose. Amongst other things he took up with zest may be mentioned some missionary efforts among the people in the country, which had already been begun by the Divines. The Society of St Vincent de Paul was established about this time, and from it our labours took their rise. From visiting the poor in their houses, we gradually developed into assembling them at a common meeting place, and a little chapel was established in a barn at Nasty, where we preached on Sunday afternoons. Mr Oakeley's sermons were very successful, to judge by the results, for there were numerous conversions'.[10]

Oakeley's otherwise happy time at Ware was rendered difficult by a public controversy that was not of his own making. In April 1847 there appeared an anonymous novel entitled *From Oxford to Rome*, the author of which was later revealed to be a Miss E. F. Harris, whom Oakeley had been advising about becoming a Roman Catholic. Not for the first time, and not for the last, did a holy man of God fall victim to the fantasies of a woman, and Miss Harris repaid Oakeley's efforts by including in the book a slanderous attack on the converts in general, and one, who though unnamed, could be clearly identified as Oakeley. The damage was done, and Oakeley, who might have hoped for a peaceful time at Ware, found himself the target of a malicious campaign of denigration. On 19 June 1847 the *Tablet* reported that the *Church and State Gazette* had published an article calling Oakeley a hypocrite in that, as an Anglican he had received holy orders too quickly, without the customary year between being ordained deacon and then ordained priest, and that the speed with which he was ordained was due to his desire to gain the Balliol fellowship.

The allegation was immediately refuted by a subsequent anonymous article in the *Tablet*. Though signed 'Fellow of Balliol', the author was almost certainly William George Ward who, with memories of Oakeley's support during his own 'trial' in the Sheldonian, sprang to the defence of his old friend. Ward, if he was the author stated rightly that although a period of a year was usual between the conferment of the orders of deacon and then priest, it was not mandatory, and could be dispensed with in the case of exceptional candidates. He also stated that Oakeley had been anticipating ordination for some time, and was far from being unprepared.

A further article appeared in *The Tablet* in August 1847, by the 'unknown' author of *From Oxford to Rome*, apologising for the slur, and was accompanied by a letter from Oakeley graciously accepting the apology. Two weeks later a second recantation was published, prompted, it seems, by undue pressure from Miss Harris' brother and the Reverend W. F. Lloyd, who complained of the lady being subjected to 'mental torture' and asserted that 'Mr Oakeley *was* an English gentlemen before he became a Romish deacon'. Both men spread rumours that the initial recantation had been forced upon the lady by Oakeley himself, and this allegation was supported by *The Church and State Gazette*.

The whole correspondence was finally published in the issue for 11 September 1845, and at this point, with the known facts in print, it becomes possible to discover the truth behind the charges. Oakeley was accused of abusing the confessional and of being in favour of the compulsory separation of wives from their husbands in the event of only one party being received into the Roman Catholic Church. This was combined with a general charge of hypocrisy over his decision to join the Roman Catholic Church and an imagined desire [on the part of Miss Harris] that he intended to rejoin the Church of England. As Oakeley and Miss Harris were both unmarried, it is a wonder that the subject of the separation of husbands and wives, in the event of one or the other becoming a Roman Catholic, should have formed so prominent a section of the charges against him. This is the allegation that arouses the suspicion that deeper and unhealthier passions were concealed beneath the outward complaints.

The charges could never be substantiated, and anyone who had known or read of Oakeley's theological and spiritual development in the years 1839–45, would realise that they were baseless. So what was really at the heart of Miss Harris' slander? Given that the principal players were an unmarried middle-aged former Anglican priest with a reputation for humility and holiness of life, and an unmarried lady who had been a member of his congregation at Margaret Chapel, the only conclusion to be drawn is that Oakeley had fallen victim to the old familiar syndrome of infatuation. In her novel, Miss Harris describes a priest named Eustace A. in language which borders on the amorous. 'The first sight of the young clergyman could not but be to everyone prepossessing in a high degree. The priest ideal of Raphael could not more than describe the expression of his pale and beautiful countenance. His large blue eyes were filled with that heavenly light which gives, perhaps, the loveliest notion of an angel's spirit; his fair hair of singularly brilliant texture, formed a natural coronet above the high and expanded brow, and gave a classic finish to the finely marked profile ... His voice and air – grave, measured, and subdued – would impress you as the manner of one eminently holy – one less of earth and than heaven'.[11] In all probability Miss Harris had become enamoured with Oakeley, and projected on to him her own desires and needs without any regard for the fact that, in relation to her, he was exercising a pastoral role and was quite unable and unwilling to return her undue advances. His departure to Rome and the prospect of him becoming a celibate Roman Catholic priest, must have been a devastating prospect for her. On this premise, she therefore becomes the archetype of a person disappointed in love who, unable to control the passionate emotions aroused within her, resorts to spite and venom in a futile effort to destroy that which she could not have.

The episode caused acute embarrassment for Oakeley, and was more public and lasted far longer than it should have done. But the story of vengefulness as a way of dealing with unrequited love is all too familiar, and Oakeley was neither the first victim nor the last.

Miss Harris's emotional outbursts did not produce an entirely negative result. One qualitative piece of literature emerged from the sorry tale, and that was Newman's novel, *Loss and Gain*. Newman was in Rome at the time that Oakeley was mired in the shattering newspaper allegations by Miss Harris, and wrote the novel for general consumption to indicate just what a convert could expect to lose and gain by conversion. Following the pattern of Miss Harris, *Loss and Gain* was first published as an anonymous work, although everyone knew the identity of the author, and Newman himself did not trouble to conceal it. Oakeley's gratitude to Newman became apparent in 1855, when he published his *Personal reminiscences of the 'Oxford Movement'*, in which there are a substantial number of quotations from *Loss and Gain*.

Oakeley's life as a Roman Catholic priest began at his ordination by Bishop Nicholas Wiseman on 14 November 1847. He was assigned to St George's Cathedral in Southwark, one of the six priests on the staff of the new cathedral that was then approaching completion. The cathedral proved to be a great success, and attracted a varied congregation, from the rich to the poor. A large number of wealthy patrons came to enjoy the high standard of music, but the basic congregation consisted of the very poor who lived in the vicinity of the building.

Oakeley would have been present in the cathedral at its dedication by Bishop Wiseman on 4 July 1848, as one of the 300 clergy and fourteen bishops present on that occasion. In the following week, a special octave of Solemn Benediction and sermon took place with a different preacher each day, and the preachers on Wednesday, Thursday and Friday were all former Oxford Movement comrades; J. B. Dalgairns on Wednesday, Frederick Faber on Thursday, and then Oakeley himself on Friday. His powers of preaching, always of a high standard, were recognised on the octave of the dedication, when he was the preacher at Benediction in the evening.

With his love of liturgy and music, he was a natural candidate for a cathedral post, and although little is known of his brief time in Southwark, it would have been mostly to his liking. The possible exception might have been his relations with Thomas Doyle, the cathedral administrator. Although Doyle was the driving force behind the construction of the cathedral, and liked organising grand ceremonies within when it was completed, he was inclined to snobbery and eccentricity and had developed a taste for writing verbose letters to various magazines and journals on a wide of variety subjects.

In July 1849, Oakeley reported that during Exposition of the Blessed Sacrament on a Sunday afternoon, a young girl had been sent to the cathedral by her mother, accompanied by a servant. 'They had not been on their knees more than a few seconds when one of our doorkeepers threw them out'. The doorman claimed that the church was always closed between Mass and Vespers. The girl's mother complained to Oakeley who discovered that there had been a misunderstanding between the cathedral administrator and the doorman. Presumably under instructions not to admit the unknown girl, he claimed that he did not know that she was a member of the congregation. Oakeley delivered a full report to the bishop on 31 July 1849, pleading only for anonymity. 'Whether the exclusion was the effect of misunderstanding between the doorkeeper and Dr Doyle I know not; certain it is that the last time at St George's, the Exposition was a failure as far as the people were concerned. Scarcely any were there. The good were kept out under the plea of protection against the innocent. Your lordship will, I am sure, act upon this information; but I shall be glad if you will not name me'.[12]

In the same year, and only four years after joining the Roman Catholic Church, Oakeley involved himself in a controversy with Bishop William Ullathorne, Vicar Apostolic of the Central District, and shortly to become the first Roman Catholic Bishop of Birmingham. The dispute began with an article in the *Rambler*, a journal founded in 1848 by a group of able laymen as an alternative to the *Dublin Review*. The *Rambler* became the active and vocal organ of liberal English Catholicism before being suppressed by Archbishop Manning in 1862. Ward and Oakeley were among the earliest contributors, and it tended to become the journal of the Oxford converts, and occasionally critical of elements of existing English Catholicism. In December 1848, an article appeared in the *Rambler*, written by a convert, which attacked the poor standard of Roman Catholic educational institutions in England; both schools for boys and seminaries for the clergy. It aroused strong reactions in a church that was still endeavouring to assimilate the new 'Oxford' converts with the old Catholics, and the article was generally regarded as exaggerated, undiscriminating, ungenerous and unjust. It aroused the wrath of Bishop Ullathorne who wrote an intemperate letter to the *Tablet*, published on 9 December 1848. Ullathorne condemned the article as a piece of mischief and impertinence on the part of one who was still a child and in pupillage, and who had no right to criticise that of which he knew nothing. 'At this time of trouble for the whole Catholic world, we are presented with our own particular and private cup of bitterness which is made up of detraction, injustice, and, I must add, of ungratefulness, towards ourselves, by a few, indeed a very few, who are but of yesterday amongst us, and whom we received with affection and confidence . . . When the children of the Martyrs, who kept the hallowed fire in secret at all perils, are detracted and defamed before the civilised world, their guardians cannot be justified in keeping silence, unless we would acquiesce in the conclusion that the body of English Catholics is a scandal to the Church'.[13]

As the original article had been criticised, so Ullathorne's letter was criticised in turn, and Oakeley reported to Wiseman that it would be unhelpful to the cause of integrating the Oxford converts with the old Catholics, and to the cause of conversion generally. 'I regret the letter, more especially on account of its probable effect on expected conversions from the Anglican body; for I know an opinion widely prevails that the more excellent of the recent converts, the more learned, devoted, self-denying, zealous, are not appreciated among us; and this opinion, most unfavourable to the conversion of similar persons, is likely, I fear, to be promoted by such a letter as Dr Ullathorne has felt it his duty to publish, not confined to a correction of the mistakes or exaggerations into which the *Rambler* has fallen on the subject, but implying a hint of confederacy on the part of certain converts to assail our existing institutions'.[14] Oakeley did his best to calm the troubled waters in an evenly tempered way, springing to the defence of Catholic education, but also taking the line that the article criticised an historical situation which had been largely remedied. That said, he was obliquely critical of Ullathorne, arguing that those who read the article should be able to accept that it did contain a large element of truth that should not be ignored.[15]

There was always to be a slightly uneasy relationship between the influx of converts in 1845 and afterwards, and those whose families were historically Catholic, and Oakeley returned to the issue in 1871. In his book *The priest on the mission*, he cautioned converts against being too critical of aspects of their new spiritual home. 'Converts are disposed to overlook the great and consistent moral and spiritual excellence of some hereditary Catholic or another, because he does not come up to their standard of refinement. They make too little account of unavoidable differences in education and social antecedents between themselves and those with whom they are suddenly thrown in later age, and with whom they ought to feel how much that is really important and valuable they have in common, rather than to dwell on points of distinction which are purely secondary and subordinate'.[16]

Although little is known of Oakeley's life at Southwark, he seems to have been generally content at the cathedral. A temporary release came in March 1848 when he returned to Ware for a short and happy visit that must have reminded him of his days as a tutor at Balliol. 'I am still here very happily and quietly preaching to the students. I suppose I cannot hope for these golden days much longer'.[17]

The golden days finished in January 1850. In the previous month, Wiseman asked Oakeley to take over the church of St John the Evangelist, Duncan Terrace, Islington. Oakeley was the fifth of a number of priests at St George's Cathedral, but now he was to be given his own charge. He was installed as Missionary Rector of the comparatively new church on 26 January 1850, and there he stayed until his death on 29 January 1880.

The Romanesque-style St John's Church is a large rectangle with an imposing semi-circular apse. There are no aisles or transepts, but a series of chapels and confessionals off the north and south sides of the nave. On the south side was the baptistery, St Francis' Chapel, St Joseph's Chapel and the Lady Chapel, and on the north side the Chapel of the Sacred Heart, a Calvary Chapel, and four confessionals. Despite the problems that he faced, Oakeley, ever with an eye to architecture and liturgy, fell in love with the church at first sight. 'I thought that it possessed great capabilities as a working church. In size it exceeded the dimensions of most of the Catholic churches then in London. It had a fine sanctuary, and a series of lateral chapels which might be fitted up for different devotions, and it had also, what I have ever considered an important requisite not often found in England, two spacious sacristies'.[18]

The church was clearly the architectural antithesis of Margaret Chapel, but the appointment was not, to use Oakeley's words, 'a bed of roses'. The church had been opened on 26 June 1843, but it was still incomplete (the towers had not been built and the side chapels were unfurnished) and heavily in debt when Oakeley arrived. 'There was a huge scaffolding at the end of the church which I soon learned was to be a fixture, pending the non-payment of the account due for the works to which it had contributed'.[19] It was later to be alleged that Oakeley had been given charge of the unfinished church because, as the son of baronet, and with a private income, and with 'connections', he would be able to attract money from his wealthy friends to complete the building and free it from debt. The allegation was not entirely unfounded; Oakeley did contribute much from his own pocket towards the work of St John's. But it was also based on resentment from one who felt that he should have occupied the position that Oakeley had been given.

When Oakeley arrived at St John's, he was faced with a delicate and unfortunate situation. Richard Boyle, the curate of Oakeley's predecessor, was still living in the rectory and refusing to leave. He was a priest of nationalist and Gallican tendencies, and had little taste for Bishop Wiseman's desire to revive Roman devotions which had fallen into disuse, and ardently felt that it was his right to be appointed parish priest of St John's in the place of his colleague who had resigned. Boyle argued that Wiseman had no right to remove him, refused to leave the house, and so Oakeley was forced to live in temporary accommodation for fourteen months during the process of persuading the recalcitrant priest to vacate the clergy house. Boyle finally agreed to go in March 1851 only after claiming and receiving compensation in the sum of £60 for money spent by him (so he alleged) on the mission house, and Oakeley was able to move into 39 Duncan Terrace, where he remained until the end of his life. 'Two priests had been in charge of it;' remembered Oakeley, 'the one had given up because he had found it impossible to pay the expenses of the church out of the receipts, the other asserted his claim to come into the place of his out-going brother against all competition. The prospect before me therefore was that of having to pay money with one hand and fight with the other . . . At length, on 22 January 1850, I finally left St George's and the same afternoon found me in the small and gloomy lodging in Charlton Place to which I was compelled to resort through the occupation of the clergy house by the priest who disputed the bishop's right to supersede him. I now felt, for the first time since my ordination, the full weight of my responsibilities and not a little of the desolation of spirit which I suppose many a priest before me has experienced in finding himself without friends or advisers in the presence of an arduous undertaking'.[20]

Boyle was offered alternative appointments, both by Wiseman and by another bishop, but refused all offers, and remained resentful of the way in which he had been treated. In 1854 he contributed to a series of articles in the French journal *Ami de la religion*, written by the Abbé Cognat, which criticised Wiseman's policy as disastrous to the interests of the Church in England and complained of the way in which Boyle had been the victim of episcopal oppression. Wiseman himself replied to the allegations by means of a statement in the *Univers*, testifying to their inaccurate and unjust statements, defending his introduction of Roman devotions, and praising Oakeley's work in rescuing St John's from the mess into which it had fallen. 'I have done all I can to encourage these practices, and certainly they are nowhere followed with more devotion, and by a greater crowd, than in the Church which was a desert when it was served by the Priest whom the Abbé Cognat presents as a victim of oppression, but which under his successors has become a garden of devotion and piety'.[21]

Boyle had developed a taste for litigation, and instituted legal proceedings against Wiseman for defamation of character. The result for the unfortunate Wiseman was that he was forced to be a defendant in three trials. At the end of the first trial, at Guildford Assizes in August 1854, Boyle's complaint was dismissed. He appealed against the decision, and at the second trial, at the Surrey Spring Assizes in April 1855, in which both judge and jury were hostile to Wiseman, the adjudication was that Wiseman should pay the sum of £1,000 damages as well as the costs of the case. During the course of the Kingston trial, Oakeley was cited in court as 'a gentleman of very considerable fortune'.[22] Wiseman appealed in turn, and the Court of Exchequer set aside the verdict on the ground of excessive damages and improper reception of evidence, and a third trial was arranged for the Croydon Assizes in August 1855. By this time Boyle was wearying of the extended legal process and nervous of defeat, and intimated that he was prepared to offer a compromise. The third trial was halted on the day that it opened, by an agreement between the two parties. Oakeley himself was relieved to find that he would not have to appear in court to give evidence. During the course of the trials, Boyle, still smarting from being deprived of what he regarded as his right, alleged that Oakeley had only been given charge of St John's because of his wealth and his influence. Oakeley found this highly amusing and said as much to Wiseman when congratulating him on the outcome of the trial. 'I really regard it as a direct answer to the prayers offered for you . . . I wonder how much of our success at Islington is due to my "ample fortune" – and how it is that my 'family influence' (as a Protestant) could subsume me on a Catholic mission'.[23]

Apart from the unfinished and debt-ridden church, Oakeley also found, with a sense of déjà vu, that the choir of the church included women. 'Disinclined as I was to a coup d'état, I yet perceived at once that the abuse was one which called for a decisive measure. I therefore determined upon expediting another arrangement by which the choir would be brought near the sanctuary, and entirely re-modelled by the substitution of exclusively male singers for that mixture of sexes which had led to very undesirable results, though to nothing which deserves the name of scandal'.[24] Within a short period of time, he had replaced the ladies with men and boys, and St John's Church, like Margaret Chapel before it, was transformed by Oakeley's musical skills and love of music into a centre of musical excellence that delighted the congregation, 'excepting only the old choir who were not unnaturally, nor as I must say unreasonably, annoyed'.[25] Murmurings in the ranks claimed that as Oakeley had worked with a mixed choir at Southwark, he should not have made so much trouble with a mixed choir at Islington. In a letter to the *Oxford Herald* in July 1852, Oakeley denied that there had ever been female voices in the choir of St George's. 'I believe I am correct in saying that the Bishop of that diocese (Southwark) shares the objection which the Cardinal Archbishop also feels to female voices of any description in Ecclesiastical choirs; in any case, I can assure you that the practice of admitting them is declining amongst us as rapidly as circumstances will allow. The mistake has probably arisen from the choir of St George's occasionally having been strengthened by other instruments than the organ, a practice to which our superiors do not object'.[26]

With the ladies exiled to the pews, the musical tradition of St John's made great strides under Oakeley's direction, and was greatly appreciated by Wiseman, who was fond both of Oakeley and of the church, and went there every year to pontificate at High Mass on St John's Day. 'He often expressed himself pleased with the manner in which the ceremonies were gone through, and especially with the music. He had a strong prejudice, which I do not share, against the plain chant and liked no deviation from the rich and varied melodies of the German and Italian schools, except in favour of the style which is used in the papal choir'. In 1864, Oakeley asked Wiseman if he would visit St John's on 6 November to pontificate at High Mass. 'We are going to perform a beautiful Mass of Gounod, the great French composer, which I should like Your Eminence to hear. It is in quite a new style, not long, and very full of melody. Pray come my dear Lord if you can'.[27] Wiseman also visited St John's to deliver addresses at the three hours devotion on Good Friday. 'He spoke with delight of the music that formed the interludes between the different meditations. It was always that of Haydn's *Passione* with full instrumental accompaniments'.[28] In 1874 Gladstone, who had been an enthusiastic worshipper at Margaret Chapel in Oakeley's day, congratulated the Roman Catholic Church on acquiring a priest with such a talent. 'Mr Oakeley (now alas! ours no more) . . . gave to its very simple services, which would now scarcely satisfy an average congregation, and where the fabric was little less than hideous, that true solemnity which is in perfect concord with simplicity. The papal church now enjoys the advantages of the labours of Mr Oakeley who united to a fine musical taste a much finer and much rarer gift in discerning and expressing the harmony between the inward purposes of Christian worship and its outward investiture, and who then had gathered round him a congregation the most devout and hearty that I (for one) have ever seen in any communion in the Christian world'.[29]

It was unfortunate for Oakeley that not only did he have to contend with the obstreperous Richard Boyle, an unfinished church and a mixed choir, but also with a vociferous public reaction to Pope Pius IX's establishment of a hierarchy for the Roman Catholic Church in England and Wales. This practical administrative re-organisation of the Roman Catholic Church in England and Wales in 1850, provoked an irrational outburst of anti-catholicism which labelled the event as the 'papal aggression'. 'I have', wrote Oakeley, 'a distinct recollection of the fifth of November in that year when the popular clamour was at its height. After having been saluted in the earlier part of the day with no-Popery cries near our door, and being startled with colossal figures of the Pope and Cardinal Wiseman peering into the windows of the first floor, we repaired as was then our wont into the church to say devotions for the holy souls in purgatory, which were illustrated rather than interrupted by constant explosions of gunpowder in the immediate neighbourhood of the church'.[30] The anti-catholic mood of the time was continued in the following year when Oakeley addressed an open and published letter to the newly-formed Islington Protestant Institute 'occasioned by a recent statement of their objects and proceedings'.

No sooner had the passions of that episode died down, than Oakeley found himself embroiled in defending William Weale, Master of the Catholic Poor School at Islington. In September 1851, Weale was charged and convicted of whipping a boy named John Farrell at the school, and sentenced to three months' imprisonment in the House of Correction at Cold Bath Fields. Weale had become a Catholic in 1848 and so fell within Oakeley's pastoral care. Oakeley produced testimonials to Weale's character, and also evidence that the boy had been whipped with his clothes on, and therefore that the slight injuries sustained by the boy had been caused after his examination by three doctors. He voiced his suspicions that, in the aftermath of the 'papal aggression' the accusations were based on malice rather than fact. 'I looked upon the matter as a mere trifle, – the effect of an extensive popular feeling against Catholics, which unhappily prevails in this neighbourhood . . . I soon became aware that influences were at work to induce the parents to prosecute, though none whatever were used on Mr Weale's side'.[31] Within four days of the flogging, Farrell was examined by a surgeon 'who pronounced the injuries upon the boy's person to be so trifling as not justify any prosecution of Mr Weale'.[32] Despite the evidence submitted by Oakeley, the Home Secretary refused to re-open the matter, and Weale served his full term in prison.

Islington in the mid-nineteenth century was not the gentrified fashionable area that it became in the last quarter of the twentieth century, and parts of the neighbourhood were severely deprived. Oakeley ministered to a large congregation of Irish immigrants who adored him and affectionately called him 'our Father O'Kelly'. The church, from its construction, had always been a centre for Irish Catholics, and Oakeley was given two Irish colleagues, Fr William Ignatius Dolan (from 1850) and Fr Andrew Mooney (from 1863). Dolan was an accomplished organist and assisted Oakeley with the formation of the men's choir, and both assistant priests remained at

St John's with Oakeley throughout most of his ministry there. For a while during the mid-1860s, Oakeley also had a French priest, a Monsieur Laboue on his staff, and in 1870, the Sisters of Notre Dame, a French teaching Order with its mother house at Namur, arrived in the parish to live in a house adjoining the church.

The pattern of Sunday worship consisted of Low Masses on Sundays at 7, 8, 9, and 10am, followed by a High Mass at 11am. Catechism classes were held at 3pm and Vespers and Benediction at 7pm. Benediction also took place on Thursdays and on feasts of Christ and the Blessed Virgin Mary. The recitation of the Rosary or devotions took place every other day at 8pm unless the Sacred Heart devotions were being recited on certain Fridays, or the Confraternity devotions on certain Wednesdays. The two confraternities in the parish were those of the Blessed Sacrament and of the Immaculate Heart of Mary. Devotions to the Blessed Virgin Mary took place daily during May, and during November for the Holy Souls.

St John's parish included Pentonville Prison, and Oakeley was responsible for visiting Roman Catholic prisoners. It was the practice at the time for prisoners requiring the ministrations of a Roman Catholic priest to have their names entered on a list for that purpose, and a priest would be denied access to any prisoner whose name was not on such a list. Oakeley discovered during the course of his ministrations at the prison that any prisoner who had, even inadvertently, attended an Anglican service in the prison chapel, was immediately removed from the list. Throughout the 1850s Oakeley waged a campaign to protect the faith of Catholic prisoners and to secure better access to them. He began in 1850 by addressing a petition to the Home Office urging that Catholic priests should be paid for their work in visiting Catholic prisoners in the same way that Protestant ministers were paid. In the aftermath of the passions surrounding the re-establishment of the Catholic hierarchy, the Home Office refused to grant his request, but Oakeley continued the pressure. In 1854, he addressed an open letter to Viscount Palmerston, complaining of a deliberate policy to prevent Catholic prisoners from having access to their priests, as the result of four years visiting experience at Pentonville. 'There are two Protestant chaplains who are part of the regular staff of that establishment. They have ample salaries, besides lodgings found them at the prison. There is also one Protestant schoolmaster, at least, whose daily duty it is to give instruction to all the prisoners ... As to public worship. It is very true that Catholics may, if they make a point of it, obtain an exemption from the duty of attending the Protestant service, which is the rule of the prison. But no effort is made to acquaint them with their power in this respect, and I often find that they are actually ignorant of its existence, and remain under the idea that they are obliged to do like the rest. I may remark, also, that the absence of any provision for worship of their own, operates in fact, as a strong temptation to violate their conscience and attend a service which, by law of their Church, is forbidden to them'.[33] In 1852, he had obtained a list of all the Catholic prisoners in Pentonville, about 70–80 individuals. In 1853, when he applied for a similar list, he was told that he could see those prisoners who had asked to see a Catholic priest, and was given a list of 20 names. In 1854, he was given the same condition, and supplied with a list of 30 names. 'A great body of the Catholics at Pentonville are, I am persuaded, by the operation of the rule in question, left without the aid of their religion during the whole time of their imprisonment'.[34] In April 1861, still not satisfied, he complained to Bishop Grant of Southwark, who liaised with the government about the well-being of Roman Catholic prisoners, and added that he believed that Roman Catholics were subjected to every possible inducement to attend Protestant services, in order substantially to reduce the number of prisoners who were entitled to access to their priests.

Oakeley has left other images of his life in Islington, all written in the same wry style and with same dry humour that he employed to record his memories of Margaret Chapel. When he introduced the practice of ringing the angelus at 6am instead of 9am, the reaction from the neighbourhood was predictable. 'One man wrote to say that Catholic priests had no feeling for fathers of families who were kept awake half the night by crying children and wished to have a little peace early in the morning. Another person wrote to me to say that he did not see the necessity of announcing to the public by a bell at six in the morning that three times three made nine. There were neighbours who said that they had no objection to the bell because it made their servants get up in good time in the morning'.[35] Despite the complaints, Oakeley refused to relent, and the angelus continued to be rung at 6am.

Oakeley did what had been hoped of him and continued the work of completing and adorning the church. Gas lighting was introduced in 1850; a new organ was installed near the sanctuary at the same time; the Chapel of the Blessed Sacrament was consecrated in 1852; the Lady Chapel was decorated in 1850; the Chapel of St Francis was decorated in 1857 to a design by Edward Armitage, RA, who some years later decorated the sanctuary; an organ and choir gallery were erected in 1862; and the entire church was decorated in 1866. By the mid-1860s he was displaying the confidence that he felt about the future of St John's. 'We seem making great way here. The church is thronged, and the local newspapers are writing it up. Last night after a service in honour of the Seven Dolours (a humble imitation of the Good Friday meditations with music) a Protestant gentleman came up to one of the priests and said, "Sir, I am not of your religion, but such an evening as this is about enough to make a convert of me". '[36]

The pinnacle of Oakeley's ministry at St John's, was the celebration, on Sunday 28 June 1868, of the twenty-fifth anniversary of the opening of the church on 24 June 1843. The sermon at the High Mass in the morning was preached by the titular Bishop of Troy, one of the few survivors of those who had been present at the ceremonies in 1843. In the evening, after Vespers, the Papal Benediction was given by Monsignor George Talbot, Domestic Chamberlain to the Pope, who had been one of Oakeley's colleagues on the staff of St George's Cathedral, Southwark. A procession of the Blessed Sacrament then passed into the cemetery where a temporary altar was erected and Benediction given, and afterwards repeated in the church. 'The weather', observed Oakeley with pleasure, 'was most delicious, and the day was observed by a very large concourse of devout worshippers'.[37]

Although the success of his work at St John's, his power of oratory and his holiness of life might have warranted it, Oakeley received no significant preferment in the church of his adoption. Like many of his fellow Oxford Movement converts in and around 1845, his age might have been against him. Forty-three at the time of his conversion, he was approaching middle-age, and the chance of becoming a bishop would only have occurred when the first generation of the restored English hierarchy had begun to die after about 1860. But it is more likely that Oakeley's activities in the one preferment that he did receive, made him sufficiently unpopular in certain quarters to remove any possibility of promotion.

In 1850, with the re-establishment of a pattern of territorial dioceses for the Roman Catholic Church in England and Wales. Nicholas Wiseman, Vicar Apostolic of the London District, became Archbishop of Westminster, and was created a cardinal. Two years later, Oakeley was appointed a canon of the newly-formed chapter of the archdiocese which in a way replaced the prebendal stall at his beloved Lichfield Cathedral that he had surrendered in 1845. As a canon and a member of the chapter, Oakeley found that he was to enter the fray of controversy, albeit on a less prominent scale. Certain members of the chapter, and Oakeley was not one of them, became critical of Wiseman over what they perceived to be his poor administration of the archdiocese, and the dispute became especially acute after 1855 with the appointment of George Errington, Bishop of Plymouth, as Wiseman's coadjutor. Errington was 'a strict and exact disciplinarian, ready at all points to apply canon law without allowance for circumstances, an absolutely punctual man of business',[38] who was not beyond berating the more relaxed and flexible Wiseman on a daily basis.

Only Henry Edward Manning, who had been appointed provost of the chapter in April 1857 by the personal decision of Pope Pius IX, remained consistently loyal to Wiseman. The other members of the chapter were not overjoyed at the imposition of a provost over their heads, and dispute began between the cardinal and the chapter which was only concluded by an appeal to the Pope. Letters from Oakeley to George Talbot in Rome prove that Oakeley, who had gone to Rome to defend Wiseman against accusations of mismanagement, had little taste for conspiracy and controversy and endeavoured to steer clear of any active involvement, but he was one with the chapter members in objecting to the appointment of Manning as provost. They considered that Manning's position as Father Superior of the Oblates of St Charles, a community that he had founded at about the time that he joined the chapter, made him unsuitable for the position of provost. Oakeley also wrote strongly to Talbot about the Oblates, considering them not really suitable for the work that they had to do in the Westminster archdiocese. Unfortunately for Oakeley and the rest of the chapter, Talbot was a close friend of Manning, and whatever Oakeley wrote to Talbot was quickly passed back to Manning. The Reverend and Honourable George Talbot was a convert of 1847 who became the chamberlain, intimate friend and constant attendant of Pope Pius IX, and therefore a person of considerable influence who should have been treated with a commensurate amount of caution.

Relations between Wiseman and Errington went from bad to worse (the two men were basically incompatible), and Errington was finally removed as coadjutor in 1860 by papal decree. After Wiseman's death in 1865, the chapter had the task of selecting three names for forwarding to the Pope, and certain members pushed strongly for the appointment of Errington. Manning was alternately suspicious and contemptuous of his fellow canons, and that included Oakeley for his devotion to Newman. Manning strongly believed, without evidence, that Oakeley would put forward the name of Newman to succeed Wiseman, because he had 'literally been playing the fool about him'.[39] Oakeley had been publicising Newman's *Apologia pro vita sua*, which offended Manning who was not even mentioned in the book, and the provost dismissed the six canons as fools in successive letters to Talbot. On 24 February: 'One thing I feel, that is, how disastrous it is that the choice of the archbishop and metropolitan, affecting therefore, not Westminster only but all England, should be even remotely effected by Maguire, Searle, O'Neal, Oakeley, Weathers and Last ... I know no six men less acquainted with Rome, or England, or the needs of the Church in England. They are busy together and mean mischief'.[40] On 31 March: 'I care less about who the next archbishop may be than to see six or eight incompetent men, who have crossed the Cardinal's great work, caressed and encouraged'.[41] On 11 April: 'I know that nothing has been left untried to mislead the decision of Rome. Oakeley has been getting Bellasis to write'.[42] Oakeley later informed Talbot that the chapter had not been aware of the extent to which the Pope would have disapproved of their recommendation of the former coadjutor bishop; a surprising statement in view of the Pope's revocation of Errington's appointment as coadjutor five years earlier. Oakeley also told Talbot that the chapter vote was almost equally divided, six votes being cast in favour of Errington and five against.

With Talbot at the Pope's side in Rome, Errington was never a serious contender, and the appointment of Manning in May 1865 ended his career. Their cause lost, the canons accepted the Pope's decision without difficulty, and Manning recorded that on the day after his nomination was made public, Oakeley was among the those who took the earliest opportunity to show 'the greatest kindness' to the archbishop-designate.[43] Thereafter Oakeley maintained good relations with Manning.

Good relations or not, Manning would not tolerate opposition from his clergy. Oakeley had maintained contact with Gladstone, who sent him one of his publications shortly before Christmas in 1864 as, 'an expression of all your generous kindness to me when I was at Margaret Chapel'.[44] In 1874 when Oakeley was invited by Gladstone to attend one of his 'Thursday breakfasts'. Oakeley courteously informed Manning of the invitation and in reply was warned that the archbishop would regard it as a personal affront if any of his priests should visit Gladstone's house. When Oakeley relayed this remark he reported that Gladstone became 'visibly affected – for a moment there was almost a vindictive gleam in his eye'.[45] Manning's antipathy was to be expected; Gladstone had launched an attack on the 1871 definition of Papal Infallibility; the ultramontane Manning regarded this as nothing short of heresy and severed all relations with Gladstone. Despite Manning's stern disapproval of Gladstone, Oakeley maintained his friendship with the politician to the end of his life, 'with the feelings of respect and gratitude which I entertain towards you'.[46]

In July and August 1867 Oakeley, at Manning's behest, endeavoured to effect a reconciliation between the archbishop and Newman, by acting as an intermediary between the two men. The process was somewhat farcical, and the result unsuccessful; but it was a measure of Manning's trust in Oakeley, that he was willing to use him as an impartial and trusted postbag until the two men had reached the point where they were to able to write directly to each other. For the time being, each addressed his letters to Oakeley, beginning with the words, 'My dear Oakeley, will you be so good as to forward to . . . these remarks on the letter which he has addressed to you about me.' The plan was doomed and Oakeley's efforts were fruitless. Manning, the icy, stern and unyielding ultramontanist, and Newman, the frighteningly brilliant but independently-minded intellectual, were as incompatible as Wiseman and Errington, and there was little that Oakeley could do beyond ferrying letters to and fro. Nonetheless, Manning was grateful to Oakeley for his efforts, and anticipated that he would in due course receive 'the reward of the peacemakers'.[47]

Throughout the rest of his life, Oakeley continued his literary output, producing books, articles and reviews on aspects of liturgy, devotion and 'practical priesthood', most of them now completely forgotten or superseded, in the two principal Catholic journals of the time, the *Rambler* and the *Dublin Review*. Of the forty-six articles identifiably by Oakeley, forty appeared in the *Dublin Review*, five in the *Rambler*, and one (his last) in *Contemporary Review*. He was at his most prolific in the years 1846–64. Articles for the *Rambler* appeared between 1849 and 1861. Articles for the *Dublin Review* appeared virtually every year, and sometimes two or three times each year between 1846 and 1859. Four articles in 1863 and 1864 were published in 1865 as *Historical Notes on the Tractarian Movement*. No doubt because of his failing eyesight, his productivity declined thereafter. Two articles on church music appeared in 1868; one, on education, in 1869, and his last, on the use and abuse of ritual, in 1875.

The *Rambler*, originally the journal of the converts, came to dominate the market, and the *Dublin Review* declined until it was nearly moribund by the mid-1850s. In 1858, Oakeley and Ward agreed to Wiseman's request to take it over and try to give it a new lease of life, and for a while the two men became joint editors. Ward was characteristically dismissive of the project. 'All of us, except Oakeley, were occupied entirely against the grain . . . I am about as competent to direct a Review as to dance on the tight rope, and Oakeley is not much better'.[48] Despite this comment, Ward went on to become sole editor from 1863 to 1878, and under his jurisdiction, the *Review* strongly supported the cause of Papal Infallibility and attacked theological liberalism.

In 1851, Oakeley was revealed as a highly knowledgeable horticulturalist, when he produced a charmingly eccentric work entitled *The Catholic florist. A guide to the cultivation of flowers for the altar . . . and fragments of ecclesiastical poetry.* 'The lovers of horticulture', he wrote, 'are here presented with a little work [it ran to 327 pages] which, as its title proclaims, and as its pages will speedily disclose, is intended to give a religious and Catholic direction to that beautiful and interesting pursuit . . . It ought to be found a useful guide to the cultivation of flowers appropriate to the successive seasons of the Church'.[49] He pointed out how many flowers have had their names changed from religious titles like 'the snowdrop whose pure white flowers are the first harbingers of spring and is noted down in some calendars as an emblem of the Purification of the Spotless Virgin Mother. It blooms about Candlemas and was formerly known by the more religious designation of "Fair maids of February".'[50] Oakeley also recalled for the benefit of his readers, the opposition that he had endured from the Bishop of London in the use of flowers on the altar at Margaret Chapel. 'As a method of Church decorations it has fallen under the ban of Church condemnation in the Establishment and not many years ago the writer of these lines was himself inhibited, when an Anglican Minister, from attempting to interest his congregation through the medium of "Flowers on the Altar" in the varying succession of Christian Festivals'.[51] It would be easy to dismiss the book as a collection of exotic trivia, were it not for the fact that the subject is both thoroughly researched and so quintessentially Oakeley, and despite its naive title, *The Catholic florist* shows that he never lost his love and talent for church decoration. 'The precious metals which lie buried in the earth are wrought into the vessels which enshrine or sustain the Adorable Presence on the altar; the labours of the delicate hand, or the products of ingenious machinery, are turned to the account of religion in the draperies of the sanctuary, or the vestments of the priest; the busy bee and the languid silk-worm are ministers in the same holy cause; for the one yields materials for the loom, and the other has its praise in the very offices of Holy Church, as the unconscious contributor of her Paschal Light. And shall it be thought that flowers – the fairest and most unblemished among the remnants of Paradise – are to have no place in this catalogue of offerings?'[52] Oakeley must have loved writing the book, but its implementation would require every church to have a full time gardener, and easy access to a comprehensively stocked garden centre to obtain the many different types of flower to be used in church every day.

If *The Catholic florist* was the product of Oakeley the horticulturalist, then *Lyra Liturgica*, published in 1865, was the product of Oakeley the florid poet and hymn writer. It was dedicated to his colleague for fifteen years, Fr William Ignatius Dolan, who had done much to raise the standard of music at St John's Church. In Oakeley's words, *Lyra Liturgica* was, 'an attempt to apply to portions of the Catholic Liturgy, the method of illustration so beautifully exemplified in [Keble's] the *Christian Year* . . . The idea upon which the work is founded has been for many years in the writer's mind; but he has delayed giving expression to it, partly from want of leisure, and partly in the hope that it might find some better exponent'.[53]

His introductory verses entitled 'Holy Ceremonies' express much of what had been important to Oakeley from the day when he arrived at Margaret Chapel in 1839.

> *I love, O Lord, the beauty of thy house,*
> *I love the place wherein thy glory dwells;*
> *I love the silent speech, and sweet accord,*
> *Of holy ceremonies, dear to faith,*
> *Wherein, as in a mirror, shows the zeal*
> *That burns around the Throne of God, and breaks*
> *Into a thousand forms of active joy.*
>
> *I love to hear the white-rob'd semi-choirs*
> *Discourse of God in David's loyal song,*
> *And sum the import of each lofty Psalm*
> *In full voic'd Antiphon, or teach in hymn,*
> *And sweet Magnificat, its Christian sense;*
> *And note in prayer, or 'memory' devout,*
> *The glories of the Saint whose aid we crave*
> *To lead us closer to the Fount of Grace.*
> *I love the long procession, as it winds*
> *Through spacious aisle or circling colonnade,*
> *With cross erect, and banners waving high;*
> *While strains of festive praise or solemn plaint,*
> *Or strong entreaty, surge upon the ear.*[54]

Oakeley became especially well-known for a little book entitled *The ceremonies of the mass.* He compiled it in 1849, while a seminarian at Ware, and it was published in 1855 and became a standard work at Rome, where it was translated into Italian by a young student named Lorenzo Santarelli. It passed to a second edition in 1859, and further editions appeared in 1860, 1885 and 1891, the last more than ten years after Oakeley's death. The book is written throughout in the style of a charmingly worded dialogue between a catechumen and a priest, the former seeking the answers to his questions about contemporary liturgical practice. '*Catechumen*. You have now, reverend Father, fully instructed me in the doctrine of the Church upon the holy Sacrifice of the Mass; I pray you to give me some explanation of its words and ceremonies to be used in it. *Priest*. Most willingly. Your devotion cannot fail to be strengthened by some acquaintance with the Liturgy of the Church, as well as with the use and meaning of those sacred rites by which this most solemn of all religious actions is accompanied'.[55] A sequel, entitled *Catholic worship, a manual of popular instruction on the ceremonies and devotions of the church*, was printed privately in 1867, but it also proved to be a popular work, and American editions were published in 1872 and 1892.

In 1856 Oakeley uncharacteristically turned his hand to the writing of a play entitled *The youthful martyrs of Rome*. The play, now hardly worth remembering, was based on a novel written in 1854 by Wiseman under the title of *Fabiola; or, the church of the catacombs*, which has itself has largely passed into obscurity. It portrayed the life of persecution and martyrdom endured by Christians in early fourth century Rome, and was intended to be the first in a series of novels evoking Christian daily life at various times in history; *The church of the basilicas* was a fancied title for a further novel that never appeared. Both *Fabiola* and *The youthful martyrs* need to be approached not as an entertaining pieces of fiction but primarily as works of propaganda, and this was Wiseman's intention with *Fabiola*. The Christian slaves for example, deliver remarkably erudite discourses of philosophical theology.

At the time of its publication, *Fabiola* was a resounding success, and translated into several European languages. Oakeley's dramatical adaptation proved to be just as successful, running to more than twelve editions. Wiseman encouraged him to attempt the task, 'under the idea that it might possibly contribute towards the important purposes of innocent and Christian recreation, whether in families, or schools and communities'.[56] The story centres on Fabiola, a highborn but pagan woman, obviously destined for conversion and death, who is taught about the nature of God by her slave Syra, in poetic theological discourses.

> *Simple as light is His nature,*
> *One and the same always and every where;*
> *Partless and passionless; untied to place,*
> *Yet in all places intimately present.*
> *Before all creation was He was and when*
> *All ending endeth, He, unending still,*
> *Shall be the same. Power, wisdom, greatness, love,*

Justice and judgement true, are His by nature,
And, like that nature, limitless and free;
Naught is, but by His word; moves, but His eye
Directs it; ceases, but at His recall.[57]

In 1857 Oakeley published *The Church of the bible*, an adapted and expanded collection of sixteen 'discourses', the substance of each of which was preached as a sermon at St John's Church and aimed at non-Roman Catholics, with the intention of demonstrating that the nature and teachings of the Roman Catholic Church were in full accordance with the words of scripture, and to answer various charges made against the church. 'The Catholic church at Islington is frequented by a large number of Protestants, whose regular attendance, and uniform propriety of demeanour, seem to indicate that they are actuated, not by mere idle curiosity, but by a sincere desire of acquainting themselves with the Catholic religion. Hence the author felt that it became a part of his pastoral responsibilities to do what he could towards the satisfaction of these apparently honest inquirers'.[58] Oakeley was critical of the widespread printing and distribution of the bible without supplying any means of guidance to interpreting the texts. This, he warned, 'supposes that each individual person is capable of arriving at their true sense, and of either forming his religion out of them, or testing by them the tenets of the religion in which he happens to have been be educated. Again the bible is commonly distributed through the medium of a translation [the Authorised Version], which Catholics cannot but regard as in a very material degree erroneous or defective'.[59] The contents included chapters on the Crucifixion, the Blessed Virgin Mary, the confessional, the sacraments, the eucharist, the use of ceremonial, spirituality, and the primacy of St Peter. Although the main body of the work is by Oakeley, the section on St Peter was followed by a long 'note' on the second chapter of the letter to the Galatians, a chapter then most quoted by Protestants in denial of the supremacy of St Peter. The author was W. G. Ward, 'a name', wrote Oakeley, 'sufficient to guarantee the argumentative ability and theological erudition of whatever can be referred to it'.[60] Looking at *The ceremonies of the mass* and *The Church of the bible*, it becomes clear that Oakeley had become a conscientious, competent and effective Catholic apologist. It was therefore not surprising that in 1868 he should be elected a member of the Roman Academy of Letters.

His last major publication appeared in 1871. *The priest on the mission*, based on a series of sermons given at St Edmund's College, Ware in 1869, was written with the purpose of reminding the clergy of the Roman Catholic Church of their duties, and to assist them in the performance of those duties by helpful pieces of practical advice. Considering the art of preaching in Chapter 2, he dismissed extempore preaching, as well as reading from a prepared script, or reciting it, having learned it by heart. 'You should be very careful to forget putting your manuscript into your pocket. I am not speaking of mere notes which may be useful to you in suggesting the order of topics, but of any such part of your composition as might supply you with the very words to be used. If, while you are preaching, you feel that this paper is at your command, you will be apt to hanker and fidget after it, instead of trying to do your best in expressing the sense, not in reproducing the words, of what you have written'.[61] Chapter 8, dealing with the reception and treatment of converts, contained a slight hint of autobiography. 'It is . . . of great importance that, in arguing for our own religion, we should give our disciples from without all due credit for the amount of truth involved in their present profession; and this is especially right in the case of those who come to us from the Established Church, and more particularly from those of what is called the High Church party, who often bring with them so much knowledge of Catholic doctrine as leaves us little to do except in the way of supplying the foundation'.[62] Other chapters deal with visiting the sick and those in prison, working with young people, and, as always, the care of the church building.

From the mid-1860s, Oakeley, increasingly lame, had to endure the additional burden of failing eyesight. In 1864 he lost the sight of one eye, and the sight of his other eye gradually deteriorated, although he was never entirely blind. He wrote to Gladstone in 1865: 'My eyes, thank you much, are not worse, though not better. The sight of one eye is totally gone, and that of its companion hangs on by a thread still however I hope [it] will stay my short time, by the great mercy of God, which I have so largely experienced in my life'.[63] When Gladstone sent him a copy of his latest publication in March 1868, Oakeley was full of gratitude, but his letter was tinged with sadness by the knowledge that he was no longer able to read. 'I would not acknowledge it till I had read it through or rather heard it read, for my sight though it allows me to write, does not admit of my reading'.[64]

He became a much-loved figure in Islington, and as late as 1943, there were still parishioners at St John's who could remember 'the humped figure of the Canon as he walked about with his stick in his later days with a kindly twinkle in his one remaining eye and a blessing for everyone he met'.[65] He was in poor health in the last few years of his life and in 1875 his illness was serious enough for Newman to visit him, in the belief that death was imminent. Oakeley had written to Ambrose St John, Newman's amanuensis, speaking of his 'long imprisonment under the combined trial of labouring breath and weak sight',[66] but Newman's visit seems to have been undertaken with little grace. 'I made a great effort to get to Canon Oakeley who had sent me a kind letter and was very ill. I thought I might not see him again. I took a cab there and back; it cost 5s 6d. I could only stop literally 5 minutes with him, yet was late at my appointment with Lady Coleridge by half an hour'.[67]

Oakeley always retained his respect and adoration for Newman, and when the latter was made a cardinal in 1879, he was delighted. 'It is the answer to a prayer I have again and again made in the Mass, that your services to the Church might receive some public recognition in your lifetime, for indeed I felt that in such a prayer I was asking something for the Church as well as for you; since I do not know of anything which is more likely to win over to her the mind and heart of England than such an act as that which our Holy Father has done in offering you the highest ecclesiastical dignity which it is his power to bestow'.[68] Oakeley retained a high regard for Newman to the end of his life. He paid tribute to him in *Historical Notes*, and the latter acknowledged it with 'sincere gratitude' in the preface to his *Apologia*, also published in 1865.

He kept in touch with the other converts of 1845 until the end of his life, and eventually contact was re-established with those who had 'stayed behind' in the Church of England. An episode in 1852 brought him into contact with two bishops with whom he had once been very familiar: Charles Sumner of Winchester and Charles James Blomfield of London. Oakeley had first met Sumner on 19 September 1817, and saw him for the last time in 1843 at his London home in St James's Square. 'I feared of course that the more decided step which I afterwards took would have completed the estrangement, but here I was happily disappointed. During the last twenty-five years [Oakeley was writing in May 1875], I have received from him the kindest, nay the most affectionate of letters'.[69] Contact was renewed in 1849 when Oakeley wrote to Sumner expressing his sadness at the death of Jennie Sumner. 'The letter which I received in answer was all that I could have desired'.[70]

In 1852 Oakeley asked Sumner for help in suppressing an anti-Catholic exhibition at Newington in Surrey, believing that it was in the diocese of Winchester. Sumner was unable to help, as Newington was in the diocese of London, but his letter to Oakeley, dated 1 August 1852, demonstrated that he retained an abiding fondness for his former pupil. 'My dear Oakeley', he wrote, 'I can never address you by any less familiar title, although circumstances unhappily have so much sundered us. But if I never think of you without a sigh, so can I never think of you otherwise than with much affection'.[71] Oakeley retained to the end of his life a similar regard for Sumner. 'I have since received several other letters from him all couched in the same terms of affectionate regard, qualified, as in the preceding extract, by a tone of natural regret, which in no case, however, took the form of reproach. This tenderness of feeling might have been expected from one who always exhibited the greatest indulgence towards conscientious convictions of others, even when most at variance with his own'.[72]

As Newington was in the diocese of London, Oakeley followed his letter to Sumner by a similar one to his old adversary, Bishop Blomfield of London. Oakeley had never enjoyed the same degree of intimacy with Blomfield that he had enjoyed with Sumner, and probably with memories of the troubles that the bishop had with the former Minister of Margaret Chapel, Blomfield's reply was formal, though not curt, and he forwarded Oakeley's complaint to the Rector of Newington, asking him to do what he could.

From the mid-1850s, Oakeley renewed contact with Pusey, Gladstone and Tait, and he always remained as respectful of Pusey as he did of Newman. In 1865, he wrote: 'I have seen with real pleasure that Dr Pusey and Mr Keble are at length heading a movement in the right direction, and they have my cordial wishes for its success. They are doing good Catholic work in trying to stem the tide of rationalism and infidelity, whencesoever and wheresoever flowing ... Dr Pusey more especially is entitled to the thanks of all Catholics for the eminent services he is rendering to the cause of Biblical literature'.[73] When Pusey's *Eirenicon* was published in 1867, a series of letters appeared in the *Weekly Register*, complaining of Pusey's criticisms of Roman Catholic doctrine. Oakeley's letter was typically gentle in its criticism of Pusey's complaint about 'overwrought devotion to the Blessed Virgin', and he began by prefacing it 'with all the real and affectionate respect which I bear to Dr Pusey'.[74] In 1871 he visited Oxford and was 'most kindly received' by Pusey.[75]

In 'Ritualism and Ritual', published in the October 1874 *Contemporary Review*, Gladstone acknowledged how fondly he remembered Oakeley and his work at Margaret Chapel, and Oakeley replied with evident pleasure to the article, which 'is so full of kindness to me and my work at Margaret Chapel, that I cannot refrain from thanking you for it with all my heart. Your words reveal a host of pleasant and painful memories. Among the former, are those of the powerful sympathy and support which I received from you during those anxious years; and among the latter, those of the pang it caused me to break [with] so many attacking associates. Truly one's lot has been cast on trying and mysterious times. Who would have thought 40 years ago that events would happen in our life time to cut clean through so many early sympathies and friendships without fault on any side. Let us hope that they will one day be renewed under happier conditions'.[76]

In 1876, Gladstone invited Oakeley to visit him, but he was too frail to accept. 'At the present moment I am suffering from the effects of a long winter's illness which has reduced me to a state of extreme weakness, and the favourable change of weather has not as yet produced its usual effect. In the meantime my blindness has made rapid strides during the last year or two though I have still sight enough to find my way about. I cannot however read a word and am generally obliged, as in the present instance to trust to the kindness of an amanuensis for writing my letters. I will not however fail to bear your kindness in mind, though without any present hope of being able to profit by it'.[78] Gladstone issued another invitation in the winter of 1878, and Oakeley was again cautious of accepting. 'I am afraid of making promises at the age of 76, and with broken health, but, should it please God that I should get as much better next summer as I have hitherto done, I shall be truly glad to avail myself of yours and Mrs Gladstone's kind hospitality'.[78]

In April 1879, Oakeley, who had witnessed not only a substantially changed attitude to English Catholics during his life time, but also the substantial changes that the Oxford Movement had wrought on the spiritual and liturgical life of the Church of England, drafted an article, submitted to Gladstone for his approval,[79] subsequently published in *Contemporary Review*. In reply, Gladstone invited him to a meeting with R. W. Church, now Dean of St Paul's Cathedral; but it was clear that time was running out. 'I will do my best to be with you on Thursday at 10 as you so kindly propose. In my present uncertain state of health I cannot absolutely promise, but nothing less than physical impossibility will prevent my coming. Thanks for what you say about the Dean of St Paul's whom I shall be glad to meet'.[80]

In the case of Archibald Tait, contact was renewed on the initiative of Tait himself. Oakeley showed genuine pleasure at the progress of Tait's career and was probably secretly proud of the success of his former pupil, warmly congratulating him on his appointment as Bishop of London in 1856. 'You will not find it hard to imagine the strange combination of feelings with which I read the announcement of your great promotion. My thoughts naturally went to the days of our intimacy at Balliol and to the marvellous and mysterious divergency of our several lines of providential destination . . . So far as it is a real subject of congratulation to you, believe me that none of your friends can regard it with a greater interest or a truer pleasure than myself ... I shall always feel very sensible of the kind way in which you have acted towards me in later times. You are about the only member of the little Balliol coterie of 1830–3 with whom I have had any communication since I became a Catholic and the renewal of friendly relations has always, as I reflect with pleasure, originated with you. I am sure therefore [that] I shall still have a place in your friendly regard notwithstanding the great difference in our relative positions, and for myself can assure you that you will always have a place in my prayers. If you should ever fall in with any of our former friends ... pray tell them that, although out of sight, they are not, with me, out of mind'.[81] Twelve years later, when Tait was promoted to be Archbishop of Canterbury, and reached the pinnacle of his career, Oakeley again put pen to paper. 'My dear friend, I have just seen in the paper that you are to be the Archbishop of Canterbury. Pray accept the sincere congratulations of one of your oldest friends upon this elevation. I remember it as also your friends' prediction ... at Balliol, and it is a proof of our prescience ... What a curious fact it is that one like myself should have been a pupil of the Bishop of Winchester and the tutor of the Archbishop of Canterbury'.[82] It was a measure of the depth of friendship between the two men that they remained fond of each other despite the divergence in their lives and, contact having been re-established, Oakeley often enjoyed dining quietly with his former pupil at Fulham Palace (when Tait was Bishop of London), and at Addington and Lambeth Palaces (when Archbishop of Canterbury).[83] At a dinner in Fulham Palace in 1860, Oakeley found himself dining with his old friend Ward as well. Oakeley much enjoyed the entertainments with his former pupil, making only the condition [after the deterioration of his eyesight] that, as his health was poor, the dinners should be quiet and private. 'It will give me great pleasure to see you ... on your return to Lambeth, though it must be in a quiet way as my failing sight ... indisposes me for company'.[84]

In 1872, with Tait and Ward, Oakeley was invited to dine on high table at Balliol College, and was touched by Tait's speech in which the archbishop said how much he owed to his old tutor. 'I was touched and gratified by the affectionate words which Your Grace spoke about me at the Balliol dinner. Among the earthly consolations of my later life is the assurance that I have place in the hearts of those old friends who have always a place in mine'.[85] There was one small venture into the area of doctrine when, in December of the same year, Oakeley sent Tait the published version of four lectures that he had delivered, defending the Athanasian Creed against criticism. 'It is also a real pleasure to me to find myself once more fighting on the side of old friends in the defence of principles which, amid whatever supervening differences, we still hold in common'.[86]

Another invitation from Tait in 1875 brought a response from Oakeley indicating that age and ill-health were beginning to take their toll. 'Your truly kind letter is very tantalising to me, because it suggests the prospect of what is at the present time impossible. I have been suffering from an unusually severe attack of asthma ever since 25 October, the very day, curiously enough, on which I was prevented from coming to you the year before. Although better in other respects, I am still too weak to leave the house. I need not say how glad I should otherwise have been to have accepted your tempting invitation, and I still hope that as the year advances I might be well enough to pass a day or two with you at Addington if you should happen to be there and able to receive me. Should such a contingency arise, I would write to you and you could reply according to circumstances. I am glad to infer from your letter that your own health continues good. We are both getting on in life, but you have some years the advantage of me, and above all have got good eyes and a free breath which are the two points in which despite so many other blessings, I am weak. My sight grows gradually worse, but it is running a race with my years and I hope will beat'.[87]

On the death of first Tait's son and then his wife in 1878, Oakeley wrote to his old friend to express his deep sympathy, and Tait duly responded with an enquiry about Oakeley's own health, that encouraged him to put pen to paper again. 'Thank you for your kind note which was more than I expected and I am therefore all the more grateful for it. I am glad to infer from it that you are bearing up with fortitude and resignation against this crushing blow which has followed so quickly upon another in which also I thought much of you. . . . I have as usual suffered much this year from chronic bronchitis, but less perhaps on the whole than might have been expected from the extraordinary severity of the winter'.[88] A little more than a year later, when Oakeley felt himself to be dying, he said to those around him, 'Let my dear friend the Archbishop of Canterbury know as soon as I am gone'.[89]

Whether or not the story is true, Tait was not notified of Oakeley's death, and only discovered the news when he read the papers on the morning of 10 February 1880. He recorded the event in his diary for the day, displaying personal affection for a man to whom he was genuinely close, despite a closing sentence indicating that he never could understand why Oakeley had left the Church of England for the Roman Catholic Church. 'Dear Frederick Oakeley – at one time one of my nearest and dearest, and always one of my most revered friends. How I felt the separation caused by his secession to Rome. Many years have kept us apart, but always since I came to London I have tried to see him often, and these renewals of old intimacy have been very precious. He was a man of God, and sacrificed all that the world holds dear to conscience. Sad that it should have led him astray'.[90] In a letter to Oakeley's nephew, the composer Sir Herbert Oakeley (who had been one of his pupils at Rugby), Tait delivered a warm tribute. 'I owed to your uncle more than perhaps to any man; he took me under his care, and helped me when I was an unknown undergraduate . . . He never ceased all through my Oxford days to be my kind helper. It was a great grief to me when our intercourse was so greatly interfered with by the step through which, though following conscience, he sacrificed so many bright earthly prospects, and gave himself to a system for which he was too good! At every trial of my life he was true to me, and I never ceased to feel deep affection for him'.[91] After the death of Ward in 1882, and within six months of his own death, Tait, the last survivor of the three, offered a generous tribute to the formerly inseparable friends. 'Two more single-hearted and devoted men I believe never lived'.[92]

Thomas Mozley and R. W. Church have left vivid portraits of Oakeley in his last years, which are valuable as the judicious judgements of his friends and contemporaries who remained in the Church of England after his departure. Inevitably, they were written from the Anglican view of those who thought Oakeley had done the wrong thing and should have remained in the Church of England where he might have been given preferment, but there is no mistaking the warm feelings that he still aroused in their thoughts.

After the storms of the *British Critic* in 1841–3, Mozley had little reason to remember Oakeley with any great affection, but he delivered this tribute less than two years after Oakeley's death. 'Nobody cared less for himself, or took less care of himself. He spent his life eventually serving a poor congregation, chiefly Irish, in the not very attractive region of Islington. He might be seen limping about the streets of London – for he was very lame – a misshapen fabric of bare bones, upon which hung some very shabby canonicals. Yet his eye was bright, and his voice, though sorrowful, was kind, and he was always glad to meet an old friend. He could sometimes be induced to dine quietly at Lambeth and talk over old days with the Primate. There was always something aristocratic in the wreck'.[93]

The austere and reserved figure of R. W. Church, wrote to Gladstone two days after Oakeley's death, and included an abiding image of his last years. 'Poor Oakeley, I have always thought of him as one of the converts of 44 or 45 who had sacrificed much that the natural man cares for. He was a man whose quality and whose craving was refinement, not strength or exactness of ascertained truth or originality of any kind, but the grace and beauty of finish. He was just the man to pass a happy and useful life writing elegant and interesting lectures and sermons, and enjoying music and art and good talk without luxury or selfishness, as a distinguished Anglican clergyman. The Romans made nothing of him, but sent him up to Islington to live poorly in a poor house with two Irish colleagues, with just a print or two remaining of the Oxford wreck, which was the overthrow of his old idea of life. And he was to the last, as far as I saw him, interested in nothing so much as in gossip of the old days; and he was always kindly and patient and gentle, not without touches of amusement when talking to people who did not think with him. It was like a genuine bit of the old Balliol common room, set in the frame of this dingy Islington parlour'.[94]

Church was Dean of St Paul's Cathedral at the time of this comment, and his observations need to be set in that context, but he need not have worried; the surviving evidence indicates that Frederick Oakeley never regretted the step that he had taken in 1845, never looked back longingly to the Church of England after he had left it, and that his thirty-four years in the Roman Catholic Church were years of contentment. On 8 June 1851, at St John's, he celebrated a mass of thanksgiving for those who had joined the Roman Catholic Church, and preached a sermon on the text 'Thou hast broken my bonds; I will sacrifice to thee the victim of praise' (Psalm 115, verse 17). During the course of his sermon, he made it quite clear that he had no regrets about the path he had chosen to follow. 'I think that if there be a word which we should feel more than another to describe our present state, that word would be – deliverance . . . Which of us does not feel that the change from without to within the Church of God, has been like the bursting asunder of chains, and the inhaling of the fresh morning air after a night of weariness and unrest? Of all the burdens which we have been called to bear, surely the most oppressive was that of being thrown, at morning, noontide and evening, upon our own evil selves; of having to try all the subjects of faith and duty by some standard of man's creating; of feeling, as it were, that a heaven of brass was over our heads, depressing and threatening to crush us, instead of a firmament so spacious as to impress us with our sense of nothingness'.[95] 'I will candidly avow,' he wrote in 1855, 'that to have to bid adieu for the term of our natural lives, to courts ecclesiastical, whether Consistory or of Arches, to the Judicial Committee of the Privy Council, to episcopal charges, to puritan sabbaths, and to that crowning misery of all, the right of private judgement, is really so unspeakably a relief that, even were there nothing else in the church to make us happy, it is no wonder we should sometimes find it hard to keep our joy within the bounds of moderation'.[96]

As Oakeley moved into old age and the last phase of his life, he began to reminisce with affection, not about the Church of England, but about his days at Balliol College. He visited the college in 1871 and reported his pleasure to Tait. 'I spent a very pleasant week lately in Balliol . . . The old College so interested me. I scarcely felt myself at home except in the Common Room which is more like its old self than the rest'.[97] On the title pages of *Historical notes on the Tractarian Movement* (1865) and *The priest on the mission* (1871) he felt the need to add below his name, office and distinctions, the words: 'Formerly Fellow of Balliol College Oxford', almost as a way of recalling and reliving a status that had once been important to him.

In December 1878, in a letter to Tait, Bishop George Moberly of Salisbury noted Oakeley's preoccupation with the past. 'Many thanks, my dear archbishop, for the sight of poor old Oakeley's letter which I return. I have met him once or twice at Church's, and have been struck to see how his whole heart is in the memories of Balliol half a century ago'.[98] As he grew older, Oakeley's memories returned to the place from where he had set out on the spiritual journey that had led him from the dreaming spires of Oxford to the back streets of Islington. He had set out from Balliol and now in his mind he was revisiting his happy memories of the college. The wheel had come full circle and the journey was finished, and this is the point at which to take our leave, because he only lived another thirteen months.

Frederick Oakeley died on 29 January 1880 at the age of seventy-seven, suffering from a catalogue of respiratory problems. The death certificate cited gastric catarrh, chronic bronchitis, acute bronchitis and exhaustion as the causes of his death. He was buried at St Mary's Roman Catholic Cemetery, Kensal Green, London on 5 February. The funeral mass was conducted by Bishop Weathers, an auxiliary bishop in the archdiocese of Westminster, and a former fellow member with Oakeley of the diocesan chapter. Cardinal Manning, who had known Oakeley since 1827, preached the panegyric. 'During the last fifteen years they had been bound together by a far closer tie, a far more intimate confidence, and therefore if anyone could speak of Frederick Oakeley, he could. He was a true disciple of Jesus Christ in the fullness of the word, loving, holy, harmless, self-denying, laborious in his master's service . . . He was a true pastor labouring for souls. He was a kind and loving friend. None that ever approached him could forget so long as they lived the humble, gentle, kindly, and even playful manner, the sweet voice and aspect with the maturity of thought and wisdom which distinguished him. For thirty years he had denied himself and given a large part of his income amounting to thousands of pounds to the church – a fact no man knew till his death. The result was a unity, a sweetness of Catholic worship that had drawn many. He had accomplished what no other priest had done – he had trained seventy boys and men to sing the praises of God about the altar. All this, although nature had laid upon him a burden through a life of seventy-eight years that made motion hard to bear, and, in his last years God had deprived him of half his sight, so that the study of His Word was painful and difficult. Yet almost with his last breath he had preached to his people'.[99]

In 1865, Oakeley had regarded the Tractarian movement as failed and vanished. In 1879, a little more than six months before his death, in what was to be his last publication, he mused on the astonishing transformation of attitudes towards Catholicism over the preceding fifty years; not only towards the Roman Catholic Church, but also towards the continuing Catholic movement within the Church of England. The conclusions that he reached, including an anonymous memory of his own work at Margaret Chapel, were quite different. 'The material type of an essentially Protestant Church has almost ceased to have any counterpart among us. The high-walled pews have given way to open benches; the pulpit is usually of more moderate dimension than heretofore, and the communion table presents a more decent if not dignified appearance than in the olden time. But at the period from which the change may be dated, the word Catholic, now so common in the vocabulary of churchmen, was entirely unknown in its relation to anything within the Church of England ... The great ritual movement in the Church of England took its rise somewhere about the year 1839, or rather earlier ... In August 1839, it was taken up with great interest by the minister of a little proprietary chapel in the neighbourhood of Cavendish Square ... The two principal objects which the new minister proposed to himself were – first, to introduce a quieter and more thoughtful style of preaching than was at that time popular in London; and, secondly, to provide such sensible aids to devotion, both in the general character of the services and in the internal arrangements and ornaments of the chapel itself'.[100] Of the movement as a whole, Oakeley was now sure that it had been of the hand of God; that it had been productive of nothing but good; and that it would continue because of its fundamental worth. 'The original movers of the great Catholic revival had themselves no idea of the direction in which their studies were leading them; and, for the most part, stopped short of what proved to be the ultimate destination of their labours. But although the issue of their work was, for a time, uncertain, there could never have been any reasonable doubt that an issue it would have, and a momentous one.

It had within it those elements of vitality and perpetuity the presence of which is always a pledge of final success, and their absence a note of sure failure – singleness of purpose, the love of truth for its own sake, and the spirit of self-sacrifice.'[101]

At the time of Oakeley's appointment as Rector of St John's in 1850, Richard Boyle in particular had spread rumours about Oakeley being given the appointment only because it was hoped that he would use his wealth to underpin the weak financial state of the church. Whether or not that was Wiseman's intention, Manning's eulogy confirmed that Oakeley had indeed used his private income for the benefit of the church. The origin of his wealth is unknown, but probably derived from a sizeable bequest from his father or mother. What is certain is that at the time of his death, probate recorded that he had less than £300 to his name.

In *The priest on the mission*, Oakeley published a series of addresses, intended to provide common sense advice to his fellow priests and to future generations of priests. No author can write a book without something of his character emerging in the text, and *The priest on the mission* includes a passage which, if not quite a self-asessment, certainly sums up the attractive amalgam of passion and humility that was Frederick Oakeley: 'I assure you, my dear brethren, that there is one thought which has painfully occurred to me . . . It is that of my own great unfitness to take a ground so high as I must needs take if I am to tell the truth. Two considerations alone have served to mitigate if not dispel this misgiving. The first of these considerations is, that I am not here by choice, but in obedience to the voice of authority. The second is that, while I have been teaching you, I have been at the same time teaching myself. For the rest, let me entreat you to receive what I have said, not because I say it, but because it is true . . . Of him whose words they are, think only that they express not so much his practice as his convictions and his aims; and for his reward, if any reward he deserve, he does but entreat you to pray that those convictions may be operative and those aims fulfilled'.[102]

In Exsequias Viri admodum Reverendi Frederici Canonici
Oakeley Nonis Februariis, MDCCCLXXX

Rapte tuis, Frederici, vale! qui carcere vitae,
  tenuia disjiciens vincla, solutus abis!
haec tua libertas minime deflenda – 'Beatus
  quem Domini elegit quem sibi sumpsit amor:' (Psalm 65, v 4)
nostra tamen superest sors flebilis: occidit almus
  pastor, oberrantis dux columenque gregis.
Qui te fraterno coluerunt more sodales,
  testantur fuerit quam pretiosa fides:
testantur qui jam sexto caelestia lustro
  munera monstrantem te didicere sequi:
turba sacerdotum haud alii devincta magistro
  testantur fidam sacra docentis opem:
his non flere nefas, sanctae quibus alma loquellae
  verba sepulcrali conticuere gelu. –
Talia volventes stipatam intravimus aedem,
  quae pia pastoris cura domusque fuit;
scilicet his adytis, haec juxta altaria, nidum (Psalm 84, v 3)
  non alio posuit pellicienda fides:
hic dubios docuit veram sperare salutem;
  dempsit onus fessis, sustinuitque pedes:
huc coeunt hodie memores cum divite pauper,
  nec fictas edunt fervida corda preces;
orant aeternam requiem lucumque perennem
  acceptasque locum det Deus inter oves.
Quis scit an his egeat precibus? qui dignior illis
  sedibus aut vitam sanctius egit homo?
Nam fallente homines quot corde domestica constans
  martyria et gravius robore ferret onus,
Scit Deus: an talis virtus mercede carebit?
  seposita, stabit nec Patris ante thronum?
O animam sine labe piam, sine crimine fortem!
  culpae si tu non integer, ecquis erit?
Nonne simul rapuit terris, in ovile beatum
  pastorem Pastor sustulit, Agnus ovem?

The Revd H Kynaston

For the funeral obsequies of a man wholly to be revered
Frederick, Canon Oakeley
5 February 1880

Farewell, Federick, torn from your own people, you cast away these gentle chains and in freedom depart from the prison of life! Shed few tears for this your freedom – 'Happy is the man whom the love of God has chosen and taken for himself'.

Our lot, however, remains a source of weeping: a gentle teacher is deapspeech have fallen silent in the cold of the tomb.

Pondering such thoughts, we have come into this crowded church which was both the home and the sacred charge of this priest: without doubt in these sanctuaries, near these altars, loyalty not to be tempted elsewhere made its nest.

Here he taught the doubtful to hope for true salvation, he took their burden from the weary and gave strength to their feet; here they gather today to remember him the poor with the rich, nor do passionate hearts utter feigned prayers: they pray that God may grant him eternal peace, everlasting light and a place among His accepted sheep.

Who knows whether he needs these prayers? What man more worthy of those habitations, or lived his life with greater holy awe? For God knows how many men whose hearts were failing them he, with constancy, supported in domestic martyrdom and bore a burden more heavy than oak: or will such virtue lack a reward? If it is set aside, will he not stand before the Father's throne.

O soul devout and without blemish, brave without reproach, if you are not free from blame, is there anyone who will be? Surely as soon as He snatched him from the earth, the Shepherd raised him to His sheepfold to be a shepherd and the Lamb raised him to be a lamb.

Bibliography

Primary sources
Blomfield Papers, Lambeth Palace Library, London
Bodleian Library (Miscellaneous Manuscripts), Oxford
Court of Arches Records, Lambeth Palace Library, London,
Gladstone Papers, British Library (Manuscript department), London
Keble Papers, Keble College, Oxford
Manning Papers, Bodleian Library, Oxford
Newman Papers, Birmingham Oratory
Oakeley Papers
- Oakeley's autobiographical manuscripts (*The story of my life* and *Canon Oakeley's memoirs*), together with his common-place book, are preserved in the library of Balliol College, Oxford (MSS 408–410)
- Oakeley's *History of St John's Church since 1850* is preserved in the archives of the archdiocese of Westminster.
- Oakeley's prize essays (1825–7), *De tribunicia apud Romanus potestate* and *The influence of the crusades upon the arts and literature of Europe*, are preserved in the Bodleian Library, Oxford (39037, ff 89–124; 39038, ff 71–104)
- The letter books of Edward Murray Oakeley are in the possession of Mr Rowland Oakeley
Pusey Papers, Pusey House, Oxford
Tait Papers, Lambeth Palace Library, London
Wilberforce Papers, Bodleian Library, Oxford

Secondary sources
Altholz, J. L., *The Liberal Catholic movement in England. The 'Rambler' and its contributors 1848–1864*, (London, 1962).
Ashwell, A. R. and Wilberforce, R. G., *Life of the Right Reverend Samuel Wilberforce*, 3 volumes, (London, 1880–2).
Baker, W. J. *Beyond port and prejudice. Charles Lloyd 1784–1829*, (Orono, 1981).
Bassett, B., *Newman at Littlemore*, (Birmingham, n.d.)
Bayford, A. F., *A full report of the proceedings in the case of the office of the judge promoted by Hodgson v. Rev. F. Oakeley before the Rt. Hon. Sir Jenner Fust, Kt., Dean of the Arches*, (London, 1845).

Bellasis, E., *Memorials of Mr Serjeant Bellasis*, second edition, (London, 1895).

Blachford, F., *Letters of Frederic, Lord Blachford*, ed. George Eden Marindin, (London, 1896).

Blomfield, A., *Memoir of Bishop Blomfield*, 2 volumes, (London, 1863).

Blomfield, C. J., *A charge delivered to the clergy of the diocese of London, at the visitation in October, MDCCCXLII*, London, 1842).

Boase, F. (ed.), *Modern English biography*, six volumes, (London, 1892–1921).

Bogan, B., *The great link. A history of St George's Cathedral, Southwark, 1786–1958*, 2nd edition, (London, 1958).

Bourne, E., 'Old Margaret Street chapel', *Merry England*, volume 4 (1884–5), 357–63.

Bouyer, L., *Newman. His life and spirituality*, (London, 1958).

Bowden, J. E., *The life and letters of Frederick William Faber*, (London, 1869).

Boyle, R., *Boyle versus Wiseman. A full statement of the causes which necessitated the action, and a complete refutation of all the allegations of libel*, (London, 1855).

Brandreth, H. R. T., *The oecumenical ideals of the Oxford Movement*, (London, 1947).

Brendon, P., *Hurrell Froude and the Oxford Movement*, (London, 1974).

Brilioth, Y., *The Anglican revival. Studies in the Oxford Movment*, (London, 1925).

Browne, E. G. K., *History of the Tractarian Movement*, second edition, (London, 1856).

Burke, Sir B., *Burke's genealogical and heraldic history of the landed gentry of Ireland*, ed. L. G. Pine, fourth edition, (London, 1958).

Burke, Sir B., *Burke's genealogical and heraldic history of the peerage, baronetage and knightage*, ed. Peter Townend, one hundred and fifth edition, (London, 1970).

Butler, C., *The life and times of Bishop Ullathorne 1806–1889*, 2 volumes, (London, 1926).

Butler, P., *Gladstone. Church, state and tractarianism*, (Oxford, 1982).

Carpenter, S. P., *Church and people 1789–1889. A history of the Church of England from William Wilberforce to 'Lux Mundi'*, (London, 1933).

Carter, J. F. M., *Life and work of the Rev. T. T. Carter*, (London, 1911).

The Catholic Encyclopaedia, 15 volumes and index, (London, 1911).

Chadwick, O., *The mind of the Oxford Movement*, (London, 1963).

Chadwick, O., *The Victorian church*, third edition, 2 volumes, (London, 1971).

Chapman, R., *Father Faber*, (London, 1961).

Church, M. C. (ed.), *Life and letters of Dean Church*, (London, 1894).

Church, R. W., *The Oxford Movement. Twelve years 1833–1845*, (London, 1891).

Clarke, B. F. L., *Parish churches of London*, (London, 1966).

Clayton, H., *Cathedral city. A look at Victorian Lichfield*, (Lichfield, 1977).

Clifton, M., *A Victorian convert quintet*, (London, 1998).

Coombs, J., *George and Mary Sumner. Their life and times*, (London, 1965).

Couch, L. M. Quiller (ed.), *Reminiscences of Oxford by Oxford men 1559-1850*, (Oxford, 1892).

Craven, A., *Life of Lady Georgiana Fullerton*, trans. Henry James Coleridge, (London, 1888).

Crosthwaite, J. C., *Modern hagiology: an examination of the nature and tendency of some legendary and devotional works published under the sanction of the Rev. J. H. Newman, the Rev. Dr Pusey, and the Rev. F. Oakeley*, (London, 1846).

Dalgairns, J. B., *Life of St Stephen Harding*, (London, 1844).

Davidson, R. T. and Benham, W., *Life of Archibald Campbell Tait, Archbishop of Cantebury*, 2 volumes, (London, 1891).

Dearmer, P., *Songs of praise discussed. A handbook to the best-known hymns and to others recently introduced*, (Oxford, 1933).

Downs, F. S., 'The Oxford Movement and church unity', (dissertation, St Andrews, 1960).

English Churchman.

Faber, F. W., *The life and letters of Frederick William Faber*, ed. John William Bowden, (London, 1869).

– *Life of St Wilfrid, bishop of York*, (London, 1844).

– *Faber. Poet and priest. Selected letters by Frederick William Faber 1833-1863*, ed. R. Addington, (London, 1974).

Faber, G. *Oxford apostles. A character study of the Oxford Movement*, (London, 1933).

Ffoulkes, E. S., *A history of the church of St Mary the Virgin, Oxford*, (Oxford, 1891).

Fitzgerald, P., *Fifty years of Catholic life and social progress*, 2 volumes, (London, 1891).

Foot, M. R. D., and C. F. G. Matthew (editors), *The Gladstone diaries 1825-1868*, 6 volumes, (London, 1968-78).

Fothergill, B., *Nicholas Wiseman*, (London, 1963).

Frost, M., (ed.), *Historical companion to hymns ancient and modern*, (London, 1962).

Froude, R. H., *Remains of the late Reverend Richard Hurrell Froude, M.A., Fellow of Oriel College*, ed. John Henry Newman and John Keble, 4 volumes, (Oxford 1838-9).

Garbett, J., *The university, the church and the new test, with remarks on Mr Oakeley's and Mr Gresley's pamphlets. A letter to the lord bishop of Chichester*, (London, 1845).

Gillow, J., *A literary and biographical history or bibliographical dictionary of the English Catholics from the breach with the Rome, in 1534, to the present time*, 5 volumes, (London, 1845).

Gladstone, W. E., *Correspondence on church and religion of William Ewart Gladstone*, ed. D. C. Lathbury, 2 volumes, (London, 1910).

– 'Ritualism and ritual', *Contemporary Review*, volume 24 (1874), 663-81.

Goode, W., *Tract XC historically refuted, or a reply to a work by the Rev. F. Oakeley, entitled 'The subject of Tract XC historically examined'*, (London, 1845).

Gorman, W. J. G., *Converts to Rome. A list of over three thousand protestants who have become Roman Catholics since the commencement of the nineteenth century*, (London, 1892).

Gray, D., *The influence of Tractarian principles on parish worship 1839-1849*, (London, 1894).

Gray, R., *Cardinal Manning. A biography*, (London, 1985).

Greenfield, R. H., 'The attitude of the Tractarians to the Roman Catholic Church 1833-1850', (dissertation, Oxford, 1956).

A history of the county of Stafford, Victoria county history, various editors, 9 volumes, (Oxford, 1908-84).

Guiney, L. I., *Hurrell Froude. Memoranda and comments*, (London, 1904).

Gwynne, D., *Lord Shrewsbury, Pugin and the Catholic revival*, (London, 1946).

Hardelin, A., *The Tractarian understanding of the eucharist*, (Uppsala, 1965).

[Harris, E.], *From Oxford to Rome: and how it fared with some who lately made the journey*, (London, 1847).

Houghton, W. E. (ed.), *The Wellesley index to Victorian periodicals 1824-1900*, 3 volumes, (Toronto 1966-79).

Holmes, J. D., 'Newman's reputation and the lives of the English saints', *Catholic Historical Review*, volume 51 (1966), 528-38.

The Hymnal 1940 Companion, third edition, (New York, 1951).

Jones, J., *Balliol College. A history 1263-1939*, (Oxford, 1988).

Jones, J., 'The civil war of 1843', *Balliol College Annual Record*. (Oxford, 1979)

Julian, J., *A dictionary of hymnology, setting forth the origin and history of Christian hymns*, 2 volumes, (London, 1907).

Knowles, D. and Hadcock, R. N. H., *Medieval religious houses. England and Wales*, (London, 1953).

Knox, E. A., *The Tractarian movement*, (London, 1933).

Law, H. W. and Law, I., *The book of the Beresford Hopes*, (London, 1925).

Leach, T., *A short sketch of the Tractarian upheaval*, (London, 1887).

Leslie, S., *Henry Edward Manning. His life and labours*, (London, 1921).

Liddon, H. P., *Life of Edward Bouverie Pusey, Doctor of Divinity; Canon of Christ Church; Regius Professor of Hebrew in the University of Oxford*, volumes 1-3 ed. J. O. Johnston and R. J. Wilson, volume 4 ed. J. O. Johnston, R. J. Wilson and W. C. E. Newbolt., 4 volumes, (London, 1893-7).

Luker, R., *All Souls, Langham Place. A history*, (London, 1979).

Lyson, R., *The environs of London: Being an historical account of the towns, villages, and hamlets, within twelve miles of that capital: interspersed wth biographical anecdotes*, 4 volumes, (London, 1792-6).

Martin, B., *John Henry Newman*, (London, 1982).

McClelland, V. A., *Cardinal Manning. His public life and influence 1865-1892*, (London, 1962).

Merlo, J. H., *The paradise of the Christian soul, delightful for its choicest pleasures of piety of every kind. A new and complete translation* [by Frederick Oakeley and H. W. Lloyd], (London, 1877).

Middleton, R. D., *Magdalen studies*, (Oxford, 1936).

- *Newman and Bloxam. An Oxford friendship*, (Oxford, 1947).

- *Newman at Oxford. His religious development*, (London, 1950).

Miller, J., *Singers and songs of the church*, (London, 1889).

Morley, J., *The life of William Ewart Gladstone*, 3 volumes, (London, 1903).

Mozley, D., (ed.), *Newman family letters*, (London, 1962).

Mozley, J. B., *Letters of the Revd. J. B. Mozley*, ed. Anne Mozley, (London, 1895).

Mozley, T., *Reminiscences, chiefly of Oriel College and the Oxford Movement*, (London, 1882).

Murray, F., *A hymnal, for use in the English Church*, (London, 1852).

The Musical Times.

Newman, F. W., *Contributions to the early history of the late cardinal*, (London, 1891).

Newman, J. H., *Correspondence of John Henry Newman with John Keble and others, 1839-45*, ed. Fathers of the Birmingham Oratory, (London, 1917).

- *Letters and correspondence of John Henry Newman during his life in the English Church*, ed. Anne Mozley, 2 volumes (London, 1891).

- *Letters and diaries of John Henry Newman*, various editors, 31 volumes, (Oxford, 1961-).

- *Newman's apologia pro vita sua. The two versions of 1864 and 1865, preceded by Newman's and Kingsley's pamphlets. With an introduction by Wilfrid Ward*, (Oxford, 1913).

- *Remarks on certain passages in the thirty-nine articles*, Tracts for the times, Number 90, (Oxford, 1841).

Newsome, D., *The parting of friends*, (London, 1966).

Norris, H., *Church vestments. Their origin and development*, (London, 1949).

Oakeley, Sir C., *Some account of the service of Sir Charles Oakeley, Bart. in India, consisting of a narrative of events, drawn up by himself; and a collection of official letters and other documents*, ed. Sir Herbert Oakeley, Bart. Dean and Rector of Bocking, second edition, (London, 1836).

Oakeley, E. F., *The Oakeley pedigree*, (London, 1934).

Oakeley, E. M., *Frederick Oakeley and some side lights on the Oxford Movement*, (Dover, 1922).

- *Some links with the past: the epic of a family epitomised*, (Clifton, 1900).

Oakeley, Frederick,

- "The Abbe Massé's 'Life of St Edmund of Canterbury'", *Dublin Review*, volume 45 (1858), 484-501.

- 'Ancient and modern ways of charity', *British Critic*, volume 29 (1841), 44–70.
- 'Allies's *Journal in France*', *Dublin Review*, volume 26, (1849), 241–62.
- 'Anglican propagandism', *Dublin Review*, volume 43 (1857), 327–49.
- *The Athanasian Creed: four lectures suggested by the present controversy*, (London, 1873).
- 'Bishop Jewel', *British Critic*, volume 30 (1841), 1–46.
- *Canon Oakeley's memoirs*, (unpublished manuscript).
- 'Cardinal Wiseman's "Essays"', *Dublin Review*, volume 34 (1853), 541–66.
- *The Catholic Church before and after conversion*, (London, 1855).
- *Catholic colleges and Protestant universities. An oratorical address spoken at the Jubilee of St Cuthbert's College, Ushaw, 21 July 1858*, (London, 1859).
- *The Catholic florist. A guide to the cultivation of flowers for the altar . . . Illustrated by historical notices and fragments of ecclesiastical poetry*, (London, 1850).
- *Catholic worship: a manual of popular instruction on the ceremonies and devotions of the church*, (London, 1867).
- 'The ceremonies of the church in their devotional and theological bearings', *Dublin Review*, volume 35 (1853), 362–82.
- 'Chanting', *British Critic*, volume 28 (1840), 371–90.
- *Christ manifested to the faithful through his church. A sermon (on Colossians 2:10) preached at Margaret Chapel on 25th Sunday after Trinity*, (Oxford, 1839).
- *Christians, the salt of the earth and the light of the world. A sermon*, (Oxford, 1838).
- 'Church music', *Dublin Review*, volume 10 (old style) 62 (new style) (1868), 307–15.
- 'Church music and choral regulations', *Dublin Review*, volume 21 (1846), 201–16.
- *The church of the bible; or scripture testimonies to Catholic doctrines and Catholic principles; collected and considered, in a series of popular discourses, addressed chiefly to non-Catholics*, (London, 1857).
- 'Church offices and devotions', *Dublin Review*, volume 30 (1851), 1–23.
- 'The church service', *British Critic*, volume 27 (1840), 249–76.
- *The claim to 'hold as distinct from teaching', explained, in a letter to a friend*, (London, 1845).
- '*The Creator and the Creature, or The Wonders of Divine Love*' (by F. W. Faber), *Dublin Review*, volume 43 (1857), 253–6.
- 'Crotchets and crotchettiness', *Dublin Review*, volume 44 (1858), 200–19.
- *De tribunicia apud potestate*, (Oxford, 1825).
- 'Devotional use of the breviary – Advent and Christmas', *Dublin Review*, volume 21 (1847), 273–305.
- *Devotions commemorative of the most adorable passion of our Lord and Saviour Jesus Christ*, (London, 1842).
- *The dignity and claims of the Christian poor: two sermons (on Luke 6:20*

and Matthew 25:36); the latter in aid of the Middlesex Hospital, (London, 1840).

- 'Dodsworth on Protestant delusions', *Dublin Review*, volume 42 (1857), 481–90.
- *The duty of maintaining the pope in his temporal sovereignty. An appeal in behalf of the collection for the pope, addressed to Catholics and others in St John's Church, Islington, on the evening of Low Sunday, 1860*, (London, 1860).
- 'English public schools in Catholic times', volume 28 (old style) 5 (third series) (1861), 346–60.
- 'English views of Catholicism', *Contemporary Review*, volume 35 (1879), 458–70.
- 'Episcopal charges of the past year', *British Critic*, volume 33 (1843), 274–81.
- *Explanation of a passage in an article on certain works of Bishop Jewel published in the British Critic for July, 1841, in a letter to the Rev C. S. Bird ... author of a 'Plea for the Reformed Church'*, (London, 1842).
- 'Faber's "Hymns"', *Dublin Review*, volume 27 (1849), 163–81.
- *A few words of affection and congratulation addressed to his fellow converts, before the mass of thanksgiving for the conversions to the church at St John's, Islington, on the octave of the Ascension, June 5th 1851*, (London, 1851).
- *A few words to those churchmen, being members of convocation, who purpose taking no part in Mr Ward's case (i.e. his proposed degradation at Oxford)*, (London, 1845).
- 'Formby on Christian psalmody', *Dublin Review*, volume 22 (1847), 135–58.
- 'Historical Notes on the Tractarian Movement', *Dublin Review*,
    Part 1, volume 1 (new style) 53 (old style) (1863), 167–90.
    Part 2, volume 1 (new style) 53 (old style) (1863), 494–508.
    Part 3, volume 2 (new style) 54 (old style) (1864), 64–79.
    Part 4, volume 3 (new style) 55 (old style) (1864), 181–99
- *Historical notes on the Tractarian Movement AD 1833–1845*, (London, 1865).
- *History of St John's since 1850*, (unpublished manuscript).
- *The holy bible, translated from the Latin Vulgate ... Revised and corrected with additions by the Very Rev Frederick Canon Oakeley and the Rev T. G. Law of the Oratory. With the approbation of his eminence the cardinal archbishop of Westminster*, 2 volumes, (London, 1874–8).
- *Homilies for holy days and seasons commemorative of our Lord and Saviour Jesus Chrust, from Advent to Whitsuntide inclusive, translated from the writings of the saints; with biographical notices of the writers*, (London, 1842).
- 'Importance of religious ceremonial', *Rambler*, volume 12 (1853), 336–8.
- 'In correspondence: Our most noble selves', *Rambler*, volume 27 (old style), 4 (third series) (1860), 117–20.

- 'In ecclesiastical register: Consecration of Bishop of Bruges', *Rambler*, volume 4 (1849), 152–5.
- *The influence of the crusades upon the arts and literature of Europe*, (Oxford, 1827).
- 'Jubilee of St Cuthbert's College', *Dublin Review*, volume 45 (1858), 131–49.
- 'The latest phenomena of Anglicanism', *Dublin Review*, volume 42, (1857), 95–123.
- *The leading topics of Dr Pusey's recent work reviewed in a letter addressed ... to the Most Rev H E Manning ... by the Very Rev Frederick Oakeley*, (London, 1866).
- *A letter on submitting to the Catholic Church. Addressed to a friend*, (London, 1845).
- *A letter to his grace the Duke of Wellington, Chancellor of the University of Oxford, upon the principle and tendency of a bill (i.e. the earl of Radnor's), now before parliament, entitled, 'A bill for abolishing subscription to articles of religion in certain cases'*, (Oxford, 1835).
- *A letter to the Lord Bishop of London, on a subject connected with the recent proceedings (of convocation) at Oxford (in reference to Mr Ward's case)*, (London, 1845).
- *A letter to the members of the Islington Protestant Institute, occasioned by a recent statement of their object and proceedings*, (London, 1851).
- *A letter to the vice-chancellor*, (Oxford and London, 1845).
- *The life of our lord and saviour Jesus Christ, from the Latin of St Bonaventure newly translated for the use of members of the Church of England*, (London, 1844).
- *The life of St Augustine of Canterbury, apostle of the English, with some account of the early British Church*, (London, 1844).
- *Lyra liturgica. Reflections in verse for holy days and seasons*, (London, 1865).
- 'The Messiah [by Handel] at Exeter Hall', *Dublin Review*, volume 44 (1858), 395–412.
- 'Meyrick on Church of Spain', *Dublin Review*, volume 32 (1852), 289–310.
- 'Miss Sellon and her sisterhood', *Dublin Review*, volume 32 (1852), 436–64.
- 'The *Month* on church choirs', *Dublin Review*, volume 11 (old style) 63 (new style) (1868), 568–74.
- 'Modern ascetic divinity: Father Faber', *Dublin Review*, volume 36 (1854), 194–212.
- 'Music, chiefly ecclesiastical', *British Critic*, volume 34 (1843), 277–320.
- 'Musical festivals', *British Critic*, volume 34 (1843), 170–94.
- 'The Newcomes', *Dublin Review*, volume 40 (1856), 299–309.
- 'The Office of Holy Week', *Dublin Review*, volume 24 (1848), 1–31.
- 'On a liberal education on its bearing on mental discipline and culture', Dublin Review, volume 13 (old style) 65 (new style) (1869), 531.
- *On the mission and prospects of the Catholic Church in England*, (n.d.).

– *The order and ceremonial of the most holy and adorable sacrifice of the Mass, explained in a dialogue between a priest and a catechumen*, (London, 1855).
– *Personal reminiscences of the 'Oxford Movement'*, (London, 1855).
– 'Popular recreations and their moral influence', *Dublin Review*, volume 42 (1857), 271–93.
– *The position of a Catholic minority in a non-Catholic country*, (n.d.)
– *Practical sermons preached in 1847-8*, (London, 1848).
– *Preces tempores ecclesiae novae aedificandus habendae. Prayers for a blessing on the work of building a new church*, (London, 1842).
– *The priest on the mission. A course of lectures on missionary and parochial duties*, (London, 1871).
– 'Prayers for England: the recent conversions', *Dublin Review*, volume 20 (1846), 83–106. (This article may have been revised by Nicholas Wiseman before publication)
– 'Preaching and public speaking', *Rambler*, volume 27 (old style) 4 (third series) (1861), 205–16.
– 'Prison and workhouse grievances', *Dublin Review*, volume 46 (1859), 424–37.
– 'Protestant ideas of confessional: 'Pascal the younger'', *Dublin Review*, volume 31 (1851), 122–44.
– 'Psalms and hymns', *British Critic*, volume 32 (1842), 1–33.
– 'Pusey's sermon on absolution', *Dublin Review*, volume 20 (1846), 224–57.
– 'Pusey's teaching and practice, *Dublin Review*, volume 30 (1851), 152–76.
– *The question of university education for English Catholics, considered principally in its moral and religious bearings. In a letter to . . . the Bishop of Birmingham*, (London, 1864).
– 'Religious disabilities of Catholic prisoners', *Dublin Review*, volume 44 (1858), 485–501.
– *The religious disabilities of our Catholic prisoners considered, with a view to their removal, in a letter to the Viscount Palmerston, MP*, (London, 1854).
– *Remarks upon Aristotelian and Platonic ethics, as a branch of the studies pursued in the University of Oxford*, (Oxford, 1837).
– 'Rite of ordination; moral training for the church', *Dublin Review*, volume 20 (1846), 500–19.
– 'Rites and ceremonies', *British Critic*, volume 30 (1841), 422–65.
– 'Sacramental confession', *British Critic*, volume 33 (1843), 295–347.
– *A second letter to the Lord Bishop of London, containing an earnest and respectful appeal on the subject of Margaret Chapel*, (Oxford, 1845).
– 'The sees of St Asaph and Bangor', *British Critic*, volume 33 (1843), 233–46.
– *A sermon (on Luke 9:59–62) preached at the general ordination of Richard (Bagot) Lord Bishop of Oxford*, (Oxford, 1836).

- *Sermons, preached chiefly at the chapel royal, at Whitehall*, (Oxford, 1839).
- 'Souperism" [i.e. proselytism], tested by its own statistics', *Dublin Review*, volume 42 (1857), 363–82.
- *Statement of the facts relative to the case of Mr William Weale, Master of the Poor School at Islington*, (London, 1851).
- *The story of my life*, (unpublished manuscript)
- *The subject of Tract XC. Historically examined with a view of ascertaining the object with which the articles were put out, and the sense in which they are allowed to be subscribed; together with testimonies of English divines to Catholic doctrine. To which is added the case of Bishop Mountague, in the reign of King James I*, (London, 1841; second edition, 1845).
- 'Sumner on justification', *British Critic*, volume 34 (1843), 63–79.
- *The teaching and practice of the Catholic Church on the subject of frequent communion*, (London, 1849).
- *Things dispensable and things indispensable: the importance of distinguishing between them with a view to true conscientiousness and Christian joy. Two sermons*, (London, 1844).
- *A treatise on indulgences . . . translated from the French. With a preface by the Rev Frederick Oakeley*, (London, 1848).
- 'Use and abuse of ritual', *Dublin Review*, volume 24 (new style) 76 (old style) (1875), 346–56.
- *The voice of creation as a witness to the mind of its divine author*, (London, 1876).
- 'Ways and means of the Church: the offertory', *Dublin Review*, volume 27 (1849), 267–91.
- 'What is meant by unprotestantising?', *British Critic*, volume 32 (1842), 211–44.
- 'Wiseman's "Tour in Ireland in 1858"', *Dublin Review*, volume 46 (1859), 499–510.
- *The youthful martyrs of Rome*, twelfth edition, (London, 1862).
O'Connell, M. R., *The Oxford conspirators. A history of the Oxford Movement 1833–1845*, (New York, 1969).
Ollard, S. L., *A short history of the Oxford Movement*, (London, 1915).
Ornsby, R., *Memoirs of James Robert Hope-Scott of Abbotsford, DCL, QC, late Fellow of Merton College, Oxford. With selections from his correspondence*, second edition, 2 volumes, (London, 1884).
Palmer, W., *A narrative of events connected with the publication of the Tracts for the Times*, (Oxford, 1843).
- *Origines liturgicae, or, antiquities of the English ritual, and, a dissertation on primitive liturgies*, 2 volumes, second edition, (Oxford, 1836).
Penny, B., *Maryvale*, (Birmingham, 1985).
Purcell, E. S., *Life and letters of Ambrose Phillipps de Lisle*, ed. Edwin de Lisle, 2 volumes, (London, 1901).
- *Life of Cardinal Manning. Archbishop of Westminster*, 2 volumes, (London, 1896).

Rainbow, B., *The choral revival in the Anglican communion 1839–1872*, (London, 1970).

Redhead, R., *Church music. A selection of chants, sanctuses and responses, together with the litany and versicles as used in the choral service; also psalm tunes, adapted to the authorized metrical versions*, (London, 1840).

– *Laudes diurnae. The psalter and canticles in the morning and evening service of the Church of England. Set and pointed to the Gregorian tones (with a preface on antiphonal chanting by the Revd. Frederick Oakeley. MA)*, (London, 1841).

Rhodes, M. R., *Letters on the 'Eirenicon:' addressed to the 'Weekly Register,' by M. R. Rhodes, Esq., M.A., and now re-printed with the replies of The Rev. Dr. Pusey, a letter from The Very Rev. Canon Oakeley, and important additions*, (London, 1867).

Rivington, S., *The publishing family of Rivington*, (London, 1919).

Rottman, A., *London catholic churches. A historical and artistic record*, (London, 1926).

Rowell, G., *The vision glorious. Themes and personalities of the Catholic revival in Anglicanism*, (Oxford, 1983).

Schiefen, R. J., *Nicholas Wiseman and the transformation of English Catholicism*, (Shepherdstown, 1984).

Shannon, R., *Gladstone*, volume 1 1809–1865, (London, 1982).

Sieveking, I. G., *Memoir and letters of Francis W. Newman*, (London, 1909).

Simms, R., *Bibliotheca Staffordiensis*, (Lichfield, 1894).

Sinclair, W., *The Chapels Royal*, (London, 1912).

Smith, B. A., *Dean Church. The Anglican response to Newman*, (London, 1958).

Squibb, G. D., *Doctors Commons. A history of the college of advocates and doctors of law*, (Oxford, 1977).

Stephen, Sir L. and Lee, Sir S., *The dictionary of national biography*, 22 volumes, (London, 1921–22).

Stirling, A. M. D. (ed.), *The Richmond papers from the correspondence of George Richmond, and his son Sir William Richmond*, (London, 1926).

Stone, J. M., *Eleanor Leslie. A memoir*, (London, 1898).

Sullivan, A., *British literary magazines. The romantic age 1789–1836*, (London, 1983).

Sumner, G. H., *Life of Charles Richard Sumner, bishop of Winchester, during a forty years episcopate*, (London, 1876).

Tait, A. C., *A letter to the reverend the vice-chancellor*, (London, 1845).

Temperley, N., *The music of the English parish church*, 2 volumes, (Cambridge, 1979).

Trevor, M., *Newman. The pillar of the cloud*, (London, 1962).

Walsh, W., *A history of the Romeward movement in the Church of England 1833–1864*, (London, 1906).

Ward, B., *History of St Edmund's College, Old Hall*, (London, 1893).

Ward, W., *The life of John Henry, Cardinal Newman*, 2 volumes, (London, 1912).

Ward. W. P., *William George Ward and the Oxford Movement*, second edition, (London, 1890).

Ward, W. P., *William George Ward and the Catholic revival*, (London, 1893).

Welch, P. J., 'Bishop Blomfield', (dissertation, London, 1952).

Whitworth, W. A., *Quam dilecta: a description of All Saints' Church, Margaret Street with historical notes of Margaret Chapel and All Saints' Church*, (London, 1891).

Williams, I., *The autobiography of Isaac Williams*, ed. Sir George Prevost, (London, 1893).

Wilberforce, H., *The foundation of the faith assailed in Oxford*, (Oxford, 1835).

References

Chapter 1

1 *Burke's genealogical and heraldic history of the peerage, baronetage and knightage*, ed. Peter Townend, p. 2013.
2 *A history of the county of Stafford*, volume 3, p. 67.
3 O. Chadwick, *The Victorian Church*, volume 1, p. 514.
4 *A history of the county of Stafford*, volume 3, p. 67.
5 ibid.
6 *Burke's peerage*, p. 2013.
7 F. Oakeley, *The story of my life*, p. 1.
8 Sir Charles Oakeley, *Some account of the services of Sir Charles Oakeley, Bart., in India*, ed. Sir Herbert Oakeley, p. 4.
9 ibid., p. 10
10 ibid., p. 29.
11 *Dictionary of national biography*, volume 14, p. 731.
12 F. Oakeley, *The story of my life*, p. 1.
13 D. Knowles & R. N. Hadcock, *Mediaeval religious houses. England and Wales*, p. 77.
14 H. E. Forrest, *The old houses of Shrewsbury: Their history and associations*, p. 86.
15 F. Oakeley, *The story of my life*, p. 1.
16 ibid., p. 3
17 F. Oakeley, *The story of my life*, p. 3.
18 ibid.
19 ibid., p. 4
20 ibid.
21 ibid.
22 ibid.
23 ibid., p. 5
24 ibid.
25 ibid., p. 6.
26 ibid.
27 ibid., p. 8
28 ibid.
29 F. Oakeley, *The story of my life*, pp. 8–9
30 ibid., p. 9.

31   H. Clayton, *Cathedral city: a look at Victorian Lichfield*, p. 137.
32   R. Simms, *Bibliotheca Staffordiensis*, p. 396.
33   F. Oakeley, *The story of my life*, p. 9.
34   ibid.
35   ibid., p. 10.
36   ibid.
37   ibid.
38   ibid., p. 11.
39   ibid.
40   ibid.
41   ibid.
42   ibid., p. 7.
43   ibid., p. 11.
44   The Venerable Sir Herbert Oakeley (1791–1845), Domestic Chaplain to Bishop Howley of London 1814–22, Vicar of Ealing 1822–34, Dean of Bocking 1834–45, Archdeacon of Colchester 1841–5. He was offered, but declined, the bishopric of Gibraltar when it was founded in 1842.
45   F. Oakeley, *The story of my life*, p. 13
46   Charles Richard Sumner (1790–1874), Dean of St Paul's Cathedral, London, and Bishop of Llandaff 1826–7, Bishop of Winchester 1827–69.
47   F. Oakeley, *The story of my life*, p. 13.
48   G. H. Sumner, *Life of Charles Richard Sumner*, p. 41, Oakeley to George Henry Sumner, 5 May 1875.
49   ibid.
50   F. Oakeley, *The story of my life*, p. 14.
51   ibid.
52   ibid.
53   ibid., p. 15.
54   G. H. Sumner, *Life of Charles Richard Sumner*, p. 41, Oakeley to George Henry Sumner, 5 May 1875.
55   ibid., p. 42.
56   F. Oakeley, *The story of my life*, p. 17.
57   G. H. Sumner, *Life of Charles Richard Sumner*, p. 42, Oakeley to George Henry Sumner, 5 May 1875.
58   'I will give you (Peter) the keys of the kingdom of heaven, and whatever you bind on earth shall be bound in heaven, and whatever you loose on earth shall be loosed in heaven'.
59   'Truly, I say to you, (the disciples) whatever you bind on earth shall be bound in heaven, and whatever you loose on earth shall be loosed in heaven'.
60   G. H. Sumner, *Life of Charles Richard Sumner*, p. 42, Oakeley to George Henry Sumner, 5 May 1875.
61   ibid., p. 43.
62   ibid.
63   F. Oakeley, *The story of my life*, p. 16.
64   ibid., p. 17.

65 ibid., p. 18.
66 G. H. Sumner, *Life of Charles Richard Sumner*, p. 44, Oakeley to George Henry Sumner, 5 May 1875.
67 ibid., p. 45.
68 F. Oakeley, *The story of my life*, p. 18.
69 ibid.
70 G. H. Sumner, *Life of Charles Richard Sumner*, pp. 45–6, Oakeley to George Henry Sumner, 5 May 1875.
71 F. Oakeley, *The story of my life*, p. 19.
72 G. H. Sumner, *Life of Charles Richard Sumner*, pp. 41–5, Oakeley to George Henry Sumner, 5 May 1875.
73 F. Oakeley, *Canon Oakeley's memoirs*, p. 1.
74 ibid., p. 2.
75 ibid., p. 1.
76 F. Oakeley, *Canon Oakeley's memoirs*, p. 1.
77 ibid.
78 Sir C. Oakeley, *Some account of the services of Sir Charles Oakeley, Bart.*, p. 121.
79 F. Oakeley, *Canon Oakeley's memoirs*, p. 29.
80 ibid.
81 ibid., p. 1.
82 ibid.
83 ibid., p. 2.
84 F. Oakeley, *The story of my life*, p. 9.
85 ibid., *Canon Oakeley's memoirs*, p. 2.
86 M. R. O'Connell, *The Oxford conspirators. A history of the Oxford Movement 1833–1845*, p. 302.
87 F. Oakeley, *Historical notes on the Tractarian Movement*, pp. 34–5.
88 ibid., p. 36.
89 The chapel was constructed in 1803, the first permanent place of worship for Roman Catholics in Lichfield since the Reformation. It was afterwards refronted and considerably enlarged, and re-opened on 23 September 1834 as the Church of St Cross.
90 F. Oakeley, *The Catholic Church before and after conversion*, p. 5
91 ibid., *Historical notes on the Tractarian Movement*, p. 35.
92 John Kirk DD (1760–1851), Roman Catholic parish priest of Lichfield 1801–51.
93 F. Oakeley, *The Catholic Church before and after conversion*, p. 5.
94 ibid.
95 ibid., *Historical notes on the Tractarian Movement*, p. 36
96 ibid., *Canon Oakeley's memoirs*, p. 2.
97 G. H. Sumner, *Life of Charles Richard Sumner*, p. 47, Oakeley to George Henry Sumner, 5 May 1875.
98 ibid., p. 42.
99 ibid.
100 *Canon Oakeley's memoirs*, p. 2.
101 ibid.

Chapter 2

1   F. Oakeley, *The story of my life*, p. 25
2   ibid.
3   L. M. Quiller Couch (ed.), *Reminiscences of Oxford by Oxford Men 1559–1850*, p. 303.
4   ibid., p. 304.
5   ibid.
6   ibid., p. 303.
7   F. Oakeley, *The story of my life*, p. 26.
8   L. M. Quiller Couch (ed.), *Reminiscences of Oxford by Oxford Men 1559–1850*, pp. 317–8.
9   ibid., p. 318.
10 Philip Shuttleworth (1782–1842), Bishop of Chichester 1840–2.
11 Sri Lanka (formerly Ceylon).
12 F. Oakeley, *The story of my life*, p. 27.
13 ibid., p. 28.
14 F. Oakeley, *Canon Oakeley's memoirs*, p. 3
15 L. M. Quiller Couch (ed.) *Reminiscences of Oxford by Oxford Men 1559–1850*, p. 330.
16 M. R. D. Foot and C. F. G. Matthew (editors), *The Gladstone diaries 1825–1868*, volume 1, pp. 370–1.
17 Thomas Vowler Short (1790–1872), Bishop of Sodor and Man 1841–6 and bishop of St Asaph 1846–70.
18 F. Oakeley, *Canon Oakeley's memoirs*, p. 4.
19 L. M. Quiller Couch (ed.), *Reminiscences of Oxford by Oxford Men 1559–1850*, p. 324.
20 F. Oakeley, *De tribunicia apud Romanus potestate* & *The influence of the crusades upon the arts and literature of Europe*.
21 B. A. Smith, *Dean Church: The Anglican response to Newman*, p. 225.
22 T. Mozley, *Reminiscences, chiefly of Oriel College and the Oxford Movement*, volume 2, p. 228.
23 ibid., p. 229.
24 Wilberforce Papers, Oakeley to Wilberforce, 11 July 1827.
25 F. Oakeley, *The Subject of Tract XC*, p. x.
26 Richard Hurrell Froude (1803–36), Robert Wilberforce (1802–57), archdeacon of the East Riding 1841–54, Roman Catholic 1854.
27 Francis Newman (1805–97), Professor of Latin, University College, London 1846–63. George Moberley (1803–85), Bishop of Salisbury 1869–85.
28 Samuel Wilberforce (1805–73), Bishop of Oxford 1845–69, Bishop of Winchester 1869–73.
29 Wilberforce Papers, Oakeley to Wilberforce, 8 (May or June) 1826.
30 ibid., Oakeley to Wilberforce, 1826 (fragment of a letter).
31 F. Oakeley, *The story of my life*, p. 32.
32 Wilberforce Papers, Oakeley to Wilberforce, 28 March 1827.
33 ibid.

34 ibid., Oakeley to Wilberforce, 11 May 1827.
35 Charles Lloyd (1784–1829), Regius Professor of Divinity 1822–9 and Bishop of Oxford 1827–9.
36 Wilberforce Papers, Oakeley to Wilberforce, 26 November 1827.
37 William Baker, *Beyond port and prejudice. Charles Lloyd 1784–1829*, pp. 214–15.
38 F. Oakeley, *Historical notes on the Tractarian Movement*, p. 13
39 L. M. Quiller Couch (ed.), *Reminiscences of Oxford by Oxford Men 1559–1850*, p. 328.
40 ibid., p. 328–9.
41 F. Oakeley, *Historical notes on the Tractarian Movement*, p. 13.
42 ibid.
43 F. Oakeley, *Canon Oakeley's memoirs*, p. 4.
44 Wilberforce Papers, Oakeley to Wilberforce, 26 November 1827.
45 F. Oakeley, *Canon Oakeley's memoirs*, p. 4
46 I. G. Sieveking, *Memoir and letters of Francis W. Newman*, (London, 1909).
47 Mrs John Mozley (1808–79), Newman's second sister.
48 J. H. Newman, *The letters and diaries of John Henry Newman*, volume 2, p. 10, Newman to Mrs Jemima Newman, 30 March 1827.
49 ibid., p. 127, Newman's Diary 3 March 1829.
50 ibid., volume 3, pp. 198–9, Newman to Isaac Williams, 16 January 1833.
51 ibid., volume 4, p. 276, Newman to Froude, 14 June 1834.
52 F. Oakeley, *Canon Oakeley's memoirs*, p. 5.
53 ibid.
54 ibid.
55 ibid., p. 7.
56 R. T. Davidson and W. Benham, *Life of Archibald Campbell Tait*, volume 1, p. 43.
57 F. Oakeley, *Canon Oakeley's memoirs*, p. 7.
58 ibid., *A letter to his grace the Duke of Wellington,* p. 10.
59 ibid., p. 14.
60 ibid., p. 16.
61 ibid., p. 20.
62 Henry Wilberforce (1807–73), Roman Catholic 1850.
63 H. Wilberforce, *The foundation of the faith assailed in Oxford*, (Oxford, 1835).
64 Renn Dickson Hampden (1793–1868), Bishop of Hereford 1848–68.
65 J. H. Newman, *The letters and diaries of John Henry Newman*, volume 5, p. 89, Newman to Froude, 27 June 1835.
66 H. P. Liddon, *Life of Edward Bouverie Pusey*, volume 1, pp. 333–4.
67 ibid., volume 2, p. 118, Pusey to Newman, 2 August 1839.
68 F. Oakeley, *Canon Oakeley's memoirs*, pp. 7–8
69 E. S. Ffoulkes, *A history of the church of St. Mary the Virgin, Oxford*, p. 461.
70 R. W. Church, *The Oxford Movement 1833–1845*, p. 296.

71   W. Ward, *William George Ward and the Oxford Movement*, p. 122.

72   Richard Bagot (1782–1854), Bishop of Oxford 1829–45, Bishop of Bath and Wells 1845–54.

73   F. Oakeley, *A sermon preached at the general ordination of Richard, lord bishop of Oxford*, p. 13.

74   ibid., *Canon Oakeley's memoirs*, p. 7.

75   ibid., p. 8.

76   ibid., p. 2.

77   ibid., p.8.

78   R. T. Davidson and W. Benham, *Life of Archibald Campbell Tait*, volume I, p. 62, Alexander Hall Hall to A. C. Tait, 20 January 1837.

79   Henry Philpot (1807–92), Bishop of Worcester 1856–90.

80   J. H. Newman, *The letters and diaries of John Henry Newman*, volume 6, p. 10, Newman to Pusey, 10 January 1837.

81   ibid., *Letters and correspondence of John Henry Newman*, ed. Anne Mozley, volume 2, p. 228, Newman to J.W Bowden, 16 March 1837.

82   John William Bowden (1798–1844), A Commissioner of Stamps 1828–40.

83   F. Oakeley, *Canon Oakeley's memoirs*, p. 8.

84   ibid.

85   R. T. Davidson and W. Benham, *Life of Archibald Campbell Tait*, volume 1, p. 75.

86   F. Oakeley, *Remarks on Aristotelian and Platonic ethics*, p. 5.

87   ibid., p. 9.

88   ibid., pp. 9–10.

89   ibid., p. 20

90   ibid., p. 21.

91   ibid., p. 22.

92   ibid., p. 23.

93   ibid., p. 53.

94   ibid., p. 49.

95   ibid., p. 54.

96   ibid., pp. 56–7.

97   The volume includes a number of sermons preached at Oxford.

98   F. Oakeley, *Sermons, preached chiefly in the Chapel Royal, at Whitehall*, p. ix.

99   ibid., pp. lvi-lvii.

100   ibid., p. iv.

101   ibid.

102   ibid., pp. ix-x.

103   ibid., p. xi.

104   ibid., p. xii.

105   ibid., pp. viii-ix.

106   ibid., pp. xii-xiii.

107   ibid., p. xv.

108   ibid., p. xvi.

109   ibid., p. xviii.

110 ibid.
111 ibid., pp. xviii-xix.
112 ibid., p. xix.
113 ibid., p. xxi.
114 ibid., p. xxii.
115 ibid., p. xxiv.
116 ibid., p. xxv.
117 ibid., p. xxvii.
118 Charles James Blomfield (1786–1857), Bishop of Chester 1824-8, Bishop of London 1828–56.
119 F. Oakeley, *Canon Oakeley's memoirs*, p. 9.
120 ibid., *Christians, the salt of the earth and the light of the world. A sermon*, pp. 19–20.
121 Edward Oakeley (1796–1870), fourth of Sir Charles' six sons.
122 F. Oakeley, *The story of my life*, p. 32.
123 W. G. Ward, *The Ideal of a Christian Church*, p. 597. This is from an anonymous and undated letter used by Ward in the Appendix to the book. The dates and experiences suggest the strong probability of Oakeley's authorship.
124 T. Mozley, *Reminiscences, chiefly of Oriel College and the Oxford Movement*, volume 2, p. 5.
125 F. Oakeley, *Sermons, preached chiefly in the Chapel Royal, at Whitehall*, p. ix.
126 Wilberforce Papers, Oakeley to Wilberforce, 28 March 1827.
127 ibid., Oakeley to Wilberforce, 11 July 1827.
128 D. Newsome, *The parting of friends*, p. 103, Wilberforce to Froude, 30 July 1827.
129 Wilberforce Papers, Oakeley to Wilberforce, 26 November 1827.
130 F. Oakeley, *Historical notes on the Tractarian Movement*, p. 6.
131 ibid., *The Subject of Tract XC historically examined*, p. x.
132 W. Ward, *William George Ward and the Oxford Movement*, p. 136.
133 F. Oakeley, *Canon Oakeley's memoirs*, p. 9.
134 ibid.
135 Richard Jenkins (1783–1854), Master 1819-54, Dean of Wells 1845–54.
136 W. Ward, *William George Ward and the Oxford Movement*, p. 116.
137 F. Oakeley, *Canon Oakeley's memoirs*, p. 9.
138 J. Jones, 'The civil war of 1843', *Balliol College Annual Record 1978*.
139 F. Oakeley, *Canon Oakeley's memoirs*, p.10.
140 Henry Ryder (1777–1836), Bishop of Gloucester 1815–24, Bishop of Lichfield and Coventry 1824–36.
141 F. Oakeley, *Canon Oakeley's memoirs*, p. 6.
142 ibid.
143 ibid., p. 10.

Chapter 3

1 F. Oakeley, Canon Oakeley's memoirs, p. 10

2 ibid., *Historical notes on the Tractarian Movement*, pp. 59–60.
3 G. H. Wakeling, *The Oxford Church Movement*, p. 84
4 Henry Drummond (1786–1860), Member of Parliament from 1810.
5 A. R. Ashwell and R. G. Wilberforce, *Life of Samuel Wilberforce*, volume 1, pp. 102–3.
6 E. Bellasis, *Memorials of Mr Serjeant Bellasis*, p. 41.
7 G. H. Wakeling, *The Oxford Church Movement*, p. 84.
8 F. Oakeley, *Historical notes on the Tractarian Movement*, p. 61.
9 ibid., Oakeley, *Personal reminiscences of the 'Oxford Movement'*, p. 10.
10 G. H. Wakeling, *The Oxford Church Movement*, p. 84.
11 F. Oakeley, *Personal reminiscences of the 'Oxford Movement'*, p. 10.
12 ibid.
13 Isaac Williams (1802–65), poet and theologian, he left Oxford in 1842 after being defeated in the election for the chair of Poetry.
14 I. Williams, *The autobiography of Isaac Williams*, ed. Sir George Prevost, pp. 86–7.
15 E. Bourne, 'Old Margaret Street Chapel', pp. 357–63.
16 G. H. Wakeling, *The Oxford Church Movement,* p. 86.
17 F. Oakeley, *Canon Oakeley's memoirs*, p. 11.
18 ibid., *Personal reminiscences of the 'Oxford Movement'*, p. 9.
19 ibid., *Historical notes on the Tractarian Movement*, p. 9.
20 ibid., *Personal reminiscences of the 'Oxford Movement'*, p. 9.
21 P. Fitzgerald, *Fifty years of Catholic life and social progress*, volume 1, p. 178.
22 A. M. W. Stirling, *The Richmond Papers,* p. 130.
23 F. Oakeley, *Historical notes on the Tractarian Movement*, p. 62.
24 ibid.
25 G. Rowell, *The vision glorious*, p. 114.
26 F. Oakeley, *Canon Oakeley's memoirs*, p. 11.
27 ibid., *Historical notes on the Tractarian Movement*, p. 63.
28 Edward Bellasis (1800–73), a distinguished parliamentary lawyer, he became a Roman Catholic in 1850.
29 E. Bellasis, *Memorials of Mr Serjeant Bellasis*, p. 41.
30 F. Oakeley, *Personal reminiscences of the 'Oxford Movement'*, p. 10.
31 ibid., *Canon Oakeley's memoirs*, p. 16.
32 ibid., *Historical notes on the Tractarian Movement*, p. 63.
33 ibid.
34 ibid., *Personal reminiscences of the 'Oxford Movement'*, p. 11.
35 ibid., *Canon Oakeley's memoirs*, p. 15.
36 ibid., pp. 15–16.
37 P. J. Welch, "Bishop Blomfield' (Dissertation, London, 1952), p. 409.
38 R. D. Middleton, *Magdalen studies*, p. 38.
39 F. Oakeley, *Historical notes on the Tractarian Movement*, p. 65.
40 William Upton Richards (1811–73). He succeeded Oakeley in charge of the Chapel in 1845, and subsequently became the first vicar of All Saints', Margaret Street.

41 P. J. Welch, 'Bishop Blomfield', p. 408.
42 F. Oakeley, *Personal reminiscences of the 'Oxford Movement'*, p. 10.
43 John Rouse Bloxam (1807–91), Fellow of Magdalen College 1836, Curate of Littlemore 1837–40, Vicar of Upper Beeding 1862–91.
44 R. D. Middleton, *Magdalen studies*, p. 34.
45 E. Bellasis, *Memorials of Mr Serjeant Bellasis*, pp. 41–2, Oakeley to Bellasis, 20 September 1839.
46 R. D. Middleton, *Newman and Bloxam*, pp. 43–4, Oakeley to Bloxam, 1 October 1839.
47 E. Bourne, 'Old Margaret Street Chapel', pp. 359–60.
48 F. Oakeley, *Christ manifested to the faithful through his church*, p. 20.
49 W. E. Gladstone, *Correspondence on church and religion*, ed. D. C. Lathbury, volume 1, pp. 408–9.
50 E. Bellasis, *Memorials of Mr Serjeant Bellasis*, p. 42.
51 F. Oakeley, 'The Church Service', *British Critic*, volume 27 (1840), 249–76.
52 F. Oakeley, *Canon Oakeley's memoirs*, p. 12.
53 ibid., p. 13.
54 ibid.
55 ibid., p. 12.
56 ibid., p. 13.
57 ibid., p. 16.
58 ibid., p. 14.
59 F. Oakeley, *Historical notes on the Tractarian Movement*, p. 69.
60 R. D. Middleton, *Magdalen studies*, p. 37.
61 J. F. M. Carter, *Life and work of the Rev. T. T. Carter*, p. 7.
62 P. J. Welch, 'Bishop Blomfield', pp. 411–12.
63 C. J. Blomfield, *Charge of 1842*, pp. 53–4.
64 ibid., pp. 48–9.
65 P. J. Welch, 'Bishop Blomfield', p. 434.
66 C. J. Blomfield, *Charge of 1842*, p. 49.
67 Blomfield Papers, volume 34, f. 94, Blomfield to Oakeley, 28 November 1842.
68 F. Oakeley, *Historical notes on the Tractarian Movement*, p. 69.
69 ibid., *Canon Oakeley's memoirs*, p. 14.
70 ibid., *Personal reminiscences of the 'Oxford Movement'*, p. 17.
71 ibid., *Christ manifested to the faithful through his church*, p. iii.
72 ibid., pp. 8–9.
73 ibid., p. iv.
74 ibid., p. 12.
75 ibid., p. 17.
76 ibid., p. 13.
77 ibid., p. 14.
78 ibid., p. 16.
79 Properly *The British Critic and Quarterly Theological Review*.
80 M. O'Connell, *The Oxford conspirators*, pp. 269–71.
81 F. Oakeley, 'The Church Service', p. 249.

82 ibid., p. 251.
83 ibid., p. 252.
84 ibid.
85 ibid.
86 ibid.
87 ibid.
88 ibid., pp. 252–3.
89 ibid., p. 253.
90 ibid.
91 F. Oakeley, *Historical notes on the Tractarian Movement*, pp. 29–30.
92 ibid., 'The Church Service', p. 254.
93 ibid., p. 255.
94 ibid.
95 ibid.
96 ibid., p. 256.
97 ibid., p. 257.
98 ibid., p. 258.
99 ibid., p. 259.
100 ibid., p. 260.
101 ibid., p. 257.
102 ibid.
103 ibid., p. 262.
104 ibid., p. 265.
105 O. Chadwick, *The Victorian Church*, volume 1, p. 212.
106 F. Oakeley, 'The Church Service', p. 266.
107 ibid., p. 269.
108 ibid., p. 270.
109 ibid., p. 271.
110 ibid.
111 ibid., p. 272.
112 ibid.
113 ibid., p. 273.
114 ibid.
115 ibid.
116 ibid., p. 274.
117 H. Norris, *Church vestments. Their origin and development*, p. 70.
118 R. W. Church, *The Oxford Movement 1833–1845*, p. 371.
119 E. Purcell, *Life of Cardinal Manning*, volume 1, p. 314.
120 S. L. Ollard, *A short history of the Oxford Movement*, p. 62.
121 M. O'Connell, *The Oxford Conspirators*, p. 410.
122 R. H. Greenfield, 'The Attitude of the Tractarians to the Roman Catholic Church 1833–1850' (Oxford, Dissertation, 1956), p. 308.
123 G. H. Wakeling, *The Oxford Church Movement*, p. 86.
124 ibid.
125 ibid., p. 87.
126 ibid., p. 89.
127 ibid., p. 88.

128 W. E. Gladstone, *Correspondence on church and religion*, volume 1, pp. 408-9.
129 Lady Georgiana Fullerton (1812-85), Roman Catholic 1846, novelist and philanthropist.
130 Presumably John, fifth Earl of Bessborough (1809-80).
131 F. Oakeley, *Historical notes on the Tractarian Movement*, p. 65.
132 ibid.
133 ibid., p. 64.
134 ibid.
135 J. H. Newman, *A packet of letters*, ed. J. Sugg, p. 51, Newman to Mrs Thomas Mozley, 8 July 1840.
136 Pusey Papers, Oakeley to Pusey, 17 August 1840.
137 F. Oakeley, *Canon Oakeley's memoirs*, p. 17.
138 ibid., pp. 17-18.
139 W. A. Whitworth, *Quam dilecta*, p. 45, W. G. Ward to A. L. Phillipps, Christmas 1841.

Chapter 4
1 E. M. Oakeley, *The life of Sir Herbert Stanley Oakeley*, p. 13.
2 J. Murray, *Hymnal for use in the English Church*, (London, 1852).
3 P. Dearmer, *Songs of praise discussed*, pp. 53-4.
4 M. Frost (ed.), *Historical companion to hymns ancient and modern*, p. 447.
5 British Library, Add MSS 57,514, ff. 188-191, Oakeley to Julian, 9 April 1873.
6 ibid., f. 193, Oakeley's response to a questionnaire sent to him by Julian.
7 F. Oakeley, *The story of my life*, pp. 4-5.
8 E. M. Oakeley, *The life of Sir Herbert Stanley Oakeley*, p. 13.
9 G. H. Sumner, *Life of Charles Richard Sumner*, p. 41.
10 B. Rainbow, *The choral revival in the Anglican Church*, p. 18.
11 W. Ward, *William George Ward and the Oxford Movement*, p. 41.
12 ibid., p. 93.
13 B. Rainbow, *The choral revival in the Anglican Church 1839-1872*, p. 3.
14 ibid., p. 5.
15 B. Rainbow, *The choral revival in the Anglican church 1839-1872*, p. 15.
16 F. Oakeley, *Canon Oakeley's memoirs*, p. 11.
17 ibid.
18 E. Bourne, 'Old Margaret Street Chapel', p. 359.
19 Richard Redhead (1820-1901), organist of Margaret Chapel, then All Saints' Church 1839-64, organist of St Mary Magdalene, Paddington 1864-94.
20 *The Musical Times*, 1 June 1901, p. 411.
21 R. Redhead, *Church Music*, p. vii.
22 ibid., p. v.

23 ibid.
24 ibid., p. vi.
25 ibid., p. vii.
26 ibid., p. vi.
27 ibid.
28 ibid., p. vii.
29 ibid.
30 B. Rainbow, *The choral revival in the Anglican Church 1839–1872*, p. 20.
31 F. Oakeley, 'Chanting',p. 372.
32 ibid., pp. 373–4.
33 ibid., p. 373.
34 ibid., p. 375.
35 ibid., pp. 377–8.
36 ibid., p. 383.
37 ibid.
38 ibid., p. 386.
39 ibid., p. 388.
40 ibid., p. 389.
41 F. Oakeley, 'Psalms and Hymns', p. 4.
42 ibid., p. 5.
43 ibid., p. 10.
44 ibid., p. 24.
45 A. R. Ashwell and R. G. Wilberfoce, *Life of Samuel Wilberforce*, volume 1, p. 237, Wilberforce to Miss L. Noel, 6 May 1844.
46 W. E. Gladstone, *Correspondence on church and religion*, volume 1, p. 408, Gladstone to W. A. Whitworth, 3 September 1893.
47 *The hymnal 1940 companion*, p. 519.
48 B. Rainbow, *The choral revival in the Anglican Church 1839–1872*, p. 20.
49 Newman Papers, Oakeley to T. Mozley, 26 July 1842.
50 B. Rainbow, *The choral revival in the Anglican Church*, p. 21.
51 N. Temperley, *The music of the English parish church*, volume 1, p. 256.
52 ibid., pp. 260–1.
53 B. Rainbow, *The choral revival in the Anglican Church 1839–1872*, p. 22.
54 F. Oakeley, 'Music, chiefly ecclesiastical', p. 295.
55 ibid.
56 E. Bourne, 'Old Margaret Street Chapel', p. 359.
57 Newman Papers, Newman to Dalgairns, 31 October 1843.
58 E. Bellasis, *Memorials of Mr Serjeant Bellasis*, p. 35, Bellasis to W. J. Garnett, 12 January 1844.
59 W.E. Gladstone, *Correspondence on church and religion*, volume 1, p. 409.
60 A. R. Ashwell and R. G. Wilberforce, *Life of Samuel Wilberforce*, volume I, p. 237, Wilberforce to Miss L. Noel, 6 May 1844.

Chapter 5

1 F. Oakeley, 'Ancient and Modern Ways of Charity', p. 46.
2 ibid., p. 55.
3 ibid., p. 68.
4 ibid., p. 46.
5 ibid., p. 50.
6 ibid., p. 56.
7 ibid., p. 55.
8 ibid.
9 ibid.
10 ibid., p. 69.
11 J. H. Newman, *Remarks on Certain Passages in the Thirty-Nine Articles*, p. 4.
12 Newman Papers, Newman to Thomas Mozley, 7 March 1841.
13 ibid., Oakeley to Pusey, 15 March 1841.
14 ibid.
15 ibid.
16 H. P. Liddon, *Life of Edward Bouverie Pusey*, volume 2, p. 216.
17 F. Oakeley, *The Subject of Tract XC*, p. 19.
18 ibid., p. 22.
19 ibid.
20 ibid., p. 23.
21 ibid., p. 31.
22 ibid., p. 32.
23 ibid., p. 35.
24 ibid., p. 40.
25 ibid., p. 58.
26 ibid., p. 36.
27 ibid., p. 57.
28 Pusey Papers, Oakeley to Pusey, 5th week in Lent 1841 (the 5th Sunday in Lent fell on 28 March in 1841).
29 ibid.
30 ibid.
31 ibid., Oakeley to Pusey, 22 June 1841.
32 ibid.
33 Tait Papers, Oakeley to Tait, 28 May 1841.
34 ibid., Oakeley to Blomfield, 25 June 1841.
35 ibid.
36 F. Oakeley, 'Bishop Jewel', *British Critic*, p. 1.
37 ibid., p. 2.
38 ibid.
39 ibid., p. 3.
40 ibid.
41 ibid.
42 ibid., p..4.
43 ibid.
44 ibid., p. 7.

45   ibid., p. 13.
46   ibid., p. 17.
47   ibid.
48   ibid., p. 21.
49   ibid.
50   ibid., pp. 26–7.
51   ibid., pp. 27–8.
52   ibid., p. 28.
53   ibid., p. 30.
54   ibid.
55   ibid., p. 32.
56   ibid., p. 34.
57   ibid., p. 44.
58   ibid.
59   ibid., p. 38.
60   ibid., p. 39.
61   ibid., pp. 44–5.
62   ibid., p. 33.
63   ibid., p. 45.
64   ibid., pp. 45–6.
65   Thomas Mozley (1806–93), married to Newman's elder sister.
66   Newman Papers, Newman to T. Mozley, 6 April 1841.
67   M. O'Connell, *The Oxford conspirators*, p. 346.
68   ibid.
69   Newman Papers, Newman to T. Mozley, 20 August 1841.
70   T. Mozley, *Reminiscences, chiefly of Oriel College and the Oxford Movement*, volume 2, p. 244.
71   Harriet Mozley (1803–52). She had no sympathy with her brother's religious development, and broke off relations with him two or three years before he was received into the Roman Catholic Church.
72   D. Mozley (ed.), *Newman family letters*, p. 107.
73   H. P. Liddon, *Life of Edward Bouverie Pusey*, volume 2, p. 220. Keble to Pusey, 4 July 1841.
74   ibid., pp. 218–9, Pusey to Newman, 20 July 1841.
75   Frederic Rogers (1811–89), Fellow of Oriel 1833–45, Lord Blachford (1871).
76   Robert Francis Wilson (1809–88), Keble's curate at Hursley.
77   F. Blachford, *Letters of Frederic, Lord Blachford*, ed. G. E. Marindin, p. 206, Rogers to Newman, 22 July 1841.
78   Newman Papers, Palmer to Newman, 25 July 1841.
79   Newman Papers, Pusey to Newman, 27 July 1841.
80   ibid.
81   J. H. Newman, *Apologia Pro Vita Sua*, p. 259.
82   H. P. Liddon, *Life of Edward Bouverie Pusey*, volume 2, p. 223.
83   Pusey Papers, Newman to Pusey, 30 July 1841.
84   Newman Papers, Pusey to Newman, 9 August 1841.
85   Pusey Papers, Newman to Pusey, 13 August 1841.

86 Richard Bagot (1782–1854), Bishop of Oxford 1829–45, Bishop of Bath and Wells 1845–54.
87 H. P. Liddon, *Life of Edward Bouverie Pusey*, volume 2, p. 230, Pusey to bishop of Oxford, 8 September 1841.
88 George Dudley Ryder (1810–80), one of Newman's students at Oriel. His wife was a sister-in-law of Henry and Samuel Wilberforce. He and his family were received into the Roman Catholic Church in 1846.
89 Newman Papers, Ryder to Newman, 9 August 1841.
90 ibid., Oakeley to T. Mozley, 31 August 1841.
91 ibid.
92 F. Oakeley, 'Bishop Jewel', p. 42.
93 ibid.
94 *The Record*, 2 August 1841, p. 4.
95 ibid., 12 August 1841, p. 4.
96 Newman Papers, Mozley to Newman, 17 August 1841.
97 ibid., Newman to T. Mozley, 23 August 1841.
98 F. Oakeley, *The story of my life*, pp. 26–7.
99 Miscellaneous Papers, M.S. Eng.hist, c1033, ff..110–111, Shuttleworth to Oakeley, 13 December 1841.

Chapter 6
1 T. Mozley, *Reminiscences, chiefly of Oriel College and the Oxford Movement*, volume 2, p. 225.
2 Newman Papers, Oakeley to Newman, 31 August 1841.
3 ibid.
4 B. Penny, *Maryvale*, pp. 9–11.
5 A. W. N. Pugin (1812–52) architect and ecclesiologist.
6 D. Gwynne, *Lord Shrewsbury, Pugin and the Catholic Revival*, pp. 77–8.
7 Edmund Purcell, *Life of Ambrose Phillipps de Lisle*, volume 1, p. 266.
8 F. Oakeley, 'Rites and Ceremonies', p. 422.
9 ibid., p. 423.
10 ibid. p. 424.
11 ibid.
12 ibid., p. 426.
13 ibid., p. 427.
14 ibid., p. 428.
15 ibid., p. 430.
16 ibid., p. 433.
17 ibid., p. 435.
18 ibid., p. 442.
19 ibid., pp. 442–3.
20 ibid., p. 447.
21 ibid.
22 R. W. Church, *The Oxford Movement*, p. 371.
23 F. Oakeley, 'Rites and Ceremonies', p. 447.
24 ibid., p. 448.

25   ibid., p. 453.
26   ibid.
27   ibid., p. 465.
28   ibid., p. 408.
29   ibid., p. 465.
30   ibid., p. 423.
31   ibid., p. 454.
32   ibid., p. 464.
33   ibid., p. 460.
34   ibid., p. 455.
35   ibid., p. 459.
36   ibid., p. 457.
37   ibid., pp. 460-1.
38   ibid., pp. 455-6.
39   ibid., p. 460.
40   ibid., p. 462.
41   ibid., p. 461.
42   ibid., p. 463.
43   Presumably the baptism of Princess Victoria.
44   F. Oakeley, 'Rites and Ceremonies', p. 464.
45   Oratory Fathers, *Correspondence of John Henry Newman*, p. 144, Newman to J. R. Hope, 7 October 1841.
46   Newman Papers, Newman to J. W. Bowden, 10 October 1841.
47   Jemima, Mrs John Mozley (1808-79).
48   Newman Papers, Newman to Mrs John Mozley, 16 November 1841.
49   F. Oakeley, 'Rites and Ceremonies', p. 465.
50   Pusey Papers, Oakeley to Pusey, 16 November 1841.
51   J. H. Newman, *Apologia pro vita sua*, p. 245.
52   H. P. Liddon, *Life of Edward Bouverie Pusey*, volume 2, p. 396.
53   Oratory Fathers, *Correspondence of John Henry Newman*, p. 159, Newman to Wood, 6 December 1841.
54   Newman Papers, Newman to Wood, 8 January 1842.
55   ibid.
56   ibid., Mozely to Newman, 30 November 1841.
57   ibid., Oakeley to T. Mozley, 3 December 1841.
58   ibid., Mozley to Newman, 28 January 1842.
59   ibid., Newman to T. Mozley, 29 January 1842.
60   Louis Bouyer, *Newman. His life and spirituality*, p. 237.
61   Newman Papers, Oakeley to T. Mozley, 4 March 1842.
62   F. Oakeley, *Homilies for holy days and seasons*, p. ix.
63   ibid., p. x.
64   ibid., p. xi.
65   ibid.
66   ibid., p. xii.
67   F. Oakeley, 'Bishop Jewel', p. 45.
68   Newman Papers, Oakeley to T. Mozley, 30 April 1842.
69   C. S. Bird, *Plea for the reformed church*, (London, 1842).

70 Newman Papers, Oakeley to T. Mozley, 27 May 1842.
71 ibid.
72 ibid., Wednesday in Whit Week 1842.
73 F. Oakeley, 'What is meant by unprotestantizing', p. 211.
74 ibid., p. 212.
75 ibid.
76 ibid.
77 ibid., p. 215.
78 ibid., p. 213.
79 ibid., p. 215.
80 ibid., p. 213.
81 ibid., p. 215.
82 ibid.
83 ibid., p. 216.
84 ibid., p. 224.
85 ibid., p. 242.
86 ibid., p. 244.
87 J. Morley, *The life of William Ewart Gladstone*, volume 1, pp. 309–10.
88 Edward Denison (1801–54), Bishop of Salisbury 1837–54.
89 Newman Papers, Mozley to Newman 9 September 1942.
90 ibid., Newman to Mozley 14 September 1842.
91 ibid., Mozley to Newman 16 September 1842.
92 ibid., Newman to Mozley 17 September 1842.
93. ibid., Mozley to Newman 20 September 1842.
94 ibid., Newman to Mozley 26 September 1842.
95 Keble Papers, John Keble to Thomas Keble, 26 September 1842.
96 Newman Papers, Newman to T. Mozley, 18 October 1842.
97 ibid., Newman to Mozley 30 October 1842.
98 ibid., Newman to Pusey, 16 October 1842.
99 ibid., Oakeley to Newman 27 October 1842.
100 ibid., Newman to Mozley 26 December 1842.
101 F. Oakeley, 'Episcopal Charges of the past year'.
102 ibid., p. 274.
103 ibid., p. 275.
103 ibid., p. 276.
105 ibid.
106 ibid.
107 ibid., p. 277.
108 ibid., p. 278.
109 ibid., p. 279.
110 ibid.
111 Newman Papers, Mozley to Newman, 9 September 1842.
112 F. Oakeley, 'The Church Service', p. 257.
113 ibid., 'Bishop Jewel', p. 3.
114 ibid., 'Episcopal Charges of the past year', p. 281.
115 ibid

116 F. Oakeley, *The Subject of Tract XC*, p. 57.
117 ibid., 'Episcopal Charges of the past year', p. 280.
118 H. P. Liddon, *Life of Edward Bouverie Pusey*, volume 2, p. 223.
119 Newman Papers, Newman to T. Mozley, 29 January 1842.

Chapter 7
  1 O. Chadwick, *The Victorian Church*, volume I, p. 135.
  2 F. Oakeley, 'The sees of St Asaph and Bangor', p. 233.
  3 ibid.
  4 ibid., p. 234.
  5 ibid.
  6 ibid., p. 235.
  7 F. Oakeley, *The story of my life*, pp. 6–7.
  8 Wilberforce Papers, Oakeley to Wilberforce, 11 July 1827.
  9 F. Oakeley, 'The sees of St Asaph and Bangor', p. 238.
 10 ibid., p. 239.
 11 ibid., p. 238.
 12 ibid., p. 239.
 13 ibid.
 14 ibid.
 15 ibid.
 16 ibid., p. 240.
 17 ibid., p. 246.
 18 Pusey Papers, Palmer to William Gresley, 28 August 1843.
 19 ibid., Palmer to Pusey, 2 August 1843.
 20 W. Ward, *W. G. Ward and the Oxford Movement*, p. 243.
 21 ibid., pp. 243–4.
 22 W. Palmer, *A narrative of events*, p. 36.
 23 ibid., p. 37.
 24 ibid., p. 43.
 25 ibid., p. 44.
 26 ibid.
 27 ibid.
 28 ibid., p. 68.
 29 ibid., p. 45.
 30 ibid., p. 45.
 31 ibid., p. 51.
 32 ibid., p. 50.
 33 ibid., p. 67.
 34 ibid.
 35 ibid., p. 68.
 36 R. H. Greenfield, 'The Attitude of the Tractarians to the Roman Catholic Church 1833–1850', p. 390.
 37 Newman Papers, Newman to Bowden, 31 October 1843.
 38 W. Palmer, *A Narrative of events*, p. 68.
 39 Francis Rivington (1806–85). The Rivington family had published the journal since its inception in 1793.

40 Newman Papers, Rivington to T. Mozley, 15 September 1843.
41 S. Rivington, *The publishing family of Rivington* p. 132.
42 T. Mozley, *Reminiscences, chiefly of Oriel College and the Oxford Movement*, volume 2, p. 391.
43 ibid., p. 392.
44 Harriet, Mrs Thomas Mozley (1803–52).
45 T. Mozley, *Reminiscences, chiefly of Oriel College and the Oxford Movement*, volume 2, p. 394.
46 ibid.
47 James Bowling Mozley (1813–78).
48 Richard William Church (1815–90). Fellow of Oriel College. Dean of Saint Paul's Cathedral 1871–90.
49 J. B. Mozley, *Letters of the Revd. J. B. Mozley*, p. 148.
50 F. Oakeley, 'Music, chiefly ecclesiastical'.
51 Newman Papers, Oakeley to T. Mozley, 23 October 1843.
52 James Hope, later Hope-Scott (1812–73). Fellow of Merton College and legal adviser to the Tractarians. Roman Catholic from 1851.
53 Newman Papers, Hope to Newman, 14 November 1843.
54 W. E. Gladstone, *Correspondence on church and religion*, volume 1, p. 289.
55 W. Palmer, *A narrative of events*, pp. 242–3.
56 S. Rivington, *The publishing family of Rivington*, p. 142.

Chapter 8
1 Newman Papers, Oakeley to Newman, 27 April 1842.
2 ibid.
3 Gladstone Papers, Add MSS 44,359, f. 122.
4 ibid.
5 F. Oakeley, *Prayers for a blessing on the work of building a new church*.
6 Newman Papers, Robert Williams to T. Mozley, 12 August 1842.
7 ibid., Oakeley to Newman, April 1843.
8 Pusey Papers, Oakeley to Pusey, no date except "St Philip' (1 May at that time, almost certainly 1844.
9 Gladstone Papers, Add MSS, 44,362, ff. 334–5, circular letter, Oakeley to Gladstone, 30 September 1845.
10 H. W. Law and I. Law, *The Book of the Beresford Hopes*, pp. 161–2.
11 F. Oakeley, *Personal reminiscences of the 'Oxford Movement'*, pp. 11–12.
12 J. H. Newman, *Apologia pro vita sua*, p. 302.
13 ibid., *Letters and correspondence*, ed. A. Mozley, volume 2, p. 345, Newman to Bowden, 4 April 1841.
14 J. H. Newman, *Apologia pro vita sua*, pp. 502–18.
15 ibid., p. 302.
16 ibid., *Letters and correspondence*, ed. A. Mozley, volume 2, pp. 412–3, Newman to Bowden, 3 April 1843.
17 Newman Papers, Oakeley to Newman, April 1843.

18 J. D. Holmes, 'Newman's reputation and the Lives of the English saints', p. 530.
19 Newman Papers, Rivington to Newman, 1 April 1843.
20 ibid., 1 August 1843.
21 George Tickell (1815–93), of University College. He became a Jesuit in 1851.
22 Newman Papers, Tickell to Newman, 4 August 1843.
23 ibid., Oakeley to Newman, 3 October 1843.
24 ibid.
25 S. Rivington, *The publishing family of Rivington*, p. 116.
26 Frederick Faber (1812–73). Fellow of University College. He became a Roman Catholic in 1845.
27 Newman Papers, Faber to Newman, 2 January 1844.
28 ibid., Hope to Newman, 14 November 1843.
29 ibid., Oakeley to Newman, 14 December 1843.
30 Newman Papers, Oakeley to Newman, 11 January 1844.
31 Oratory Fathers, *Correspondence of John Henry Newman*, pp. 280–1, Newman to Hope, 2 November 1843.
32 ibid., p. 288, Newman to Hope, 16 December 1843.
33 Newman Papers, Oakeley to Newman, 10 January 1844.
34 ibid., 17 January 1844.
35 ibid., Toovey to Newman, 24 January 1844.
36 ibid.
37 ibid., Oakeley to Newman, 26 January 1844.
38 ibid., Toovey to Newman, 20 March 1844.
39 ibid., Newman to R. H. Gray, 28 June 1844.
40 ibid., Oakeley to Newman, Tuesday.
41 ibid., Toovey to Newman, 17 January 1844.
42 ibid., 20 January 1844.
43 John Dalgairns (1818–76). Roman Catholic from 1845.
44 Mark Pattison (1813–84). Rector of Lincoln College 1871–84.
45 J. H. Newman, *Apologia pro vita sua*, p. 303.
46 J. E. Bowden, *Life of Frederick William Faber*, p. 223.
47 F. W. Faber, *Life of St Wilfrid*, p. 4.
48 ibid., p. 63.
49 ibid., p. 84.
50 ibid., p. 172.
51 J. E. Bowden, *Life of Frederick William Faber*, p. 226.
52 J. Dalgairns, *Life of St Stephen Harding*.
53 J. H. Newman, *Apologia pro vita sua*, p. 303
54 O. Chadwick, *Mind of the Oxford Movement*, pp. 173–4.
55 F. Oakeley, *Life of St Augustine*, p. 9.
56 ibid., p. 10.
57 ibid., p. 12.
58 ibid., p. 13.
59 ibid., p. 16.
60 ibid., p. 18.

61 ibid., p. 38.
62 ibid.
63 ibid., pp. 54–6.
64 ibid., pp. 96–9.
65 ibid., pp. 105–9.
66 ibid., pp. 182–6.
67 ibid., pp. 192–3.
68 ibid., p. 189.
69 ibid., p. 190.
70 ibid., p. 247.
71 ibid., p. 259.
72 F. Oakeley, 'Bishop Jewel', p. 3.
73 Newman Papers, Oakeley to T. Mozley, 24 January 1843.
74 Pusey Papers, Oakeley to Pusey, 2 December 1843.
75 ibid.
76 ibid.
77 Newman Papers, Oakeley to Newman, 11 January 1844.
78 Gladstone Papers, Add MSS 44,361, ff. 13–15, Prospectus, 9 January 1844.
79 Pusey Papers, Oakeley to Pusey, 2 December 1843.
80 ibid., 13 January 1844.
81 ibid.
82 ibid., 22 January 1844.
83 ibid.
84 ibid.
85 ibid., 24 January 1844.
86 Pusey Papers, Oakeley to Pusey, 22 January 1844.
87 Oratory Fathers, *Correspondence of John Henry Newman*, p. 298.
88 Newman Papers, Oakeley to Newman, 9 February 1844.
89 Oratory Fathers, *Correspondence of John Henry Newman*, p. 306.
90 Pusey Papers, Oakeley to Pusey, 24 June 1844.
91 Gladstone Papers, Add MSS, 44,459, ff. 299–301, Oakeley to Gladstone, 24 April 1876.
92 J. H. Newman, *Letters and correspondence*, ed. A. Mozley, volume 2, p. 177.
93 H. P. Liddon, *Life of Edward Bouverie Pusey, DD,* volume 2, p. 146.
94 J. H. Newman, *Letters and correspondence*, ed. A. Mozley, volume 2, p. 347, Newman to Keble, 23 July 1841.
95 Pusey Papers, Oakeley to Pusey, 20 November 1843.
96 ibid., Oakeley to Pusey, 12 March 1844.
97 ibid., Oakeley to Pusey, 24 June 1844.
98 H. P. Liddon, *Life of Edward Bouverie Pusey,* volume 2, p. 396.
99 M. Frost, *Historical companion to hymns ancient and modern*, p. 194.
100 F. Oakeley, *The life of our Lord and Saviour Jesus Christ*, p. vii.
101 J. C. Crosthwaite, *Modern hagiology*, p. 259.
102 ibid., p. 257.
103 ibid., p. 260.

104   F. Oakeley, *The life of our Lord and Saviour Jesus Christ*, p. xv.
105   ibid., p. 97.
106   ibid., pp. xv-xvi.
107   J. C. Crosthwaite, *Modern hagiology*, p. 262.
108   ibid., p. 263.
109   ibid.
110   ibid., p. 286.
111   ibid., p. 288.
112   F. Oakeley, *The life of our Lord and Saviour Jesus Christ*, p. iv.
113   ibid p. ix.
114   ibid., p. xiv.
115   ibid., p. vi.
116   J. C. Crosthwaite, *Modern hagiology*, p. 293.
117   ibid., p. 254.
118   ibid., p. 256.

Chapter 9
  1   F. Oakeley, *Life of St Augustine of Canterbury*, Advertisement, pages unnumbered.
  2   F. Oakeley, *Canon Oakeley's memoirs*, p. 19.
  3   Pusey Papers, Oakeley to Pusey, 24 June 1844.
  4   Newman Papers, Newman to Ambrose St John, 16 September 1844
  5   J. M. Stone, *Eleanor Leslie*, p. 91
  6   F. Oakeley, *Canon Oakeley's Memoirs*, p. 19.
  7   Newman Papers, Newman's Diary, 14 August 1844.
  8   F. Oakeley, *Canon Oakeley's memoirs*, p. 19.
  9   William Bence-Jones (1812–82). A barrister and author, he had been an undergraduate at Balliol in the 1830s and was a friend of Manning and Tait. His family estate was at Lisselane in Co. Cork.
 10   F. Oakeley, *Canon Oakeley's memoirs*, p. 19.
 11   ibid.
 12   J. M. Stone, *Eleanor Leslie*, pp. 91–2.
 13   F. Oakeley, *Canon Oakeley's memoirs*, p. 20.
 14   Newman Papers, Newman to Ambrose St John, 16 September 1844.
 15   Oratory Fathers, *Correspondence of John Henry Newman*, p. 537, Newman to Faber, 1 December 1844.
 16   *English Churchman*, 21 November 1844, p. 742.
 17   ibid.
 18   Oratory Fathers, *Correspondence of John Henry Newman*, p. 537, Newman to Faber, 1 December 1844.
 19   *English Churchman*, 21 November 1844, p. 742.
 20   ibid., p. 743.
 21   W. Ward, *William George Ward and the Oxford Movement*, pp. 250–1.
 22   W. G. Ward, *The Ideal of a Christian Church*, p. 16.
 23   F. Oakeley, *Life of St Augustine of Canterbury*, p. 189.
 24   *English Churchman*, 21 November 1844, p. 743.

25 ibid.
26 ibid.
27 ibid.
28 F. Oakeley, *Life of St Augustine of Canterbury*, Advertisement.
29 ibid., *Canon Oakeley's memoirs*, p. 20.
30 F. Oakeley, *The life of our Lord and Saviour Jesus Christ*, pp. xxviii-xxix.
31 *English Churchman*, 21 November 1844, p. 743.
32 ibid., p. 744.
33 ibid., p. 761.
34 ibid., p. 762.
35 Pusey Papers, Oakeley to Pusey, November 1844.
36 W. G. Ward, *The Ideal of a Christian Church*, p. 565.
37 ibid., p. 567.
38 R. W. Church, *The Oxford Movement 1833–1845*, p. 323.
39 Y. Brilioth, *The Anglican revival*, p. 176.
40 E. A. Knox, *The Tractarian Movement*, p. 320.
41 R. D. Middelton, *Newman at Oxford*, p. 219.
42 M. O'Connell, *The Oxford conspirators*, p. 399.
43 L. Bouyer, *Newman. His life and spirituality*, p. 238.
44 F. Oakeley, *Historical notes on the Tractarian movement*, p. 85.
45 ibid, *Canon Oakeley's memoirs*, p. 20.
46 ibid, *Historical notes on the Tractarian movement*, p. 86.
47 Pusey Papers, Oakeley to Pusey, 17 December 1844.
48 ibid., Oakeley to Pusey, 21 December 1844.
49 ibid.
50 W. G. Ward, *The Ideal of a Christian Church*, pp. 474–81.
51 F. Oakeley, *The Subject of Tract XC*.
52 Pusey Papers, Oakeley to Pusey, 21 December 1844.
53 ibid.
54 ibid.
55 ibid., Oakeley to Pusey, 24 December 1844.
56 ibid.
57 ibid.
58 ibid, Oakeley to Pusey, undated, probably December 1844.
59 Manning Papers, Oakeley to Manning, 12 December 1844.
60 ibid.
61 ibid.
62 ibid, Manning to Oakeley, 21 December 1844.
63 ibid.
64 ibid.
65 ibid.
66 ibid.
67 Pusey Papers, Pusey to Oakeley, 24 December 1844.
68 F. Oakeley, *The Subject of Tract XC*, p. v.
69 ibid., p. vi.
70 ibid., p. vii.

71   ibid., p. vii-viii.
72   ibid., p. viii.
73   ibid., p. ix.
74   ibid.
75   ibid., p. xii.
76   ibid.
77   ibid., p. xii.
78   ibid., p. xiii.
79   ibid., p. xiv.
80   ibid.
81   ibid., p. xv.
82   ibid., p. xvi.
83   Manning Papers, Manning to Oakeley, 25 January 1845.
84   ibid.
85   ibid.
86   ibid., Oakeley to Manning, 27 January 1845.
87   ibid.
88   ibid.
89   ibid.
90   ibid.
91   ibid., Manning to Oakeley, 31 January 1845.
92   ibid., Oakeley to Manning, 3 February 1845.
93   J. Garbett, *The University, the Church and the new Test*, p. 8.
94   W. Goode, *Tract XC historically refuted*, p. 8.
95   ibid., p. 9.
96   ibid.
97   ibid., p. 10.
98   ibid., p. 131.
99   ibid., p. 191.
100 ibid.
101 F. Oakeley, *A few words to those churchmen being members of convocation who purpose taking no part in Mr Ward's case*, p. 14.
102 ibid., p. 15.
103 ibid., p. 16.
104 ibid., p. 18.
105 ibid., pp. 19–20.
106 ibid., p. 20.
107 ibid., p. 21.
108 ibid.
109 ibid., p. 22.
110 ibid., p. 27.
111 ibid.
112 ibid., p. 29
113 Gladstone Papers, Add MSS 44,362, ff. 21-4, Oakeley to Gladstone, 25 January 1845.
114 R. W. Church, *The Oxford Movement 1833–1845*, p. 325.
115 Richard Whateley (1787–1863), Archbishop of Dublin 1831-63.

116 R. W. Church, *The Oxford Movement 1833–1845*, p. 327.
117 ibid., pp. 327–8.
118 A. C. Tait, *A letter to the reverend the vice-chancellor*.
119 ibid., p. 19.
120 R. W. Church, *The Oxford Movement 1833–1845*, p. 329.
121 F. Oakeley, *Historical notes on the Tractarian Movement*, p. 90.
122 E. Ffoulkes, *A history of the church of St Mary the Virgin Oxford*, p. 460.
123 This figure is also given by R. W. Church in *The Oxford Movement 1833–1845*, p. 331, also by H. P. Liddon in *Life of Edward Bouverie Pusey*, volume 2, p. 434. W. Ward in *W. G. Ward and the Oxford Movement*, p. 342, gives 777 to 391. M. O'Connell in *The Oxford conspirators*, p. 406, gives 777 to 341. E. J. K. Browne in *History of the Tractarian Movement*, p. 81, gives 777 to 368.
124 R. W. Church, *Life and letters of Dean Church*, ed. A. Church, p. 57.
125 R. W. Church, *The Oxford Movement 1833–1845*, p. 331.
126 H. P. Liddon, *Life of Edward Bouverie Pusey*, volume 2, p. 437, Pusey to Gladstone, 18 February 1845.
127 ibid., Gladstone to Pusey, 17 February 1845.
128 Pusey Papers, Oakeley to Pusey, 21 December 1844.

Chapter 10
  1 E. Bourne, 'Old Margaret Street Chapel', p. 362.
  2 F. Oakeley, *A second letter to the Lord Bishop of London*, p. 28.
  3 E. G. K. Browne, *History of the Tractarian Movement*, p. 97.
  4 ibid.
  5 ibid.
  6 ibid., p. 98.
  7 ibid., p. 99.
  8 ibid.
  9 ibid., p. 98.
 10 ibid.
 11 Newman Papers, Newman to Ward, 15 February 1845.
 12 Pusey Papers, Keble to Pusey, 26 February 1845.
 13 W. E. Gladstone, *Correspondence on church and religion*, volume 1, p. 326.
 14 *English Churchman*, 20 February 1845, p. 117.
 15 F. Oakeley, *Canon Oakeley's memoirs*, p. 21.
 16 ibid.
 17 ibid.
 18 *The Times*, 4 March 1845, p. 5.
 19 F. Oakeley, *Canon Oakeley's memoirs*, p. 22.
 20 ibid.
 21 ibid., *A second letter to the Lord Bishop of London*, pp. 19–20.
 22 ibid., p. 19.
 23 ibid., p. 20.

24   ibid., *Canon Oakeley's memoirs*, p. 22.
25   ibid., *A letter to the Lord Bishop of London*, p. 10.
26   ibid., p. 11.
27   ibid., p. 13.
28   ibid., p. 15.
29   ibid., pp. 16–17, George Chandler (1770–1859), Rector of All Souls, Langham Place 1825–47, Dean of Chichester 1830–59.
30   ibid., pp. 17–18.
31   ibid., p. 14.
32   ibid., p. 21.
33   ibid., p. 22.
34   ibid., p. 24.
35   ibid.
36   ibid., p. 25.
37   ibid., p. 36.
38   ibid.
39   ibid., p. 37.
40   ibid., p. 38.
41   Blomfield Papers, volume 42, f. 115, Blomfield to Oakeley, 19 February 1845.
42   ibid.,
43   *The Times*, 4 March 1845, p. 5.
44   Blomfield Papers, volume 42, ff. 117–18, Blomfield to Oakeley, 20 February 1845.
45   Gladstone Papers, Add MSS 44,362, f. 95, Oakeley to Gladstone, 20 February 1845.
46   ibid., f. 99, Oakeley to Gladstone, 21 February 1845.
47   ibid., f. 101, Bellasis to Gladstone, 22 February 1845.
48   W. E. Gladstone, *Correspondence on church and religion*, volume 1, p. 335, Gladstone to Blomfield, 22 February 1845.
49   Pusey Papers, Oakeley to Pusey, 21 February 1845.
50   H. P. Liddon, *Life of Edward Bouverie Pusey*, volume 2, p. 438.
51   Blomfield Papers, volume 42, ff. 124–5, Blomfield to Chandler, 24 February 1845.
52   R. Luker, *All Souls Langham Place. A history*, p. 22.
53   J. B. Mozley, *Letters of the Revd. J. B. Mozley*, ed. A. Mozley, p. 165.
54   E. S. Purcell, *Life of Cardinal Manning*, volume 1, p. 379.
55   Pusey Papers, Oakeley to Pusey, 21 February 1845.
56   ibid.
57   ibid., Oakeley to Pusey, 22 February 1845.
58   ibid.
59   ibid.
60   ibid.
61   ibid., Oakeley to Pusey, 24 February 1845.
62   ibid.
63   ibid.

64 Baptist Wriothesley Noel (1798–1873), minister of St John's Chapel, Bedford Row 1827–48. He had close links with evangelical nonconformity, and joined the Baptists in 1849 as a result of the Gorham Judgement.
65 Pusey Papers, Oakeley to Pusey, 24 February 1845.
66 ibid.
67 ibid.
68 ibid., Chandler to Pusey, 25 February 1845.
69 ibid.
70 ibid.
71 ibid., Oakeley to Pusey, 24 February 1845.
72 *The Times*, 3 March 1845, p. 5.
73 The preface is dated 24 February.
74 Pusey Papers, Pamphlet 11525, F. Oakeley, *A second letter to the Lord Bishop of London*, p. 6.
75 ibid., p. 7.
76 ibid., pp. 7–8.
77 ibid., pp. 8–9.
78 Sir John Taylor Coleridge (1790–1876), a Judge of the King's Bench. He was a Tractarian and published a biography of his friend John Keble in 1869.
79 E. Bellasis, *Memorials of Mr Serjeant Bellasis*, p. 49.
80 F. Oakeley, *A second letter to the Lord Bishop of London*, p. 11.
81 ibid., p. 12.
82 ibid., p. 15.
83 ibid., pp. 15 and 31.
84 ibid., p. 17.
85 ibid., p. 18.
86 ibid., p. 21.
87 ibid.
88 ibid., p. 22.
89 ibid., p. 23.
90 ibid.
91 ibid., pp. 23–4.
92 ibid., p. 26.
93 ibid.
94 Court of Arches Records, H672/6, Oakeley to Blomfield, 25 February 1841.

Chapter 11
1 Sir Stephen Lushington (1782–1873), Dean of the Arches 1858–67.
2 E. Bellasis, *Memorials of Mr Serjeant Bellasis*, p. 49, Bellasis to C. Blandy, 28 February 1845.
3 Blomfield Papers, volume 42, f. 133, Blomfield to Oakeley, 26 February 1845.
4 ibid.
5 ibid.

6 E. Bellasis, *Memorials of Mr Serjeant Bellasis*, p. 49.
7 Gladstone Papers, Add MSS 44,362, f. 104, Oakeley to Gladstone, 26 February 1845.
8 ibid.
9 Newman Papers, Newman to Crawley, 27 February 1845.
10 Oratory Fathers, *Correspondence of John Henry Newman*, p. 373, Newman to Keble, 28 February 1845.
11 ibid.
12 Pusey Papers, Keble to Pusey, 1 March 1845.
13 Newman Papers, Ward to Pusey, 26 February 1845.
14 ibid.
15 ibid.
16 ibid.
17 ibid.
18 ibid.
19 ibid.
20 ibid.
21 ibid.
22 Pusey Papers, Oakeley to Pusey, 27 February 1845.
23 *English Churchman*, 27 February 1845, p. 134.
24 ibid.
25 ibid.
26 ibid.
27 Pusey Papers, Oakeley to Pusey, 27 February 1845.
28 Blomfield Papers, volume 42, f. 133, Blomfield to Oakeley, 26 February 1845.
29 Gladstone Papers, Add MSS 44,362, f. 104, Oakeley to Gladstone, 27 February 1845.
30 *The Times*, 28 February 1845, p. 6.
31 ibid., 1 March 1845, p. 6.
32 ibid., 4 March 1845, p. 5.
33 *English Churchman*, 6 March 1845, p. 147.
34 ibid., p. 148.
35 ibid.
36 ibid., p. 150.
37 Blomfield Papers, volume 42, ff. 145-7, Blomfield to the Bishop of Gibraltar, 3 March 1845.
38 ibid., f. 157, Blomfield to Oakeley, 10 March 1845.
39 Edward Lowth Badeley (1803-68). A lawyer, he became a Roman Catholic in 1850.
40 John David Chambers (1805-93), Recorder of Salisbury 1844-93.
41 R. Ornsby, *Memoirs of James Robert Hope-Scott*, volume 2, p. 66, Hope to Gladstone, 10 March 1845.
42 ibid., Gladstone to Hope, 10 March 1845.
43 E. S. Purcell, *Life of Cardinal Manning*, volume 1, p. 300, Gladstone to Manning, 17 March 1845.
44 R. Ornsby, *Memoirs of James Robert Hope-Scott*, volume 2, p. 65.

45 ibid., p. 66.
46 Newman Papers, Oakeley to Newman, 10 March 1845.
47 F. Oakeley, *Canon Oakeley's memoirs*, p. 22.
48 Court of Arches records, H672/1, Letters of request, 8 April 1845.
49 ibid.
50 Newman Papers, Newman to Mrs John Bowden, 7 April 1845.
51 Court of Arches records, H672/6, 10 May 1845.
52 Newman Papers, Newman to Ambrose St John, 17 April 1845.
53 Ambrose St John (1815–75). Newman's confidant until his death.
54 Newman Papers, Newman to ? (the letter begins 'My dear D.'), 27 April 1845.
55 ibid., Newman to ? (the letter begins 'My dear D.'), 9 May 1845.
56 ibid.
57 ibid., Newman to Hope, 14 May 1845.
58 ibid.
59 ibid.
60 ibid.
61 ibid.
62 ibid., Newman to ? (the letter begins 'My dear D.'), 18 May 1845.
63 ibid., Newman to ? (the letter begins 'My dear H.'), 16 May 1845.
64 ibid., Newman to ? (the letter begins 'My dear D.'), 18 May 1845.
65 ibid., Oakeley to Newman, 20 May 1845.
66 Pusey Papers, Oakeley to Pusey, 20 May 1845.
67 ibid., Newman to Bellasis, 30 May 1845.
68 ibid.
69 ibid.
70 ibid.
71 ibid., Newman to Bellasis, 3 June 1845.
72 ibid.
73 *The Times*, 6 June 1845, p. 5.
74 ibid., Oakeley to Blomfield, 3 June 1845.
75 Newman Papers, Newman to Bellasis, 4 June 1845.
76 *English Churchman*, 5 June 1845, pp. 358–9.
77 ibid., p. 359.
78 ibid.
79 *The Times*, 6 June 1845, p. 4.
80 ibid.
81 ibid., p. 5.
82 ibid. 10 June 1845, p. 5.
83 G. D. Squibb, *Doctors Commons. A history of the college of advocates and doctors of law.*
84 *English Churchman*, 12 June 1845, p. 374.
85 Sir Herbert Jenner Fust (1778–1852), Dean of the Arches 1834–52.
86 Sir John Dodson (1780–1858), Dean of the Arches 1852–7.
87 *English Churchman*, 12 June 1845, p. 375.
88 ibid.
89 ibid., p. 376.

90 ibid.
91 Newman Papers, Newman's diary, 6 June 1845.
92 F. Oakeley, *The claim to 'hold as distinct from teaching', explained in a letter to a friend*, p. iii.
93 ibid., p. iv.
94 ibid., pp. 5–6.
95 ibid., p. 5.
96 ibid., *A letter to the Lord Bishop of London*, pp. 16–17.
97 ibid., *The claim to 'hold as distinct from teaching', explained in a letter to a friend*, p. 6.
98 ibid.
99 ibid., pp. 7–8.
100 Pusey Papers, Oakeley to Pusey, 27 June 1845.
101 F. Oakeley, *Canon Oakeley's memoirs*, p. 23.
102 H. P. Liddon, *Life of Edward Bouverie Pusey*, volume 2, p. 439.
103 *English Churchman*, 3 July 1845, p. 420.
104 A. F. Bayford, *A full report of the proceedings of the office of the judge promoted by Hodgson v. Rev. F. Oakeley*, p. 167.
105 p. 166.
106 Court of Arches records, H672/12.
107 A. F. Bayford, *A full report of the proceedings of the office of the judge promoted by Hodgson v. Rev. F. Oakeley*, p. 167.

Chapter 12
1 F. Oakeley, *Canon Oakeley's memoirs*, p. 23.
2 Pusey Papers, Oakeley to Pusey, no date except 'Saturday evening'.
3 ibid.
4 ibid.
5 ibid.
6 Court of Arches records, H672/12.
7 F. Oakeley, *Canon Oakeley's memoirs*, p. 23.
8 ibid.
9 ibid.
10 ibid., pp. 23–4.
11 ibid., p. 24.
12 Pusey Papers, Oakeley to Pusey, 18 September 1845.
13 F. Oakeley, *Canon Oakeley's memoirs*, p. 24.
14 F. Oakeley, *A few words of affection and congratulation*, p. 6.
15 Newman Papers, Newman's diary, 29 August 1845.
16 F. Oakeley, *Canon Oakeley's memoirs*, p. 25.
17 Pusey Papers, Oakeley to Pusey, 18 September 1845.
18 ibid.
19 ibid.
20 ibid.
21 ibid.
22 ibid.
23 ibid.

24 Manning Papers, Oakeley to Manning, 27 January 1845.
25 ibid.
26 Pusey Papers, Oakeley to Pusey, 23 September 1845.
27 ibid.
28 *English Churchman*, 2 October 1845, pp. 626–8.
29 Pusey Papers, Oakeley to Pusey, 25 September 1845.
30 ibid.
31 ibid.
32 ibid.
33 Newman Papers, Newman's diary, 1 September 1845.
34 Keble Papers, Oakeley to ? (the letter begins 'My dear John'), 7 October 1845.
35 ibid.
36 M. Trevor, *Newman. The pillar of the cloud*, p. 357.
37 ibid., p. 358.
38 Keble Papers, Oakeley to ? (the letter begins 'My dear John'), 7 October 1845.
39 ibid.
40 F. Oakeley, *Canon Oakeley's memoirs*, p. 25.
41 ibid.
42 Keble Papers, Oakeley to ? (the letter begins 'My dear John'), 7 October 1845.
43 F. Oakeley, *Canon Oakeley's memoirs*, pp. 25–6.
44 John Lonsdale (1788–1867), Bishop of Lichfield 1843–67.
45 Keble Papers, Oakeley to ? (the letter begins 'My dear John'), 15 October 1845.
46 Newman Papers, Oakeley to Newman, 24 October 1845.
47 F. Oakeley, *A letter on submitting to the Catholic Church*, p. 11.
48 ibid., p. 12.
49 F. Oakeley, *A letter to his grace the Duke of Wellington*, p. 16.
50 F. Oakeley, *A letter on submitting to the Catholic Church*, p. 12.
51 ibid.
52 ibid., p. 18.
53 ibid., p. 16.
54 ibid., p. 18.
55 ibid., p. 20.
56 ibid., pp. 21–2.
57 ibid., p. 33.
58 ibid.
59 ibid., p. 34.
60 ibid.
61 ibid.
62 ibid., pp. 34–5.
63 Fr Robert Newsham (1783–1859), parish priest of St Clements ?-1849.
64 Newman Papers, Oakeley to Newman, 24 October 1845.
65 F. Oakeley, *Canon Oakeley's memoirs*, p. 26.
66 ibid.

67 ibid.
68 ibid.
69 ibid., p. 27.
70 ibid.

Chapter 13
1 J. H. Newman, *Apologia pro vita sua*, p. 259.
2 L. Bouyer, *Newman. His life and spirituality*, p. 237.
3 T. Mozley, *Reminiscences, chiefly of Oriel College and the Oxford Movement*, volume 2, p. 4.
4 W. Ward, *William George Ward and the Oxford Movement*, p. 122.
5 ibid., p. 123.
6 ibid., p. 121.
7 ibid.
8 ibid.
9 F. W. Newman, *Contributions to the early history of the late cardinal*, p. 72.
10 R. W. Church, *The Oxford Movement 1833–1845*, p. 322.
11 J. H. Newman, *Apologia pro vita sua*, p. 260.
12 ibid., p. 259.
13 ibid.
14 R. H. Froude, *Remains of the late Reverend Richard Hurrell Froude*, ed. J. H. Newman and J. Keble, volume 1, p. 403.
15 F. Oakeley, *Historical notes on the Tractarian Movement*, p. 65.
16 R. W. Church, *The Oxford Movement 1833–1845*, p. 322.
17 J. H. Newman, *A packet of letters*, ed. J. Sugg, p. 37, Newman to John William Bowden, 2 March 1836.
18 R. W. Church, *The Oxford Movement 1833–1845*, p. 56.
19 P. Brendon, *Hurrell Froude and the Oxford Movement*, p. x.
20 J. H. Newman, *The letters and diaries of John Henry Newman*, volume 4, p. 276, Newman to Froude, 14 June 1834.
21 T. Mozley, *Reminiscences, chiefly of Oriel College and the Oxford Movement*, volume 2, p. 228.
22 ibid., p. 229.
23 I. Williams, *The autobiography of Isaac Williams*, ed. G. Prevost, p. 89.
24 R. W. Church, *The Oxford Movement 1833–1845*, p. 321.
25 B. A. Smith, *Dean Church. The Anglican response to Newman*, p. 225.
26 Oakeley Papers, Letter Books of E. M. Oakeley, Gladstone to E. M. Oakeley, 26 March 1880.
27 F. Oakeley, *Personal reminiscences of the 'Oxford Movement'*, p. 9.
28 *English Churchman*, 5 June 1845, p. 359.
29 E. Bourne, 'Old Margaret Street Chapel', p. 360.
30 R. W. Church, *The Oxford Movement 1833–1845*, p. 321.
31 E. M. Oakeley, *The life of Sir Herbert Stanley Oakeley*, p. 14.
32 R. T. Davidson and W. Benham, *Life of Archibald Campbell Tait*, volume 1, p. 106, W. C. Lake to R. T. Davidson, 23 March 1888.

33 W. Ward, *William George Ward and the Oxford Movement*, p. 123.

34 T. Mozley, *Reminiscences, chiefly of Oriel College and the Oxford Movement*, volume 2, p. 244.

35 B. A. Smith, *Dean Church. The Anglican response to Newman*, p. 225.

36 W. Ward, *William George Ward and the Oxford Movement*, p. 122.

37 ibid., p. 130.

38 E. Bourne, 'Old Margaret Street Chapel', p. 361.

39 ibid.

Chapter 14

1   F. Oakeley, *Historical notes on the Tractarian Movement*, p. 5.

2   ibid., p. 1.

3   ibid., pp. 101–102.

4   Gladstone Papers, Add MSS 52,485, ff. 133–4, Oakeley to ?Gladstone [The letter begins 'My dear Sir'], 19 August 1874.

5   F. Oakeley, The recent conversions'.

6   W. Ward, *The life of John Henry Cardinal Newman*, volume 1, p. 109, Newman to Dalgairns, 10 December 1845.

7   ibid., Newman to Dalgairns, 16 December 1845.

8   B. Ward, *History of St Edmund's College, Old Hall*, p. 252.

9   Newman Papers, Oakeley to Newman, 1 April [1846].

10 B. Ward, *History of St Edmund's College, Old Hall*, p. 253–4.

11 [E. Harris], *From Oxford to Rome*, pp. 35–6.

12 Wiseman Papers, Oakeley to Bishop Nicholas Wiseman, 31 January 1849.

13 *Tablet*, 9 December 1848.

14 C. Butler, *The life and times of Bishop Ullathorne 1806–1889*, volume 1, p. 160.

15 *Rambler*, January 1849.

16 F. Oakeley, *The priest on the mission*, p. 146.

17 E. Bellasis, *Memorials of Mr Serjeant Bellasis 1800–1873*, third edition, p. 159, Oakeley to Bellasis, 15 March 1848.

18 F. Oakeley, *History of St John's Church since 1850*.

19 ibid.

20 ibid.

21 W. Ward, *The life and times of Cardinal Wiseman*, volume 2, p. 92.

22 R. Boyle, *Boyle versus Wiseman*, p. 9.

23 Wiseman Papers, Oakeley to Wiseman, 14 August [1855].

24 F. Oakeley, *History of St John's Church since 1850*.

25 ibid.

26 M. Clifton, *A Victorian convert quintet*, p. 82.

27 ibid., p 88.

28 F. Oakeley, *History of St John's Church since 1850*.

29 W. E. Gladstone, 'Ritualism and ritual', p. 181.

30 F. Oakeley, *History of St John's Church since 1850*.

31 F. Oakeley, *Statement of the facts relative to the case of Mr William Weale*, p. 11.
32 ibid.
33 F. Oakeley, *The religious disabilities of our Catholic prisoners*, pp. 5–9.
34 ibid., p. 18.
35 F. Oakeley, *History of St John's Church since 1850*.
36 Wiseman Papers, Oakeley to Wiseman, 21 September 1863.
37 F. Oakeley, *History of St John's Church since 1850*.
38 W. Ward, *The life and times of Cardinal Wiseman*, volume 2, p. 257.
39 E. S. Purcell, *Life of Cardinal Manning. Archbishop of Westminster*, volume 2, p. 206, Manning to Talbot, 24 February 1865.
40 ibid.
41 ibid., p. 210, Manning to Talbot, 31 March 1865.
42 ibid., p. 215, Manning to Talbot, 11 April 1865
43 ibid., p. 222.
44 Gladstone Papers, Add MSS 44,404, f. 180, Gladstone to Oakeley, 20 December 1864.
45 E. S. Purcell, *Life of Cardinal Manning. Archbishop of Westminster*, volume 2, p. 487.
46 Gladstone Papers, Add MSS 44,445, ff. 41–2, Oakeley to Gladstone, 10 November 1874.
47 ibid., Manning to Oakeley, 14 August 1867.
48 W. Ward, *William George Ward and the Catholic revival*, pp. 141–2, W. G. Ward to John Henry Newman, 8 March 1859.
49 F. Oakeley, *The Catholic florist*, p. i.
50 ibid., p. xi.
51 ibid., p. xvii.
52 ibid., p. iii.
53 F. Oakeley, *Lyra liturgica*, p. i.
54 ibid., pp. 5–6.
55 F. Oakeley, *The ceremonies of the mass*, second edition, p. 1.
56 F. Oakeley, *The youthful martyrs of Rome*, p. iii.
57 ibid., pp. 48–9.
58 F. Oakeley, *The church of the bible*, p. ix.
59 ibid., p. 4.
60 ibid., p. xii.
61 F. Oakeley, *The priest on the mission*, pp. 34–45.
62 ibid., p. 136.
63 Gladstone Papers, Add MSS 44,408, ff. 168–70, Oakeley to Gladstone, 23 November 1865.
64 ibid., Add MSS 44,414, f. 151, Oakeley to Gladstone, 13 March 1868.
65 *St John the Evangelist Islington, 1843–1943*.
66 Newman Papers, Frederick Oakeley to Ambrose St John, 15 February 1875.
67 ibid., Newman to Emily Bowles, 29 March 1875.

68 W. Ward, *The life of John Henry, Cardinal Newman*, volume 2, pp. 578–9, Oakeley to Newman, 18 February 1879.
69 G. H. Sumner, *Life of Charles Richard Sumner*, p. 46, Oakeley to George Henry Sumner, 5 May 1875.
70 ibid.
71 ibid., Charles Richard Sumner to Oakeley, 1 August 1852.
72 ibid., p. 47, Oakeley to George Henry Sumner, 5 May 1875.
73 F. Oakeley, *Historical notes on the Tractarian Movement*, p. 101.
74 M. R. Rhodes, *Letters on the 'Eirenicon'*, p. 4.
75 Newman Papers, John Henry Newman to J. R. Bloxam, 30 April 1871.
76 Gladstone Papers, Add MSS 44,444, f 276, Oakeley to Gladstone, 1 October 1874.
77 ibid., Add MSS 44,449, f 299, Oakeley to Gladstone, 24 April 1876.
78 ibid., Add MSS 44,459, f 248, Oakeley to Gladstone, 16 April 1879.
79 ibid., Add MSS 44,786, f 69, Oakeley to Gladstone, 26 April 1879.
80 Tait Papers, volume 79, ff. 7–9, Frederick Oakeley to Archibald Campbell Tait, 18 September 1856.
81 ibid., volume 85, ff. 216–17, Oakeley to Tait, 16 November 1868.
82 T. Mozley, *Reminiscences, chiefly of Oriel College and the Oxford Movement*, volume 2, p. 5.
83 Tait Papers, volume 86, ff. 336–8, Oakeley to Tait, 15 November 1869.
84 ibid., volume 103, ff. 296–7, Oakeley to Tait, 8 June 1872.
85 ibid., volume 91, ff. 249–50, Oakeley to Tait, 31 December 1872.
86 F. Oakeley, *The Athanasian Creed: four lectures suggested by the present controversy*, p. v.
87 Tait Papers, volume 94, f. 165, Oakeley to Tait, 24 March 1875.
88 ibid., volume 98, ff. 203–204, Oakeley to Tait, 24 December 1878.
89 R. Davidson and W. Benham, *Life of Archibald Campbell Tait*, volume 2, p. 44.
90 ibid., volume 2, p. 525.
91 E. M. Oakeley, *The life of Sir Herbert Stanley Oakeley*, p. 14, Archibald Campbell Tait to W. W. Wodehouse, 3 February 1880.
92 W. Ward, *W. G. Ward and the Oxford Movement*, second edition, p. 124.
93 T. Mozley, *Reminiscences, chiefly of Oriel College and the Oxford Movement*, volume 2, p. 5.
94 Gladstone Papers, Add MSS 44,127, ff. 184–6, Church to Gladstone, 2 February 1880.
95 F. Oakeley, *A few words of affection and congratulation addressed to his fellow converts, before the mass of thanksgiving for the conversions to the church at St John's, Islington, on the octave of the Ascension, June 5th 1851*, p. 4.
96 F. Oakeley, *Personal reminiscences of the 'Oxford Movement'*, p. 22.
97 Tait Papers, volume 89, ff. 215–16, Oakeley to Tait, 10 June 1871.
98 ibid., volume 98, f. 221, Moberly to Tait, 29 December 1878.

99 *Tablet*, 7 February 1880, p. 179.
100 F. Oakeley, 'English views of Catholicism', pp. 463–4.
101 ibid., p. 470.
102 F. Oakeley, *The priest on the mission*, p. 228.

Index